Title Withdrawn

Biography Today

Profiles
of People
of Interest
to Young
Readers

Volume 19—2010
Annual Cumulation

Cherie D. Abbey
Managing Editor

Omnigraphics

P.O. Box 31-1640
Detroit, MI 48231-1640

Cherie D. Abbey, *Managing Editor*

Peggy Daniels, Joan Goldsworthy, Jeff Hill, Kevin Hillstrom, Laurie Hillstrom, Justin Karr, Leslie Karr, and Diane Telgen, *Sketch Writers*

Allison A. Beckett and Mary Butler, *Research Staff*

* * *

Peter E. Ruffner, *Publisher*
Matthew P. Barbour, *Senior Vice President*

* * *

Elizabeth Collins, *Research and Permissions Coordinator*
Kevin Hayes, *Operations Manager*
Cherry Stockdale, *Permissions Assistant*
Shirley Amore, Martha Johns, and Kirk Kauffmann, *Administrative Staff*

Special thanks to Frederick G. Ruffner for creating this series.

Copyright © 2010 EBSCO Publishing, Inc.
ISSN 1058-2347 • ISBN 978-0-7808-1063-1

Library of Congress Cataloging-in-Publication Data

The information in this publication was compiled from sources cited and from sources considered reliable. While every possible effort has been made to ensure reliability, the publisher will not assume liability for damages caused by inaccuracies in the data, and makes no warranty, express or implied, on the accuracy of the information contained herein.

This book is printed on acid-free paper meeting the ANSI Z39.48 Standard. The infinity symbol that appears above indicates that the paper in this book meets that standard.

Printed in the United States of America

Contents

Preface

Biography Today is a magazine designed and written for the young reader—ages 9 and above—and covers individuals that librarians and teachers tell us that young people want to know about most: entertainers, athletes, writers, illustrators, cartoonists, and political leaders.

The Plan of the Work

The publication was especially created to appeal to young readers in a format they can enjoy reading and readily understand. Each issue contains approximately 10 sketches arranged alphabetically. Each entry provides at least one picture of the individual profiled, and bold-faced rubrics lead the reader to information on birth, youth, early memories, education, first jobs, marriage and family, career highlights, memorable experiences, hobbies, and honors and awards. Each of the entries ends with a list of easily accessible sources designed to lead the student to further reading on the individual and a current address. Retrospective entries are also included, written to provide a perspective on the individual's entire career.

Biographies are prepared by Omnigraphics editors after extensive research, utilizing the most current materials available. Those sources that are generally available to students appear in the list of further reading at the end of the sketch.

Indexes

Cumulative indexes are an important component of *Biography Today*. Each issue of the *Biography Today* General Series includes a Cumulative Names Index, which comprises all individuals profiled in *Biography Today* since the series began in 1992. In addition, we compile three other indexes: the Cumulative General Index, Places of Birth Index, and Birthday Index. See our web site, www.biographytoday.com, for these three indexes, along with the Names Index. All *Biography Today* indexes are cumulative, including all individuals profiled in both the General Series and the Subject Series.

Our Advisors

This series was reviewed by an Advisory Board comprising librarians, children's literature specialists, and reading instructors to ensure that the concept of this publication—to provide a readable and accessible biographical magazine for young readers—was on target. They evaluated the title as it developed, and their suggestions have proved invaluable. Any errors, however, are ours alone. We'd like to list the Advisory Board members, and to thank them for their efforts.

Our Advisory Board stressed to us that we should not shy away from controversial or unconventional people in our profiles, and we have tried to follow their advice. The Advisory Board also mentioned that the sketches might be useful in reluctant reader and adult literacy programs, and we would value any comments librarians might have about the suitability of our magazine for those purposes.

Your Comments Are Welcome

Our goal is to be accurate and up-to-date, to give young readers information they can learn from and enjoy. Now we want to know what you think. Take a look at this issue of *Biography Today*, on approval. Write or call me with your comments. We want to provide an excellent source of biographical information for young people. Let us know how you think we're doing.

Cherie Abbey
Managing Editor, *Biography Today*
Omnigraphics, Inc.
P.O. Box 31-1640
Detroit, MI 48231-1640
www.omnigraphics.com

Congratulations!

Congratulations to the following individuals and libraries who have received a free copy of *Biography Today* for suggesting people who appear in this volume.

Adrian Alvarez, San Saba, TX
Paul Bishette, Silas Bronson Library, Waterbury, CT
Michael Bosquez, San Saba, TX
Susannah Chase, Englewood High School, Jacksonville, FL
Judi Chelekis, Vassar Junior/Senior High School Library, Vassar, MI
Ashley Daly, Ardmore High School, Ardmore, AL
Rachel Q. Davis, Thomas Memorial Library, Cape Elizabeth, ME
Lori Drummond, Washington Middle School, Aurora, IL
Regina Floyd, Chicago, IL
Kathleen Gorman, Cardinal Joseph Bernardin Catholic School, Orland Hills, IL
Bershard Horton, Longview, TX
Cierra Huggins, Toledo, OH
Tyisha James, Tampa, FL
Richard Kimball, Sherman, ME
Kimberly Lentz, North Rowan High School, Spencer, NC
Ricza Lopez, Bronx, NY
Amy Lucio, Cedar Creek Intermediate, Cedar Creek, TX
Michelle D. Lyons, Jennings High School Library, Jennings, LA
Laurie Martucci-Walsh, McKenna Elementary School, Massapequa, NY
Jennifer McGuire, Esther Dennis Middle School, Dayton, OH
Steven Ott Jr., Covington School, Oak Lawn, IL
Melina Rangel, Bell Gardens, CA
Jessica Sanchez, Dr. William R. Peck Middle School, Holyoke, MA
Lisa Scharf, Memorial Junior High, Mentor, OH
S.A. Schene, Homecroft Elementary, Indianapolis, IN
Laurie Skien, Bushnell-Prairie City Jr. High School, Bushnell, IL
Jim Steinke, Cottage Grove High School, Cottage Grove, WI
Shreya Subramanian, Martell Elementary School, Troy, MI
Loretta Talbert, North County Regional Library, Huntersville, NC
Owen V., McKenna Elementary School, Massapequa, NY
Josh Wallace, Joliet Public Library, Joliet, IL
Judy Yamane, Aliamanu Middle School, Honolulu, HI

Beyoncé 1981-
American Singer, Songwriter, Producer, and Actress
Grammy-Winning Creator of *I Am ... Sasha Fierce*
and Star of *Dreamgirls*

[An entry on the group Destiny's Child, with significant coverage of Beyoncé, appeared in Biography Today, *April 2001, and the* Biography Today *2001 Annual Cumulation.]*

BIRTH

Beyoncé Giselle Knowles was born on September 4, 1981, in Houston, Texas. She was the first child of Mathew Knowles, a medical equipment salesman, and his wife Tina, a hairdresser and salon owner. Her unusual first name, which rhymes with "fiancé," was taken from Beyincé, which was Tina Knowles's maiden name. Beyoncé has a younger sister, Solange, who also became a professional performer and songwriter.

Beyoncé started out her professional career with the group Destiny's Child, and at that point she used her full name, Beyoncé Knowles. Later, after she became a solo performer, she began using just her first name, Beyoncé.

YOUTH

Beyoncé's parents had loved music in their own youth, and their daughters grew up with music in the house. "My parents used to sing to me all the time," the singer remembered. "My dad tells me that as a baby, I would go crazy whenever I heard music, and I tried to dance before I could even walk." Since Beyoncé was a shy child, her parents hoped to bring her out of her shell by giving her dance lessons. Her teacher discovered her singing talent and encouraged her to perform in a school talent show. She won the competition by singing John Lennon's "Imagine," astonishing her parents with her powerful voice. This led to singing lessons and many more victories in talent shows. By 1990, Beyoncé had joined Girl's Tyme, a local girl group managed by Andretta Tillman. Although the lineup changed as girls dropped in and out, Beyoncé became a mainstay of Girl's Tyme, which performed at events around the Houston area.

When Tillman became ill, Mathew Knowles helped manage Girl's Tyme, which by now included Kelly Rowland. Because Rowland's mother worked as a nanny and often lived away from home, Kelly came to live with Beyoncé's family. The Knowleses gave the girls every opportunity to polish their skills. Mathew Knowles made them sing while jogging, so they could develop the stamina to sing and dance at the same time. He built a deck in their back yard, providing a place to practice routines. Tina Knowles had the girls perform for customers in her hair salon, and their feedback helped the girls develop their stage presence. Summer vacations were full of dance rehearsals, voice lessons, and interview training, which Beyoncé considered fun. "It was my time to create dance routines and vocal arrangements. It seemed like playtime," she recalled. Girl's Tyme was excited when they made the finals of the nationally syndicated television talent show "Star Search" in 1992. When they lost to an adult rock band the group was crushed, thinking their dream of a music career was over. "We almost went crazy from crying," Beyoncé noted. "A lot was riding on that performance."

Mathew Knowles had faith in his daughter's talent. After the loss on "Star Search," he left his high-paying job at Xerox to take over management of the group. By this time it had settled on four members—Beyoncé, Rowland, LeToya Luckett, and LaTavia Roberson—and had gone through several name changes before settling on Destiny's Child. Mathew Knowles took the group to California for record company auditions. In 1993 they signed with Elektra Records and moved to Atlanta to work on a first recording. Unfortunately, the record company dropped them in 1995 before they could produce an album. The girls returned home, seemingly to start all over again. The efforts put a strain on the Knowles family, and Beyoncé's parents separated briefly when she was 14. By 1996, however, the family was reunited and Destiny's Child had a new contract, this time with Columbia Records.

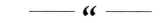

"My parents used to sing to me all the time," Beyoncé remembered. "My dad tells me that as a baby, I would go crazy whenever I heard music, and I tried to dance before I could even walk."

EDUCATION

Beyoncé attended private elementary schools as a child, earning mostly As and Bs. She briefly attended Houston's High School for Visual and Performing Arts and the Alief Elsik High School. Because she was a working performer by the time she was in ninth grade, she was privately tutored for the rest of her teens. She earned the equivalent of a high school diploma in 2000.

CAREER HIGHLIGHTS

Destiny's Child

It took a while for Destiny's Child to create their first album, as the record company sought appropriate material for a young girl group to record. They paired the group with superstar producers like Wyclef Jean and Jermaine Dupri, who helped the group record tracks over the next two years. In the meantime the group contributed the single "Killing Time" to the *Men in Black* soundtrack in 1997 and got to meet the film's co-star, rapper-actor Will Smith. Tina Knowles took over as the group's stylist during this time, using her sewing experience, fashion sense, and knowledge of the girls' personalities to craft an image they felt comfortable with. They released their first single in 1997, and "No, No, No" hit No. 1 on the R&B (rhythm & blues) chart and No. 3 on the *Billboard* Hot 100 list. When they

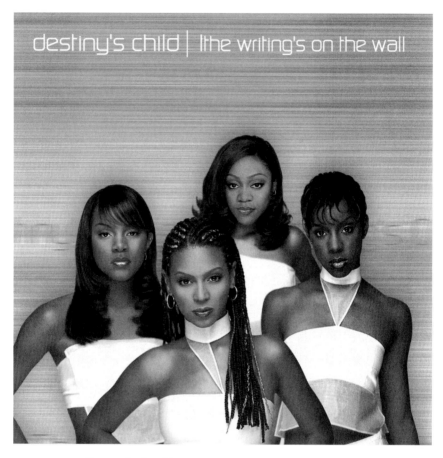

Beyoncé's first big success came with Destiny's Child.

released the self-titled album *Destiny's Child* in 1998, it hit No. 15 on the R&B album charts and was certified gold.

The group quickly followed up their first album with a second, *The Writing's on the Wall,* in 1999. This time Beyoncé co-wrote 10 of the tracks, rather than just a couple, including the first single, "Bills, Bills, Bills." The song, featuring Beyoncé and Rowland telling a deadbeat boyfriend to leave, became the group's first No. 1 single. A second single, "Bug a Boo," only reached No. 33, but it helped establish the group's style: fast singing (usually featuring Beyoncé) that sometimes approached rapping, and themes of strength, independence, and girl power. Controversy struck before the group released their next single, when Luckett and Roberson asked for a new manager. They accused Mathew Knowles of favoring Beyoncé and Rowland. In response, he kicked the girls out of the group and found replacements. He brought in Michelle Williams and Farrah Franklin to fill in for public appearances. Eventually Franklin left too, claiming control issues were the reason for her departure.

But the controversy didn't slow the group down. Even as Luckett and Roberson sued the group and their manager, Destiny's Child continued as a trio made up of Beyoncé, Kelly Rowland, and Michelle Williams. Their next single produced the monster hit "Say My Name," which spent 11 weeks in the Top 10, including three weeks at No. 1. It boosted *The Writing's on the Wall* to No. 5 on the album chart, selling more than 10 million copies worldwide. A fourth single, "Jumpin', Jumpin'" landed in the Top 20 for radio airplay. In 2000 the group also earned their first Grammy Awards, with "Say My Name" earning statues for Best R&B Song and Best R&B Vocal Performance by a Duo or Group. Beyoncé was philosophical about all the turmoil: "I think in order for your group to be successful your story has to be interesting. Our story was very squeaky clean, so I thank God for the controversy. I'm happy because it helps me sell records." Later, however, she admitted to a period of depression following the departure of her childhood friends from the group. During this time, she sought solace in church services and worked out her emotions by writing songs.

Those songs appeared on the trio's next album, the 2001 smash *Survivor.* Not only did Beyoncé co-write all but one track on the album, she co-produced most of the tracks as well. The first single, "Independent Women, Part 1," debuted as part of the *Charlie's Angels* film soundtrack and sat at No. 1 for 10 weeks. The second single, "Survivor," charted at No. 2, but also inspired a defamation lawsuit from Luckett and Roberson, who claimed the line "You thought I wouldn't sell without ya/ sold 9 million" violated the terms of their agreement in settling their previous lawsuit. That suit was also settled out of court, and Destiny's Child continued to rule the charts: the single "Bootylicious" spent two weeks at No. 1, "Emotion" hit No. 10, and the album *Survivor* debuted at No. 1 and sold over 3.7 million copies in 2001. It earned the group a slew of awards, including a Grammy for Best R&B Vocal Performance by a Duo or Group ("Survivor"), an MTV Video Music Award for Best R&B Video ("Survivor"), American Music Awards for Favorite Soul/R&B Group and Favorite Pop/Rock Album, and a Teen Choice Award for Choice Pop Group.

Going Solo

Destiny's Child was one of the hottest groups of the early 2000s, but there was also speculation that Beyoncé, as the group's lead singer and song-

Scenes from Beyoncé's early career: performing with Destiny's Child (top); appearing with Mike Myers in Austin Powers in Goldmember; *and releasing her first solo album,* Dangerously in Love.

writer, was looking toward a solo career. It was Beyoncé, not the group, who won the ASCAP Songwriter of the Year Award in 2002—only the second woman, and the first African-American one, to capture that prize. After the singer commented she needed a break from four years of constant rehearsing and touring, rumors spread that Destiny's Child was breaking up. The rumors increased as members took a break to pursue their individual interests. In 2002, Rowland released a solo R&B album and Williams had the best-selling gospel album of that year. Beyoncé, however, decided to focus on developing her acting career.

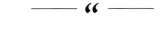

The singer had her first acting experience in the 2001 made-for-MTV musical, "Carmen: A Hip-Hopera." It set the story of Bizet's classic opera *Carmen* in modern times, with Beyoncé in the title role of an aspiring actress whose seduction of a policeman leads to ruin. A *Variety* reviewer noted that "Knowles makes a fine acting debut, and once again makes it clear that she's got a surplus of star power." Although the film was more like an extended music video, it brought her to the attention of Holly-

Over the years, Beyoncé has developed a separate persona for her stage shows. "I have someone else that takes over when it's time for me to work and when I'm on stage, this alter ego that I've created that kind of protects me and who I really am."

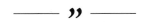

wood. For her next film, she earned her first feature film role working with Mike Myers in *Austin Powers in Goldmember* (2002). She played Foxxy Cleopatra, a sexy agent who recalled the heroines of the 1970s black-centered action films. While *Goldmember* didn't get great reviews, several critics noted Beyoncé demonstrated good screen presence in the role. The film earned over $200 million in the U.S. and earned her nominations for Teen Choice, Kids' Choice, and MTV Movie Awards.

In 2003 Beyoncé released her own solo singing project. The album showcased a different, more vulnerable side. "I always held back in Destiny's Child, because I was comfortable in a group," she explained. "I would not lose myself or go all the way." *Dangerously in Love* debuted at No. 1 on the *Billboard* album charts, with help from its first single, "Crazy in Love." This collaboration with rapper (and rumored boyfriend) Jay-Z was the hit of summer 2003, spending eight weeks at No. 1. The next single, "Baby Boy," topped the charts for nine weeks, and the album also produced the Top 10 hits "Naughty Girl" and "Me, Myself, and I." The album earned acclaim from her peers as well, garnering three MTV Music Video Awards and five Grammy Awards, tying a record for a female artist in a single Grammys. *Dangerously in Love* earned Best R&B Album; "Crazy in Love" won Best Rap/Sung Collaboration and Best R&B Song (a songwriting award); "Dangerously in Love 2" brought a trophy for Best Female R&B Vocal Performance; and Beyoncé's duet with Luther Vandross, a remake of "The Closer I Get to You," won Best R&B Performance by a Duo or Group with Vocals.

Not long after her solo release, Beyoncé appeared in her first lead film role, opposite Oscar-winner Cuba Gooding, Jr. in *The Fighting Temptations* (2003). She played Lilly, a single mom who has been kicked out of her church for having a child out of wedlock and who then teams up with Darrin (played by Gooding) to win a choir competition. "I saw a lot of comedic and dramatic opportunities in playing this character, and I knew I'd have a lot of fun with it," she remarked. Although the film didn't perform well at the box office, Beyoncé earned nominations for best actress from the NAACP Image Awards and Black Reel Film Awards. She also co-wrote songs for the film, including "He Still Loves Me," which earned her a Black Reel Film Award for Best Song.

Saying Goodbye to Destiny's Child

By 2004, Beyoncé was a full-fledged superstar, singing the national anthem at the Super Bowl and earning endorsement deals with many major companies. People were surprised when Destiny's Child announced they would release a new album that year, but it made sense to Beyoncé. While seeing how they could grow as solo artists was important, she said, "it's really beautiful to do that and then also have the opportunity to come back together and have the fun we have when we are together. When you have that sort of friendship, recording doesn't feel like work." Their 2004 release *Destiny Fulfilled* was the group's last original album. It debuted at No. 2 on the album charts and topped the R&B album charts. It generated two No. 3 hits, "Lose My Breath" and "Soldier," as well as the Top 25 singles "Girl" and "Cater 2 U." The group—which according to some measurements was the best-selling female group of all time—went on a final tour in 2005 and announced midway they would disband for good after it was over. Nevertheless, they had one last number one album, the 2005 greatest hits collection *#1's*.

Beyoncé had plenty to keep her occupied once Destiny's Child broke up in 2005. Besides her growing acting and solo singing careers, she founded the fashion company House of Deréon with her mother, Tina, who had long been her daughter's costume designer and stylist. The company name—and its designs—were inspired by Beyoncé's grandmother and Tina's

*Beyoncé performing with Jay-Z, her future husband, at the
2003 MTV Video Music Awards.*

mother, Agnéz Dereon, who had worked as a seamstress. House of Deréon created higher-end gowns, women's wear, and accessories and was sold in boutiques and prestige department stores like Neiman Marcus and Bloomingdale's. Later they created another line with Beyoncé's sister Solange, called Deréon. This line focused on lower-priced sportswear for juniors, to be sold in department stores like Dillard's and Macy's.

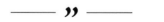

Beyoncé is rarely the focus of tabloid stories, is never caught behaving badly by paparazzi, and declines to speak about her private life. "I've worked too hard and sacrificed too much to do something silly that would mess up the brand I've created all of these years," she noted. *"The older I get, the more I think about the amount of influence I have on these young girls, and it's scary sometimes. But I also understand how lucky I am to have that."*

In 2006, on her 25th birthday, Beyoncé released her second solo album, *B'Day*. It debuted at No. 1 on the album chart on the way to selling more than three million copies. Its first single, "Déjà Vu," reached No. 4 and "Ring the Alarm" hit No. 11. But "Irreplaceable" was the monster hit from the album, staying at No. 1 for 10 weeks. *B'Day* won a Grammy for Best Contemporary R&B Album. In spring 2007 Beyoncé released an expanded deluxe edition of the album with several new tracks, some in Spanish. One was a duet with Colombian singing star Shakira, "Beautiful Liar," which became the fastest moving single in *Billboard* history, going from No. 94 to No. 3 in a single week. The song also earned an MTV Video Music Award. Beyoncé supported the album with a lavish worldwide tour called "The Beyoncé Experience," which featured an all-female backing band and dancers, video screens, multiple costume changes, and complex choreography. It played to enthusiastic audiences all over the world, and in 2007 Beyoncé was voted Best International Artist at the American Music Awards, the first African American to earn that honor.

A *Dream* Acting Role

Even as she dominated the music charts, Beyoncé was working on developing her acting career. In 2006 she appeared in *The Pink Panther* with

Beyoncé with Jennifer Hudson in Dreamgirls.

comedy superstar Steve Martin. The film was inspired by the classic 1963 comedy of the same title, about a bumbling French detective (played by Peter Sellers in the original) who manages to solve mysteries in spite of his clumsiness. In this prequel, Beyoncé plays Xenia, a pop star who becomes a suspect when her soccer coach-boyfriend is murdered at the same time his diamond ring is stolen. The actress found filming both fun and challenging. "Many of my scenes were with Steve [Martin], and it was really difficult to stay in character because he is so funny and I never knew what he was going to do," she said. While the film received tepid reviews, it opened at No. 1 and made a respectable $82 million in U.S. box office. Beyoncé recorded a new version of her song "Check on It" for the film—it was originally released with the Destiny's Child collection #1's—and it shot to the top of the pop charts and stayed at No. 1 for five weeks.

Later that year the budding actress appeared in the role of a lifetime: a starring turn in *Dreamgirls,* a film based on the Tony Award-winning stage musical from 1982. The story is loosely based on the journey of the Supremes, a Motown girl group of the 1960s whose lead singer, Diana Ross, later became a superstar solo artist. Beyoncé had studied the Supremes' moves as a young singer, and she was thrilled to be cast in the role of Deena Jones, a backup singer in the "Dreamettes" who is promoted to lead singer because of her stunning looks and pop-style voice. This angers former lead singer Effie (played by Oscar-winner Jennifer Hudson), leading the group to break up and Deena to rise to solo stardom under the control of her manager-husband (played by Jamie Foxx). Beyoncé dropped 20 pounds to play the role, which required her to portray both inexperience and independence. She was successful, as a *Daily Variety* critic observed: "Knowles is poised, quietly determined, and beautiful beyond belief, blossoming from innocent teenager to self-possessed star."

Dreamgirls was a both a popular and critical success, earning over $100 million at the box office and landing on many critics' lists of top films of the year. Beyoncé earned several nominations for acting awards, most notably the Golden Globe for best actress in a musical or comedy, but also the NAACP Image, MTV Movie, Satellite, and Black Reel Awards. A new song she co-wrote for the film, "Listen," won a Critics Choice Award for best song from the Broadcast Film Critics Association and was also nominated for a Golden Globe.

Beyoncé worked even harder for her next role, in *Cadillac Records* (2008), which tells the true story of the pioneering record label that introduced artists like Chuck Berry and Bo Diddley to mainstream America. This time she was playing a real person, legendary blues singer Etta James, who broke barriers in the music business but also struggled with heroin addiction. The actress—who also helped produce the film and wrote four songs for the soundtrack—gained 15 pounds for the role and researched drug addiction by visiting rehab centers. (She later donated her entire $4 million salary for the film to Phoenix House, a nationwide group of rehab centers.) The film earned her the best notices of her career, with critics using words like "surprise," "soulful," "bitter and beautifully vulnerable," "inspired and persuasive," and "revelatory" to describe her performance. Beyoncé admitted that she had been particularly inspired by playing James: "She was bold and she did not try to change who she was for anyone," she wrote on her website. Playing her on screen "gave me the strength and the confidence to step out of my comfort zone even more." As she later added in an interview, "That is why I love doing movies so much, because it's not just an art form. It changes my life and my music and the way I look at things."

Expanding Her Horizons

The singer brought that sense of change and exploration to her next recording project, the 2008 double album *I Am … Sasha Fierce*. The first CD, *I Am…*, was filled with self-reflective ballads like the top five singles "If I Were a Boy" and "Halo." The second disc featured up-tempo numbers, like the smash No.1 hit "Single Ladies (Put a Ring on It)," that represent the booty-shaking performer nicknamed "Sasha Fierce." "I have someone else that takes over when it's time for me to work and when I'm on stage, this alter ego that I've created that kind of protects me and who I really am," Beyoncé explained. *I Am … Sasha Fierce* debuted at No. 1 on the album chart, selling over four million copies worldwide in its first year. The supporting tour was a top earner of summer 2009, and the video for "Single Ladies" became an internet sensation that was copied throughout pop culture. Inspired by a dance routine by Broadway choreographer Bob Fosse, the video earned the MTV Video of the Year Award and was parodied on television shows like "Saturday Night Live" and "Glee."

In 2009, Beyoncé also made her first movie appearance in a role that didn't involve music. In *Obsessed*, she played a wife whose marriage is threatened by a woman stalking her husband. The singer also helped produce the film and was excited about the challenge: "It's the first time I didn't have that [musical] crutch, but after *Cadillac Records*, I had a confidence that I never had before." Although the film was critically panned, it opened at No. 1 and earned over $68 million in U.S. box office. That year also saw the singer-actress featured at the Academy Awards, performing a musical number with host Hugh Jackman. Her most memorable moment of the year, however, was her performance at one of the inaugural balls for President Barack Obama. For many observers, her emotional version of the Etta James's standard "At Last," sung as the first African-American president and first lady danced together, helped symbolize this historic moment.

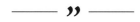

Her "Sasha Fierce" image may be sexy and sassy, but Beyoncé considers herself a simple, spiritual woman: "It's a way of life for me. What's more important to me [over image] is the way I treat people, what I think, what I give to other people. When I go back to Houston and go to church and see those people, I feel like the same country girl."

Beyoncé's most recent release, I Am … Sasha Fierce, *showcased two sides of her performing persona.*

Beyoncé decided to take a different approach in 2010. Early in the year, she announced that she wanted to spend time not working. "It's definitely time to take a break, to recharge my batteries," she said. "I'd like to take about six months and not go into the studio. I need to just live life, to be inspired by things." Her new attitude was due, in part, to the previous year, which had been hectic. On the *I Am … Tour,* Beyoncé visited 110 cities around the world. She managed to visit many great sites along the way, including the pyramids in Egypt, the Great Wall in China, and whales in Australia. When she got home, "I wrote out a contract with myself. I made a list of everything I want to do that has nothing to do with music. . . . I promised myself I would not go back on tour or in the studio until I finished these things." Her list was a bit random—take a class, go to restaurants, see some movies and Broadway shows, spend time with her nephew. She admitted, though, that relaxing isn't easy for her. "It will be the hardest thing in the world for me to make myself not do an album and shoot a video and turn it in and say, 'I'm ready!' I already have all these melodies and ideas in my head. I have to tell myself, 'Sit down! Sit down!'" She did make an exception for the Grammy Awards, where she won six trophies, winning the most trophies ever by a female artist in one year.

Despite the potential pitfalls of attaining fame at a young age, Beyoncé has maintained a reputation as a class act, something she first determined to do when she was at a *Men in Black* signing with Will Smith. "He was so nice to every person," she remembered. "I watched him. I knew he had to be tired, and I couldn't believe how nice he was." At the time, she told herself, "I don't care if I ever get that famous, I will always be like him." One example occurred at the 2009 MTV Video Music Awards. When Taylor Swift won Best Female Video Award, she was rudely interrupted during her acceptance speech by rapper Kanye West, who stormed the stage and insisted that Beyoncé should have won. Then, when Beyoncé won the Video of the Year Award, she offered the microphone to Swift. Beyoncé is rarely the focus of tabloid stories, is never caught behaving badly by paparazzi, and declines to speak about her private life. "I've worked too hard and sacrificed too much to do something silly that would mess up the brand I've created all of these years," she noted. "The older I get, the more I think about the amount of influence I have on these young girls, and it's scary sometimes. But I also understand how lucky I am to have that."

MARRIAGE AND FAMILY

Beyoncé married rapper and music mogul Shawn Corey Carter, known professionally as Jay-Z, on April 4, 2008. The two first worked together on Jay-Z's 2003 hit "Bonnie and Clyde" and dated for several years before their marriage. While they appeared in public at various events, they never spoke of their relationship to the press, and it was several months before they publicly confirmed the wedding took place. The couple has an apartment in Manhattan, as well as a mansion in Scarsdale, New York.

Although her life is filled with glamour and excitement, Beyoncé stresses that family is the most important thing to her. Without it, she said, she would be nowhere, because "nobody in the world had confidence and believed in us like my mom and dad." Her father is still her manager as the head of the Urban/Gospel division of Music World Entertainment, the management company that he founded and later sold for $10 million. Her

Beyoncé in an appearance on the "Today" show.

mother is still her stylist and design partner in House of Deréon; her cousin is her personal assistant and frequent songwriting partner; and her sister Solange has joined her on tour as a backup dancer or opening act. Her "Sasha Fierce" image may be sexy and sassy, but Beyoncé considers herself a simple, spiritual woman: "It's a way of life for me. What's more important to me [than image] is the way I treat people, what I think, what I give to other people. When I go back to Houston and go to church and see those people, I feel like the same country girl."

HOBBIES AND OTHER INTERESTS

As a superstar in multiple fields, Beyoncé has little time for hobbies. She enjoys relaxing at home and likes to watch movies or makeover shows. She enjoys fashion, collecting clothes and old costumes, which she may later sell for charity. She devotes time and money to many charitable causes, including public school music programs, children's charities, hunger and disaster relief, cancer and AIDS charities, and church programs. After Hurricane Katrina forced many New Orleans families to relocate to her hometown of Houston, the Knowles family and Kelly Rowland set up the Survivor Foundation, which founded "Destiny Village" to provide cost-free housing for 100 families. The singer also uses her tours to inspire others to help; the final Destiny's Child tour contributed 25 cents of every ticket to Ronald McDonald House Charities, while she partnered with General Mills during her "Beyoncé Experience" tour to include a food drive with each concert.

RECORDINGS

With Destiny's Child

Destiny's Child, 1998
The Writing's on the Wall, 1999
Survivor, 2001
8 Days of Christmas, 2001
This Is the Remix, 2002
Destiny Fulfilled, 2004
#1s, 2005

As Beyoncé

Dangerously in Love, 2003
Live at Wembley, 2004
B'day, 2006, deluxe edition, 2007
I Am … Sasha Fierce, 2008

MOVIE AND TELEVISION CREDITS

"Carmen: The Hip-Hopera," 2001
Austin Powers in Goldmember, 2002
The Fighting Temptations, 2003
The Pink Panther, 2006
Dreamgirls, 2006
Cadillac Records, 2008
Obsessed, 2009

SELECTED HONORS AND AWARDS

With Destiny's Child

Grammy Awards (National Academy of Recording Arts and Sciences): 2000, Best R&B Song and Best R&B Vocal Performance by a Duo or Group, both for "Say My Name"; 2001, Best R&B Vocal Performance by a Duo or Group, for "Survivor"

MTV Video Music Awards (MTV): 2000, Best R&B Video, for "Say My Name"; 2001, Best R&B Video, for "Survivor"

American Music Awards: 2001, Favorite Soul/R&B Band, Duo or Group; 2002, for Favorite Soul/R&B Band, Duo or Group, and Favorite Pop/Rock Album, for *Survivor*

Image Award (NAACP): 2001, for Outstanding Duo or Group; 2005, for Outstanding Duo or Group

Soul Train Music Awards: 2001, Sammy Davis Jr. Award for Entertainer of the Year

ASCAP Pop Music Awards, Pop Songwriter of the Year (American Society of Composers and Publishers): 2002

World Music Award: 2002, for World's Best-selling Artist or Group, Pop Group, and R&B Group

Caring Hands, Caring Hearts Award (Ronald McDonald House Charities): 2005

As Beyoncé

Grammy Awards (National Academy of Recording Arts and Sciences): 2004 (five awards), for Best R&B Song and Best Rap/Sung Collaboration (with Jay-Z), both for "Crazy in Love," Best Female R&B Vocal Performance, for "Dangerously in Love 2," Best Contemporary R&B Album, for *Dangerously in Love,* and Best R&B Performance by a Duo or Group with Vocals (with Luther Vandross), for "The Closer I Get to You"; 2006, Best R&B Performance by a Duo or Group with Vocals (with Stevie Wonder), for "So Amazing"; 2007, Best Contemporary R&B Album, for *B'day;* 2010 (six awards), Song of the Year, for "Single Ladies (Put a Ring

On It)," Best Female Pop Vocal Performance, for "Halo," Best Female
R&B Vocal Performance, for "Single Ladies (Put a Ring On It)," Best Traditional R&B Vocal Performance, for "At Last," Best R&B Song, for "Single Ladies (Put a Ring On It)," Best Contemporary R&B Album, for *I
Am...Sasha Fierce*
MTV Video Music Awards (MTV): 2003 (two awards), Best Female Video
and Best R&B Video, both for "Crazy in Love"; 2004, Best Female Video,
for "Naughty Girl"; 2006, Best R&B Video (with Slim Thug and Bun B),
for "Check on It"; 2007, Most Earthshattering Collaboration (with Shakira), for "Beautiful Liar"; 2009 (three awards), Video of the Year, Best
Choreography, and Best Editing, all for "Single Ladies (Put a Ring On It)"
Soul Train Music Awards: 2004, Sammy Davis Jr. Award for Entertainer of
the Year
Image Award (NAACP): 2004, for Entertainer of the Year
Broadcast Film Critics Association Awards: 2007, Best Song, for "Listen"
from *Dreamgirls*
American Music Awards: 2007, International Artist Award
Teen Choice Awards: 2009, Choice Music: R&B Artist, Choice Music: R&B
Track, for "Single Ladies (Put a Ring On It)"; 2010, Choice Music: R&B
Artist

FURTHER READING

Books

Arenofsky, Janice. *Beyoncé Knowles: A Biography,* 2009
Bednar, Chuck. *Beyoncé: Singer-Songwriter, Actress, and Record Producer,*
2009
Biography Today, April 2001
Knowles, Beyoncé, Kelly Rowland, and Michelle Williams. *Soul Survivors:
The Official Autobiography of Destiny's Child,* 2002

Periodicals

Allure, Feb. 2010, p.130
Current Biography Yearbook, 2001
Daily Variety, Dec. 1, 2006, p.2
Ebony, July 2002, p.36; Dec. 2005, p.148
Essence, Nov. 2008, p.126
Forbes, June 22, 2009, p.80
In Style, Jan. 2007, p.60; Nov. 2008, p. 286
Jet, Sep. 22, 2003, p.58; Dec. 6, 2004, p.60; Feb. 13, 2006, p.60
Junior Scholastic, Apr. 12, 2010, p.3
New York Times, Nov. 16, 2008, p.1L

New Yorker, Feb. 9, 2009, p.98
People, Oct. 6, 2003, p.87; Apr. 21, 2008
Texas Monthly, Apr. 2004, p.175; July 2009, p.54
Time, June 30, 2003, p.56
USA Today, Aug. 17, 2007, p.D14; Jan. 12, 2010, p.D1
Vanity Fair, Nov. 2005, p.336
Vogue, Apr. 2009, p.214

ADDRESS

Beyoncé
Music World Entertainment
1505 Hadley Street
Houston, TX 77002

WORLD WIDE WEB SITE

http://www.beyonceonline.com

Justin Bieber 1994-
Canadian Musician
Creator of the Hit Albums *My World* and *My World 2.0*

BIRTH

Justin Bieber was born on March 1, 1994, in Stratford, Ontario, Canada. His parents broke up when he was 10 months old. His father, Jeremy, eventually moved to Winnipeg, Manitoba, where he works in construction. He has kept up a relationship with his son, but Bieber has been raised by his mother, Pattie Mallette. She eventually remarried, and Bieber now has two younger half-siblings.

YOUTH

Bieber's mother was 19 years old when he was born. She had dreamed of becoming an actress, but as a young, single parent, she found she had to work more than one job just to support herself and her baby. She designed web sites, did office work, and played music for a church group. Her parents lived nearby, and they helped her out, but it was still very difficult. "We were living below the poverty line," she recalled. "We had a roof over our heads and we had food in the house, but we really struggled."

"I've always loved music, especially percussion," Bieber said. "My mom bought me my first drum kit when I was four because I was banging on everything around the house, even couches. I picked up the guitar when I was six and taught myself to play, but I didn't really start singing until I was 10."

Although she didn't have much money, Mallette did whatever she could to encourage her young son to develop his talent, which was obvious even when he was very young. "I've always loved music, especially percussion," Bieber said. "My mom bought me my first drum kit when I was four because I was banging on everything around the house, even couches. I picked up the guitar when I was six and taught myself to play, but I didn't really start singing until I was 10." He also taught himself to play keyboards and the trumpet. "When he was five, he'd hear something on the radio and go to the keyboard and figure it out," his mother remembered. He liked to sing, too, though he was more focused on instrumental music at first.

EDUCATION

Bieber attended the Stratford Northwestern Secondary School, where he played hockey and soccer. Since his singing career has taken off, he has a private tutor who makes sure that he gets at least 15 hours a week of class time. He also has voice lessons on a regular basis.

CAREER HIGHLIGHTS

When Bieber was 12 years old, he entered a local talent competition. Styled after the popular television program "American Idol," it was called "Stratford Idol." "The other people in the competition had been taking singing lessons and had vocal coaches. I wasn't taking it too seriously at the time," he recalled. "I would just sing around the house." Despite his relaxed approach, he was a strong, confident singer. Performing Ne-Yo's "So Sick" and Matchbox Twenty's "3 a.m.," he took second place in the "Stratford Idol" contest.

A few months later, Bieber was short on cash. His friends were going golfing, and he didn't have the money he needed to go along. So he came up with a plan. Stratford is home to the Stratford Shakespeare Festival, which stages a variety of plays and attracts many visitors each summer. Bieber took his guitar to one of the theaters where the festival is held. On the sidewalk outside, he opened his guitar case so that people passing by could toss money into it, and began to sing and play. Over the next few days, he earned enough money for the golfing trip—and a trip to Disneyland for himself and his mother. It was the first vacation they'd ever been able to afford.

YouTube Sensation

After "Stratford Idol," Bieber and his mother posted video clips of his performance on the YouTube web site. They wanted friends and relatives who hadn't been able to attend the show to be able to watch his performance. They also posted some new videos of him singing covers of songs by Chris Brown and Justin Timberlake. Before long, Bieber's postings were getting thousands of hits. Word was spreading, far beyond his family and friends, that Justin Bieber was a talent to be seen. It wasn't long before Mallette was contacted by people in the music business who wanted to sign Bieber to a contract. Without money to hire a lawyer, she didn't know how to sort out legitimate offers from those that would take advantage of her and her son. Not wanting to make a bad decision, she started trying to avoid the calls altogether.

That situation changed after Mallette was contacted by a talent agent named Scooter Braun. Best known for discovering rapper Asher Roth, Braun had worked as a marketing representative at So So Def Records before starting his own company. He had been looking for someone else's video on YouTube when he found Bieber's posting. Braun was very impressed. "I thought, 'I gotta find this kid.'" It took him a while to track down Mallette and get a message to her, and when he did, she only called him back "to get rid of him," according to Bieber. Instead, "they ended up having a two-hour conversation," he recalled. "My mom had that gut feeling. I think moms generally know when they have their gut feelings." Braun offered to fly Bieber and Mallette to Atlanta, Georgia, to meet with him, and they accepted. Braun won her trust and confidence, and she agreed to let him handle her son's music career.

Braun had some unusual ideas about the best way to get Bieber's career going. Many popular young music stars—including Britney Spears, Justin Timberlake, and Miley Cyrus—got their start in television programs on the Disney channel. Doing so allowed them to gain exposure and build confidence in their singing skills before trying to launch a full-blown music career. Braun felt that Bieber could, and should, take a different path. Without launching any sort of traditional publicity blitz, Braun began adding more videos to Bieber's YouTube channel. The videos didn't use backup musicians or expensive production elements; they were simply homemade videos showing off his voice, his musicianship, and his charm. Braun was counting on word of mouth to spread his young client's reputation. He thought fans would like to feel they had discovered Bieber on their own. He was right. Buzz about Bieber's videos spread quickly through the Internet, and his YouTube channel began to get millions of hits.

Wanted by Top Producers

Thanks to YouTube, Bieber had a large and growing fan base even before he had released a single. It wasn't just young girls who were talking about him, either. His reputation was growing in the music industry, but he still wasn't committed to any record company. Two influential producers emerged as the top competitors, trying to get him to sign with their labels: Justin Timberlake and Usher. Both of them had started out as teen singers and continued their success as adult artists and producers. Both of them saw huge potential in Bieber. "He had all the nuances of a classic artist," Usher recalled. "Very cute, for all the young girls, gotta have that. He had swagger. And most important, he had talent." Usher and Timberlake each felt that they could use their own experiences to help Bieber start a long-lasting career. The singer and his mother felt good about both producers, but in the end, Usher made a better offer. In October 2007, Bieber signed a contract with Usher's record label, Island Def Jam.

Even before signing Bieber, Usher saw his potential. "He had all the nuances of a classic artist," Usher recalled. "Very cute, for all the young girls, gotta have that. He had swagger. And most important, he had talent."

In spring 2008, Bieber and his mother left Stratford to move to Atlanta to focus on developing his career. The next months were busy. In addition to doing schoolwork with a tutor, Bieber spent time at voice lessons, working on original songs, and communicating with his fan base by way of Internet sites like Twitter, Facebook, MySpace, and, of course, YouTube. He also made guest appearances on television shows.

Knowing that the pressures on a rising teen star can be tough, Usher felt protective of his young protégé and spent plenty of time with him. "He's like a big brother to me," Bieber said of Usher. "We just hang out and don't really talk about music a lot. We go go-karting and to arcades and movies."

Bieber with Usher, his mentor, who signed him to the record label Island Def Jam.

My World

Bieber's first single, a love song titled "One Time," was released in spring 2009 and soon shot to the top of the *Billboard* Hot 100 chart. It was produced by Antonio "L.A." Reid, a Grammy Award-winning songwriter and producer who is also the chairman of Island Def Jam. The song's video featured a cameo appearance by Bieber's mentor, Usher. "Bieber's first *Billboard* Hot 100 single, 'One Time,' was an insanely catchy ode to young love that immediately won over fans. And so were his second, third, and fourth," wrote Monica Herrera, a music reviewer for *Billboard*. "It's hardly a stretch to imagine Bieber racking up more hits in the next decade to come."

Bieber's way of adding a dash of urban style and rhythm to sweet love songs was a winning combination, as shown in "One Time" and the songs that followed, "One Less Lonely Girl," "Favorite Girl," and "Love Me." With these songs, as reviewer Crystal Bell wrote in *Billboard*, "Bieber makes a strong case for why he's the next pop/R&B heartthrob." All of them shot to No. 1 on the charts, making him the first recording artist ever to have four No. 1 singles without having released an album. With each new single, his popularity increased still more. His promotional appearances around the U.S. and Canada began to attract thousands of wildly enthusiastic fans. In October 2009 Bieber appeared on "The Today Show" and drew a bigger crowd than any other musical artist that year, including Miley Cyrus.

My World was released in November 2009. With only seven tracks, it was really an extended-play (EP) recording, rather than a full-length album. In addition to the four hit singles that had already been released, it contained the tracks "Down to Earth," "Bigger," and "First Dance," which featured Usher. "Down to Earth" stood out from the romantic songs that made up the rest of the recording, with lyrics about painful relationships and a family breaking up. Despite its EP status, *My World* was included on the *Billboard* album charts, where it started out in the No. 6 spot. Within four months, over a million copies of *My World* had been sold.

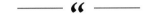

Biebermania

By that point, Bieber was already very popular with fans. But after the release of *My World,* the mobs of fans that greeted him at his appearances became even larger and more intense. The singer's road manager,

"He's like a big brother to me," Bieber said of Usher. "We just hang out and don't really talk about music a lot. We go go-karting and to arcades and movies."

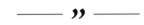

Ryan Good, described it as "mass hysteria. Loud screaming, crying, passing out. It's amazing." On November 20, a scheduled appearance by Bieber at the Roosevelt Field Mall in Garden City, New York, turned into a near-riot. It was an afternoon event, but fans began arriving early in the morning. About 3,000 people eventually gathered. The crowd got out of control, and five people had to be sent to the hospital with minor injuries. By the time Bieber arrived, the police refused to let him enter the mall because the situation with the crowd was too dangerous. Similar mob scenes took place in Paris and in Australia. In both places, crowds were dispersed due to safety concerns.

Bieber appreciates his fans, and he enjoys performing. But the level of excitement from fans has been surprising to him. "I don't really understand it, because I've never had a musician I was that into," he said. "I just try to make it as fun for them as possible. For some of them, this might be the only time they'll get to meet me." He says that the crowds rushing at him can be a little scary. He now travels with bodyguards, who keep over-eager fans at a safe distance. He tries to maintain a personal connection with his fans by way of Twitter, Facebook, and other web sites, but at the same time, he's careful not to share too much detailed personal information. With over 162 million views of his videos on YouTube, 2.6 million fans on Facebook, and 1.7 million Twitter followers, privacy has become an issue.

Bieber with some of his fans at the Nickelodeon Kids' Choice Awards.

Singing for President Obama

Throughout late 2009 and early 2010, Bieber was busy performing. During one hectic weekend in December, he took part in a Christmas show at Madison Square Garden in New York City, flew to Las Vegas to tape a New Year's Eve television special, flew to Chicago for another performance, and ended up in Washington DC, where he was part of the annual "Christmas in Washington" concert. His fellow performers there included Mary J. Blige, Neil Diamond, Sugarland, Rob Thomas, and Usher. Bieber sang "Someday at Christmas," a song by Stevie Wonder. President Barack Obama and First Lady Michelle Obama were in the audience.

In February 2010, Bieber was part of "We are the World: 25 for Haiti," a recording made by a chorus of celebrity musicians to raise money for the victims of the earthquake that struck Haiti on January 12, 2010. The song was a remake of one written and produced 25 years earlier to raise money for famine relief in Africa. In March, Bieber performed at the Kids' Choice Awards in Los Angeles. He also celebrated his 16th birthday, receiving a Range Rover as a gift from Usher. In April, he performed for the Obamas again, this time at the White House Easter Egg Roll.

My World 2.0

On March 23, 2010, Bieber's album *My World 2.0* was released. It sold 283,000 copies that first day, putting it in the No. 1 spot on the *Billboard* album chart. He was the youngest solo male artist to have a No. 1 album since Stevie Wonder had done it at age 13, in 1963. Furthermore, Bieber's first album was still at No. 5. *My World 2.0* contained 10 tracks, and despite the album's title, the material was all new. Bieber got support from older artists such as Ludacris, who contributed to "Baby," the album's first hit single, and Sean Kingston, who took part in the playful "Eenie Meenie," about a girl who can't choose between two guys. On "Overboard," Bieber sang with Jessica Jarrell, an up-and-coming female vocalist.

Reviewing *My World 2.0* for the *Washington Post,* Chris Richards found it somewhat overproduced, but praised the young singer's abilities. "If we truly want the best of America's children, let us pause and give thanks for Justin Bieber," Richards wrote. "At its best, his voice is both powerful and adorable." More praise came from Jody Rosen, a reviewer for *Rolling Stone.* Rosen noted that while "Bieber's talent is not fully formed," those who dismiss *My World 2.0* because they think he is just another cute singer "are missing out on a seriously good pop record." Bieber supported the release of *My World 2.0* with still more high-profile appearances, including appearing as a musical guest on "Saturday Night Live." He also began preparing to launch his first full-blown tour late in June 2010. Talking about the fast-paced changes that have taken place in his life since he won the "Stratford Idol" competition, he said, "It has been overwhelming, but I love it."

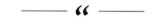

"I think that as my audience grows with me, that my lyrics will change and they'll be more directed for the older audience," Bieber commented. "I mean, right now I'm singing to young and old. I'm singing to basically anybody who wants to listen."

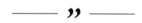

In 2010, Bieber announced plans for a couple of new projects. He will star in an autobiographical 3-D movie based on footage from his current tour. In a statement, he said that the movie was "our chance to give something very special back to all the fans who have been a huge source of inspiration and support throughout my entire career thus far." Speaking of his fans, Bieber also said that "They simply make my dreams come true every day." In addition, he signed a deal to write his memoirs for the publisher HarperCollins. *Justin Bieber: First Step 2 Forever: My Story* will be released in late 2010. Described as an "illustrated memoir," the book will chart his rise to stardom and include previously unpublished photos.

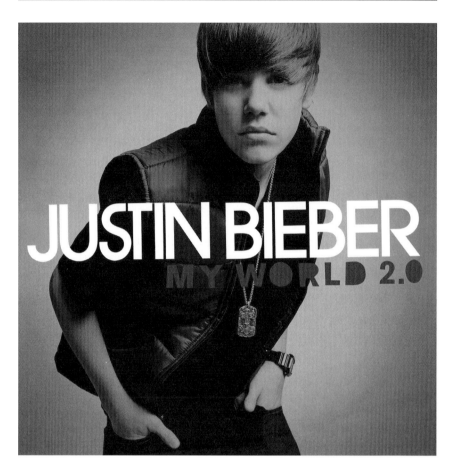

Bieber's first full album, My World 2.0, *debuted at the No. 1 spot on the charts.*

Thinking ahead, Bieber hopes to attend college. He may major in English, because he likes writing. He has thought about getting into acting, and he wants to continue with his music, which he hopes will just keep getting better. "I think that as my audience grows with me, that my lyrics will change and they'll be more directed for the older audience," he commented. "I mean, right now I'm singing to young and old. I'm singing to basically anybody who wants to listen."

HOME AND FAMILY

Although they have a home base in Atlanta, Bieber and his mother are usually on the road, traveling in a group that includes his tutor, music company representative, bodyguards, publicists, vocal coach, and road manager/stylist. "It's quite different coming where we're coming from to being driven around in limos," said Mallette. Despite his busy schedule, Bieber tries to make sure he has some time each week to do the things any kid his age would usually do, even if it means flying in a couple of his best friends from Stratford to hang out with him.

Bieber's mother is very important to him, and she travels everywhere with him. "She's been there since the beginning and has given up a lot for me, I'm very blessed to have her," he said. Mallette says she is proud of her son. "He's working really, really hard," she added. "But I'd probably be proud of him no matter what he did if he did his best and he was doing what he wanted to do and what God wanted him to do." Bieber also gives credit to his grandparents for helping to provide comfort and security for him and his mother in the days when she was a struggling single parent. "I definitely did not have a lot of money," Bieber recalled. "I couldn't afford to get a lot of new clothes a lot of times. But I had a roof over my head. I was very fortunate. I had my grandparents, I saw them a lot, they were very kind. So I grew up getting everything that I wanted."

FAVORITE MUSIC

Although Bieber likes all types of music, some of his favorite artists are Stevie Wonder, Michael Jackson, Boyz II Men, Ne-Yo, Drake, and Taylor Swift, about whom he said: "She tells stories that actually happened. Her songs are amazing."

HOBBIES AND OTHER INTERESTS

Bieber's favorite sports team is the Toronto Maple Leafs. He has played hockey with the Atlanta Knights, a AAA team. He enjoys soccer, go-karts, skateboarding, video games, and chess.

RECORDINGS

My World, 2009
My World 2.0, 2010

HONORS AND AWARDS

Teen Choice Awards: 2010 (four awards): Choice Music: Male Artist, Choice Music: Breakout Artist—Male, Choice Music: Album—Pop, for My World 2.0, and Choice Summer Music Star

FURTHER READING

Periodicals

Billboard, Nov. 14, 2009, p.31; Mar. 27, 2010, p.18
Los Angeles Times, Apr. 10, 2010, p.D1
Maclean's, Dec. 28, 2009, p.16
New York Times, Dec. 14, 2009, p.C1; Jan. 3, 2010, p.1
People, Apr. 19, 2010, p.66
Rolling Stone, Jan. 21, 2010, p.22
Washington Post, Dec. 20, 2009, p.E1; Mar. 23, 2010, p.C1

Online Articles

http://www.msnbc.com
   (MSNBC, "The Safe Sex Appeal of Justin Bieber," Apr. 21, 2010)
http://www.people.com
   (People, "Five Things to Know about Justin Bieber," Jan. 8, 2010)
http://www.rollingstone.com/music/reviews
   (Rolling Stone, "My World 2.0," Apr. 27, 2010)

ADDRESS

Justin Bieber
Island Records
825 Eighth Avenue
New York, NY 10019

WORLD WIDE WEB SITES

http://www.myspace.com/justinbieber
http://www.justinbiebermusic.com

Charles Bolden 1946-
American Astronaut and NASA Administrator
Retired United States Marine Corps Major General
First African American to Head NASA

BIRTH

Charles Frank Bolden Jr. was born in Columbia, South Carolina, on August 19, 1946. His father, Charles Frank Bolden Sr., was a social studies teacher and respected high school football coach, and his mother, Ethel M. Bolden, was a librarian, educator, and community leader. He has a younger brother, Warren Maurice Bolden. "Despite long hours and low wages, my parents made the hard choice to remain in public education, motivated by the opportunity to put young students on the path to success," Bolden commented. "They helped launch countless black students toward local, state, and national leadership positions. I was one of them."

YOUTH

When Bolden was growing up in South Carolina, life was very hard for African Americans. Many white people felt a deep and abiding prejudice against black people. African Americans were often treated as inferior, and they were expected to act subservient. During his childhood, segregation— the separation of African Americans and whites—was common in the South. The South was still segregated under what were called "Jim Crow" laws. These laws were founded on the legal principle of "separate but equal," which made it legal to discriminate against African Americans. Jim Crow laws forced the segregation of the races and created "separate but equal" public facilities—housing, schools, transportation, bathrooms, drinking fountains, movie theaters, restaurants, and more—for blacks and whites. Although these separate facilities were called equal, in reality those for blacks were miserably inadequate. African Americans usually attended dilapidated, impoverished schools with underpaid teachers. After leaving school, their opportunities for work were often just as limited.

This was the society in which Bolden was raised. Despite these challenges, he became fascinated at a young age with the nighttime sky and the idea of becoming an astronaut. But he did not think a career in space exploration was possible. "When I was a kid, all astronauts were male, all astronauts were test pilots, all astronauts were white, and all astronauts were the same size," Bolden explained. "I didn't fit into most of these categories." Although his dream seemed out of reach, he grew determined to excel at his chosen path in life and began his journey by dedicating himself to his studies.

EDUCATION

Bolden was an exemplary student and was particularly interested in the subjects of science and math. He was also active in sports, notably swimming and football, and played percussion in the school band. His parents instilled a strong sense of academic discipline in their son. "I was always encouraged to study," he recalled. "I'm very thankful for that now." Demonstrating his ingenuity and persistence, he wrote to his senators and congressmen to express his interest in attending the United States Naval Academy. He also wrote to Vice President Lyndon Johnson, who responded and asked him to contact him again when he was old enough to apply. Despite the challenges of being educated in a segregated school system, he graduated with honors in 1964 from C. A. Johnson High School in Columbia. At Bolden's repeated request, President Johnson arranged for his appointment to the U.S. Naval Academy in Annapolis, Maryland. Bolden was voted president of his class and earned a bachelor's degree in electrical science in 1968. He was one of only four African Americans out of over 800 students to graduate from the academy that year.

Following graduation, Bolden was commissioned as a second lieutenant in the Marine Corps. In 1970 he completed flight training to become a naval aviator. During this time, the United States was involved in the Vietnam War. The U.S. got involved in Vietnam in the late 1950s, when it was essentially a civil war between North Vietnam and South Vietnam. The political makeup of these two countries contributed to the decision by the U.S. to get involved there. It was the Cold War at that time, a period of extreme distrust, suspicion, and hostility between, on the one side, communist countries like the Soviet Union, China, and their allies, and, on the other side, the United States and its allies. North Vietnam was controlled by communists, who wanted to bring their political system to South Vietnam also. Many people in the U.S. felt that it was important to support South Vietnam in order to stop the spread of communism to other nations. In the late 1950s the U.S. began

When Bolden was growing up, he did not think a career in space exploration was possible. "When I was a kid, all astronauts were male, all astronauts were test pilots, all astronauts were white, and all astronauts were the same size," he explained. "I didn't fit into most of these categories."

sending in military advisers to help South Vietnam; by the early 1960s, the U.S. began sending in military troops to fight in the war. By the mid to late 1960s, there were strong voices of dissent in the U.S. against American involvement, as President Lyndon Johnson escalated the war and sent hundreds of thousands of soldiers to Vietnam.

After completing his flight training, Bolden was stationed in Thailand from 1972 to 1973. He flew more than 100 combat missions over Vietnam and surrounding areas. Upon returning to the United States, Bolden served as a recruiting officer for the Marine Corps in Los Angeles. He earned a master's degree in systems management from the University of Southern California in 1977, and then attended the United States Naval Test Pilot School at Patuxent River, Maryland, graduating in 1979.

On his first space flight, Bolden is shown at the pilot's station on the Columbia *flight deck prior to re-entry, 1986.*

CAREER HIGHLIGHTS

Bolden's training allowed him to get a job as a test pilot at the Naval Air Test Center's Systems Engineering and Strike Aircraft Test Directorates. He flew various ground-attack test projects before embarking on a long and accomplished career as an astronaut, military officer, and executive.

Joining NASA

During the late 1970s, NASA (the National Aeronautics and Space Administration) began responding to changing attitudes regarding race in America. "As we went through the sixties and through the civil rights movement," Bolden recounted, "NASA realized that it would be untenable for them to have another astronaut selection in the 1970s and 1980s and not include a culturally diverse group of people." He submitted his application to NASA and was admitted into the space shuttle program at the Lyndon B. Johnson Space Center in Houston in 1980. After undergoing rigorous training, he became a qualified astronaut in 1981.

Bolden held a variety of positions with NASA, including special assistant to the director of the Johnson Space Center, technical assistant to the director of flight crew operations, chief of the safety division at Johnson, and lead astronaut for vehicle test and checkout at the Kennedy Space Center in Florida. In addition, he took part in several space flights. The first was the Space Shuttle *Columbia* mission in 1986 (STS-61-C), followed by the Space Shuttle *Discovery* mission in 1990 (STS-31), the Space Shuttle *Atlantis* mission in 1992 (STS-45), and the Space Shuttle *Discovery* mission in 1994, a joint U.S.-Russian space flight (STS-60).

Flights in Space

Bolden's first trip to space, the *Columbia* mission in 1986, involved deploying the SATCOM KU satellite to analyze the effects of microgravity on materials processing, seed germination, and chemical reactions. The crew also conducted experiments concerning protein crystal growth and infrared imaging of Halley's Comet. On the *Discovery* mission in 1990, the crew deployed the powerful Hubble Space Telescope. This telescope, which orbits above the Earth's atmosphere, revolutionized the field of astronomy by providing detailed views of the universe that aren't distorted by the Earth's atmosphere. They also used a variety of cameras, including both the IMAX in-cabin and cargo bay cameras, for Earth observations from their record-setting altitude. Bolden served as the pilot on these first two trips to space.

Bolden's third trip to space was the *Atlantis* mission in 1992, for which he served as mission commander. This mission carried part of NASA's Space-

———— " ————

"The highlights of any flight always include the spectacular views of the earth," Bolden recalled. "We had some absolutely phenomenal passes over the United States as well as other parts of the world at night. At night you have the opportunity to see all the beautiful lights and the outlines of the cities.... It's really breathtaking."

———— 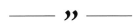 ————

lab, an orbiting laboratory designed to allow scientists to conduct experiments in a weightless environment. The crew planned to study the sun, the upper reaches of the Earth's atmosphere, and other astronomical objects using a special array of instruments for a series of experiments that constituted ATLAS-1 (Atmospheric Laboratory for Applications and Science). The ATLAS-1 experiments obtained a vast array of detailed measurements of atmospheric properties, including the chemistry of the atmosphere, solar radiation, space plasma physics, and ultraviolet astronomy. These tests contributed significantly to improving scientists' understanding of the Earth's climate and atmosphere.

Bolden's last space flight was the first joint U.S.-Russian mission. Here, five NASA astronauts and a Russian cosmonaut squeeze through the tunnel that connects the space shuttle Discovery and a module in the payload bay. Mission commander Bolden is upper right; clockwise from Bolden are mission specialists Ronald M. Sega and N. Jan Davis; payload commander Franklin R. Chang-Diaz; mission specialist cosmonaut Sergei Krikalev; and pilot Kenneth S. Reightler Jr.

In 1992 Bolden was appointed assistant deputy administrator at NASA headquarters in Washington DC. While in that position, he was selected as commander of the 1994 *Discovery* mission, the first joint U.S.-Russian space expedition. The mission became Bolden's fourth and final space flight. This mission initiated a new era of cooperative efforts in space between the United States and Russia, as Russian cosmonaut Sergei Krikalev joined the STS-60 crew. The shuttle flight was the beginning of an ongoing program in developing the international space station. STS-60 crew members did a range of experiments on the mission, and they also took on the role of teacher as they educate students in the United States and Russia about their mission objectives and what it is like to live and work in space. Bolden later claimed that working with Russian cosmonaut Sergei Krikalev caused him to undergo "a great cultural metamorphosis." He added, "I learned a lot of things from Sergei about operating in space."

After logging more than 680 hours in space, Bolden left NASA to return to military life. He became the deputy commandant of midshipmen at the U.S. Naval Academy in 1994.

Building a Military Career

After returning to active duty in the Marines in 1994, Bolden served as commanding general of 1st Marine Expeditionary Force (I MEF) during Operation Desert Thunder. Mounted in 1998 under President Bill Clinton, Operation Desert Thunder was directed against the President of Iraq, Saddam Hussein. It was part of an attempt to force the government of Iraq to allow the United Nations to inspect the country for signs of weapons of mass destruction. That same year Bolden was promoted to the rank of major general and named deputy commander of U.S. forces in Japan. From 2000 to 2002, he served as commanding general of the 3rd Marine Aircraft Wing at Marine Corps Air Station Miramar in San Diego. In 2002 President George W. Bush nominated him for the position of deputy administrator of NASA. But Bush later withdrew the nomination, opting to "keep key military personnel engaged in the battle against terrorism," according to a NASA announcement. White House spokeswoman Jeanie Mamo explained this decision, stating that Bolden's "expertise and talent is most needed in the Marines."

In 2003 Bolden entered into a new phase of his life and career when he retired from the United States Marine Corps after 34 years of service. His contributions to his country earned him the Defense Superior Service Medal and the Distinguished Flying Cross, among other honors. After his retirement, he reflected upon the difficulties and triumphs of his military career. "As an officer of Marines who happened to be black, I faced some distinct challenges from time to time," he disclosed. "The Marine Corps, however, afforded me opportunities to assume leadership roles and influence the attitudes and actions of Marines and their families, as well as civilians in nearby communities."

After his retirement, Bolden entered into the civilian workforce for the first time in his life. He took high-level jobs at such corporations as American PureTex Water, Marathon Oil, and TechTrans International. He also served as the chief executive officer of JackandPanther LLC, a military and aerospace consulting firm.

Heading NASA

Bolden's highest recognition to date came on May 23, 2009, when President Barack Obama nominated him for the position of NASA administrator, the top position in the organization. He was sworn in on July 17, 2009, becoming the first African American and the second astronaut to head NASA. "It is an honor to have been nominated by President Obama and confirmed by the Senate to lead this great NASA team," he said at his con-

The 1994 launch of the space shuttle Discovery.

firmation. He then outlined his goals for NASA: "We must build on our investment in the International Space Station, accelerate development of our next generation launch systems to enable expansion of human exploration, enhance NASA's capability to study Earth's environment, lead space science to new achievements, continue cutting-edge aeronautics research, support the innovation of American entrepreneurs, and inspire a rising generation of boys and girls to seek careers in science, technology, engineering, and math." The NASA community wholeheartedly embraced Bolden and his vision. "He's a real leader," former Johnson Space Center Director George Abbey told the *Washington Times.* "NASA has been looking for a leader like this that they could have confidence in."

A test of Bolden's leadership came early when he was faced with a difficult financial situation. NASA didn't have sufficient government funding to finance upcoming missions and projects, and he had to figure out how to compensate for the insufficient funding. To remedy the situation, he proposed that NASA seek out privately owned companies to invest in its future. "The government cannot fund everything that we need to do, but we can inspire and open the door for commercial entrepreneurial entities to become involved, to become partners with NASA." He specifically reached out to the African-American business community, encouraging black entrepreneurs to invest in space travel and technology. As he proclaimed in his 2009 address to the Congressional Black Caucus, "We believe that the development of commercial space is a great future frontier of American economic growth. It offers to African-American risk takers, men and women with ideas and the courage to pursue them, a place at the table not just at NASA, but also on the space frontier. That spirit—of risk bringing rewards; of creativity and innovation—is the spirit that America will need now more than ever to strengthen our economy and remain competitive in the global marketplace."

Creating an International Alliance

As part of his ongoing efforts to expand the resources available to NASA, Bolden signed cooperative agreements with a number of countries and organizations. He oversaw pacts with the governments of Canada and France for future space projects designed to study the atmosphere of Mars and survey the surfaces of the Earth's oceans. Similarly, he reached an agreement with the European Space Agency (ESA) regarding cooperation in the field of space transportation. "From shuttle Spacelab missions to the International Space Station, ESA has a long history of participating with NASA in human

"He's a real leader," former Johnson Space Center Director George Abbey said when Bolden was named NASA administrator. "NASA has been looking for a leader like this that they could have confidence in."

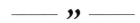

spaceflight," he asserted. "With this agreement, it is our intent to continue to build this relationship, sharing valuable engineering analyses and technology concepts that will help transport humans to low Earth orbit and beyond." He also signed an agreement with the government of Japan, outlining the terms of international collaboration on the Global Precipitation Measurement (GPM) mission, a project to track climate information.

As he lays the groundwork for new NASA projects, Bolden is keeping his eye on future endeavors, especially the possibility of landing on Mars. "In my lifetime, I will be incredibly disappointed if we have not at least reached Mars," he admitted. Another of his future goals is to extend the operation of the international space station beyond its planned closing date of 2016.

Promoting Space Education.

Before Bolden became NASA administrator, he began to notice a lack of enthusiasm from young people about space exploration. "If I go to a classroom today, it's different than when I went as an astronaut in 1980," he explained. "I could ask then, 'How many of you want to be an astronaut?' and every hand went up in the class. When I go to a school today and ask that question, I may see three hands." After his confirmation, he reached out to students in the hopes of promoting interest in NASA. "We can continue to inspire the next generation of NASA scientists and engineers by holding more competitions to help high-school and college students turn their creative talents to exploring our planet, solar system, and galaxy [and] ensuring more government scientists and engineers are mentoring and tutoring in classrooms," he said.

"If you have the ideas, the courage, the hard work, nothing in space is out of reach," Bolden has advised young people. "Don't ever give up on yourself or your dreams. Don't listen to people that tell you what you can't do! If you can dream it, you can do it! I am living proof of that."

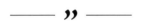

To this end, Bolden took the time to meet with students in DEVELOP, a NASA training and development program that brings the concepts of space research to local communities. In addition, he gave an address at the Charles F. Bolden Elementary/Middle School in Beaufort, South Carolina, where he serves as an inspiration in terms of both his accomplishments and his character. The school's principal, Jacque Taton-Saunders, told the *Beaufort Gazette*, "Around the halls of our school, you hear things like, 'We don't do things like that at Bolden,' 'That's not the Bolden way,' or 'Do you think Gen. Bolden got to be an astronaut acting like that?' He's been a great role model."

MARRIAGE AND FAMILY

Bolden is married to Alexis "Jackie" Walker of Columbia, South Carolina. They have known each other since Bolden was three years old, and Bolden

Bolden and NASA Kennedy Space Center Director Bob Cabana welcome home the crew of the space shuttle Endeavour *after they completed a 16-day journey of more than 6.5 million miles.*

has praised her as "a loving and supportive wife who suffered through the difficult periods along with me." Their son Anthony Che was born in 1971 and became a lieutenant general in the Marine Corps. Their daughter Kelly Michelle was born in 1976 and became a plastic surgeon. They have three granddaughters, Mikaley, Kyra, and Talia.

MAJOR INFLUENCES

Bolden has cited Captain Frederick C. Branch as an inspiration on his life and career. The first African-American officer in the U.S. Marine Corps, Branch met Bolden in 1975 at a military convention held in honor of the first black Marines to train at the formerly segregated Montford Point Camp in North Carolina. Bolden has also named Frank Peterson—the first African-American aviator in the Marine Corps and the first black Marine to be promoted to the rank of lieutenant general—as a source of inspiration. Bolden has acknowledged the strength that he has drawn from such leaders. "Though my 34-year journey as an active duty Marine Corps officer was not without its challenges, I was blessed with the legacy of strong and dynamic men."

Bolden has also credited the pioneers of the civil rights movement with paving the way for his successes by fighting against the odds, and he has

*Bolden with Anatoly Perminov, head of the Russian Federal Space Agency,
shown at the Mission Control Center in Russia.*

consistently tried to spread that spirit of bold accomplishment to subsequent generations. "Believe in yourself," he urged in J. Alfred Phelps's book *They Had a Dream.* "Don't let anybody else determine what your life is going to be. Pick some goal that's just slightly out of your reach, then go for it. Be persistent and don't be afraid of failing. Some of my best accomplishments … have come after I've failed, picked myself up, and tried again." By demonstrating this sense of determination and dedication, Bolden has become a role model himself. "If you have the ideas, the courage, the hard work, nothing in space is out of reach," he has advised young people. "Don't ever give up on yourself or your dreams. Don't listen to people that tell you what you can't do! If you can dream it, you can do it! I am living proof of that." As Senator Lindsey Graham declared in an interview, "There's no better example of what we can do in America than what General Bolden has achieved."

MEMORABLE EXPERIENCES

During his four space missions, Bolden saw many sights that he will never forget. "The highlights of any flight always include the spectacular views of the earth," he recalled. "We had some absolutely phenomenal passes over the United States as well as other parts of the world at night. At night you have the opportunity to see all the beautiful lights and the outlines of the cities.... Down south towards Antarctica you would frequently see what they call the 'southern lights'; the Aurora Australis," he explained. "The lights are caused by electrically charged particles coming into the atmosphere from outer space and causing energy to be given off in the form of light.... It's really breathtaking."

In contrast to the awe-inspiring beauty and thrill of space travel, an astronaut's job also encompasses great risks. The dangers associated with his career, however, have never deterred Bolden. When the Space Shuttle *Columbia* tragically exploded over Texas in 2003, he mourned the loss of his colleagues but remained unshaken in his dedication to space flight. "Why would I do something different when I've been blessed with a life like I've had," he explained. The *Columbia* tragedy also served as a reminder of the destruction of the Space Shuttle *Challenger*, which exploded shortly after take-off in 1986. "Every time I watch a launch, even today, [the *Challenger*] is on my mind," he confessed. Remaining committed to the shuttle program despite such concerns served to strengthen his legacy as an astronaut.

— **"** —

"Believe in yourself. Don't let anybody else determine what your life is going to be. Pick some goal that's just slightly out of your reach, then go for it. Be persistent and don't be afraid of failing. Some of my best accomplishments . . . have come after I've failed, picked myself up, and tried again."

— **"** —

Bolden's accomplishments as a marine and an astronaut were recognized by his home state in 1999 when he was inducted into the South Carolina Hall of Fame. During the induction ceremony, he urged a crowd of local schoolchildren to follow in his footsteps. "Do the best you can and dream big dreams," he advised. "A dreamer, that's what I was, what I am, and what our youth should be." In 2006 he was honored for his NASA career by being inducted into the Kennedy Space Center's U.S. Astronaut Hall of Fame in Florida.

HOBBIES AND OTHER INTERESTS

When he is not involved with his daily duties as NASA administrator, Bolden enjoys such sports as soccer and racquetball, and keeps in shape by running and swimming. He is also an active member of the Marine Corps

Association, the University of Southern California Alumni Association, and the Naval Academy Alumni Association.

HONORS AND AWARDS

University of Southern California Outstanding Alumni Award: 1982
National Technical Association Honorary Fellow: 1983
Defense Superior Service Medal: 1986
NASA Space Flight Medal: 1986; 1991; 1992; 1994
NASA Exceptional Service Medal: 1988; 1989; 1991
University of Southern California Alumni Award of Merit: 1989
Defense Meritorious Service Medal: 1990
AAS (American Astronautical Society) Flight Achievement Award: 1991
NASA Outstanding Leadership Medal: 1992
NASA Distinguished Service Medal: 1993; 1995
Yuri A. Gagarin Gold Medal: 1995
Inducted into the South Carolina Hall of Fame: 1999
Inducted into the Kennedy Space Center's U.S. Astronaut Hall of Fame: 2006

FURTHER READING

Books

Encyclopedia Britannica, 2009
Gubert, Betty Kaplan, Miriam Saywer, and Caroline M. Fannin. *Distinguished African Americans in Aviation and Space Science,* 2002
Phelps, J. Alfred. *They Had a Dream: The Story of African-American Astronauts,* 1994
Walton, Darwin McBeth. *Overcoming Challenges: The Life of Charles F. Bolden, Jr.,* 1999 (juvenile)
Who's Who among African Americans, 16th ed., 2003

Periodicals

Jet, Feb. 21, 1994, p.9
New York Times, Mar. 3, 1986, p.9; May 16, 2009, p.A11
Washington Post, Feb. 3, 2003, p.C1
Washington Times, May 24, 2009, p.A1; July 20, 2009, p.E7

Online Articles

http://www.news.cnet.com
(CNET, "Obama Picks Former Astronaut to Lead NASA," May 23, 2009)
http://www.jsc.nasa.gov/Bios/htmlbios/bolden-cf.html
(NASA, Lyndon B. Johnson Space Center, "Astronaut Biography:

Charles Bolden, Major General, USMC Ret., NASA Administrator," Sep. 2009)
http://topics.nytimes.com/topics/reference/timestopics/people/b/charles_f_bolden_jr/index.html
(New York Times, "Times Topics: Charles Bolden," multiple articles, various dates)
http://www.time.com
(Time Magazine, "Charles Bolden: The Next Boss at NASA?" May 19, 2009)

ADDRESS

Charles Bolden
NASA Headquarters
300 E Street SW
Washington, DC 20546-0001

WORLD WIDE WEB SITES

http://www.nasa.gov/audience/forstudents
http://www.jsc.nasa.gov/Bios/htmlbios/bolden-cf.html
http://raahistory.com
http://www.nasm.si.edu/blackwings

Drew Brees 1979-

American Professional Football Quarterback with
the New Orleans Saints
Most Valuable Player of Super Bowl XLIV in 2010

BIRTH

Drew Christopher Brees was born on January 15, 1979, in Dallas, Texas. His parents, Chip Brees and Mina (Akins) Brees, were both lawyers. They named their first child after Drew Pearson, a star wide receiver for the Dallas Cowboys of the National Football League (NFL).

When Brees was seven years old, his family moved to Austin, Texas. Although his parents divorced a short time later, they maintained a friendly relationship. Drew and his younger brother, Reid, divided their time evenly between their parents' houses. Chip Brees later married Amy Hightower, and they had a daughter, Audrey, who is Drew's half-sister. Mina Brees later married Harley Clark, who originated the famous "hook 'em horns" hand gesture used by fans of the University of Texas Longhorns.

YOUTH

As a boy, Brees loved to play sports with his brother and neighborhood friends. "We played in the street, in the yard, using the garage as a backstop for pitching to each other," he recalled. "We were always going to the park. It was constant sports and activity."

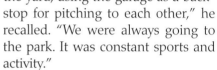

As a boy, Brees loved to play sports with his brother and neighborhood friends. "We played in the street, in the yard, using the garage as a backstop for pitching to each other," he recalled. "We were always going to the park. It was constant sports and activity."

Brees was an athletic kid who showed talent in a variety of sports. In baseball he played pitcher, shortstop, and third base. When he was 12 years old, he broke the Little League home run record for the city of Austin. He always wore jersey number 9 to be like his idol, Major League Baseball Hall of Famer Ted Williams.

Brees learned to play tennis from his mother, who had been a highly regarded player in her youth. "I wanted both Drew and his brother to be great tennis players, because that's my favorite sport," she admitted. "I was hoping he could be the next Pete Sampras or Andre Agassi." Brees ranked first in the state of Texas in the under-12 age group before he drifted away from the game. Still, the graceful footwork he developed as a tennis player has served him well in his football career.

Growing up, Brees's main exposure to football came from his maternal grandfather, Ray Akins. After fighting in the Pacific during World War II, Akins launched a career as a high-school football coach. The military discipline he instilled in his players helped make him a coaching legend in football-crazy Texas. Brees often visited his grandfather during the summer and attended his team's practice sessions. "He would tell us stories about the war and about football and about the value of hard work," he remembered. "He was an amazing man."

EDUCATION

Short and skinny as a kid, Brees did not play organized football until his freshman year at Westlake High School in Austin. Even then, he saw little action as the third-string quarterback on the junior varsity team. But Brees worked hard to learn the game and develop his skills. By the time he reached his junior year in 1995, he had earned the starting quarterback job on the varsity squad. Over the next two years, Brees led the Westlake Chaparrals to an amazing record of 28 wins, 0 losses, and 1 tie. Showing remarkable poise and accuracy as a passer, he threw for 5,416 yards and 50 touchdowns during those two seasons. Brees capped off his senior year in 1996 by leading his team to the Texas Class 5A state championship.

Despite his impressive performance on the football field, Brees attracted very little interest from college football recruiters when he graduated from high school in 1997. He was particularly disappointed not to receive scholarship offers from the two college football powerhouses in his home state, the University of Texas and Texas A&M University. "Believe me, we told them he was the most accurate passer we'd ever seen, that he was a great leader and a tough kid," remembered Westlake's offensive coordinator, Neal Lahue. "Nobody listened." Most college recruiters seemed concerned about his size. Brees was barely six feet tall, and recruiters worried that he would not be able to see over the opposing team's defensive line. "I just never believed that [height] mattered," he noted. "To play the quarterback position, it's all in the heart and the mind."

Purdue University Boilermakers

One of the few teams that offered Brees a full football scholarship was Purdue University in West Lafayette, Indiana. He jumped at the chance to play in the Big Ten Conference and to attend Purdue's prestigious Krannert School of Management. He spent his freshman year in 1997 learning Coach Joe Tiller's complex offensive system as the Boilermakers' backup quarterback.

As a sophomore in 1998, however, Brees won the starting job and showed phenomenal accuracy as a passer. He set Big Ten records in pass attempts (569), completions (361), completion percentage (63.4), passing yards (3,983), and touchdowns (39). "This guy has thrown the ball better than anybody we've had in this system," Tiller declared. Brees led the Boilermakers to an impressive 9-4 record for the season. He topped off his great year by throwing a last-second, game-winning touchdown pass in the Alamo Bowl to upset fourth-ranked Kansas State.

This outstanding 1998 season did not earn Brees much respect at the national level. Most football analysts gave credit for Purdue's success—and his

*Brees's accuracy as a passer was evident early on, as in this
1999 Purdue game against Penn State.*

impressive passing statistics—to Tiller's offensive system. "A lot of credit should go to the system," Brees acknowledged. "If you weren't throwing so many passes, you wouldn't be putting up all those numbers. But you still have to complete them. You have to know where to go with the football. The system does provide the opportunity, but you still have to execute."

Brees began to win over his doubters by turning in another strong performance during his junior season in 1999. He completed 337 of 554 passes (60.8 percent) for 3,909 yards and 25 touchdowns. He ranked third in the nation in total offense with 340.5 yards per game and finished fourth in the voting for the Heisman Trophy, awarded each year to the top player in college football. Brees also won the NCAA's first Socrates Award, presented annually to the nation's finest player in terms of academics, athletics, and community service. But his personal accolades did not translate into team success. Purdue finished the year with a 7-5 record and a loss to Georgia in the Outback Bowl.

Brees was disappointed not to receive scholarship offers from the two college football powerhouses in his home state, the University of Texas and Texas A&M University. "Believe me, we told them he was the most accurate passer we'd ever seen, that he was a great leader and a tough kid," remembered Westlake's offensive coordinator, Neal Lahue. "Nobody listened."

Rather than leaving early for the NFL, Brees decided to return to Purdue for his senior year in 2000. His goal was to lead the Boilermakers to a Big Ten championship and earn a trip to the Rose Bowl for the first time since 1967. He had another outstanding year, completing 309 of 512 passes (60.4 percent) for 3,668 yards and 26 touchdowns. Purdue posted an 8-4 record to claim a share of the Big Ten title and a spot in the Rose Bowl.

Although the Boilermakers lost to the Washington Huskies by a score of 34-24, Brees won the Maxwell Award as the nation's top collegiate player and finished third in the Heisman voting.

Brees graduated from Purdue in 2001 with a bachelor's degree in industrial management and manufacturing. His 3.4 grade point average earned him Academic All-American Player of the Year honors and an NFL post-graduate scholarship. He left Purdue as the Big Ten's all-time career leader in passing yards (11,792), total yards (12,693), touchdown passes (90), pass attempts (1,678), completions (1,026), and completion percentage (.611).

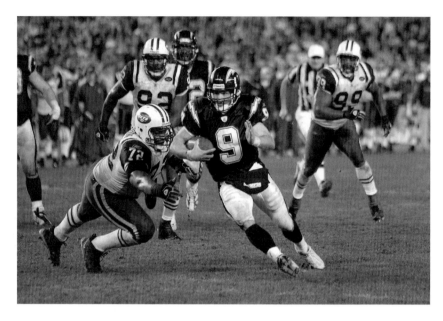

In 2005, Brees led the Chargers to the first round of the playoffs, where they lost to the New York Jets in overtime. Here, Brees runs for a first down at the one-yard line to set up the tying score.

CAREER HIGHLIGHTS

NFL—The San Diego Chargers

After completing his college football career, Brees was selected as the first pick in the second round of the 2001 NFL draft (32nd overall) by the San Diego Chargers. Although the Chargers had posted a dismal 1-15 record the previous year, fans hoped that the addition of Brees and running back LaDainian Tomlinson (San Diego's first-round pick) would revitalize the franchise. Brees signed a four-year contract with the Chargers worth $3.6 million, plus a $2 million signing bonus. He spent most of his rookie season watching from the bench as veteran quarterback Doug Flutie led the team to a 5-11 record.

Brees took over the starting job at the beginning of the 2002 season. He raised the expectations of Chargers fans early in the season by winning 6 of the first 7 games he started. San Diego came back to earth in the second half of the season, however, to finish the year at 8-8. The team continued to struggle at the outset of the 2003 season, losing 7 of the first 8 games. Brees threw 15 interceptions and only 11 touchdowns during this frustrating stretch. "I just felt helpless," he recalled. "I mean, it was hard on everyone, but I was very, very disappointed. Nothing ever felt right. We lost our first two games; then all of a sudden we were 0-5. Then people started pointing fingers, and the wheels just fell off the bus. I started pressing, trying to win each game on every play." Brees was benched for the final five games of the season in favor of Flutie, and the Chargers ended the year with a 4-12 record.

By the end of the disappointing 2003 season, San Diego management decided that the team needed to find a new quarterback. They used the first pick of the 2004 NFL draft to select quarterback Eli Manning, who quickly indicated that he had no desire to play for the Chargers. The team responded by trading Manning for another rookie quarterback, Philip Rivers. With Rivers on the roster, Brees found himself facing a major threat to his career. "People were turning their back on me and saying I couldn't play and I wasn't the right guy for this team," he acknowledged. "It was devastating. I was angry. No one wants to hear that he's not wanted. But once I got past it, I knew I could only worry about things in my control."

"People were turning their back on me and saying I couldn't play and I wasn't the right guy for this team," Brees acknowledged. *"It was devastating. I was angry. No one wants to hear that he's not wanted. But once I got past it, I knew I could only worry about things in my control."*

Making a Comeback

Prior to the start of the 2004 season, Brees analyzed every aspect of his game. He changed his training regimen and diet, and he redoubled his commitment to hard work and preparation. The changes paid off for both him and the Chargers. With Brees starting 15 games, San Diego went from worst to first in a single season and claimed the AFC West Division title with a 12-4 record. Brees led the way by passing for 3,159 yards, 27 touchdowns, and only 7 interceptions. His 104.8 passer rating ranked third in the NFL, and he earned his first Pro Bowl appearance. "I'm sure there was a lot of pressure on people that if I wasn't getting the job done, it was time to pull the plug and put the new guy in, you know, the future," he noted. "I don't play to prove people wrong. I don't want success so I can shove it in other people's faces. I play to win." Although the Chargers lost to the New York Jets in the first round of the playoffs, the league recognized Brees's remarkable career turnaround by naming him Comeback Player of the Year.

The successful 2004 campaign created a dilemma for San Diego management. They had signed Rivers to a six-year, $41 million contract, but now it appeared that Brees—who was eligible to become a free agent—gave the team its best chance to reach the playoffs again in 2005. They ultimately decided to designate Brees as the Chargers' "franchise player," which prevented him from becoming a free agent for one year in exchange for an $8 million contract. Brees responded by turning in another strong performance in 2005, throwing for 3,576 yards and 24 touchdowns with only 15 interceptions. It was not enough to lift the Chargers into the playoffs, however, as the team finished the season with a 9-7 record.

———— " ————

"When I visited New Orleans, I saw it all, the good and the bad," Brees recalled. "The city was devastated.... Cars lying on top of houses. Boats through living-room windows. I felt like I was driving through a World War II documentary. But I just thought, 'This is a chance to be part of something incredible—the rebuilding of an American city.' I felt like it was a calling. Like I was destined to be here."

———— " ————

Brees's departure from San Diego became a certainty in the final game of 2005 against the Denver Broncos. The quarterback dove to recover a fumble, and an opposing player landed on his throwing arm. Brees suffered a serious injury to his shoulder that required offseason surgery. "As much as I wanted the Chargers to resign me, I had a bad feeling that that might have been my last snap in a Chargers uniform," he related. "It was."

Joining the New Orleans Saints

The injury to Brees's throwing arm not only made the Chargers hesitant to resign him, but also limited his prospects on the free-agent market. One of the few teams that showed a consistent interest in acquiring his services was the New Orleans Saints. The Saints were beginning a rebuilding phase unlike any other in NFL history. On August 28, 2005, the city of New Orleans and other parts of the Gulf Coast had been devastated by Hurricane Katrina. This natural disaster took the lives of over 1,800 people and caused more than $80 billion in property damage. The Superdome, where the Saints played their home games, had served as an emergency shelter for 20,000 people during and immediately after the hurricane, and it sustained serious damage from wind and flooding. During the 2005 season, the Saints were forced to practice at a local high school, lift weights in

Brees joined the New Orleans Saints soon after Hurricane Katrina devastated the region. The Superdome, the team's home, was severely damaged by the disaster.

a tent, watch game films at a convention center, and play their home games in Baton Rouge, San Antonio, and even New Jersey. Partly as a result of all the disruptions, the Saints posted a dismal 3-13 record.

When Brees entered into negotiations with the Saints six months after Katrina, he and his wife came to New Orleans to survey the damage. "When I visited New Orleans, I saw it all, the good and the bad," he recalled. "The city was devastated. Brittany and I saw the Lower Ninth Ward. Unbelievable. Cars lying on top of houses. Boats through living-room windows. I felt like I was driving through a World War II documentary. But I just thought, 'This is a chance to be part of something incredible—the rebuilding of an American city.' I felt like it was a calling. Like I was destined to be here."

Brees signed a six-year, $60 million contract with the Saints. He became part of a major rebuilding process that included a new head coach, Sean Payton, and 27 new players. "The opportunity to come to a place that needs that rebuilding and resurgence, there's something to be said for being a part of that," Brees declared. "Obviously this city's trying to rebuild, trying to get back on track. We as a franchise are trying to rebuild, get back on track. The fact that we're going to be doing it together is a great thing."

Making the Playoffs

Everything came together to make 2006 a magical season for the Saints. With repairs completed at the Superdome, the team sold out every home game to season ticket holders—a first for any NFL team. The incredible fan support helped lift New Orleans to an 11-6 record and the second seed for the playoffs. Brees led the way with 356 completions for an NFL-leading 4,418 yards, with 26 touchdowns and only 11 interceptions. "We had a whole new offensive line, a rookie split end, other guys with little experience," Payton noted. "That's a lot of new pieces to the puzzle, and Drew has been the guy to bring them all together."

The Saints received a bye in the first round of the playoffs, then defeated the Philadelphia Eagles 27-24 to earn a spot in the NFC Championship game for the first time in franchise history. Although the Saints fell one game short of reaching the Super Bowl, losing to the Chicago Bears 39-16 in the NFC title game, New Orleans fans enjoyed the highly successful season. Brees was named to the 2006 NFL All-Pro Team in recognition of his contributions. "Really, the only team that believed in me was the Saints, and I feel like I owe them a big debt of gratitude," he said afterward. "I want to give them what they saw in me, which was a guy who could lead this team to a championship."

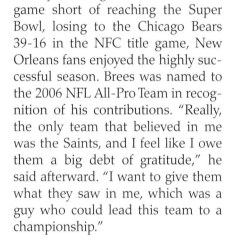

"*Really, the only team that believed in me was the Saints, and I feel like I owe them a big debt of gratitude,*" *Brees stressed.* "*I want to give them what they saw in me, which was a guy who could lead this team to a championship.*"

Brees continued to put up great numbers in 2007. He finished the season with a league-leading 440 completions for 4,423 yards, with 28 touchdowns and 18 interceptions. The Saints struggled with injuries to several key players, however, and missed the playoffs with a 7-9 record. Brees had a remarkable year in 2008, when he became only the second quarterback in NFL history to pass for more than 5,000 yards in a season. His total of 5,069 yards narrowly missed beating the all-time record of 5,084 set by Dan Marino in 1984. Brees also led the league in completions with 413 and tied for first in touchdowns with 34. He was named Offensive Player of the Year and voted to his third career Pro Bowl appearance. Unfortunately, the Saints' defense struggled throughout the season and the team missed the playoffs with an 8-8 record. Still, Brees saw a great deal of potential for fu-

In 2007, the Saints made it to the NFC Championship game for the first time in franchise history. Brees is shown being sacked by Chicago Bears defender Israel Idonije (71) and Lance Briggs (55), and the Saints went on to lose 39-16.

ture success. "Three, four, five games all came down to one or two plays for us," he noted, "and if we make those plays, that's us in the Super Bowl."

The Saints Make It to the Super Bowl

Shortly before the start of the 2009 season, Brees received the sad news that his mother had passed away. But he did not allow his personal loss to distract him from his professional goal—marching the Saints all the way to the Super Bowl. The team got off to a fantastic start in the 2009 season, winning its first 13 games. The entire city of New Orleans rejoiced with each victory. Fans came up with a chant to express their belief that the Saints were unstoppable: "Who dat say they gonna beat them Saints?" The phrase "Who Dat" appeared on signs, T-shirts, and other merchandise all over town.

With Brees at the helm, Payton built the most potent offense in the NFL, averaging 40 points per game. "Drew and Sean have such a special relationship," said Brittany, Brees's wife. "They're so similar, such hard workers. They weren't the biggest or strongest. But they're smart guys who are going to figure out a way to win." Brees set a new NFL record by completing 70.62 percent of his passes (363 of 514), breaking a 27-year-old mark set by Ken Anderson. Adding 34 touchdowns and only 11 interceptions, Brees also earned a league-leading passer rating of 109.6.

After clinching a spot in the playoffs, New Orleans took the opportunity to rest some injured players and lost its final three games of the season. The Saints broke their losing streak as soon as the playoffs began, however, crushing the Arizona Cardinals 45-14 to win the division. The Saints moved on to the NFC Championship game, where they faced the Minnesota Vikings. The two teams waged an epic, seesaw battle through three quarters. With the game tied 28-28 and five minutes left to play, veteran quarterback Brett Favre drove the Vikings to the Saints' 33-yard line. Minnesota was then called for a penalty for having too many players on the field. The loss of yardage forced Favre to throw a pass, and Saints cornerback Tracy Porter picked it off for an interception. New Orleans kicked a field goal on its first possession of overtime to win 31-28 and reach the Super Bowl for the first time in franchise history.

Winning the Super Bowl and Earning the MVP Award

As Super Bowl XLIV approached, most analysts described the Saints as heavy underdogs. After all, Brees and his teammates had little playoff experience compared to their opponents, four-time league MVP Peyton Manning and the Indianapolis Colts. When the game got underway, the

In 2009, Brees led the league in passing, completing 70.62 percent of his passes and earning a rating of 109.6.

The Saints beat the Indianapolis Colts to win the 2010 Super Bowl 31-17, and Brees won the MVP award in recognition of his superlative play: 32 out of 39 passes completed for 288 yards and 2 touchdowns.

Colts jumped out to a 10-0 lead in the first quarter. The Saints overcame their early jitters, however, and scored two field goals in the second quarter to cut the deficit to 10-6 at halftime. Kicking off to start the second half, Payton shocked the Colts—as well as the millions of people watching the game—by trying an onside kick. The gamble worked perfectly, and the Saints drove straight down the field for a touchdown on the ensuing offensive possession to take a 13-10 lead. The Colts answered with a touchdown of their own, but the Saints added another field goal to close the gap to 17-16 at the end of the third quarter.

Still trailing by a point with 10 minutes left in regulation, Brees took matters into his own hands. He called his teammates into a huddle and told them, "Let's be special." Then he proceeded to hit seven passes to seven different receivers for a touchdown, followed by yet another pass to an eighth receiver for a 2-point conversion and a 24-17 lead. Porter, the Saints' defensive back who had made the key interception against Favre, sealed the victory by intercepting a Manning pass with three minutes remaining and running it back for a touchdown. The Saints won the Super Bowl by a score of 31-17.

Brees was an obvious choice for Most Valuable Player honors. He set a Super Bowl record by completing 82.1 percent of his passes (32 out of 39) for 288 yards and 2 touchdowns. "We played for so much more than ourselves—we played for our city. We played for the entire Gulf Coast region. We played for the entire 'Who Dat Nation,'" Brees said afterward. "Whoever thought that this could be happening? Eighty-five percent of the city was underwater. People were evacuating to places all over the country. Most people left not knowing whether New Orleans would ever come back, or if the organization would ever come back. But not only did the organization and the city come back. And so many of our core group of players came in that year as free agents, and we all looked at one another and said, 'We're going to rebuild together. We're going to lean on each other.' And that's what we've done."

In winning the Super Bowl MVP award, Brees proved that hard work, preparation, intelligence, and leadership ability can overcome limitations in physical size and strength. Since joining the Saints in 2006, he has passed for more yards (18,298) than any other NFL quarterback. He has raised the Saints franchise from the lowest point in its history all the way to the pinnacle of professional football. In the process, he has become a hero to the people of New Orleans and played a vital role in restoring the city's pride. "I get people stopping me on the street every day, like 20 times a day, telling me how great it makes them feel and how it just helps them go about their day and rebuild their life," Brees stated. "It means a tremendous amount."

MARRIAGE AND FAMILY

Brees married Brittany Dudchenko, whom he met while they were both students at Purdue. They have a son, Baylen Robert Brees, who was born on his father's 30th birthday in 2009, and they are expecting another child in late 2010.

HOBBIES AND OTHER INTERESTS

Other than spending time with his family, Brees's main hobby is collecting military coins. He is also known as one of the most active NFL players in terms of volunteer work and community service. Since founding the Brees Dream Foundation in 2003, he and his wife have raised or committed over $4.5 million for various causes. The foundation has helped rebuild schools, parks, playgrounds, and athletic fields in New Orleans. It gives away 300 bicycles to needy children every year at Christmas. It also provides care for

———— *"* ————

By leading the Saints to a Super Bowl championship, Brees became a hero to the people of New Orleans and played a vital role in restoring the city's pride. "I get people stopping me on the street every day, like 20 times a day, telling me how great it makes them feel and how it just helps them go about their day and rebuild their life," he stated. "It means a tremendous amount."

———— *"* ————

cancer patients and funding to advance cancer research.

The foundation sponsors a number of annual charity events, including an NFL players golf tournament, a youth football gridiron challenge, and Habitat for Humanity home-building projects. One of Brees's favorite events is the Brees on the Seas deep-sea fishing excursion, in which he takes seriously ill children and their families out on a boat in the Gulf of Mexico. "When you see the look on these kids' faces when they catch a fish—some of them have never caught a fish in their life—sometimes that's the best therapy, as good as any medicine you could give them," he related.

Finally, Brees serves as a spokesman for the NFL Play 60 program, which encourages American kids to engage in physical activity for at least 60 minutes per day to prevent obesity and achieve better health. Brees has received several honors for his community service, including the 2006 Walter Payton Man of the Year Award from the NFL and the 2008 Horizon Award from the U.S. Congress.

WRITINGS

Coming Back Stronger; Unleashing the Power of Adversity, 2010 (with Chris Fabry)

HONORS AND AWARDS

Texas High School 5A Offensive Player of the Year: 1996
Big Ten Conference Player of the Year: 1998, 2000
Socrates Award: 1999
Maxwell Award: 2000
Academic All-American Player of the Year: 2000
NFL Comeback Player of the Year: 2004
NFL Pro Bowl: 2004, 2006, 2008, 2009

NFC Offensive Player of the Year: 2006, 2008, 2009
NFL Walter Payton Man of the Year: 2006
Horizon Award for Making a Difference in the Lives of Youth (U.S. Congress): 2008
NFL Offensive Player of the Year: 2008
Super Bowl XLIV Most Valuable Player: 2010
ESPY Awards (ESPN): 2010 (four awards, Best Male Athlete, Best Championship Performance, Best NFL Player, and Best Team (with the New Orleans Saints)

FURTHER READING

Books

Brees, Drew, and Chris Fabry. *Coming Back Stronger: Unleashing the Power of Adversity,* 2010
DiPrimio, Pete. *Drew Brees,* 2010 (juvenile)
Donnes, Alan, and Chris Myers. *Patron Saints: How the Saints Gave New Orleans a Reason to Believe,* 2007
Savage, Jeff. *Amazing Athletes: Drew Brees,* 2010 (juvenile)

Periodicals

Austin Business Journal, Nov. 30, 2001, p.23
Los Angeles Times, Feb. 8, 2010, p.C1
San Diego Union Tribune, Jan. 21, 2007
Sporting News, Aug. 21, 2000, p.78; Nov. 6, 2000, p.58; Aug. 17, 2009, p.55
Sports Illustrated, Aug. 16, 1999, p.56; Apr. 30, 2001, p.56; Nov. 15, 2004, p.61; Sep. 21, 2009, p.52; Jan. 18, 2010, p.54; Feb. 15, 2010, p.30
Sports Illustrated Kids, Winter 2008, p.21; Dec. 2009, p.24
Texas Monthly, Jan. 2002, p.82
USA Today, Nov. 17, 2004, p.C1; Sep. 8, 2006, p.F14; Oct. 2, 2009, p.C1; Oct. 26, 2009, p.C5; Feb. 8, 2010, p.C8

ADDRESS

Drew Brees
New Orleans Saints
5800 Airline Drive
Metairie, LA 70003

WORLD WIDE WEB SITES

http://www.drewbrees.com
http://www.neworleanssaints.com

Ursula M. Burns 1958-

American Business Executive
CEO of Xerox
First African-American Woman to Head a Fortune
500 Company

BIRTH

Ursula M. Burns was born on September 20, 1958, the second
of her mother's three children. Her father played little role in
her life, and it was her mother, Olga, who supported the family by running a home-based daycare business, taking in ironing, and cleaning offices.

YOUTH

Burns grew up in New York City, living with her mother, brother, and sister in a low-income housing project on Delancey Street on the Lower East Side of Manhattan. "The gangs were there, and the drug addicts were there," she recalled in the *New York Times*. "There were lots of Jewish immigrants, fewer Hispanics and African Americans, but the common denominator and great equalizer was poverty."

> "I came from a very poor single-parent household," Burns explained, "but from a woman who was extremely confident, very amazing, and had nothing but outstanding expectations of me and my siblings. So while business wasn't the goal, success was the goal.... My mother was the person who instilled in me that it is possible to just go after it."

Despite the difficult circumstances, Burns's mother dedicated herself to providing for her children and insisted that they take responsibility for their lives. Her example and guidance were a great influence on her daughter. "I came from a very poor single-parent household," Burns explained, "but from a woman who was extremely confident, very amazing, and had nothing but outstanding expectations of me and my siblings. So while business wasn't the goal, success was the goal.... My mother was the person who instilled in me that it is possible to just go after it." Decades later, after she became a high-ranking executive, she paid tribute to her mother by placing a motto on her office wall: "Don't do anything that wouldn't make your Mom proud."

EDUCATION

Another important factor in Burns's childhood was her schooling, and in this area, too, her mother played a decisive role. Even though the family had very little money, Olga Burns found a way to send all of her children to private Catholic schools because she believed that doing so would keep them safe and provide them a quality education. Ursula Burns spent the final years of her secondary schooling at Cathedral High School in New York City and earned her diploma in 1976.

Throughout her school years, math was a favorite subject for Burns, and she decided to pursue college studies in engineering. Accepted into a number of universities, including several prestigious Ivy League schools, she opted to attend Polytechnic Institute of New York University. She was able to afford her college tuition because of assistance she received from the New York State Higher Education Opportunity Program, which provides scholarship funds and other help to deserving students from disadvantaged backgrounds. She graduated in 1980 with a Bachelor of Science (BS) degree. She then enrolled in a graduate program in mechanical engineering at Columbia University and earned a Master of Science (MS) degree in mechanical engineering the following year.

CAREER HIGHLIGHTS

In the summer of 1980, right after she completed her undergraduate degree, Burns began an internship at the Xerox Corporation, a large U.S. company that had helped pioneer the development of photocopying technology and went on to become a leading manufacturer of document production equipment. Impressed with her abilities, Xerox helped pay for her graduate studies at Columbia and gave her a position as a contract worker and then as a full-time employee after she earned her master's degree.

Burns began working as an engineer in the areas of product planning and development. "From the day I walked in, I was trained by Xerox to believe that what I did was real and had real impact," she recalled. "It was, 'Here's a problem; can you solve it?' ... So therefore I got confident." She advanced through a number of different positions during the early 1980s, and in 1987 she moved into management, overseeing engineering teams working on Xerox products. At that point, she was still less than 30 years old, and she often encountered individuals who were surprised that a woman of her age was supervising important projects. "People would ask, 'So where is the boss?'" Burns later recalled. "I'd say, 'I am.' And they'd ask, 'How old are you?'"

Race, Gender, and Performance

While her age attracted a certain amount of attention, Burns was also unique for another reason: she was a high-ranking black female in a profession where there were relatively few minorities and even fewer females of color. Throughout her career, she was something of a pioneer in this regard, and her presence was a sign of change. Since the 1960s, Xerox had been making a focused effort to create greater racial and gender diversity among its employees, one of many businesses to undertake that step. As Burns rose through the ranks, she was often viewed as a symbol of the progress that Xerox had made in that regard.

While the corporation's diversity policy brought a wider array of people into important positions in the workforce, it also created controversy.

Burns with a colleague at Xerox.

When minorities and women were hired and promoted, questions were sometimes raised about whether they were truly qualified for their new positions or whether they were simply being advanced in order to meet the company's goal of becoming more inclusive.

Burns has faced this issue throughout her career. While she agreed that Xerox's policies aided her progress, she has argued that the main factors behind her success are her abilities and her accomplishments. "I'm in this job because I believe I earned it through hard work and high performance," she explained. "Did I get some opportunities early in my career because of my race and gender? Probably.… I imagine race and gender got the hiring guys' attention. And then the rest was really up to me." In another interview, she explained her views in a different way. "Being a black woman is who I am and I can't control that. But being the youngest person to pass through all the gates is what I did have control over.… The fact that I did it faster than others has nothing to do with race and gender. It was my performance."

Telling It Like It Is

In addition to her skills as an engineer and manager, Burns developed a reputation for being a "straight shooter" who was not afraid to speak her mind. It was that quality that led to the next phase of her career at the company. In 1989, she attended a meeting where Wayland Hicks, the vice president of marketing and customer operations at Xerox, responded to a question about the company's diversity initiatives. Feeling that Hicks did not defend the program forcefully enough, she debated the senior executive openly at the meeting. Soon after, Hicks summoned her to his office. Burns feared that she might be fired, but instead, the vice president asked if she would be interested in meeting with him on a regular basis to discuss issues at the company. "She was enormously curious," Hicks explained. "She wanted to know why we were doing some things at the time, and she was always prepared in a way that I thought was very refreshing."

In early 1990, Burns became executive assistant to Hicks. In that role, she attended high level meetings, traveled on business trips, and helped her boss to get things accomplished. She also received a crash course in senior management, with Hicks passing on his knowledge about leadership. The job brought her in frequent contact with other executives at Xerox, and she got the opportunity to share her opinions with them as well. Paul Allaire, the person who then headed Xerox as chief executive officer (CEO), was impressed with her candor and ideas, and in 1991, he asked her to become his executive assistant. In that position, Burns spent even more time away

For Burns, the main factors behind her success are her abilities and her accomplishments. "I'm in this job because I believe I earned it through hard work and high performance," she explained. "Did I get some opportunities early in my career because of my race and gender? Probably.... I imagine race and gender got the hiring guys' attention. And then the rest was really up to me."

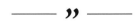

from home, devoting 40 percent of her work hours to corporate trips in which she and the CEO courted new clients and kept tabs on Xerox's far-flung global operations.

The next assignment for Burns was to oversee various business units within the company. Her success in that role led to a promotion to vice president and general manager of the Workgroup Copier Business in 1995, which required her to relocate to London, England. After two years there, she returned to the United States to head the Departmental Copier Business Unit. In 1999, she took another step toward the top when she was named vice president of Worldwide Business Services.

Troubled Times at Xerox

While Burns's personal career was thriving, Xerox was not faring so well. By the late 1990s, the company was teetering on the edge of bankruptcy due to changing market conditions and several major missteps. Faced with tough competition from other copier companies, it lagged behind its rivals in developing cutting-edge products and technology. A new CEO replaced Allaire in 1999 and shook things up by cutting 14,000 jobs and reorganizing the sales force, but the changes did little to improve business. Profits fell sharply, and in 2000, the U.S. Securities and Exchange Commission began investigating accounting problems at Xerox. The value of the company's stock plummeted as shareholders lost faith in its direction.

"Being a black woman is who I am and I can't control that," Burns pointed out. *"But being the youngest person to pass through all the gates is what I did have control over.... The fact that I did it faster than others has nothing to do with race and gender. It was my performance."*

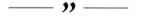

Burns began to have her own doubts about her employer during this period and decided to leave. "It was not because of more money," she said. "It was just, 'What's going on here? What is this place?'" Once she informed her superiors of her decision, however, they pleaded with her to stay and help the ailing company. Surprised that they valued her so much, she ultimately decided to remain with Xerox, and she began to realize that she might have a chance of rising to the very top of the corporation. Around this time, she was handed new responsibilities, becoming senior vice president of Corporate Strategic Services in 2000.

Meanwhile, Xerox looked to a new CEO, company veteran Anne M. Mulcahy, to change its fortunes. Shortly after taking the helm in August 2001, Mulcahy began putting together a "turnaround team" to guide the corporation out of trouble, and she asked Burns to join the group. The two women quickly formed a very productive partnership. As the senior executive, Mulcahy focused on the corporation's finances and on convincing people inside and outside the company that Xerox could turn the corner.

Burns with Anne M. Mulcahy, whom she succeeded as CEO.

For her part, Burns was given responsibility for managing many of the details of how the business was run. "Anne had so many other things to focus on," Burns later explained. "The employee base was nervous, our customers were really unhappy, our investors were panicking. While she was focusing on other things, she just gave me a mandate to fix this thing."

Managing a Crisis

Burns's assignment was especially challenging because she had to make the company smaller and more efficient. Xerox was too far in debt and spending too much money, and Mulcahy asked Burns to find a way to cut $2 billion in costs. To accomplish that goal, she had to make many tough decisions that had a profound effect on the company. She masterminded a plan to hire other businesses to handle much of Xerox's manufacturing, and she greatly reduced the number of managers in the corporation. Moreover, Burns negotiated new contracts with unionized employees that helped save additional money. In the end, the Xerox workforce was reduced by nearly 40 percent.

While drastically cutting costs, Mulcahy and Burns also needed to improve the products offered by Xerox. Towards that end, a new line of copiers and printers was introduced, including innovative color models. In time, the changes put in place by the two executives began to pay off. By 2007, the company's debt was half of what it had been five years before, net earnings had greatly increased, and its stock price was on the rebound. The fear of bankruptcy that had previously hung over Xerox had been banished.

> **"This old notion that work is drudgery is nonsense,"** Burns asserted at a commencement ceremony, and she encouraged the young graduates to find a similar sense of excitement and dedication in their own careers. "Most days—even back when Xerox was under siege—I could not wait to get to the office," she recalled. "I love my work—and you should too."

While the company's turnaround was a collaborative effort, Burns has claimed credit for much of the restructuring that took place, noting that "Ten percent of that was Anne [Mulcahy], 90 percent was me." Mulcahy agrees that Burns was instrumental in the changes that took place and has explained that "Ursula absorbs problems like a sponge. Once she takes them on, it's 'Let's go!'" Burns has been equally appreciative of Mulcahy and has viewed her as a role model, not only for her business achievements but for her ability to pursue a high level career while raising a family.

Reaching the Top

Burns acquired a series of new job titles while helping Xerox return to health. In 2001, she became president of Document Systems and Solutions, and the following year, she was named senior vice president of Business Group Operations, which provides more than 80 percent of the company's sales. With her success in helping guide the Xerox turnaround, there was a great deal of speculation that Burns was destined to one day become CEO.

Burns is shown accepting the National Medal of Technology of behalf of Xerox from President George W. Bush.

As with most large corporations, Xerox employs a senior leadership system in which an individual who is expected to become CEO first takes the position of president, which is the second-highest office in the business. In April 2007, Burns officially received that title and was also made a member of the board of directors—the group that governs the company and represents its stockholders.

It was Mulcahy who had chosen Burns as her successor, but the two women found that the leadership transition was not entirely smooth, despite their close relationship. They engaged in several weeks of intense discussions to

*As CEO of Xerox, Burns has taken a prominent role,
which often includes public speaking.*

decide how they would divide their responsibilities during the period before Burns finally became CEO. But, as in their previous collaborations, the two reached a successful compromise. "I definitely want to lead this company," Burns said in *Fortune.* "But I do not want to lead it until Anne doesn't want to." Over the next two years, Burns got further guidance about the CEO's responsibilities and learned that there were many fine points to leading the company. Mulcahy provided her with valuable advice, which included tips on how to motivate employees and suggestions about keeping a "poker face" so that others would not be able to easily read Burns's emotions.

Finally, on July 1, 2009, the preparation came to an end, and Ursula Burns took over as the chief executive officer of the Xerox Corporation. In addition to being a major achievement for Burns herself, it was a significant milestone in American business history. She was the first African-American woman to become the CEO of a Fortune 500 company, and when Mulcahy turned the leadership over to Burns, it was the first time that a woman succeeded another woman in heading a corporation of that size.

Looking to the Future

Once she took her place in the CEO's office, or "C-suite," Burns quickly showed that she was willing to take the company in a new direction. In

September 2009, less than two months after she took charge, Xerox announced that it was buying another business, Affiliated Computer Services. The move is intended to strengthen the corporation's ability to provide a full range of document services. Rather than simply selling and servicing equipment, as it has in the past, Xerox plans to help customers with tasks such as payroll, accounting, and other information-related functions. Burns has identified this as an important new area that will be a major focus in the years ahead.

Another important element that Burns has stressed since taking charge of the company is the need for employees to talk honestly with one another about important issues in the workplace. This emphasis is not surprising given her own history of speaking her mind. "I want us to stay civil and kind, but we have to be frank," she said, "and the reason we can be frank is because we are all in the same family."

In directing her corporate "family," Burns plans to lead by example, which means showing her employees that she has is extremely involved in the company and working as hard as they are to attain success. This is the same approach that she has followed since moving into management, and she believes it is much more important than trying to appear calm and assured at all times, as many senior executives strive to do. "One of the things I was told early on is that you should never let them see you sweat," she noted. "I remember hearing that and saying: 'Oh my God! I think that they have to see you sweat.'"

Though her job comes with many challenges, Burns remains passionate about what she does. "This old notion that work is drudgery is nonsense," she asserted in a 2009 commencement address, and she encouraged the young graduates to find a similar sense of excitement and dedication in their own careers. "Most days—even back when Xerox was under siege—I could not wait to get to the office," she recalled. "I love my work—and you should too."

MARRIAGE AND FAMILY

Burns lives in Rochester, New York, with her husband, Lloyd F. Bean. She and Bean, a former scientist at Xerox, were married in 1988. She has two children, a stepson named Malcolm and a daughter named Melissa. Though her total yearly compensation for 2009 was estimated to be more than $11 million, she refuses to adopt all the trappings of an affluent lifestyle. She still does her own shopping and drives her own car rather than using chauffeured vehicles.

As is common with high level executives, Burns devotes a lot of hours to her work and has had to be creative in finding ways to meet both her professional and personal responsibilities. At certain points in her career, she was away from home for extended periods. Back in 1992, for instance, she noted that "I see my husband two, maybe three times a month. We've been married for three years, but we've only had the same home base for one year. He lives in our official home in Rochester, and I live in a townhouse in Stamford [Connecticut]."

> "
>
> *"I meet a lot of women today who actually say they are not going to have a family because they want to be executives. My response is what do the two have to do with each other? You can do all those things ... if you aren't trying to balance them perfectly."*
>
> "

To deal with the great demands, of her job, Burns tries to remain flexible and allows herself to take time away from work when necessary. "If you do call in [to the office] or just don't show up occasionally, nobody will die," she said. "People will actually applaud that you made a reasonable choice." Overall, she feels that having children need not be a hindrance to a successful career as long as female employees remain realistic about what can be accomplished. "I meet a lot of women today who actually say they are not going to have a family because they want to be executives. My response is what do the two have to do with each other? You can do all those things ... if you aren't trying to balance them perfectly."

HOBBIES AND OTHER INTERESTS

Burns assists a number of charitable and educational organizations, serving on the boards of the National Center on Addiction and Substance Abuse at Columbia University, the National Academy Foundation, the Massachusetts Institute of Technology, and the University of Rochester. Encouraging young people to become interested in technology is one of her major priorities. She is a board member for FIRST (Foundation for the Inspiration and Recognition of Science and Technology). Moreover, in November 2009 President Barack Obama named her as one of the people to lead the "Educate to Innovate" campaign that is intended to improve students' skills in science, technology, engineering, and math (STEM).

Because of the expertise that she has gained in her many years as a senior manager, Burns has also been invited to help guide other companies and organizations. She is a member of the boards of directors for American Express Corporation, Boston Scientific Corporation, and the National Association of Manufacturers.

HONORS AND AWARDS

50 Most Powerful Black Executives in America (*Fortune*): 2002

Annual List of Global Business Influentials (*Time*/CNN): 2003

50 Most Important Blacks in Technology (*U.S. Black Engineer and Information Technology*): 2003-05

75 Most Powerful African Americans in Corporate America (*Black Enterprise*): 2005

50 Most Powerful Black Women in Business (*Black Enterprise*): 2006

50 Most Powerful Women in American Business (*Fortune*): 2006

Inductee, Denice Dee Denton Women Engineers Hall of Fame (Maseeh College of Engineering and Computer Science, Portland State University): 2009

National Equal Justice Award (NAACP Legal Defense and Educational Fund): 2009

75 Most Powerful Women in Business (*Black Enterprise*): 2010

FURTHER READING

Periodicals

Black Enterprise, Feb. 1992, p.246; Feb. 2010, p.88

BusinessWeek, June 8, 2009, p.18

Current Biography Yearbook, 2007

Fortune, Oct. 15, 2007, p.78

International Herald Tribune, May 2, 2007, p.14

New York Times, June 1, 2003; May 22, 2009; Sep. 29, 2009; Feb. 21, 2010

Online Articles

http://people.forbes.com/profile/ursula-m-burns/4692
    (Forbes, "Ursula M. Burns," no date)

http://topics.nytimes.com
    (New York Times, "Ursula M. Burns," multiple articles, various dates)

http://www.nytimes.com/2010/02/21/business/21xerox.html
    (New York Times, "Xerox's New Chief Tries to Redefine Its Culture," Feb. 20, 2010)

http://topics.wsj.com/person/index
  (Wall Street Journal, "Ursula M. Burns," no date)

ADDRESS

Ursula M. Burns
Xerox Headquarters
45 Glover Avenue
PO Box 4505
Norwalk, CT 06856-4505

WORLD WIDE WEB SITE

http://news.xerox.com/pr/xerox/ursula-m-burns.aspx

Robin Chase 1958-

American Entrepreneur and Transportation Innovator
Founder of Carsharing Company Zipcar and
Ridesharing Network GoLoco

EARLY YEARS

Robin Maria Chase was born on September 19, 1958, in The
Hague, Netherlands. The Hague is the third largest city in the
Netherlands. Although it is not the nation's capital city, The
Hague is the center of the Netherlands government. Her
mother, Shirley Gustafson Chase, was a physical therapist and
an artist. Her father, Robert W. Chase, was a U.S. Foreign Service officer who held diplomatic posts in many international

Robin as a baby with her mother.

cities. At the time of Robin's birth, her father was posted in Beirut, Lebanon. There was an outbreak of civil war, and the family was evacuated. Her mother decided to go to The Hague, which she knew would be safe. Robin has five siblings: Linwood, Kristenna, Ragnar, Ruth, and Mark.

Chase grew up all over the world. Her family moved a lot when she was growing up, depending on where her father's work required him to live. They spent time in many different cities, including Alexandria, Virginia; Alexandria, Egypt; Beirut, Lebanon; Damascus, Syria; Jeddah, Saudi Arabia; Jerusalem, Israel; Mbabane, Swaziland; and Tangier, Morocco.

Chase attended college in the United States. She graduated from Wellesley College in 1980 with a Bachelor of Arts degree (BA) in English, French, and philosophy. She then attended the Massachusetts Institute of Technology (MIT) Sloan School of Management, where she earned a Master of Business Administration degree (MBA) in 1986.

MAJOR ACCOMPLISHMENTS

Robin Chase has created unique new transportation programs that help people arrange carpools, share rides, and rent cars in small blocks of time instead of by the day. Chase works to help people become less dependent on personally owned cars, both to save money and to reduce the amount of pollution produced by cars.

Chase has always been interested in creative problem-solving. After graduating from Wellesley, Chase worked for various nonprofit organizations. During this time, she realized that many of these organizations needed people with business management skills in order to successfully bring their innovative ideas to life. This need inspired Chase to enroll in graduate school at MIT, where she first became interested in the many ways that transportation problems can influence people's lives. The need for reliable, affordable transportation can affect people's choices about where they live, where they work or go to school, and how far and how often they can travel to the other places they need to go.

Chase began to see that typical American transportation habits were inefficient and wasteful—with most people owning their own car and driving alone most of the time. She saw a few big problems with the American system of individual car ownership. First, it results in a much larger number of vehicles on the road every day than are strictly necessary. All of these cars use a large amount of gas and oil and produce too much pollution and traffic congestion, particularly in cities. Second, having a car isn't a good solution for everyone because of the high cost of owning, operating, and maintaining a car. But some people need a car to get to work or school, and public transportation doesn't serve every community. And individual car ownership is a fundamental part of modern American culture. Chase wanted to change people's attitudes about car ownership and get people to consider other options—both for their own personal benefit and to reduce the environmental impact of overcrowded highways.

Chase thought that if people understood the real cost of owning and driving a car, they might be more open to new ideas. "If everyone really understood and paid for the cost of each car trip, we would likely sometimes choose another more efficient way to travel: by foot, by bike, subway, bus, or train." With individual car ownership, each car owner bears the full burden of paying for the car, insurance, maintenance, repairs, gas, and sometimes parking fees. "According to the National Households Consumer Survey, across the nation it costs $24 per day on average that people are spending in America on their car, day in and day out," Chase explained. "If I were to tell you that it was going to cost $125 a week to go to work, you would say, no way, I'm not going to do it. But we are doing it—we just don't realize we're doing it."

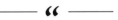

> "If everyone really understood and paid for the cost of each car trip, we would likely sometimes choose another more efficient way to travel: by foot, by bike, subway, bus, or train."

Developing a Big Idea: Zipcar

By 1999, Chase was working on an idea for a community carsharing system based on similar programs common in European cities. The idea came partly from her own need for part-time access to a car, and she thought there would be others with a similar need. "This is what I wanted personally. I have three kids and one car that my husband takes to an office where it sits, unused, for eight hours a day, so I never have access to a car.

Zipcar members have access to a wide array of vehicles, allowing them to use different types of vehicles for different situations.

Plus, I live in a city and there's no way … I want to have a second car that I have to maintain and own and park. The lightbulb went off: the costs for car ownership definitely outweigh the benefits for me in the city, and wireless and the Internet can make this easy."

Some people were initially skeptical that Chase's carsharing idea would work. Would Americans willingly give up their own cars in order to share a car with strangers? She thought they would, once they understood the benefits and how easy it would be to use her program. However, initial research with potential carsharing users revealed that many people didn't like the idea of sharing. "Forty percent of the people I talked to had an extremely negative reaction to the word 'sharing,' Chase recalled. "The word makes people nervous. They feel they're being scolded or told to wait their turn. At one point I banned my staff from using the phrase 'car sharing.' Do we call hotels 'bed sharing'? That's way too intimate. Do we call bowling 'shoe sharing'? Who would want to bowl?"

After thinking for a long time about how to convince reluctant potential customers to give her idea a try, Chase chose to name her new program Zipcar. She thought the name conveyed the sense that car sharing was a fun new way of getting around, without all the hassles and expense of car ownership. "I wanted people to feel that they were the smart ones, the cool, hip, urban insiders who figured out that to live in a city and to own a car was stupid." By January 2000, Chase had officially founded Zipcar with business partner Antje Danielson.

The Zipcar plan combined Internet and wireless technology to create what Chase envisioned as "the perfect web application—creating an online community to share a common resource." Wireless technology was new at that time and was only really being used for mobile phones. Chase saw the potential for so much more. "I thought, 'Wow, this is what the Internet was made for: sharing a scarce resource among many people. This is what wireless was made for: we can make transactions very easy for end users and brokering those transactions will cost us next to nothing."

"It costs $24 per day on average that people are spending in America on their car, day in and day out," Chase explained. *"If I were to tell you that it was going to cost $125 a week to go to work, you would say, no way, I'm not going to do it. But we are doing it—we just don't realize we're doing it."*

Zipcar has revolutionized the way that people use cars. Instead of owning their own car and paying all of the associated costs, Zipcar members have on-demand access to a car and pay only when they need to use it. Cars are parked in various locations, usually near high-traffic areas or public transportation stops. Members use Zipcar's web site (www.zipcar.com) to reserve a car for any amount of time they need. A special wireless-enabled keycard is coded with the individual member's information and is used to unlock the car at the reserved time. The amount of time and mileage per trip is recorded and transmitted wirelessly to Zipcar's database, and members' accounts are automatically charged at the end of each trip. Many Zipcar members find the service more convenient than public transportation and cheaper than a taxi or a traditional rental car.

Zipcar Grows Rapidly

Zipcar launched in Boston, Massachusetts, with a single lime green Volkswagen Beetle. More cars were added as membership grew quickly in the first few months, with an average of 25 new members joining the service each week. The company continued to grow by leaps and bounds during

The Zipcar iPhone app is a perfect example of Chase's interest in both transportation and technology.

its early years. As word of the new service spread, Zipcar swelled to more than 800 members in the Boston area within its first year. Zipcar began operating in Washington DC in 2001 and New York City in early 2002. Soon other cities were added in the U.S., Canada, and Europe. Businesses and government agencies began to replace their vehicle fleets with Zipcar contracts. "When you share a car, it's great for companies, great for individuals, great for cities," Chase explained.

But the rapid growth was unexpected and nearly overwhelmed the small company. "You have your brilliant idea, and you have your future vision, but you can't anticipate the path immediately in front of you. And it's a good thing you can't, because if you could, you would be too tired to start," Chase recalled. "There were moments when I had serious second thoughts, but it was too late. I never expected there would be a point when there was no turning back." By 2009, Zipcar was maintaining a fleet of more than 6,500 vehicles serving more than 350,000 individual members. Research has shown that every Zipcar is responsible for a reduction in private car ownership of eight to ten vehicles. "The environmental piece of it was obvious," Chase stressed. "I don't think I would have started a business that had no social benefits because I wasn't interested in spending 120 hours a week for years doing something that was just to make money."

In 2003, Chase stepped down as Chief Executive Officer (CEO) of Zipcar. Soon after, she won the competitive Loeb Fellowship from the Harvard University Graduate School of Design for 2004-2005. The fellowship is awarded to people working to improve the built environment—meaning, all the parts of the world that have been constructed by humans. Chase decided to use the fellowship to study transportation policy, urban design, and city planning. "My experience with Zipcar illuminated for me the tight links between how we build our cities, the resulting mobility options, and our ability to curb CO_2 emissions," she explained. "Think about how we built out the national highway interstate network in the '50s. We built highways, we ripped out all the trolleys, and we didn't build any trains. We created our destiny as a car-dependent nation because that's the infrastructure we built up.... We built our houses on one-acre lots and now our choices for interaction are defined by that." At Harvard, Chase focused her work on reducing the environmental impact of personal transportation. "How can we reduce CO_2 emissions in a world in love with the car and with a built environment that is totally dependent on it?"

After completing the fellowship, Chase founded the Meadow Networks consulting firm. Meadow Networks advises governments and businesses about wireless applications for transportation and the many ways in which innovative approaches to transportation can help communities grow and thrive.

> ———— " ————
>
> *"My experience with Zipcar illuminated for me the tight links between how we build our cities, the resulting mobility options, and our ability to curb CO_2 emissions,"* Chase explained. *"Think about how we built out the national highway interstate network in the '50s. We built highways, we ripped out all the trolleys, and we didn't build any trains. We created our destiny as a car-dependent nation because that's the infrastructure we built up."*
>
> ———— " ————

Beyond Carsharing: GoLoco

In 2007, Chase founded GoLoco, the world's first organization that combines social networking, ridesharing (also known as carpooling), and online payment. Chase chose the name to convey the flexibility and freedom of cooperative transportation. She explained, "GoLoco: It means go *loco*—go crazy, go free-spirited. Go location to location with local transportation. Go low cost. Go low carbon dioxide."

Chase envisioned GoLoco as a natural extension of the Zipcar service. "Carsharing only works in dense metropolitan areas or in cases where people don't need a car to get to work. If you need a car to get to work, you're going to have to own your own car. The cost of carsharing is too high for a daily commute.... That's why I did GoLoco—I said, what about all those other people who are feeling similar transportation and mobility pains but they need a car to get to work? Ride sharing is for those people." Chase designed GoLoco to help people improve their own quality of life while helping the environment. "I see GoLoco as an immediate solution. It means I don't have to wait for the government to introduce carbon taxes or congestion charges, or put in smart development or light rail or transit. Today, with the infrastructure we have, we can do something which dramatically reduces costs and emissions."

GoLoco helps people quickly set up shared car trips using concepts of social networking. Members create a profile for themselves and can invite or add friends, neighbors, coworkers, classmates, or anyone else to their personal group. Members post requests for trips they want to share, and other members respond to join the trip. "Think about standing in a mall, looking at a parking lot," Chase said in explaining the basic idea of GoLoco. "You know that a large number of people there are going exactly where you're going in the next five minutes." GoLoco members use the service to carpool to the mall or any other destination, instead of driving separately. The social networking function allows GoLoco members to choose to restrict access to their posted trip requests to only those people in their group. In this way, members can feel safer about arranging trips with trusted friends or acquaintances rather than with strangers.

> "
>
> "My goal is to reshape the way people feel about car ownership," Chase declared. "I think when we look back at ourselves sitting alone in our 120 square feet of car, driving down these highways with incredible storage costs and incredible operating costs, I think we will look back at how we travel today and just be astounded: astounded at the cost, astounded at the waste."
>
> "

The GoLoco web site also handles online payment transactions, making it easy for people to share the cost of a car trip. Chase wanted to include online payments in the GoLoco service to help people avoid any awkwardness about asking for or accepting payment from friends and to make it extremely easy to use the service. Passengers pay the driver for part of the

Chase continues to explore new ideas about transportation and technology.

cost of the trip, which is agreed upon in advance. If there is one passenger, they pay the driver for half the cost of the trip. If there are two passengers, each one will pay the driver one third the cost of the trip. Payments are automatically transferred from passenger accounts to the driver's account. GoLoco users like the system because it is easier than trying to handle cash and make change during a trip.

Creating Change

Chase's work to pioneer new ideas and methods of transportation has earned praise and recognition from the environmental and business communities alike. *Time* magazine called her work an illustration of the best use of the Internet, saying her ideas are "not well-intentioned yet futile do-goodism but business that's also a community service. It's about people using the Internet to work together in the service of one another." She has been recognized as an international transportation expert known for having big ideas and the skills to bring her ideas to life. "My secret was just believing that the world could be the place I wanted it to be," Chase said. "Small actions add up to big actions. And we can't get to the big results without all the small ones on the way."

"My goal is to reshape the way people feel about car ownership," Chase declared. "I think when we look back at ourselves sitting alone in our 120 square feet of car, driving down these highways with incredible storage costs and incredible operating costs, I think we will look back at how we travel today and just be astounded: astounded at the cost, astounded at the waste. It's such a wacky idea that we'd want to be alone in our cars spending huge sums of money and all that parking space, when it was less fun and more expensive and kind of crazy."

HOME AND FAMILY

Chase lives in Cambridge, Massachusets, with her husband, Roy Russell. They have three children.

HONORS AND AWARDS

100 Hottest Ideas List (*Fortune Small Business*): 2001, for Zipcar
100 Hottest Technology Ideas (*CIO*): 2001, for Zipcar
Top 100 Innovators (*InfoWorld*): 2001
Fast 50 Champions of Innovation (*Fast Company*): 2002
Start-Up Woman of the Year (Women's Business Hall of Fame): 2002
Alternative Transportation Innovator of the Year (AltWheels Transportation Festival): 2003
Governor's Award for Entrepreneurial Spirit (Massachusetts): 2003
Small Business Excellence in Customer Service Award (Dell/National Federation of Independent Business): 2004, for Zipcar
Entreprenuer of the Year (Ernst & Young): 2005
Top 35 Travel Innovators (*Travel & Leisure*): 2006
Top 10 Designers (*BusinessWeek*): 2007
Time 100 Most Influential (*Time*): 2009

FURTHER READING

Periodicals

Boston Globe, Apr. 23, 2007
Boston Globe Sunday Magazine, Nov. 18, 2007
Business Week, Aug. 13, 2007
New York Times, Mar. 1, 2002; Sep. 2, 2007; Mar. 3, 2009
Time, Apr. 30, 2009; Sep. 24, 2009

Online Articles

http://www.boston.com/business/articles/2007/04/23/carpooling_gets
_a_new_dash_of_green
   (Boston Globe, "Carpooling Gets a New Dash of Green," Apr. 23, 2007)

http://www.boston.com/bostonglobe/magazine/articles/2007/11/18/earth
_angels_the_entrepreneur
(Boston Globe Sunday Magazine, "Earth Angels: The Entrepreneur,"
Nov. 18, 2007)
http://www.businessweek.com
(Business Week, "Share a Car, Save the World," Aug. 13, 2007)
http://www.nytimes.com/2002/03/01/automobiles/may-i-borrow-the-car
-new-service-says-yes.html
(New York Times, "May I Borrow the Car? New Service Says Yes," Mar. 1,
2002)
http://www.nytimes.com/2007/09/02/automobiles/02LOCO.html
(New York Times, "Thumbing Rides Online," Sep. 2, 2007)
http://www.nytimes.com/2009/03/08/magazine/08Zipcar-t.html
(New York Times Magazine, "Share My Ride," Mar. 8, 2009)
http://www.oswego.edu/news/index.php/site/news_story/it_all_matters
(State University of New York at Oswego, "It All Matters," May 16, 2009)
http://www.time.com/time/specials/packages/completelist/0,29569,189441
0,00.html
(Time, "The 2009 Time 100: Robin Chase," Apr. 30, 2009)
http://www.time.com/time/specials/packages/article/0,28804,1898067_192
6040_1926049,00.html
(Time, "Time 100 Roundtables," Sep. 24, 2009)
http://urbanomnibus.net
(Urban Omnibus, "A Conversation with Robin Chase," June 10, 2009)

ADDRESS

Robin Chase
GoLoco
40 Cottage Street
Cambridge, MA 02139

WORLD WIDE WEB SITES

http://www.robinchase.org
http://www.meadownetworks.com/?page_id=3

Hillary Rodham Clinton 1947-

American Political Leader
Former U.S. Senator and Former U.S. First Lady
U.S. Secretary of State

BIRTH

Hillary Rodham Clinton was born Hillary Diane Rodham on October 26, 1947, in Chicago, Illinois. She was the first child of Hugh E. Rodham, the owner of a drapery-making business, and Dorothy Howell Rodham, a homemaker. She grew up with two brothers: Hugh Jr., three years younger, and Tony, seven years younger.

YOUTH

Rodham grew up in the middle-class suburb of Park Ridge, Illinois, northwest of Chicago. She was a good student and was active in her church and community. She was a Girl Scout and organized a fundraiser for the United Way when she was only 10. Her father stressed the importance of being thrifty, so she took her first summer job at 13, walking a few miles three days a week to supervise a local park. She also learned an interest in politics from her father, a staunch Republican who liked to debate at the dinner table; she volunteered for an anti-voter fraud effort when she was in eighth grade. She considered herself a tomboy and learned to play football and baseball from her father. She also spent a lot of time hunting, hiking, swimming, and playing cards while visiting her family's summer cabin in rural Pennsylvania.

> "I was fortunate because as a girl growing up I never felt anything but support from my family," Clinton claimed. "There was no distinction between me and my brothers or any barriers thrown up to me that I couldn't think about doing something because I was a girl. It was just: if you work hard enough and you really apply yourself, then you should be able to do whatever you choose to do."

Rodham continued to excel in high school, first at Park Ridge's Maine East High School and then at Maine South, where she was moved her senior year. She belonged to the National Honor Society and student government and was named a National Merit Scholarship finalist; during the summers she worked as a lifeguard and played softball. Although she considered herself a Republican and worked for Barry Goldwater's 1964 presidential campaign, she was also very interested in civil rights and social justice, values she had learned from her mother and her Methodist faith. She often baby-sat for local migrant workers and enthusiastically participated in events organized by her youth minister, the Reverend Don Jones. These included cultural exchanges with young Hispanic and African Americans from the inner city and attendance at a 1962 speech by the civil rights leader Martin Luther King, Jr.

Rodham's parents set high expectations for her and encouraged her to succeed. "I was fortunate because as a girl growing up I never felt anything but support from my family," she claimed. "There was no distinction between me and my brothers or any barriers thrown up to me that I couldn't think about doing something because I was a girl. It was just: if you work hard enough and you really apply yourself, then you should be able to do whatever you choose to do." So Rodham never even considered that being a girl might hamper her success. In fact, she was shocked when she wrote to NASA as a teenager to volunteer for astronaut training and was told that women weren't admitted to the program. "It was the first time I had hit an obstacle I couldn't overcome with hard work and determination, and I was outraged," she wrote in her memoir *Living History.* It made her more determined to fight against discrimination of all kinds. She herself received nothing but encouragement from her own parents and teachers and was voted "most likely to succeed" by her classmates.

EDUCATION

Rodham graduated from Maine South High School in 1965 and chose to attend Wellesley College, a highly regarded women's college in Massachusetts. She earned a Bachelor of Arts degree (BA) in political science with high honors in 1969. She performed just as well outside of the classroom: she was president of the college's chapter of Young Republicans during her freshman year, and she served in the House Republican Conference in Washington DC during a summer internship. She was active in student government and was elected president her senior year. Her commencement speech to her classmates—the first ever given at Wellesley by a student—demonstrated her increasingly liberal views when she spoke of the "indispensable task of criticizing and constructive protest" and called for an end to the Vietnam War. "We feel that our prevailing, acquisitive, and competitive corporate life … is not the way of life for us," she intoned. "We're searching for more immediate, ecstatic, and penetrating modes of living." The speech earned her a profile in *Life* magazine and an invitation to join the League of Women Voters' Youth Advisory Committee. She became a Democrat sometime during this period.

After graduating from Wellesley College, Rodham entered Yale University in fall 1969 to attend law school. She was one of only 27 women in a class of 235, and she quickly became involved with activities on campus. In her first year she served on the board of editors of the alternative law journal *Yale Review of Law and Social Action* and helped mediate between groups of student protesters. During her first summer break she did research on the health and education of migrant children and her report was used by a

Bill and Hillary at Yale Law School, 1972.

U.S. Senate subcommittee. She returned to Yale determined to focus on family and children's issues. After that, she took classes at the Yale Child Study Center and worked on family law cases for the New Haven Legal Services Office. Clinton received her law degree (Juris Doctor, or JD) from Yale in 1973.

FIRST JOBS

After graduating from Yale, Rodham took a job with the Children's Defense Fund, a nonprofit group founded by Marian Wright Edelman to advocate for the rights of children. (For more information on Edelman, see *Biography Today* 1993 Annual Cumulation.) Rodham traveled the country investigating conditions in juvenile jails and uncovering discrepancies between census lists and school enrollment lists. Although she found the work rewarding, she left for an opportunity to make history.

In early 1974, Rodham accepted a position with the U.S. House Judiciary Committee. At that time, the Committee was leading an inquiry into the possible impeachment of President Richard Nixon. Rodham spent long days researching legal grounds for removal of the president, who was accused of covering up a criminal burglary of his political opponents' offices at the Watergate Hotel. The committee eventually recommended three articles of impeachment, but Nixon resigned in August 1974, before Congress could vote on them. Out of a job, Rodham decided to follow her heart to Arkansas.

"We feel that our prevailing, acquisitive, and competitive corporate life ... is not the way of life for us," Clinton said in her college commencement address. "We're searching for more immediate, ecstatic, and penetrating modes of living."

MARRIAGE AND FAMILY

Hillary Rodham first met William "Bill" Jefferson Clinton in 1970, while they were both attending Yale Law School. In her autobiography, she remembered him staring at her across the library, so she walked up and said, "If you're going to keep looking at me, and I'm going to keep looking back, we might as well be introduced." After a long courtship, the couple married on October 11, 1975. In 1980 they had their only child, Chelsea Victoria, a hedge fund consultant who has often campaigned on behalf of her mother. The Clintons maintain residences in Chappaqua, New York, and Washington, DC.

In the years since her marriage, Hillary Rodham Clinton has used several different forms of her name. When she was first married she used her maiden name, Hillary Rodham. That became a political issue after her husband was elected to office, and she was criticized for failing to take her husband's name. Since then, she has used the names Hillary Clinton and Hillary Rodham Clinton. This issue has cropped up again at various times throughout her career.

CAREER HIGHLIGHTS

Double Career in Arkansas

In 1974, shortly before she was married, Rodham had moved to Fayetteville, Arkansas, to be with her future husband. At that time, Bill Clinton was running for Congress as a Democrat. She and her family helped him campaign, but he lost to the incumbent by four percent of the vote. At the same time, Rodham became an assistant professor at the University of Arkansas School of Law. She taught classes in criminal law and also directed the school's legal aid office, where law students helped provide counsel to the poor and those in prison. In 1976 Bill Clinton ran for Arkansas attorney general, so Rodham spent much of her time assisting with his campaign. After he won the Democratic nomination—ensuring victory in a general election without a Republican opponent—she worked as field coordinator for Democrat Jimmy Carter's presidential campaign in Indiana. After Carter took office in 1977, he appointed Rodham to the board of the Legal Services Corporation, which helps fund legal aid offices across the country.

Bill Clinton's election as state attorney general meant a move to the state capital of Little Rock. Rodham left her university job and joined the Rose Law Firm, the oldest practice in the state. She was the firm's first female associate, and she later became a partner in 1979. Although some of her trials were corporate cases, she also worked for families and children. She took a case in which a family had been denied the right to adopt the foster child who had lived with them for over two years because it was against state policy. She won the case, successfully arguing that the policy was against the child's best interests, and eventually the state followed this precedent. Believing Arkansas needed an organization to promote children's rights, she and a professor of child development founded Arkansas Advocates for Children and Families soon after.

In 1978 Bill Clinton ran for governor of Arkansas and won the seat by a vote of almost two to one. Although Rodham was now first lady of Arkansas, she continued her full schedule of legal and advocacy work. She was now a board member of the Children's Defense Fund and helped chair meetings in Washington, DC; in addition, her husband appointed her to chair the state's Rural Health Advisory Committee. Many voters, however, were perplexed by their untraditional first lady, who kept her own name and kept working after having a baby in 1980. Bill Clinton ran for governor again in

While serving as first lady of Arkansas, Clinton chaired the state's Educational Standards Committee, which proposed ways to improve school performance.

1980 but he lost this time, mainly due to an untimely car tag tax hike. But some observers felt that Rodham's image contributed to his defeat. She didn't fit the image that Arkansans at that time wanted in a first lady: she was an accomplished professional in her own right; she paid little attention to her appearance, with thick glasses and long frizzy hair; and, most importantly, she hadn't changed her name when she got married. After Clinton lost the governor's race in 1980, Rodham bowed to political pressure. She took his name and had a complete makeover, exchanging glasses for contacts and styling her hair. The strategy helped, and the 1982 election returned Bill Clinton to office as governor. The family returned to the governor's mansion, where they would stay for the next 10 years.

The governor continued to depend on his wife after the 1982 election, appointing her to chair the Arkansas Educational Standards Committee, which was charged with finding ways to improve some of the nation's poorest performing schools. Under her leadership, the committee was able to push through several education reforms, including a controversial provision for teacher competency testing. Over the next few years, Bill Clinton continued to win re-election to the governor's office, while Hillary Rodham Clinton worked for Rose Law and served on the American Bar Association's Commission on Women in the Profession. She also served on the boards of nonprofit groups, including the Arkansas Children's Hospital, and of Arkansas corporations, including discount retailer Wal-Mart and frozen yogurt chain TCBY. In 1988 and 1991 the *National Law Journal* ranked her among the 100 most influential lawyers in the country.

First Lady of the United States

As a popular southern Democrat and the co-chair of the National Governors Association, Bill Clinton had first been approached about running for president before the 1988 election. He declined that year because he didn't want to spend so much time away from his young daughter, but in 1991 he announced his intent to seek the office. He formed a campaign staff, and, in an unusual move, so did Hillary Rodham Clinton, who planned to participate as fully in his presidential campaign as she had in his state ones. Her help was needed before the first primary elections in January 1992, when rumors surfaced about Bill's supposed womanizing. The accusations threatened to derail his campaign, until he and Hillary appeared on the TV news show "60 Minutes," where she defended his character and their marriage. Later, defending her own choices as a working mother and political wife, she was accused of belittling other women who had decided not to work outside the home. The Clintons' political opponents took her words out of context and accused her of being power-hungry and opposing the traditional family. Clinton found it difficult not to take the political attacks personally. As she recalled in *Living History*, "I was being labeled and categorized because of my positions and mistakes, and also because I had been turned into a symbol for women of my generation."

> *In her memoir, Clinton recalled feeling that becoming first lady meant "I would have a 'position' but not a real 'job.' How could I use this platform to help my husband and serve my country without losing my own voice?"*

Nevertheless, many women were excited by the prospect of an energetic young couple in the White House. Aided by a majority of votes from women and young people, Bill Clinton won the 1992 election in a three-way race with Republican President George H. W. Bush and Independent Ross Perot. For Hillary Rodham Clinton, it meant new challenges. As first lady, she had to resign from her law practice and board work. Becoming first lady meant "I would have a 'position' but not a real 'job,'" she recalled in her memoir. "How could I use this platform to help my husband and serve my country without losing my own voice?" The Clintons decided she would serve as a full-fledged presidential advisor. She would have her own office, alongside other presidential advisors in the West Wing of the White House, and she would oversee efforts to reform the country's health care system. In support of her plan, she became the first first lady to testify before Congress as the lead witness on a major policy initiative. Although many people found her testimony detailed and well-reasoned, others were uncomfortable with the idea of the first lady having so much political influence.

Bill Clinton and Hillary Rodham Clinton on Inauguration Day, January 1993.

Ultimately, the Clinton plan for health care reform failed, observers have said, partially because it was too ambitious and partially because the Clintons did not make enough political alliances that might have earned the plan more support. She kept a lower political profile after this failure, focusing on smaller issues that had always been important to her, especially those involving children and families. She hosted White House Conferences on early childhood development and on child care, and contributed to efforts that eventually led to the passage of legislation. These laws included the Children's Health Insurance Program, which provided health care for poor children; the Family and Medical Leave Act, which ensured employees with new babies or sick relatives the right to unpaid leave; and the Adoption and Safe Family Act of 1997, which encouraged moving foster children to adoption. Clinton also began communicating more directly with the American public. She began writing a syndicated newspaper column in 1995, and released a book on children and families, *It Takes a Village,* in 1996.

Although Clinton was sometimes a polarizing figure at home, she was very popular abroad and frequently traveled on behalf of the United States as an official representative. Clinton made visits to ordinary women part of her

Clinton testifying before the U.S. House of Representatives Energy Committee, which was holding hearings on health care reform.

schedule, looking for programs that could improve women's lives. Her speech at the Fourth United Nations World Conference on Women, given in China in 1995, inspired women worldwide. Decrying abuses against women in China and all over the world, Clinton concluded, "If there is one message that echoes forth from this conference, let it be that human rights are women's rights and women's rights are human rights, once and for all." To continue assisting women worldwide in developing their political and economic skills, Clinton founded the Vital Voices Democracy Initiative in partnership with Madeleine Albright, secretary of state during Bill Clinton's second term. Vital Voices has since become an important nonprofit, non-governmental organization that holds conferences and training sessions for women and advocates for human rights, including laws against human trafficking and programs to support people with HIV and AIDS.

During her husband's presidency, Clinton became both a figure of controversy and of sympathy. The controversy came from the Whitewater investigation, named after a parcel of Arkansas land. The Clintons had invested in the project with a developer who later ran a shady savings and loan company. Although the Clintons lost money on their investment, they were accused of using their political influence to assist the developer, then covering up their involvement. Although an initial report cleared them of any wrongdoing, there was an extended investigation that was promoted by their political enemies. Clinton was called to testify before a grand jury in 1996, and the Senate also investigated her actions. These further investigations concluded there was no evidence to show any criminal wrongdoing, but they also revealed that the president had conducted an inappropriate sexual relationship with a young intern. Again, Hillary Clinton was called to defend her husband to save his political career, and again she demonstrated her support. By October 1998 her approval ratings were near 70 percent, although many questioned why such a strong woman would stay with a husband who had cheated on her. Clinton addressed the issue in her memoir: "All I know is that no one understands me better and no one can make me laugh the way Bill does. Even after all these years, he is still the most interesting, energizing, and fully alive person I have ever met."

U.S. Senator from New York

As the Clinton presidency was nearing its end in 1999, many Democrats believed Hillary Clinton's strong public profile and policy experience would make her an excellent candidate for public office. Clinton had thought of running a university or foundation after leaving the White House and was hesitant to stay in the harsh media spotlight as a political candidate. Finally, however, she decided it wasn't enough to talk about empowering women when she could make a difference by holding an office of her own. In 1999 she decided to target the open Senate seat in New York, although she had never lived there and would be running against Rudy Giuliani, the popular mayor of New York City. She and the president bought a house in Chappaqua, and she began a "listening tour" of New York state. During her campaign, she emphasized improving education and helping boost the upstate economy, outside of New York City. When Giuliani dropped out of the race to deal with prostate cancer, Clinton ended up running against Congressman Rick Lazio, whose aggressive campaign tactics turned off many voters. Clinton won the race 55 to 43 percent, becoming the first sitting first lady to be elected to office in her own right.

Although her critics expected her to barge ahead with big policy issues in the Senate, Clinton showed she had learned from her early days in the White House. She started out slowly, getting acquainted with her fellow Senators and limiting her legislative proposals to bills designed to help economically depressed upstate New York. "The importance of building relationships among colleagues, of trying to create coalitions behind the issues that you are championing, was not something I ever had much insight into until I was elected and started serving in the Senate," she noted. After the terrorist attacks of September 11, 2001, brought down the World Trade Center in New York City, Clinton focused on getting disaster aid to

Senator Clinton in the halls of the U.S. Senate.

the city. By the end of 2001, she had introduced or co-sponsored some 70 pieces of legislation and had won the respect of colleagues in both parties.

Perhaps Clinton's most important vote during her first term was when she joined with Republicans and 22 other Democrats in October 2002 to authorize President George W. Bush to take military action against Iraq. Although she later criticized how the administration waged the Iraq War, she noted that "I don't regret giving the president authority because at the time it was in the context of weapons of mass destruction, grave threats to the United States, and clearly, Saddam Hussein had been a real problem for the international community for more than a decade." During her first Senate term, Clinton also served on several Senate committees, including those for the Budget; Environment and Public Works; Health, Education, Labor and Pensions; and the Armed Services. When she joined the Armed Services Committee in 2003, many believed it was to gain foreign policy experience for a future presidential run of her own. She was one of the country's most visible Democrats, and when she became chair of the Senate Democratic Steering Committee in 2003, she became a leading voice in setting policy for the party. Clinton, however, said her new assignment was merely part of serving the citizens of New York, who had a vested interest in homeland security and national defense after 9/11.

Although many thought (and others hoped) Clinton would run for president in 2004, she ruled out the possibility early on and declared she had no interest in joining the Democratic ticket as vice president. "I'm having the time of my life," she said of her work as a senator. "I pinch myself every morning." She was easily re-elected to the Senate in 2006, beating her Republican challenger by a vote of more than two to one. She had spent $34 million, more than any other Senate candidate that year, a move some believed was designed to raise her national profile for the 2008 presidential election. There was no question Clinton was the biggest fundraiser in the Democratic Party, able to appear almost anywhere in the country and bring in political contributions. She was popular outside the party, as well: her 2003 memoir *Living History* sold over 1.5 million copies in the U.S. during its first year alone.

Making History as a Presidential Candidate

In early 2007, Clinton announced her intention to run for president. She was considered the immediate frontrunner in a field that also included fellow Senators Barack Obama of Illinois and John Edwards of North Carolina (a candidate for vice president in 2004), as well as New Mexico Governor Bill Richardson. Not only did Clinton have greater name recognition and experience, she also performed well in early candidate debates and raised the most money for her campaign. For many Democrats, it was a difficult choice between her, the first strong female candidate for president, and Barack Obama, the first strong African-American contender. Clinton emphasized her "deep experience over the last 35 years" and stated "I wouldn't be in this race and working as hard as I am unless I thought I am uniquely qualified at this moment in our history to be the president we need."

The lead-up to a presidential election is a long process. The Democratic and Republican parties each hold a series of special elections in states around the country to determine who will win the party's nomination for president. These special elections, called primaries and caucuses, begin in winter of the election year and continue through the spring. During this time, the candidates from a single party vie against each other to win votes and win each state's election. In late summer, each party holds a convention to officially select their nominees for president and vice president. The battle between parties' candidates continues until the election in November, followed by the inauguration in January.

Clinton suffered a setback in the first caucus of the year, where she came in third behind Obama and Edwards. Observers thought her campaign was over, but she came back to win the next primary after sharing an emotional moment with voters about why she kept going despite the challenges of campaigning. "I listened to you, and in the process I found my own voice," she later commented. Still, the contest became increasingly competitive, as Obama's message of change resonated more with voters than Clinton's emphasis on experience. The Clinton campaign focused more on primaries, which are conducted by secret ballot, effectively leaving the caucus states, where open votes are held after meetings, to the Obama camp. On February 5—called Super Tuesday because over 20 state elections were held—Clinton and Obama earned nearly the same number of votes and delegates, although Obama carried more states. His lead kept growing over the next few months, but Clinton stayed competitive, hoping that she could gain enough votes from superdelegates—important officials in the Democratic Party—to win the nomination.

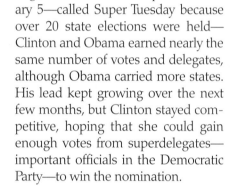

In the 2008 presidential race, Clinton said, "I wouldn't be in this race and working as hard as I am unless I thought I am uniquely qualified at this moment in our history to be the president we need."

After the final primary on June 3, 2008, however, it was clear that Barack Obama would clinch the Democratic presidential nomination. In conceding the race, Clinton referred to making history as the first woman to win a presidential primary and also to the number of votes she had received from her supporters: "Although we weren't able to shatter that highest, hardest glass ceiling, this time, thanks to you, it has about 18 million cracks in it and the light is shining through like never before." She quickly gave her endorsement to Obama, and many Democrats hoped that he might select Clinton as his vice-presidential running mate. Although Obama chose Delaware Senator Joseph Biden instead, Clinton continued to campaign around the country on behalf of the Democratic ticket, appearing at more than 200 rallies and fundraisers for more than 80 candidates.

After Obama won the presidential election in November 2008, many speculated Clinton might seek a role in his cabinet, a Supreme Court position, or even the governorship of New York. She told reporters she looked forward to returning to the Senate. "I'm not interested in just enhancing my visibility," she remarked. "I'm interested in standing on the South Lawn of the White House and seeing President Obama signing into law quality affordable health care for everybody, and voting in a big majority for clean, renewable energy and smarter economic policies.

*Clinton on the campaign trail, campaigning for president in
Charleston, West Virginia, March 2008.*

That's what I'm all about, and I'm going to use every tool at my disposal
to bring it about." Nonetheless, few were surprised when the president-
elect announced he had chosen Clinton to become his secretary of state,
the person responsible for implementing U.S. foreign policy and the
highest ranking position in the president's cabinet.

U.S. Secretary of State

Clinton was hesitant to take the job at first; she wanted to get back to the
Senate and work on issues important to her and her constituents, like
health care. Also, it had been a bruising political campaign, with hard feelings on all sides. But eventually, Obama persuaded her to say yes. "It came
down to my feeling that, number one, when you president asks you to do
something for your country, you really need a good reason not to do it,"
she explained. "Number two, if I had won and I had asked him to please
help me serve our country, I would have hoped he would say yes. And finally, I looked around our world and I thought, you know, we are in just so
many deep holes that everybody had better grab a shovel and start digging
out." She was easily confirmed by the Senate, by a vote of 94 to two.

The secretary of state is part of the Executive branch of the government.
She advises the president on foreign policy, heads up the State Department, and supervises the nation's relationships with other countries. She
also works to ensure the security of the United States. As Clinton took of-

As secretary of state, Clinton has many different roles: advising President Barack Obama (shown here in the Oval Office) on issues related to foreign affairs and national security; participating in a ceremonial tree planting in Nairobi, Kenya; talking to female artisans about how they have achieved economic self-sufficiency in Mumbai, India.

fice, there were many challenges around the world facing the U.S.: military conflicts in Iraq and Afghanistan; nuclear proliferation in Iran and North Korea; a trade imbalance with a rapidly growing China; and the need to work with other countries on issues of economics and security. But Clinton was undaunted by these challenges, as she told the Senate confirmation committee: "I don't get up every morning thinking only about the threats and dangers we face. With every challenge comes an opportunity to find promise and possibility in the face of adversity and complexity. Today's world calls forth the optimism and can-do spirit that has marked our progress for more than two centuries."

Clinton immediately identified five strategies to advance American foreign policy: first, appoint special envoys for hot spots and issues; second, engage in dialogue with adversaries; third, establish aid and development "as a core pillar of American power"; fourth, coordinate civilian and military efforts, as in Iraq and Afghanistan; and fifth, use the power of America's example to inspire the world. She got off to a fast start on these goals by naming special envoys for Afghanistan and Pakistan, Iran, North Korea, and the Israeli-Palestinian conflict. She also got more funds earmarked for the State Department, to add staff and increase foreign aid.

In her first few years as secretary of state, Clinton has been a visible advocate for American interests. She has traveled thousands of miles and made trips to dozens of countries, including Mexico, Brazil, Israel, Russia, China, Indonesia, India, Pakistan, Afghanistan, South Korea, and Vietnam, as well as other countries in Africa, Europe, Asia, the Middle East, Central and South America, and the Caribbean. She has continued the policy she began as first lady of meeting everyday citizens, and holding town hall meetings to answer questions about American policy. As she said in a speech to the Council on Foreign Relations: "In every country I visit, I look for opportunities to bolster civil society and engage with citizens, whether at a town hall in Baghdad [Iraq]—a first in the country; or appearing on local popular television shows that reach a wide and young audience; or meeting with democracy activists, war widows, or students." To date, Clinton has used her role as secretary of state to focus on several important issues: the war in Iraq and Afghanistan; the Mideast peace process among the Israelis, the Palestinians, and others in the Middle East; the aid crisis in Haiti; nuclear disarmament in North Korea and Iran; Internet censorship in China; and international agreements on climate change, among other critical issues.

Many commentators wondered what the working relationship would be like between Clinton and Obama and what role she would take within the administration. While their relationship did not appear to be close at first, it has improved greatly over time, according to Washington insiders.

———— " ————

"I always find those moments of grace, and I always see something that makes it important enough to keep going," Clinton said. "When somebody says that if it hadn't been for me they aren't sure their son would have survived because I fought with some insurance company to get them health care, I think, well, that's what politics is supposed to be about. I love that, and that's why I do what I do."

———— " ————

Clinton has developed a close partnership with the president and has come to wield greater influence on foreign policy. "I feel very much in the center of helping to devise the policies, carry out the policies, pick the people who will implement the policies," she said. "I see the president every week. We spend a lot of time talking." According to *Time* magazine, "she has the potential to become the most powerful public diplomat the U.S. has fielded in quite some time."

Clinton's long-term plans remain unclear. As an appointee of the president, Clinton will hold her job only as long as Obama is in office. Many observers have questioned whether she would run for office again—some have suggested she might run for governor of New York, while others have suggested she might run for president again. By adding experience as secretary of state to her résumé, according to political analysts, she would make an even more formidable candidate the second time around. But Clinton has said that "I have a very committed attitude toward the job I'm doing now," so another run is "not anything that is at all on my radar screen." Whatever her future plans, Clinton is clearly dedicated to a life of public service. Despite the challenges, "I always find those moments of grace, and I always see something that makes it important enough to keep going," she said. "When somebody says that if it hadn't been for me they aren't sure their son would have survived because I fought with some insurance company to get them health care, I think, well, that's what politics is supposed to be about. I love that, and that's why I do what I do."

HOBBIES AND OTHER INTERESTS

Her busy schedule leaves Clinton little time for hobbies, although she is known to enjoy ballet, art, and sculpture. A devout Methodist, she makes time for prayer groups and Bible study. In order to facilitate charitable giving, she cofounded the Clinton Family Foundation with her husband and daughter in 2001. Since then, the Foundation has donated more than $7 million to various charities, churches, hospitals, and arts and education organizations, including more than $2 million in 2008 alone.

SELECTED WRITINGS

It Takes a Village, 1996
Dear Socks, Dear Buddy: Kids' Letters to the First Pets, 1998 (compiler)
An Invitation to the White House: At Home with History, 2000 (with Carl Anthony)
Living History, 2003

SELECTED HONORS AND AWARDS

National Humanitarian Award (National Conference of Christians and Jews): 1987 (with Bill Clinton)
Named to 100 Most Influential Lawyers in the U.S. list (*National Law Journal*): 1988 and 1991
Albert Schweitzer Leadership Award (Hugh O'Brian Youth Foundation): 1993
Friend of Family Award (American Home Economics Association): 1993
Claude D. Pepper Award (National Association for Home Care): 1993
Distinguished Service, Health Education and Prevention Award (National Center for Health Education): 1994
Special Achievement Award (Hispanic Public Corporation): 1994
Living Legacy Award (Women's International Center): approx. 1994
Grammy Award (National Academy of Recording Arts and Sciences): for best spoken word album, 1997, for *It Takes a Village*
United Arab Emirates Health Foundation Prize (World Health Assembly): 1998
Lifetime Achievement Award (Children of Chernobyl Relief Fund): 1999
Mother Theresa Award (Government of Albania): 1999
German Media Prize: 2004
President's Vision and Voice Award (American Women's Medical Association): 2005
National President's Award (Reserve Officers Association): 2005
Energy Leadership Award (Energy Efficiency Forum): 2006
Trailblazer Award (Vital Voices Global Partnership): 2009
Margaret Sanger Award (Planned Parenthood Federation of America): 2009

FURTHER READING

Books

Bernstein, Carl. *A Woman in Charge,* 2007
Clinton, Hillary Rodham. *Living History,* 2003

Periodicals

Atlantic, Nov. 2006, p.56

Chicago Tribune, Jan. 21, 2007

Christian Science Monitor, Mar. 10, 2003, p.1

Current Biography Yearbook, 2002, 2009

Economist, Feb. 9, 2008, p.28

New York Times, Sep. 6, 1995, p.A10; July 19, 1998, p.1; May 23, 2006, p.1; June 8, 2008, p.A1; Dec. 3, 2008, p.A20; Feb. 5, 2009, p.12; Apr. 18. 2009, p.A4; May 2, 2009, p.A5; July 16, 2009, p.A1; Mar. 18, 2010

New York Times Magazine, May 23, 1993

New Yorker, Oct. 13, 2003, p.63

Newsweek, Jan. 21, 2008, p.60; Dec. 29, 2008, p.44; May 3, 2010, pp.31 and 36

People, Dec. 28, 1998, p.104; July 1, 2002, p.101

Time, Nov. 17, 2008, p.80; Nov. 16, 2009, p.24

USA Today, June 11, 2009, p.1A

Wall Street Journal, June 4, 2008, p.A1

Washington Post, Sep. 8, 2005, p.A12; July 16, 2009, p.A3; Aug.13, 2009, p.A8

Online Articles

http://www.CNN.com
(CNN, "Hillary Rodham Clinton Scores Historic Win in New York," Nov. 8, 2000; "Hillary Clinton: No Regret on Iraq Vote," Apr. 21, 2004; "Hillary Clinton: I Said No, At First, to Secretary of State Job," June 7, 2009)

http://www.firstladies.org
(National First Ladies Library, "First Lady Biography: Hillary Clinton," no date)

http://topics.nytimes.com
(New York Times, "Hillary Rodham Clinton," multiple articles, various dates)

http://topics.newsweek.com/people/politics
(Newsweek, "Hillary Rodham Clinton," multiple articles, various dates)

http://www.time.com
(Time, "The 2009 Time 100 Finalists," no date)

http://www.whitehouse.gov/about/first_ladies/hillaryclinton
(White House, "Hillary Rodham Clinton," no date)

http://www.clintonpresidentialcenter.org/the-administration/hillary-rodham-clinton
(William J. Clinton Presidential Center, "Hillary Rodham Clinton," no date)

ADDRESS

Hillary Clinton
U.S. Department of State
2201 C Street NW
Washington, DC 20520

WORLD WIDE WEB SITE

http://www.state.gov/secretary

Gustavo Dudamel 1981-

Venezuelan Classical Music Conductor
Music Director of the Los Angeles Philharmonic

BIRTH

Gustavo Adolfo Dudamel Ramirez was born on January 26, 1981, in Barquisimeto, the capital city of Lara, Venezuela. He comes from a musical family—his father, Oscar, played trombone in a salsa band for a living and worked with the local orchestra from time to time, while his mother taught voice lessons at a nearby conservatory. Due to his parents' occupations and the rich tradition of popular music in his hometown, he attended numerous live performances before he could even speak.

YOUTH

Dudamel's parents lived with his grandparents while he was a child, and his grandmother, Engracia de Dudamel, introduced him to classical music at an early age. She remembers taking Dudamel to see his father perform in a classical concert in Barquisimeto. "He was very small, I thought he was going to fall asleep," she recounted to the *New York Times*. "And he was completely attentive to details of the instruments. He said, 'Grandmother, I like this music.'"

Inspired to take up an instrument, Dudamel tried to play the trombone like his father, but discovered that his arms were too short. Instead, he entertained himself by setting up an imaginary orchestra of Lego figures. "I identified with the conductor a lot," he explained. "I thought, how interesting that the conductor uses an instrument that no one hears. I fell in love with it. I began to conduct in my house, arranging dolls as the orchestra. I'd put on a record and conduct, like theater." He wasted no time becoming familiar with the classics. "The first score that I had in my hand was Beethoven's Fifth, when I was seven years old," he remembered. "The first piece I played with an orchestra was Beethoven's Fifth."

> "I identified with the conductor a lot," Dudamel explained. "I thought, how interesting that the conductor uses an instrument that no one hears. I fell in love with it. I began to conduct in my house, arranging dolls as the orchestra. I'd put on a record and conduct, like theater."

Dudamel's strong reaction to this particular piece of music is something that he shares with his fellow countrymen. "In Venezuela we have a special connection with Beethoven. For us Beethoven is a symbol," he explained. "In Beethoven, you have more than music. It teaches you not only about music but about life, real life. The Fifth of Beethoven is a man searching for his destiny, and trying to live with his destiny. And for a kid who lives in our society today, it's a great thing to learn. Because a big percentage of the musicians come from very poor backgrounds, they've had a tough life. And to have the chance to get in touch with this symphony means not only to play music but also to give a very special meaning to that music." Moreover, Dudamel has acknowledged his supportive family for providing him with a strong personal foundation. "[It's] about values, and I think my values are really, really [down to] earth," he claimed. "My fami-

Dudamel developed a passion for conducting at a young age.

ly was giving me values, and the [educational] system of Venezuela was giving me values, to know what I am."

EDUCATION

At age four, Dudamel began taking violin lessons through El Sistema, a music education system designed to help Valenzuela's poor children. El Sistema was founded in 1975 by José Antonio Abreu, a Venezuelan economist who wanted to nurture his country's young musicians. Noting that many of the players in Venezuela's orchestras were foreigners, Abreu convinced the government to fund his program, which exists to this day. In fact, El Sistema has been so successful that it has inspired similar programs in other countries and has served as the focus of a documentary entitled *El Sistema: Music to Change Life*, which features Dudamel conducting the Simón Bolívar Youth Orchestra of Venezuela (SBYOV).

El Sistema trains children to play an instrument and then places them in a youth orchestra. Not only does this provide an educational structure for musically oriented kids, but it also presents a positive alternative to a criminal lifestyle. "[Many] boys from my school got pulled into gangs and drugs," Dudamel explained. "But those who came along to the sistema were saved. In a youth orchestra you must be in harmony with those around you. This makes you a good person, I think." According to Abreu,

Dudamel is an excellent example of El Sistema's importance and success. "Gustavo is the highest and most sublime expression of what [El Sistema] is," Abreu told the *Los Angeles Times*. "His musical and intellectual condition were acquired within the bosom of [El Sistema] and within the country." Now that Dudamel has risen to international fame, he has expressed great pride in his roots and is a champion of the music program that nurtured his talent. "I am a product of the sistema, and in the future, I will be here, working for the next generations," he affirmed.

———— *"* ————

At an early age, Dudamel learned the importance of the relationship between a conductor and his players. "I can be very firm," he explained, "but I also believe that the conductor is just another musician in the orchestra. When you are clear about this, it creates a magical atmosphere where everyone feels they can contribute."

———— *"* ————

During his training in El Sistema, Dudamel studied violin under José Luis Jiménez at the Jacinto Lara Conservatory at age 10. When he was 13, Jiménez allowed him to conduct a program that consisted of renaissance dances and Wolfgang Amadeus Mozart's "Ein kleine Nachtmusik." He then studied at the Latin American Academy of Violin under noted maestro José Francisco del Castillo. Proving himself a musical prodigy, he began taking lessons to become a conductor at age 15 and was named director of the state youth orchestra that same year. One of his instructors, conductor Rodolfo Saglimbeni, was instantly impressed by the young student. "When [Dudamel] was leading the state youth orchestra," Saglimbeni recalled in the *Los Angeles Times*, "maestro Abreu asked me to go there and give him some advice and I immediately knew I was in front of a special person with extraordinary capacities for music."

At an early age, Dudamel learned the importance of the relationship between a conductor and his players. "I can be very firm," he explained, "but I also believe that the conductor is just another musician in the orchestra. When you are clear about this, it creates a magical atmosphere where everyone feels they can contribute." As he continued to perform with many of the same musicians throughout his teenage years, he discovered that this bond grows stronger over time. "The relationship between the orchestra and me is so easy that sometimes in rehearsal I don't have to tell them anything—they are waiting for my hands and my movements," he commented.

CAREER HIGHLIGHTS

At the age of 18, Dudamel was appointed music director of the Simón Bolívar Youth Orchestra of Venezuela (SBYOV). Based in the Venezuelan capital of Caracas, the SBYOV was designed to place the most advanced students from El Sistema into a working environment that emphasizes the importance of the group while fostering the talents of the individual. Holding this position allowed him to hone his skills as a community leader of sorts. "In Venezuela, the most important thing is the orchestra," he stated. "You create a community, with a shared objective. That's why [the SBYOV] has such a special sound: we have learned together, as a collective."

In 2000, Dudamel performed throughout Germany with the SBYOV. This tour included a critically acclaimed performance at the prestigious Berlin Philharmonie. Later that year he was appointed as music director of the Youth Orchestra of the Andean Countries and was selected as principal conductor of the Youth Orchestra of the Americas. Incredibly, he achieved all of this before he turned 20.

"The relationship between the orchestra and me is so easy that sometimes in rehearsal I don't have to tell them anything—they are waiting for my hands and my movements," Dudamel commented.

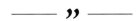

Breaking onto the World Stage

Dudamel gained more exposure in 2002 when he was chosen to perform during the UNICEF Children's Summit in New York City. That same year he won a Conductor's Academy competition that granted him a weeklong master class with renowned conductors Kurt Masur and Christoph von Dohnanyi. In 2004 he traveled to Bamberg, Germany, to compete in the Gustav Mahler International Conducting Competition. Not only did this mark his first performance with a professional orchestra, but he also won the competition. One of the judges for the Mahler Prize was Finnish composer Esa-Pekka Salonen, who was the music director of the Los Angeles Philharmonic at the time. Salonen was so impressed by Dudamel's performance that he invited him to conduct the Los Angeles Philharmonic at the Hollywood Bowl.

The concert was a huge success, prompting Mark Swed of the *Los Angeles Times* to proclaim that Dudamel "accomplished something increasingly rare and difficult at the Hollywood Bowl. He got a normally restive audience's full, immediate, and rapt attention. And he kept it." His reputation began to

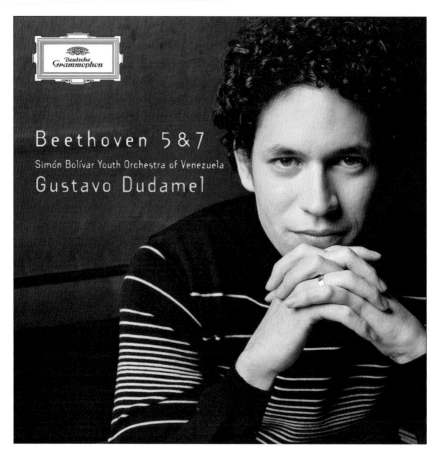

Deutsche Grammophon

Beethoven 5&7
Simón Bolívar Youth Orchestra of Venezuela
Gustavo Dudamel

*Dudamel has always felt a special connection with Beethoven's music,
which he selected for his first recording.*

spread, with critics comparing him to Simon Rattle, the highly esteemed British conductor who rose to prominence at a very young age during the 1970s. In fact, Rattle himself told London's *Daily Telegraph* that Dudamel was "the most astonishingly gifted conductor I've ever come across."

When asked whether older musicians ever felt resentful about being led by a person half their age, Dudamel acknowledged that "Of course, it sometimes happens. But for me the most important thing is to keep their respect, and from those people I always feel like I have something to learn. I always try to share something with all the musicians, but especially with those musicians that maybe gave me some resistance, I always try to get closer to them."

Signing a Record Deal and Performing Abroad

In 2005 Dudamel was offered a recording contract by Deutsche Grammophon, one of the leading classical music recording labels. For his debut he recorded *Ludwig van Beethoven: Symphonies nos. 5 & 7,* an SBYOV performance of Beethoven's symphonies. A hit with critics and audiences alike, it earned Dudamel an ECHO Award for New Artist of the Year from the German music industry. Also in 2005, he was selected as a last-minute replacement for the famous conductor Neeme Järvi for a well-received concert at London's Royal Albert Hall.

Dudamel's reputation continued to spread around the world over the next couple of years. He was awarded the 2006 Pegasus Prize at the Festival dei due monde (Festival of Two Worlds) in Spoleto, Italy. The festival jury claimed that they chose him due to his "talent, his conducting style, and for the indelible memory that his extraordinary concert left in the memory of the festival." He received more good news when Sweden's national orchestra, the Gothenburg Symphony, hired him as their principal conductor for the 2007-08 season. Having previously performed with the orchestra, he was delighted to commit to a schedule with them. "When I first conducted the Gothenburg Symphony … last year, I was very impressed by their skill and openness," he said. "It was wonderful—I simply fell in love with the orchestra!"

Never one to shy away from work, Dudamel was able to balance his Gothenburg appointment with his duties as the leader of the SBYOV, to which he has remained very loyal. As Edward Smith, the chief executive of the Gothenburg Symphony, told the *Los Angeles Times*: "Every day that he's out of Caracas I think he feels that he should be there. It's not a duty; it's a passion, it's a religion." To top it off, he was offered a spot as a guest conductor with the Chicago Symphony Orchestra. Those around him took note of his frantic schedule. "He said to me the other day he wishes there were 600 days in a year," Smith told the *Los Angeles Times.* "Of course, he's doing too much, by anybody's normal standard, and I think he's beginning to realize it. But what is too much for Gustavo? What might be too much for an ordinary guy isn't too much for Gustavo." According to his manager, Mike Newbanks, "The problem with Gustavo is just simply one of demand, that so many people want to work with him." Dudamel's hard work continued to pay off when he received the 2007 Premio de la latinidad, an award given by the Union Latina for outstanding contributions to Latin cultural life.

Appreciation of Dudamel's work grew during his 2007 North American tour, as he wowed audiences with his exuberance, passion, and talent. Critics were impressed, comparing his charisma to that of conducting legend Leonard Bernstein. *New York Magazine* deemed his debut at New York's Carnegie Hall with the SBYOV the best performance of the year. The excitement building around him prompted the *Los Angeles Times* to coin the term "Dudamelmania" to describe it all. As the *Boston Globe* put it: "Dudamel and [the SBYOV] are now officially the most exciting thing in classical music. Over the last year or so, the excitement surrounding the frizzy-haired Dudamel has blossomed into all-out frenzy.... Rarely has one musician's potential seemed so limitless." His fellow musicians were impressed as well. "With Gustavo, the chops are all there," raved violinist Gil Shaham in *Newsweek*. "The technique, the mastery—he has it all."

Ever the professional, Dudamel does not let the pressure of media attention or high-profile events affect him. "I don't feel nervous in front of any orchestra," he shared. "I feel only excitement, adrenalin, pleasure. I love to conduct. It's what I was born to do. It's what I have done all my life."

"*Dudamel and [the SBYOV] are now officially the most exciting thing in classical music. Over the last year or so, the excitement surrounding the frizzy-haired Dudamel has blossomed into all-out frenzy," said a reviewer for the* **Boston Globe**. "*Rarely has one musician's potential seemed so limitless.*"

Worldwide Accolades and Media Appearances

Dudamel soon earned even more praise, receiving the 2007 Young Artists Award from the Royal Philharmonic Society in Great Britain and, along with Abreu, the 2008 "Q" Prize for extraordinary advocacy on behalf of children from the Harvard University School of Public Health.

Also in 2008, the SBYOV won the Prince of Asturias Award for the Arts and recorded an album of Latin American musical pieces called *FIESTA*. His first performance with the Berlin Philharmonic at the Berlin Waldbühne, one of Europe's largest concert venues, was broadcast on German television that same year.

In addition, Director Enrique Sánchez Lansch filmed a documentary about Dudamel and the SBYOV called *The Promise of Music*. Released in 2008, the film follows the maestro and orchestra as they ready themselves for a concert at Beethovenfest in Bonn, Germany. By showcasing both the historical development of the SBYOV as well as their triumphant performance at Bonn, *The Promise of Music* illustrates the power of music to change lives.

As Dudamel took on new challenges over the years, he maintained his connection with SBYOV, shown here at a 2004 performance at Boston's Symphony Hall.

Dudamel achieved another first in 2008 when a recording of his performance of Hector Berlioz's *Symphonie fantastiqe* topped the *Billboard* classical chart. The following year, the French government named him a Chevalier dans l'ordre des arts et des lettres, one of the country's highest honors. In recognition of his many accomplishments and his meteoric rise to fame, *Time* magazine named him one of the 100 most influential people of 2009.

While Dudamel has enjoyed the attention and the new experiences that come with it, he has not allowed outside pressures to detract from what music really means to him. "It's only to have fun. This is the secret," he emphasized. "When you are sitting there, you need to have fun. Enjoy each moment. If your feelings are a little bit sad, you have to be there, to get it with the happy people. And all this energy." He has also recognized that being a professional is not the same thing as being a perfectionist. When asked if it mattered to him whether a performance was flawless, he responded, "I don't care. Even if it's not perfect, it's more about, 'Wow. I will remember this forever.'"

Leading the Los Angeles Philharmonic

When Esa-Pekka Salonen was preparing to step down as the leader of the Los Angeles Philharmonic, Dudamel was tapped to take his place. In fact, the organization was so excited about hiring the young conductor that it did

Dudamel has developed a warm relationship with members of the Los Angeles Philharmonic, where he became music director in 2009.

not consider any other candidates and announced its transition plan two-and-a-half years in advance. The city of Los Angeles welcomed Dudamel with open arms, posting billboards and banners announcing his arrival and presenting a fireworks display in his honor. "He's a genuine star," former movie executive and University of Southern California professor Martin Kaplan proclaimed in the *New York Times.* "He's young. He has amazing hair. He has a great back story. He has a fantastic name. He's the dude!"

Commenting on the news, Salonen said, "The right successor has been found. Gustavo Dudamel's remarkable talent, intelligence, and energy are the absolute right match for the orchestra and Los Angeles. I am peaceful and joyous about the artist to whom we will pass the baton. There could not be a more forward looking choice." In turn, Dudamel expressed his gratitude. "I am honored to be chosen to succeed the great conductor/composer Esa-Pekka Salonen, who has given me so much support," he stated. "Playing with the Philharmonic in the magnificent Walt Disney Concert Hall is a great privilege, and I look forward to many happy years together."

On October 3, 2009, Dudamel began his inaugural season as the Los Angeles Philharmonic's music director with an event called *¡Bienvenido Gusta-*

vo!, a daylong musical celebration. The sold-out program included a variety of music—including gospel, jazz, pop, and blues—and culminated with Dudamel conducting Beethoven's Ninth Symphony. Five days later, he led the Los Angeles Philharmonic in the world premiere of composer John Adams's *City Noir* and a performance of Mahler's Symphony no. 1 at the Walt Disney Concert Hall. The entire event was broadcast on PBS and is-sued on DVD by Deutsche Grammophon.

Overall, the musicians of the Philhar-monic greeted Dudamel warmly, sharing in the audience's enthusiasm for the young conductor. They ex-pressed admiration for the maestro's technical know-how and his impres-sive ability to seduce, inspire, and lead the orchestra despite his young age. "It was noticeable from the very first rehearsal that Gustavo was paying a lot of attention not only to the string sound and intensity of expression, but to how the sound is produced," vio-linist Mark Kashper commented in the magazine *Strings*. As violist Dana Hansen explained on National Public

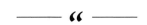

"I don't feel nervous in front of any orchestra," Dudamel shared. "I feel only excitement, adrenalin, pleasure. I love to conduct. It's what I was born to do. It's what I have done all my life."

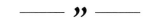

Radio's "Morning Edition": "He looks young on the podium, but he doesn't act young. I've never heard of anyone conducting as much as he has in his young life." Clarinetist David Howard added, "If you look at what this man has to offer musically, it's really independent of his age."

During the 2009-10 season, Dudamel launched YOLA: Youth Orchestra Los Angeles, an initiative to provide underserved communities with access to exceptional music education, a program he modeled after Venezuela's *El Sistema*. He also directed the Los Angeles Philharmonic in the *Americas and Americans* festival, a series of concerts celebrating the cultural and mu-sical traditions of North, Central, and South America. In addition to his work in Los Angeles, he has continued to conduct the Gothenburg Sym-phony and lead the SBYOV. In May 2010 he embarked on a coast-to-coast U.S. tour with the Los Angeles Philharmonic.

In Los Angeles, a city that emphasizes celebrity, Dudamel has become a superstar. When asked what it meant to have classical music become so popular, he had this to say. "If you're famous, you have to use your image for the other people," he stressed. "If I have the opportunity to be famous now, I want to show the kids and the new generation that it's possible—

*Dudamel at a rehearsal of YOLA (Youth Orchestra Los Angeles),
which he formed to provide music education to children who might not
otherwise have the opportunity.*

it's possible to make it to reality, that you can have a career, be successful, enjoy.... And now to bring this orchestra to the people who don't have the opportunity to have classical music. It's really important—one of the most important things. Because that is *our* future, and we have to be in the future. Especially here in L.A.—especially in my home."

MARRIAGE AND FAMILY

In 2006, Dudamel married Eloísa Maturén, a ballet dancer, choreographer, and journalist. As his workload and fame continued to increase, she helped her husband make artistic decisions and served as his translator while he was learning English. Gothenburg Symphony's Edward Smith told the *Los Angeles Times* that Maturén "will say things to Gustavo, usually in Spanish, extraordinarily perceptive things about a performance or a performer that [others may] feel more inhibited" about expressing. After Dudamel became conductor of the Los Angeles Philharmonic, the couple moved to the Hollywood Hills to start a new life. "This is a great time for him to slow down a bit and spend some more time with his wife," his manager Mark Newbanks commented in the *Los Angeles Times*. "They love to cook together, they love to read together, they love to listen to music together, they love to dance together."

Dudamel has claimed that things have worked well between him and his wife ever since they first met. "Eloísa came in the right time in my life," he said. "She came when I won the competition in Bamberg, and all the big orchestras were starting to call me, you know.… I was conducting a lot in Venezuela, but I started to do more traveling around with different orchestras. And when she arrived in my life, it was like, 'Wow.'" He has told the press that he hopes to have "a big, big family" someday.

HOBBIES AND OTHER INTERESTS

Although his first passion is classical music, Dudamel enjoys listening to a wide variety of other styles. "I love, of course, Latin music—salsa, merengue, boleros," he explained. "I love Beatles, Pink Floyd, Led Zeppelin. It's amazing! I can speak to you a lot in the way of pop music." He's also a big fan of Los Angeles's local eateries. "I love hot dogs," he admitted. "They made a hot dog for me, with my name, at Pink's [a famous L.A. hotdog stand], with jalapeño, guacamole, nachos, everything. It's not very Venezuelan, it's more Mexican. But it doesn't matter. I love to eat." He also enjoys playing soccer, swimming, and watching the L.A. Lakers.

RECORDINGS

Ludwig van Beethoven: Symphonies nos. 5 & 7, 2006 (with the Simón Bolívar Youth Orchestra of Venezuela)
Béla Bartók: Concerto for Orchestra, 2007 (with the Los Angeles Philharmonic)
Birthday Concert for Pope Benedict XVI, 2007 (DVD)
Gustav Mahler: Symphony no. 5, 2007 (with the Simón Bolívar Youth Orchestra of Venezuela)
FIESTA, 2008 (with the Simón Bolívar Youth Orchestra of Venezuela)
Hector Berlioz: Symphonie fantastique, 2008 (with the Los Angeles Philharmonic)
The Promise of Music, 2008 (DVD)
El Sistema: Music to Change Life, 2009 (DVD)
Gustavo Dudamel and the Los Angeles Philharmonic: The Inaugural Concert, 2009 (DVD)

HONORS AND AWARDS

Bamberger Symphoniker Gustav Mahler Conducting Competition: 2004, Winner
Pegasus Prize (Festival dei due monde, Italy): 2006
Classic FM Gramophone Award: 2007, WQXR Gramophone Special Recognition Award (with the Simón Bolívar Youth Orchestra of Venezuela)

Culture Award (*New York Magazine*): 2007, Best Performance of the Year, for debut at Carnegie Hall with the Simón Bolívar Youth Orchestra of Venezuela

ECHO Award (German Recording Industry): 2007, New Artist of the Year

Premio de la latinidad (Union Latina): 2007, for outstanding contributions to Latin cultural life

Young Artists Award (Royal Philharmonic Society, Great Britain): 2007

City of Toronto Glenn Gould Protégé Prize (Glenn Gould Foundation): 2008

Prince of Asturias Award for the Arts (Spain): 2008 (with the Simón Bolívar Youth Orchestra of Venezuela)

"Q" Prize (Harvard University School of Public Health): 2008, for extraordinary advocacy on behalf of children (with Dr. José Antonio Abreu)

Chevalier dans l'ordre des arts et des lettres (France): 2009

100 Most Influential People (*Time* magazine): 2009

Eugene McDermott Award in the Arts (Massachusetts Institute of Technology): 2010

FURTHER READING

Periodicals

BBC Music Magazine, June 2008, p.24

Gramophone, Nov. 2006, p.25

Los Angeles Times, Dec. 31, 2006, p.F1; Apr. 11, 2007, p.E1

Los Angeles Times Magazine, Aug. 8, 2009, p.28

New York Times, Nov. 13, 2009, p.A1; Nov. 22, 2009, p.23

New Yorker, Dec. 14, 2009, p.90

Newsweek, Jan. 7, 2008, p.92

Vogue, Sep. 2009, p.518

Online Articles

http://www.boston.com
(Boston Globe, "The Maestro at 25: Venezuelan Conductor Gustavo Dudamel Has Had a Meteoric Rise to Prominence," Aug. 25, 2006)

http://www.latimes.com
(Los Angeles Times, "Gustavo Dudamel Learns to Conduct His Career," Sep. 26, 2009)

http://www.latimes.com
(Los Angeles Times Magazine, "Gustavo Dudamel: Passion Play," Aug. 2009)

http://www.npr.org
(National Public Radio Morning Edition, "Dudamel Leads L.A. Philharmonic in Concert," Oct. 8, 2009)
http://www.nytimes.com
(New York Times, "The Kid's Got Energy. Now Watch Him Conduct," Nov. 30, 2007)
http://www.nytimes.com
(New York Times Magazine, "Conductor of the People," Oct. 28, 2007)
http://www.topics.nytimes.com
(New York Times, "Gustavo Dudamel," various articles, multiple dates)
http://www.cbsnews.com
(60 Minutes, "Gustavo the Great," Feb. 17, 2008)
http://www.time.com
(Time Magazine, "Gustavo Dudamel," May 11, 2009)
http://entertainment.timesonline.co.uk
(Times Online, "True Class: South America's Lightning Conductor," Feb. 15, 2007)

ADDRESS

Gustavo Dudamel
Los Angeles Philharmonic
151 South Grand Avenue
Los Angeles, CA 90012-3034

WORLD WIDE WEB SITES

http://www.gustavodudamel.com
http://elsistemausa.org
http://www.laphil.com/gustavo/index.html
http://vadimrepin.com/artistmicrosite/DUDGU/en/index.htms
http://www.fesnojiv.gob.ve/en.html

Eran Egozy 1971-
Alex Rigopulos 1970-

American Video Game Designers
Creators of the Award-Winning Video Games *Guitar Hero* and *Rock Band*

EARLY YEARS

Eran B. Egozy was born in Israel, a Middle Eastern country located on the eastern shore of the Mediterranean Sea. His family moved to the U.S. when he was 12 years old. As a child, Egozy was interested in music. He learned to play the clarinet, a woodwind instrument most often used in classical and jazz music.

Alexander P. Rigopulos was born in Massachusetts and grew up in the Boston area. When he was three years old, his parents bought a Magnavox Odyssey, the first video game console made for use with home televisions. Rigopulos loved playing video games, and he soon became interested in the computer technology that made the games work. He also enjoyed playing the drums.

EDUCATION

Egozy attended the Massachusetts Institute of Technology (MIT), where he studied electrical engineering and music. As a classical clarinet player, Egozy often performed as a soloist with the MIT Symphony Orchestra, the MIT Chamber Music Society, and MIT's Gamelan Galak Tika orchestra.

> "Playing music is, I think, one of the most fundamentally joyful experiences that life has to offer," Rigopulos declared. "Just about everyone tries at some point in their life to learn to play music: piano lessons as a kid, guitar lessons as a teenager, or whatever."

("Gamelan" means "to hammer" and is the name for percussion groups that perform the traditional music of the Indonesian islands of Bali and Java.) Throughout his years at MIT, he studied music and technology at the MIT Media Lab, a research department that focuses on developing new technologies. In 1995, Egozy earned both a Bachelor of Science degree (BS) in electrical engineering and computer science and a Master of Science degree (MS) in electrical engineering and computer science.

Rigopulos also attended MIT, and he was a student there at the same time as Egozy. Rigopulos studied music with a focus on composition, keyboards, and percussion. He sang with the MIT Concert Choir and was among the first members of MIT's Gamelan Galak Tika orchestra. He also played the drums in a local rock band that was known for performing songs by groups like Led Zepplin and Pink Floyd. Rigopulos earned a Bachelor of Science degree (BS) in humanities in 1992. He also stayed at MIT as a graudate student, where he studied computer music at the MIT Media Lab. Rigopulos earned a Master of Science degree (MS) in computer music in 1994.

At the MIT Media Lab, Egozy and Rigopulos were assigned to share an office. Although their paths had crossed before, they did not know each

Egozy and Rigopulos first became partners while students at Massachusetts Institute of Technology (MIT), while working at the Media Lab.

other very well before then. Egozy and Rigopulos soon discovered that they shared an interest in combining music and technology. They both loved playing music, and they wanted everyone to be able to do that too, regardless of talent or experience. "Playing music is, I think, one of the most fundamentally joyful experiences that life has to offer," Rigopulos declared. "Just about everyone tries at some point in their life to learn to play music: piano lessons as a kid, guitar lessons as a teenager, or whatever."

143

They realized that learning to play music was difficult for most people, and it took a lot of time to master a musical instrument. "The overwhelming majority of people give it up after six months or a year in frustration, just because it's too difficult to learn to play music the old-fashioned way," Rigopulos explained. "Consequently, this profound joy that comes from making music is only accessible to this tiny percentage of the people of the world." Egozy and Rigopulos began to work together to find a way for technology to make it easier for people to share the fun of making music.

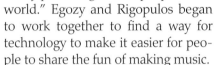

"When we handed someone a game controller and said they would be making music, as opposed to playing a game, they were skeptical, self-conscious," Rigopulos admitted. "But if we said here is a game, they were happy to dive in. So we learned that we needed to present this experience as a video game if we were to realize our secret, clandestine mission to make musicians out of people."

According to Egozy, "Alex and I got interested in the question, 'How do you get average people to be able to express themselves musically by using technology?'" He and Rigopulos created several different computer programs that allowed people to make music by pressing buttons or moving a mouse or joystick. These early programs became very popular at the Media Lab, and were often used as examples of the new technologies that were being developed at MIT.

When their time at the Media Lab was coming to an end, Egozy and Rigopulos decided to continue working together outside MIT. "We joked around about how no one would hire us, so we started a company," Egozy said. "We wanted to keep doing what we were doing. But it wasn't just that; it was that we saw the appeal, the sparkle in people's eyes and the smile that came to their faces when they touched this thing and were able to express themselves. We thought, 'Wow, we actually have something here.'"

CAREER HIGHLIGHTS

In 1995, Egozy and Rigopulos founded Harmonix Music Systems with one goal in mind: to help non-musicians have the experience of making music. "We created this company to try to invent new ways to give music-loving non-musicians—the millions of passionate air guitarists in the world—[a chance] to play music," explained Rigopulos. "Our mission was to show non-musicians how it feels when you finally get to the other side. And hopefully, to inspire them to start making music the old-fashioned way."

As the creators of the wildly popular and critically acclaimed video games *Guitar Hero* and *Rock Band*, Egozy and Rigopulos are seen as video gaming pioneers. Harmonix is recognized as one of the leading developers of music-oriented video games in the world. But success did not come quickly or easily. It took ten years of hard work, frustration, and many disappointments before Harmonix released its first successful product.

Getting Started

When Egozy and Rigopulos worked together at MIT, their goal was to create computer programs called prototypes. These prototypes served as examples—they showed how technology could help people make music. At MIT, it was enough that their prototypes worked and that people were impressed with the technology. However, Egozy and Rigopulos quickly learned that the business world is very different from MIT's research labs. Impressive technology was not enough anymore, and it turned out to be very difficult to turn their ideas into something that people would buy. Rigopulos said, "We had this naïve assumption that if we made something that had a lot of 'Wow, how'd they do that?' factor, it would sell."

Harmonix struggled with one failure after another in its first few years. Rigopulos now refers to that time as "the dark ages." Egozy and Rigopulos were creating new technology and pushing the capabilities of computer programming, but they were not making a profit from their work. "I don't mean we were earning no money," Rigopulos explained. "I mean we had near zero revenue. We were raising money and spending it, building stuff that no one actually wanted to pay for." Even with the financial support of investors, Harmonix nearly went out of business more than once. Rigopulos said, "We were on the brink of death, I don't know, 10 times."

Harmonix released its first official product in 1997. *The Axe* was a computer program that turned the movements of a mouse or joystick into musical notes, similar to the early prototypes that Egozy and Rigopulos created at MIT's Media Lab. *The Axe* was not a video game; there were no goals to reach or points to be scored. Egozy and Rigopulos thought that creating improvised music was entertaining enough on its own. "We weren't really thinking about video games," Rigopulos stressed. "We were making interactive music-making, free-form creative experiences." At the time it was released, *The Axe* was a completely new idea for computer software. "You couldn't really explain it to anyone," Egozy conceded. "People would actually have to physically sit down and try it to see what it was doing. We could guide them through it, and then they'd smile and we'd know they got it, but of course that is no way to market a product on a large scale."

The innovative new technology of *The Axe* was praised by computer software reviewers. A music critic for the *Boston Globe* called *The Axe* "armchair entertainment at its best," while a writer for *Keyboard* magazine said that "using the program is as easy as it gets." In spite of the impressive technology and positive reviews, ultimately only about 300 copies of *The Axe* were sold. In 1998, some of the technology created for *The Axe* was used for a new music-making exhibit at Disney World's Epcot Center theme park. The exhibit allowed park visitors to create music just by waving their hands in the air. Although the technology was admired by people working in the computer industry, the lack of commercial success was another disappointment for Harmonix. Egozy and Rigopulos moved on to develop new software that they hoped more people would want to buy.

Creating Video Games

In 2001, Harmonix released *Frequency*, its first music video game. The release of a second music game, *Amplitude,* followed in 2003. Harmonix hoped that combining music-making and game play would attract more buyers. In both games, players create music while navigating through futuristic environments, with eye-dazzling computer graphics and songs from such artists such as David Bowie, No Doubt, Pink, and Weezer. *Frequency* and *Amplitude* were also the world's first online multiplayer music games. "*Frequency* and *Amplitude* introduced the notion of game play," Egozy explained. "That was another big turning point. The root of this whole thing was combining music with joysticks, which was really a gaming thing, but it took us about four years to realize that we should actually be building a game." At first, it was hard to encourage people to try to make music. "When we handed someone a game controller and said they would be making music, as opposed to playing a game, they were skeptical, self-conscious," Rigopulos admitted. "But if we said here is a game, they were happy to dive in. So we learned that we needed to present this experience as a video game if we were to realize our secret, clandestine mission to make musicians out of people."

A game reviewer for IGN.com called *Frequency* an "amazingly good game" that is easy to play, even for non-gamers. *Amplitude* was nominated for the 2003 Best PS2 Game award, named by *Rolling Stone* magazine as one of the four Best Console Games of 2003, and listed as one of IGN.com's 2003

Amplitude *and* Frequency, *two early offerings from Harmonix, were their first video music games.*

Reader Top 10 PS2 games. Despite such high praise from the press and the video gaming industry, neither game sold very well. Harmonix was still attracting fans among video game professionals, but had yet to impress video game players.

> *When it was released in 2005,* **Guitar Hero** *was advertised as "a shrine to the glory of rock guitar and a fiendishly addictive fusion of music and gameplay."*

Harmonix's next attempt at creating a successful product was *Karaoke Revolution*, a series of singing games released from 2003 to 2005. Here, Rigopulos describes the design process for *Karaoke Revolution:* "We took a step back and said, 'Well, what kind of game can we create that has incredibly broad, mainstream appeal so even people who don't consider themselves 'gamers' would be willing to pick up this game and give it a try? How can we turn the tide and help expand people's understanding of what music gaming is, and put it on the map as a mainstream category?' That was a big part of the conception of *Karaoke Revolution*."

Karaoke Revolution won the 2003 Gaming Innovation of the Year award from *Electronic Gaming Monthly* and was named *Time* magazine's No. 1 Video Game of 2003. It was also nominated for 1UP.com's 2003 Game of the Year award. A video game reviewer for GameDaily.com called *Karaoke Revolution* "fantastic" and "the perfect game for anyone who celebrates the joys of music." Sales of Karaoke Revolution were good, and Harmonix finally earned its first profits—10 years after starting out.

In 2004, Harmonix released *EyeToy: AntiGrav*, its only non-music video game. An extreme sports hoverboarding game, *EyeToy: AntiGrav* was the world's first video game in which players moved their whole body to control a video game character. The game helped to define the new "physical gaming" technology, which was just beginning to emerge at that time. At first, physical gaming was unfamiliar and strange to most video game players. There also some problems with the camera that was used to sense a player's movements. Reviews of *EyeToy: AntiGrav* were mixed, with criticism focusing on the camera's occasional inconsistent motion sensing. A staff game reviewer for GameSpot.com praised the game's "inventive design" and "totally immersive experience," but complained that the game's technology was not yet able to track accurately the full-body motions required to control the game. The staff of 1UP.com said the motion control worked "amazingly well" but noted that it was difficult to play the game in certain situations, for example if the room's lighting was too dim or too bright for the camera. Once again, Harmonix had pushed the capabilities of video gaming technology almost beyond the limits of what was possible.

Guitar Hero

In 2005, Egozy and Rigopulos were contacted by RedOctane, a small company that made such video game hardware as the special mats used for the home version of the popular *Dance Dance Revolution* video game. RedOctane wanted to produce a new version of a Japanese video game called *Guitar Freaks*. RedOctane proposed that Harmonix would create a guitar-based music game, and RedOctane would manufacture the plastic guitars needed to play it. Egozy and Rigopulos were initially skeptical, doubting that this was a good idea. "Any rational analysis told you this game was not going to be successful," Rigopulos later said. He and Egozy weren't sure how well it would sell, because the guitar that was included with the game increased the price as well as the space needed to display the larger box on store shelves. But the idea did present an opportunity to create a new kind of music-making game for non-musicians. Rigopulos eventually decided that Harmonix should go into partnership with RedOctane. "Even though it wasn't going to make us any money, it was a game we were going to love to make."

Released in 2005, *Guitar Hero* was advertised as "a shrine to the glory of rock guitar and a fiendishly addictive fusion of music and gameplay." To play the game, players strum and push colored buttons on a small plastic guitar to match the rhythm and tempo of the game's music, indicated by colored dots that appear on the screen. Much to everyone's surprise, *Guitar Hero* became an overnight sensation. It became the runaway hit of the 2005 holiday shopping season, selling so fast that most stores could not keep the game in stock. *Guitar Hero* sold faster than any other video game in history, reaching $15 million in sales in its first two months—more than Harmonix had earned in the previous 10 years combined. The game also quickly became a pop culture phenomenon, attracting celebrity fans, appearing on magazine covers, and being featured in television shows. Egozy said, "We had no idea it would become this huge." In an interview with *Game Developer* magazine, Harmonix team members said, "We on the *Guitar Hero* team are all somewhat astonished that we actually got paid to make this game....It was pure fun from beginning to end."

In addition to being a huge hit with game players, game critics and industry professionals also loved *Guitar Hero*. A reviewer for *Official PlayStation Magazine* called the game "ridiculously awesome," while *Inc.* magazine

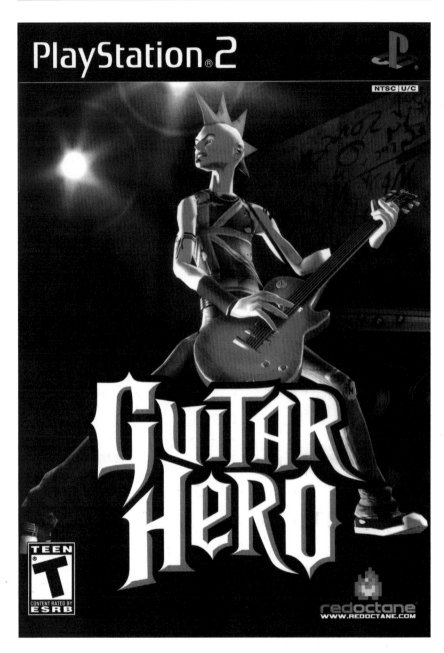

Egozy and Rigopulos had their first big hit with Guitar Hero.

said *Guitar Hero* is "shockingly fun." *Newsweek* praised *Guitar Hero* as a "cultural and high-tech phenomenon that is changing the way we interact with music." *Guitar Hero* won five Interactive Achievement Awards, two Game Developers Choice Awards, and was nominated for Game of the Year by both organizations. *Guitar Hero II*, released in 2006, continues to be ranked as one of the Top 10 games for PlayStation 2.

The phenomenal success of *Guitar Hero* and *Guitar Hero II* also captured the attention of large media entertainment companies looking to invest in new products. In 2006 Harmonix was purchased by Viacom, a large media conglomerate that also owns MTV. Around the same time, RedOctane was acquired by Activision, a major video game publisher. Because RedOctane owned the right to publish *Guitar Hero*, the game went with the sale. Activision and Viacom were fierce competitors and were unwilling to collaborate on the development of future games. Because of this conflict, Harmonix was no longer allowed to develop games for the *Guitar Hero* series. So once again, Egozy and Rigopulos turned their attention to new projects.

Rock Band

Although Harmonix could no longer release games under the *Guitar Hero* name, Egozy and Rigopulos still held patents on the technology used in the game. This gave them the right to use *Guitar Hero*'s computer programs to create new games based on the same concept. The result was *Rock Band*, a complete music performance simulation game that expanded *Guitar Hero* by combining guitar, bass guitar, drums, and singing in one game. *Rock Band* allows simultaneous play by up to four people, with each player using small replica instruments to play or sing their part of a song. Players can join together to form a band in the same room, or they can connect to

Egozy has credited their success to their early years working at the MIT Media Lab. "MIT really instills in you the notion of wanting to do original work, and not being satisfied by copying what someone else has done, and building new things. I think it's been sewn into the fabric of the company that being creative and original and innovative is just the way to do things. It's just kind of second nature. You look at the products we've made, and we're always trying to do new things in new ways."

others through an online version of the game. *Rock Band* can also be played by fewer people, with the computer filling in the parts of the missing instruments.

Rock Band was released in 2007 and quickly became another phenomenal success for Harmonix. As the first multiplayer music performance game, *Rock Band* was a hit with music fans, video game players, and reviewers. *Inc.* magazine called it "the most realistic rock-star simulation yet" and praised Harmonix for producing "another monster hit." *Wired* magazine called *Rock Band* "the ultimate music game," and *Time* said it was "the best party game ever made." *Rock Band 2* was released in 2008 and featured more music tracks and additional downloadable content. By the end of that year, more than seven million copies of *Rock Band* games and 26 million downloadable songs for the game had been sold.

In 2009, a new version of *Rock Band* was released focusing on the music of The Beatles. The British rock band first became famous in the 1960s and went on to become one of the world's most influential and successful rock bands of all time. "I think particularly younger players or listeners probably don't have an appreciation of just the sheer magnitude of the phenomenon, that there was nothing before and frankly, has not been anything like it since," Rigopulos stressed. "There are no rock bands in the world today that are the same kind of magnitude or phenomenon that The Beatles were."

The Beatles: Rock Band game spans the group's entire career, including performances on stage and in the recording studio. The usual computer animation found in *Rock Band* is combined with film recordings of the real band members, creating a unique visual experience that is new for music performance video games. Another innovation for music games is the introduction of multiple singing parts in *The Beatles: Rock Band.* As Rigopulos explained, "For the singing game play in our previous games, we've always focused on a single singer singing a single part, but harmonies are such a critical aspect of The Beatles music that this was an area we felt we had to innovate in this game."

Egozy and Rigopulos are widely credited with being groundbreaking leaders in their field, and in 2008 they were both included in *Time* magazine's list of the 100 most influential people in the world. "People talk about music games as a new category of games, but for me, music games are a new category of musical entertainment," Rigopulos said. "We make music games, but we consider it to be music first and games second. We really consider what we do in this category to be making new kinds of music experiences and to let people experience music in a new way. Our goal with

Scenes from Rock Band, *which expanded on the success of* Guitar Hero *by allowing multiple players at one time.*

Rock Band has always been to go beyond making music games and create a true music platform."

Egozy and Rigopulos are widely recognized as innovators in the field of video gaming. In 2009, they received the Game Developers Choice Pioneer Award, considered by many industry professionals to be the highest honor in game development. Egozy has credited their success to their early years working together as graduate students at the MIT Media Lab. "MIT really instills in you the notion of wanting to do original work, and not being satisfied by copying what someone else has done, and building new things. I think it's been sewn into the fabric of the company that being creative and original and innovative is just the way to do things. It's just kind of second nature. You look at the products we've made, and we're always trying to do new things in new ways."

HOBBIES AND OTHER INTERESTS

Egozy enjoys playing the clarinet and has been a member of Boston's Radius Ensemble chamber music group since 2001. He is a frequent participant in the Apple Hill Chamber Music Festival in New Hampshire. He also mentors entrepreneurs through the MIT Enterprise Forum, the MIT 100K competition, and other organizations.

In his spare time, Rigopulos plays the drums and sometimes performs in the Boston area with his brother in their band, Yeast.

Through Harmonix, Egozy and Rigopulos support music education and enrichment programs for young people. The Harmonix Music and Youth Initiative provides free music education to young people in the greater Boston area. Harmonix supports Music Drives Us, an organization that promotes music education throughout New England. Harmonix also works with the Starlight Foundation to bring music opportunities to children facing chronic and life-threatening illnesses.

HONORS AND AWARDS

Editor's Choice Award (IGN.com): 2001, for *Frequency*
Gaming Innovation of the Year (*Electronic Gaming Monthly*): 2003, for
    Karaoke Revolution
Number 1 Video Game of 2003 (*Time*): 2003, for *Karaoke Revolution*
Best Console Game of 2003 (*Rolling Stone*); 2003, for *Amplitude*
Family Game of the Year (Academy of Interactive Arts and Sciences): 2006,
    for *Guitar Hero;* 2007, for *Guitar Hero II*; 2008, for *Rock Band*

Interactive Achievement Award (Academy of Interactive Arts and Sciences): 2006, for *Guitar Hero*

Outstanding Achievement in Game Design (Academy of Interactive Arts and Sciences): 2006, for *Guitar Hero*

Outstanding Innovation in Gameplay Engineering (Academy of Interactive Arts and Sciences): 2006, for *Guitar Hero*

Best Hardware/Peripheral (Game Critics Award): 2007, for *Rock Band*

Best of Show (Game Critics Award): 2007, for *Rock Band*

Best Social/Casual/Puzzle (Game Critics Award): 2007, for *Rock Band*

Outstanding Achievement in Soundtrack (Academy of Interactive Arts and Sciences): 2007, for *Guitar Hero II*; 2008, for *Rock Band*; 2009, for *Rock Band 2*

100 Most Influential People in the World (*Time*): 2008

Entertainment Marketers of the Year (Advertising Age): 2008, for *Rock Band*

Outstanding Achievement in Gaming (Academy of Interactive Arts and Sciences): 2008, for *Rock Band*

Pioneer Award (Game Developers Choice Awards): 2009

FURTHER READING

Periodicals

Inc., Oct. 2008, p.124
Newsweek, Jan. 29, 2007; Jan. 7, 2008, p.78; May 5, 2008
Rolling Stone, Mar. 18, 2009
Time, Apr. 29, 2008
Wired, Sep. 14, 2007

Online Articles

http://arstechnica.com
(Ars Technica, "King of Rock: Ars Talks to Harmonix CEO Alex Rigopulos," Jan. 15, 2009)
http://blastmagazine.com
(Blast, "E3 2009: Harmonix CEO Alex Rigopulos interviewed by *Blast*," June 3, 2009)
http://www.gamecritics.com
(GameCritics, "Interview with Alex Rigopulos," Mar. 31, 2004)
http://freakonomics.blogs.nytimes.com/2009/01/13/the-guitar-hero-answers-your-questions
(New York Times, "The *Guitar Hero* Answers Your Questions," Jan. 13, 2009)
http://www.newsweek.com/id/134023
(Newsweek, "Rock-and-Roll Fantasy: Harmonix, Creator of *Rock Band* and *Guitar Hero*, Is Changing Videogames," May 5, 2008)

http://www.portfolio.com/culture-lifestyle/goods/gadgets/2007/09/17
  /Harmonix-Profile
  (Portfolio, "The Guitar Heroes," Sep. 17, 2007)
http://www.rollingstone.com
  (Rolling Stone, "The RS 100 Agents of Change," Mar. 18, 2009)
http://www.technologyreview.com/article/22213
  (Technology Review, "Music for the Masses," Mar./Apr. 2009)

ADDRESS

Eran Egozy
Alex Rigopulos
Harmonix Music Systems, Inc.
625 Massachusetts Ave., 2nd Floor
Cambridge MA 02139

WORLD WIDE WEB SITE

http://www.harmonixmusic.com

Neil Gaiman 1960-

British Comic Book Creator and Author of Books for
Children and Young Adults
Creator of *The Sandman, Coraline,* and the Newbery
Award-Winning *The Graveyard Book*

BIRTH

Neil Richard Gaiman was born on November 10, 1960, in
Porchester, England. He was the oldest child of David and
Sheila Gaiman. David was a director of a vitamin and supple-
ment company and Sheila was a pharmacist. Neil has two sisters, Claire and Lizzy.

YOUTH

Gaiman's childhood was full of the pleasures of books. He learned to read at age four and was soon devouring everything he could get his hands on; he claims to have read every book in the youth section of his local library. "I was a reader," he later said. "I loved reading. Reading things gave me pleasure. I was very good at most subjects in school, not because I had any particular aptitude in them, but because normally on the first day of school they'd hand out schoolbooks, and I'd read them—which would mean that I'd know what was coming up, because I'd read it."

Gaiman's early influences included everything from classic fantasy writers to the operas of Gilbert and Sullivan. Among his favorite authors were J.R.R. Tolkien, C.S. Lewis, and Lewis Carroll, whose works he read throughout his childhood. He first read Tolkien's *Lord of the Rings* at his school library. The library only had the first two volumes of the trilogy, and he took them out over and over. When he won the school English prize and the school reading prize in the same year, he got the third Tolkien volume and a collection of English poetry. Gaiman vividly remembers receiving Lewis's seven-volume series *The Chronicles of Narnia* for his seventh birthday. He was captivated by Lewis's prose style and the narrative voice in the work. "I admired his use of parenthetical statements to the reader, where he would just talk to you.…I'd think, 'Oh, my gosh, that is so cool! I want to do that! When I become an author, I want to be able to do things in parentheses.' I liked the power of putting things in brackets." Another much-loved title was Carroll's *Alice in Wonderland*, which Gaimain called "a favorite title forever. Alice was default reading to the point where I knew it by heart." In all this mix of classic children's literature, he had time for comics, too. *Batman* was an early favorite.

> "I was a reader," Gaiman recalled. "I loved reading. Reading things gave me pleasure. I was very good at most subjects in school, not because I had any particular aptitude in them, but because normally on the first day of school they'd hand out schoolbooks, and I'd read them—which would mean that I'd know what was coming up, because I'd read it."

Deciding to Become a Writer

Gaiman knew from a very young age that he wanted to be a writer. In an

Gaiman signing autographs for a young fan in China.

interview with his youngest daughter, Maddy, he said that his first composition was a poem, which he created at the age of three and which was transcribed by his mother. When he was 15, he told his school career counselor that he wanted to be a writer, specifically of "American comic books." The counselor recommended he become an accountant.

EDUCATION

Gaiman attended Ardingly College, a local grammar school, from the ages of 10 to 14, then went on to Whitgift School, the equivalent of an American high school, from the ages of 14 to 17. At 17, he decided to leave school and begin his life as a writer.

CAREER HIGHLIGHTS

In a career that has already spanned over 20 years, Neil Gaiman has become one of the finest fantasy writers of his generation, an author who has made comics and graphic novels an accepted literary art form. In addition, he won the 2009 Newbery Medal, as the author of the finest work of American literature for children. He has published works in an astonishing variety of genres, including novels, short stories, poetry, comics, graphic novels, screenplays, music, and journalism, and for a wide variety of read-

———— `` ————

When he was 15, Gaiman told his school career counselor that he wanted to be a writer, specifically of "American comic books." The counselor recommended he become an accountant.

———— `` ————

ers, from fantasy and comic book fans to adults, young adults, and young children.

One of the interesting aspects of Gaiman's work is the ways in which he has recreated many of his works in new genres and new formats. For example, he first wrote a famous comic book series *The Sandman,* then later created a graphic novel series also titled *The Sandman,* then published *The Absolute Sandman,* an enhanced collection of the original comic books. Similarly, he wrote *Stardust* as a comic book, then reimagined it as a novel. His beloved work *Coraline* was first published as a young adult novel, then recreated as a graphic novel, and then later made into a movie.

Early Journalism

Gaiman first made his living as a journalist, writing book and film reviews for English newspapers and magazines. He was also sending off his own short stories to publishers and receiving nothing but rejection letters. He was determined to stay in journalism, however, because he was writing about the world he wanted to be a part of, the world of fantasy and science fiction. "I'm a journalist," he told himself at the time. "As of right now, I'm a freelance journalist specializing in science fiction, fantasy, and horror in the world of publishing, because that's what I want to understand."

Gaiman began pitching ideas to publishers, saying he had an interview with a well-known fantasy writer, like Gene Wolfe, and hoping they would buy the piece. And they did. Gaiman also took on a book project, a biography on the rock group Duran Duran. He has claimed the book was bad, but the band was so popular the first printing sold out. Convinced he was going to be awash in royalty payments, Gaiman went to the publisher's office only to discover that they'd gone bankrupt.

Then, Gaiman got a job offer from a magazine, *Penthouse,* that publishes nude photos. He thought long and hard about it. It would be a steady source of income, and by then he had a wife and two young children to support. But he knew that was the wrong path to take, and he turned the job down. "I had this amazing, complete confidence in my ability, totally unjustified," he recalled. Then he found the right path.

First Comics

In 1987, Gaiman began work on his first comic, *Violent Cases*, which was illustrated by his long-time collaborator and friend, Dave McKean. As in most of Gaiman's work, it depicts alternate worlds: the real world and a dream, or parallel, world. The comic drew the interest of DC Comics, the powerhouse that publishes such blockbusters as *Superman* and *Batman*. They asked Gaiman and McKean for another comic, and the duo produced *Black Orchid*. Karen Berger, head of the Vertigo line at DC Comics, saw potential in the work, and she offered Gaiman a great opportunity: to produce a new comic series, based on an old DC character, the Sandman, but reimagined by him. The result is considered one of the greatest comics of all time, the work that paved the way for the success and respectability of the graphic novel.

The Sandman

Gaiman's *Sandman* comic originally appeared in 75 monthly installments, 24 pages each, published by DC Comics from December 1988 to March 1996. Beginning with the earliest issues, Gaiman's concept was clear: his Sandman, known as Dream or Morpheus, was not a gumshoe type of detective, as he was first envisioned. Instead, he is the mystical, brooding ruler of the dream world, who has been around for eternity and is part of a family of godlike beings known as the Endless. Each of them represents some aspect of humanity, with names like Destiny, Death, Destruction, Desire, Despair, and Delirium. When readers first encounter Dream, he is being held captive by an evil human. But what could have been a conventional revenge story takes on a different aspect early on.

In *Sandman*, there are a number of characters who've fallen prey to a sleeping sickness and who live in their dreams; Dream can enter, and affect, those dreams. These and other themes are presented in a series that is flavored with myth and fairy tale, encompassing a timeline that covers centuries, with characters of a depth and richness not before seen in comics. Episodes feature real figures, like Shakespeare and Marco Polo; figures from religion and myth, like the Devil and Cain and Abel; and startling new creations. There's an emotional richness, too, that brought many new readers to the world of comics. *Sandman* was the first comic that was popular with female readers, who became part of Gaiman's devoted following.

Gaiman is always quick to note that he was part of a collaborative team that created *Sandman*, including a writer, artist, letterer, inker, colorist, and cover artist. The writer, Gaiman, provided the story line, dialogue, and art

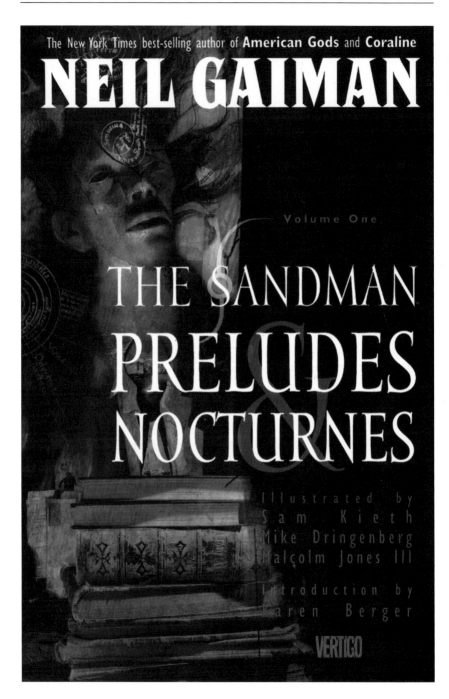

The first volume of The Sandman, *the graphic novel series that Gaiman based on his ground-breaking comic books.*

direction. The artists, Sam Kieth, Mike Dringenberg, and Malcolm Jones III, created the sketches and placement of the panels. Todd Klein did the lettering, and Robbie Busch was the colorist. The *Sandman* covers were done by Dave McKean. Together, they set a new standard for verbal and visual expression in comics. The series won many awards and a wide following among readers, critics, and other authors.

Sandman was also an important "first" in many ways. Gaiman was able to gain partial control of the character, which normally stays in the hands of the publisher. He was also able to end the comic series, which he did in 1996, while launching separate works based on some of Dream's siblings. Gaiman also published works based on *Sandman* in several other genres. He created a graphic novel series based on the comics that was one of the earliest attempts at the new genre. It's interesting to note that in early response to the series, several writers thought that graphic novels would never be accepted by the reading community; Gaiman has proven how wrong they were. *Sandman* has also appeared in a third format, the *Absolute Sandman* series, a complete multivolume book set of the comic book series.

While still working on *Sandman*, Gaiman and his family decided to move to the United States. They settled outside of Minneapolis, near his wife's family, in 1992.

Expanding His Range

Around this time, Gaiman decided to spread his wings to create works in different formats and for different ages. He wrote several novels for adults, beginning with *Good Omens*, a collaborative novel he wrote with Terry Pratchett in 1990 that became a bestseller. While continuing to produce work in other genres, Gaiman added to his adult novel line with *American Gods* in 2001 and *Anansi Boys* in 2005, both critical and popular successes.

Gaiman has also created screenplays for television and movies. In 1996, he wrote a fantasy TV series for the BBC in England called *Neverwhere*. It tells the story of a man whose life is changed when he stops to help an injured girl on a London sidewalk and is plunged into an alternate world below the streets of the "real" city. Gaiman developed a novel from the series, which he published in 1997 and which went on to become a bestseller. He's also written a screenplay for a movie version, which was purchased by Jim Henson Productions, a company run by the family of the famous creator of the Muppets. The Jim Henson company also produced the 2005 movie *MirrorMask*, whose screenplay was written by Gaiman. It also tells a story about an alternate world, this time featuring a 15-year-

Gaiman's first book for younger readers.

old girl, Helena, who is drawn into a strange and dangerous fantasy world. After writing the movie script, Gaiman went on to create two works based on that movie: a picture book for young adult readers and a heavily illustrated book containing the movie screenplay, art work, and story boards from the film.

In addition to these works, Gaiman wrote the screenplay for the English-language version of *Princess Mononoke*, the 1999 anime classic by the famed Japanese artist Hayao Miyazaki, as well as the screenplay for an adaptation of the famous epic *Beowulf.* And he wrote and directed a movie entitled *A Short Film about John Bolton* in 2002. He's produced many different screenplays based on his novels and comics, some of which have been produced and some of which are still under consideration or in revision.

Works for Younger Readers

In 1997, Gaiman published his first work for young readers, *The Day I Swapped My Dad for Two Goldfish*, with illustrations by his frequent collaborator Dave McKean. The story describes how a little boy, left in his distracted father's care, is visited by a friend showing off his two goldfish. The boy wants them badly and makes a proposition to his friend: he'll trade his dad for the goldfish. The deal takes place and havoc ensues, until his mother comes home and sets things right. Gaiman says the book was inspired by his son, Michael. When told to go to bed one night as a little boy, Michael said, "I wish I didn't have a Dad. I wish I had … a goldfish!" Such knowing insights into children and their ways make this one of Gaiman's most delightful works for young people.

Gaiman's next book for young readers was *The Wolves in the Walls* (2003). It was inspired by his daughter Maddy, who woke up one night from a nightmare claiming there were wolves in the walls. With illustrations by Dave McKean, the book describes what happens when a girl named Lucy tries to convince her family that there is a pack of menacing wolves lurking in the house. They don't believe her until the wolves come out of the walls. Lucy is full of courage and outwits the wolves in this scary and funny tale. In 2008, Gaiman published *The Dangerous Alphabet*. This picture book, originally created as a kind of Christmas card, presents a story told in 26 alphabetical lines. It features two children with a treasure map who sneak out of their house and into a world of monsters and pirates beneath the city.

"You can do so many things with fantasy," Gaiman explained. *"At a rock-bottom level, you can concretize a metaphor. Part of it is that, if you're a writer, you can play God. This is my world, you are welcome to come, but I get to call the shots, and I won't be embarrassed to pull in anything I need or want."*

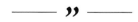

In 2009, Gaiman published several new books for young readers. *Blueberry Girl* is a beautiful picture book based on a poem that Gaiman originally wrote for his friend, musician Tori Amos, when she found out she was going to have a baby girl. It is full of all the blessings that parents everywhere want for their beloved children. *Crazy Hair*, inspired in part by his own wild hair, and by his daughter Maddy's comments on it, is another recent favorite. Illustrated by Dave McKean, it features a girl named Bonnie who attempts to bring some control to her friend's "crazy hair." Another recent work, *Odd and the Frost Giants,* reflects Gaiman's love for myth, especially Norse myth. Set in Norway, the book features a boy named Odd who meets some fantastical creatures during his quest to help the Norse gods. In 2010, he published *Instructions: Everything You'll Need to Know on Your Journey,* an illustrated book based on a poem first published in *A Wolf at the Door* (2000). In *Instructions,* a cat travels through a fairy tale world, guided by a narrator whose instructions seem as relevant and helpful to the reader as the cat.

Books for Teens and Young Adults

Some of Gaiman's most beloved works are those written for teenagers and young adults. His first work for this audience was the 1998 young adult novel version of *Stardust,* based on his earlier comic book of the same name. This novel is set in England many years ago, in the town of Wall. There's a young man, Tristan Thorn, who wants to impress the girl he loves, Victoria Forester. He claims that he will catch a falling star and bring it back to her. He climbs the wall for which the town is named, and, as often happens in Gaiman's tales, he enters another world, the land of Faerie, which is full of magic and fantastic adventure. The book inspired a movie of the same name, which came out in 2007 and brought Gaiman even more fans.

Coraline

Gaiman came to the attention of many teen readers for the first time in 2002, with the publication of his novel *Coraline.* Like most of Gaiman's works, it features parallel worlds, alike but unalike, with dangers and delights. Coraline Jones is a young girl who moves into a house her family shares with several strange and unusual neighbors. She is an only child, and a lonely one, too. Her self-involved parents sit at their computers working hours every day and have little time for their curious child. One day, while exploring the new house, Coraline discovers a door in the wall. She goes through it and finds a world much like her own, but distinctly different. Her parents are there, but her "other mother" is nurturing and kind and loves to cook Coraline mountains of delicious food. Her father, too, has all the time in the world for his little girl.

At first, Coraline thinks of her new world as a dream come true. But it's strange, too, in ways that are weird and inexplicable. Her "dream" mother changes: instead of nurturing, she becomes witchlike and controlling and tries to force Coraline to stay on "her" side of the house. Soon, Coraline

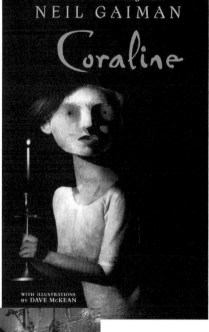

Gaiman's novel Coraline *was turned into an animated movie and a graphic novel, too.*

realizes both she and her "real" parents are in great danger. It takes all of her courage and ability to win back her real world from the menacing forces of the "other" world.

The novel was a great success and won Gaiman many awards and many new readers, both young and old. *Coraline* became even more popular in 2009 with the release of a film based on the novel. The film version of *Coraline* was directed by Henry Selick, who also directed Tim Burton's *Nightmare Before Christmas*, and was shot in 3-D stop motion animation, a technique that for many enhanced the novel's atmosphere of weirdness and adventure.

More Books for Teens and Young Adults

In 2005, Gaiman published *MirrorMask*. This funny and scary fantasy tale tells the story of a 15-year-old girl, Helena, who works for her family circus. She wants to run away and join the "real" world, to live an ordinary life. Instead, she ends up in a magical dream world filled with strange, fantastic, and dangerous creatures. Helena must fulfill a quest to escape the alternate world and return home to her own life. Like many of Gaiman's works, *MirrorMask* appeared in several formats. He first wrote the screenplay for the 2005 movie of the same name, which he followed with a picture book for young adults based on the movie.

Another work enjoyed by young adults is *M Is for Magic* (2007), a collection of 10 short stories plus a poem. Here, Gaiman created stories that seem to rely on the familiar but are all entirely different, with unexpected twists and turns. All showcase his vivid imagination, his storytelling skill, and his knowledge of what will appeal to teen readers. In *InterWorld* (2007), which Gaiman wrote with Michael Reeves, a young boy named Joey Harker discovers that his world exists within an alternate world, the "Altiverse," where there's infinite number of Earths in infinite dimensions. After Joey develops the power to travel between these dimensions, he discovers that he's in danger, because others—the armies of magic and science—want this special power, too. Joey, and the others like him, band together to protect their world.

The Graveyard Book

In 2008, Gaiman published *The Graveyard Book*. It begins with a scene of terror: a family is murdered in their beds by a killer. Only the family toddler escapes death. Unaware of the carnage taking place, he scoots out of his crib, climbs down the stairs, and steals through the open front door. From there, he wanders down the street and into the local graveyard. Once again, Gaiman creates a brilliant parallel world: a community of the dead,

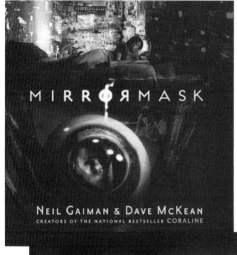

MirrorMask *came out in several different forms: first Gaiman wrote the movie screenplay, then he wrote a novel for teens and also created an illustrated film script.*

with their own society and rituals. The ghosts who make the graveyard their home take in the little boy and decide to raise him. Mr. and Mrs. Owens become his father and mother, and he is renamed Nobody Owens, called Bod for short.

> *Gaiman is a fierce defender of the rights of authors to publish what they wish without censorship. "The First Amendment is something that I think is really, really cool," he argued. "I'm from England. There is no First Amendment there, no guaranteed freedom of speech."*

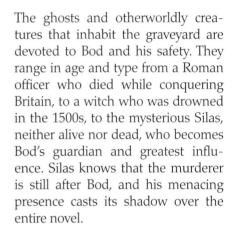

The ghosts and otherworldly creatures that inhabit the graveyard are devoted to Bod and his safety. They range in age and type from a Roman officer who died while conquering Britain, to a witch who was drowned in the 1500s, to the mysterious Silas, neither alive nor dead, who becomes Bod's guardian and greatest influence. Silas knows that the murderer is still after Bod, and his menacing presence casts its shadow over the entire novel.

The book chronicles Bod's life from his toddler years to his early teens and is in many ways a "coming-of-age" novel. Gaiman stated that his greatest influence in writing the book was Rudyard Kipling's *Jungle Book*, in which wild animals take in and raise a young human. He also recalled his first vision of the book: in the mid-1980s, he and his family were living in a tall, narrow house in England, with no yard where his son Michael, then a toddler, could play. Instead, Gaiman would take Michael to the local graveyard. He remembers having a brief glimpse of what would become *The Graveyard Book* as his son rode his tricycle up and down the cemetery.

But it took the urging of his daughter Maddy to get the book done. Gaiman had written what would become Chapter Four, "The Witch's Headstone," and he read it to her. She responded in the way that every author wants to hear: "What happens next?" Gaiman resolved to find out, and the result was *The Graveyard Book*, which became a best seller and a critical success.

Winning the Newbery Medal

In January 2009, Gaiman learned that he had won the prestigious Newbery Medal, given every year by the American Library Association to the most distinguished work of American literature for children. He was overwhelmed, and as a creature of the modern age of communication, he sent out a tweet that contained some foul language. That, and the novel's dark atmosphere and themes of murder and death, led some concerned adults to wonder whether the book was appropriate for young readers. On his web site for young people, Gaiman addressed the issue. In answer to the question, "Are you ever worried that you will introduce a world to children that is too horrific for them to handle?" his reply was simply, "No."

In 2010, Gaiman was awarded the Carnegie Medal, considered the most prestigious award for children's fiction in Great Britain. It's considered the equivalent of the Newbery Medal for British writers. In fact, Gaiman was the first author to win both the Newbery and Carnegie awards for the same book.

Speaking about His Ideas

Gaiman is frequently asked why he's devoted to the genre of fantasy. Recently, he said this: "You can do so many things with fantasy. At a rock-bottom level, you can concretize a metaphor. Part of it is that, if you're a writer, you can play God. This is my world, you are welcome to come, but I get to call the shots, and I won't be embarrassed to pull in anything I need or want." Asked to defend fantasy as a genre for children's literature, especially in *Coraline,* he said this: "The whole point of *Coraline* is summed up in the little quote from G. K. Chesterton I put at the beginning of the book. It reads, 'Fairy tales are more than true: not because they tell us that dragons exist, but because they tell us that dragons can be beaten.'"

Gaiman is a fierce defender of the rights of authors to publish what they wish without censorship. He is a passionate member of the Comic Book Legal Defense Fund, which defends authors in censorship cases. "The First Amendment is something that I think is really, really cool," he argued. "I'm from England. There is no First Amendment there, no guaranteed freedom of speech." Now that he lives in America, he works hard to keep writing and speech free.

Fans and His Online Journal

Gaiman keeps in close contact with his many fans through his blog, a journal that is accessible through his web site. He has hundred of thousands of fans worldwide, and his site receives thousands of hits each day, as they follow his constant creative activity.

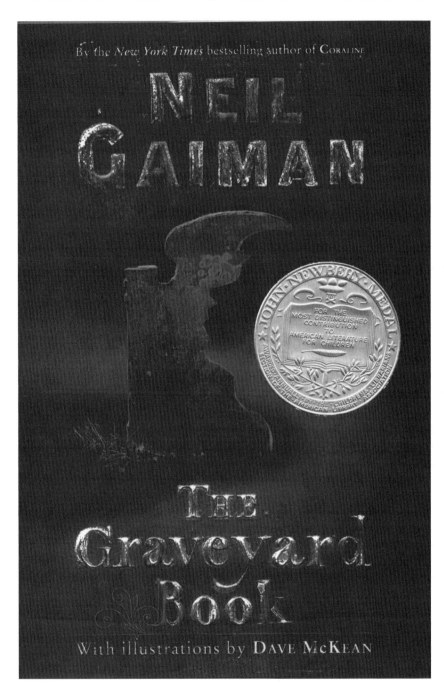

Gaiman's novel The Graveyard Book *won the Newbery Medal, given to the most distinguished book of American literature for children.*

Advice to Young Writers

Gaiman is frequently asked for advice on writing by his young fans. Here's a sampling of his replies: "Write. Finish things. Keep writing."

MARRIAGE AND FAMILY

Gaiman married Mary Therese McGrath on March 14, 1985. They have three children: Michael, born in 1983; Holly, born in 1985, and Madeleine, called Maddy, born in 1994. The Gaiman family moved to the outskirts of Minneapolis, Minnesota, in 1992, where they lived in a house the author describes as looking like something "out of a Charles Addams cartoon." He and Mary are now divorced, but are still friendly and live next door to each other in rural Wisconsin.

Gaiman loves being a dad, and his children have inspired his work for years. He says of his daughter Maddy, "It's been fun doing things like *Coraline* and having a daughter to try them out on. It's simply lovely having somebody who thinks this stuff is fun. From Maddy's point of view, really, the cool thing is the fact that I know Lemony Snicket, that she got to have dinner with Daniel Handler, the fact that R.L. Stine says hello. I am now cool."

SELECTED WRITINGS

Comics

Violent Cases, 1987 (comic book)
Black Orchid, 1988 (comic book)
The Sandman, 1988-97 (comic book)
The Books of Magic, 1989 (comic book)
The Books of Magic, 1993 (comic book collection)
Stardust, 1997-99 (comic book)
Stardust, 1998 (comic book collection)
The Absolute Sandman, Vols. 1-4, 2006-08 (comic book collection)

Graphic Novels

The Sandman, 1991-2003
Preludes & Nocturnes, 1991
The Doll's House, 1991
Dream Country, 1991
Season of Mists, 1992
A Game of You, 1993
Fables & Reflections, 1993
Brief Lives, 1994

World's End, 1995
The Kindly Ones, 1996
The Wake, 1996
Endless Nights, 2003
Coraline, 2009

Books for Children and Young Adults

The Day I Swapped My Dad for Two Goldfish, 1997
Stardust, 1998
Coraline, 2002
The Wolves in the Walls, 2003
MirrorMask, 2005
InterWorld, 2007 (with Michael Reaves)
M Is for Magic, 2007
The Dangerous Alphabet, 2008
The Graveyard Book, 2008
Blueberry Girl, 2009
Crazy Hair, 2009
Odd and the Frost Giants, 2009
Instructions: Everything You'll Need to Know on Your Journey, 2010

Novels for Adults

Good Omens, 1990 (with Terry Pratchett)
Neverwhere, 1997
American Gods, 2001
Anansi Boys, 2005

Other

Neverwhere, 1996 (screenplays for television series)
A Short Film about John Bolton, 2002 (author and director)
MirrorMask, 2005 (screenplay)
Beowulf, 2007 (screenplay; with Roger Avary)

HONORS AND AWARDS

International Horror Guild Award: 1995, for *Angels & Visitations: A Miscellany*
Defender of Liberty Award (Comic Book Legal Defense Fund): 1997
Mythopoeic Fantasy Award (Mythopoeic Society): 1999, for *Stardust*
Geffen Award (Israeli Society for Science Fiction and Fantasy): 2000, for *Stardust;* 2002, for *American Gods;* 2004, for *Smoke and Mirrors*

Bram Stoker Award (Horror Writers Association): 2000, for *The Sandman: The Dream Hunters;* 2002, for *American Gods;* 2003, for *Coraline;* 2004, for *The Sandman: Endless Nights*

Hugo Award (World Science Fiction Society): 2002, for *American Gods;* 2003, for *Coraline;* 2004, for *A Study in Emerald;* 2009, for *The Graveyard Book*

Locus Award (*Locus* magazine): 2002, for *American Gods;* 2003 (two awards), for *Coraline* and *October in the Chair;* 2004 (three awards), for *The Sandman: Endless Nights, A Study in Emerald,* and *Closing Time;* 2009, for *The Graveyard Book*

Nebula Award (Science Fiction and Fantasy Writers of America): 2002, for *American Gods;* 2003, for *Coraline*

Best Book for Young Adults (American Library Association): 2003, for *Coraline;* 2009, for *The Graveyard Book*

Best Book of the Year (*Publishers Weekly*): 2003, for *Coraline*

Bulletin Blue Ribbon Book Award (*Bulletin of the Center for Children's Books*): 2003, for *Coraline*

Children's Choice Award (International Reading Association): 2003, for *Coraline;* 2004, for *Wolves in the Walls*

Notable Children's Book Award (American Library Association): 2003, for *Coraline;* 2009, for *The Graveyard Book*

British Science Fiction Award: 2003, for *Coraline;* 2004, for *The Wolves in the Walls*

British Fantasy Award for Best Novel/ August Derleth Award (British Fantasy Society): 2006, for *Anansi Boys*

Top Ten Fiction Books (*Time* magazine): 2008, for *The Graveyard Book*

Newbery Medal (American Library Association): 2009, for *The Graveyard Book*

Carnegie Medal (Chartered Institute of Library and Information Professionals, Great Britain): 2010, for *The Graveyard Book*

FURTHER READING

Books

Wagner, Hank, Christopher Golden, and Stephen R. Bissette. *Prince of Stories: The Many Worlds of Neil Gaiman,* 2008

Periodicals

American Libraries, Mar. 2009, p.49
Booklist, Aug. 2002, p.1949
Children & Libraries, Spr. 2003, p.26
Horn Book, July/Aug. 2009, p. 351

Los Angeles Times, Sep. 3, 1995, Magazine, p.14
New York Times, Jan. 27, 2009, p.C1
New Yorker, Jan. 25, 2010, p.48
Publishers Weekly, July 28, 2003, p.46
Reading Today, Apr./May 2009, p.19
School Library Journal, Mar. 2009, p.30
Time, Aug. 6, 2007, p.62
Voice of Youth Advocates, Dec. 2002, p.358
Washington Post, Nov. 1, 1995, p.B1

Online Periodicals

http://www.avclub.com
   (AV Club, "Neil Gaiman," Sep. 28, 2005)
http://www.bookpage.com/0308bp/neil_gaiman.html
   (BookPage, "Crossing Over: Adult Author Neil Gaiman Enters the
   World of Children's Books," 2003)
http://www.indiebound.org/author-interviews/gaimanneil
   (IndieBound, "Neil Gaiman Interview," Aug. 1, 2005)
http://www.januarymagazine.com/profiles/gaiman.html
   (January Magazine, "January Interview: Neil Gaiman," Aug. 2001)
http://www.locusmag.com/2005/Issues/02Gaiman.html
   (Locus Magazine, "Neil Gaiman: Different Kinds of Pleasure," Feb. 2005)
http://www.wildriverreview.com/worldvoices-neilgaiman.php
   (Wild River Review, "Myth, Magic, and the Mind of Neil Gaiman," Aug.
   2007)

ADDRESS

Cat Mihos
for Neil Gaiman
4470 Sunset Blvd. #339
Los Angeles, CA 90027

WORLD WIDE WEB SITES

http://www.neilgaiman.com
http://www.mousecircus.com (Gaiman's site for younger readers)
http://www.harpercollins.com/Author/Browse.aspx

Tavi Gevinson 1996-

American Fashion Blogger
Creator of the Blog "Style Rookie"

EARLY YEARS

Tavi Gevinson was born on April 22, 1996. She is the youngest of three daughters born to Steve Gevinson and Berit Engen. They live in the western suburbs of Chicago, Illinois. Her mother is an artist, and her father teaches English at a high school in Oak Park, Illinois. Gevinson and her two sisters learned to speak Norwegian from their mother, who is origi-nally from Oslo, Norway. Although she can't speak the language as well as she could when she was younger, Tavi says that she knows "enough to get by and travel."

MAJOR ACCOMPLISHMENTS

Starting the "Style Rookie" Blog

Gevinson is currently a high school student in the Chicago area. She has become famous in the world of high fashion for a blog that she started writing when she was only 11 years old. She first started getting interested in fashion in early 2008. "Before then I just dressed for comfort," she said. "I was more into just a T-shirt and jeans or pajama pants. Practicality and comfort." Then, a friend's teenage sister started a blog that discussed fashion trends and featured photos of herself. This sparked Gevinson's interest. She began reading *Seventeen* magazine and watching the television show "America's Next Top Model" to soak up more fashion facts and ideas.

Gevinson's first post began simply: "Well I am new here.... Lately I've been really interested in fashion, and I like to make binders and slideshows of 'high-fashion' modeling and designs. I'd like to know of neat websites and magazines, so comments are welcome. I plan on posting pictures in the future, but for now, I'm just getting started. Yours truly, Tavi."

On March 31, 2008, Gevinson made her first post to her blog, originally called "Style Rookie/New Girl in Town" and later changed to simply "Style Rookie." She started out using the name Tavi Williams, but she now identifies herself with her real name, or "Tavi G." Her first post began simply: "Well I am new here.... Lately I've been really interested in fashion, and I like to make binders and slideshows of 'high-fashion' modeling and designs. I'd like to know of neat websites and magazines, so comments are welcome. I plan on posting pictures in the future, but for now, I'm just getting started. Yours truly, Tavi." She was just 11 years old when she made that first post.

As Gevinson became more interested in fashion, she began to dress in a unique and offbeat personal style. Her approach to fashion sometimes attracted the attention of her middle school classmates, many of whom weren't aware that she was writing a fashion blog. "Not that many know about it," she commented. "My closest [friends] do, but it's embarrassing to talk about." She was really happy the day a classmate said "I watch your outfits every day; it's like something new and I'm excited to see it." Gevinson relished the compliment. "He doesn't know about my blog. Some people at my school who know about my blog and then compliment my outfits a lot but it's like, before they knew about my blog, they sort of like snorted at them. So I know it's more sincere, coming from him, because he doesn't know about it."

As her blog developed, Gevinson developed a writing style that was youthful, yet insightful and sophisticated. She found writing for her blog a totally new experience, one she enjoyed. "I never really liked writing before because at school I never got to write about what I like," she admitted. "With my blog, it's my thoughts, like my brain is being translated onto the computer." In addition to writing, she also included pictures of styles that interested her, and pictures of herself in outfits she put together. For the most part, she took these herself, using a Canon Powershot A590IS. She says this "takes good pictures but

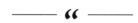

"I never really liked writing before because at school I never got to write about what I like," Gevinson admitted. "With my blog, it's my thoughts, like my brain is being translated onto the computer."

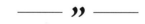

is still easy to use." With an old tripod of her dad's to hold the camera in place and a self-timer button, she was easily able to photograph herself. When finished, she uploaded them to her computer, sometimes using PhotoFiltre software to create special effects.

In the beginning, her posts typically only drew a few comments from readers, but that soon changed. Gevinson hadn't asked her parents' permission when she started her blog—something she now says was irresponsible. Her father only became fully aware of his daughter's blog when she had to ask his permission to be featured in an article in the *New York Times Style Magazine* about teenage fashion bloggers. At 12 years old, Gevinson was the youngest person mentioned in the article.

Backlash Begins

As Gevinson's name began to be heard around the fashion world, some people began questioning if her blog was really her own work. Her writing voice at times sounded very mature, and her thoughts about

Gevinson sitting at home amongst the fashion magazine clippings she's using to make a collage for her blog.

the fashion world were certainly more insightful than what anyone would expect from a girl her age. Some influential columnists suggested that there was really a "Team Tavi" and that the blog was the work of several people older than her. Furthermore, it was suggested that even if the blog really was put together by Gevinson, it was ridiculous to give so much attention to the thoughts of a middle school student, and the only reason her blog drew attention was because she was very young, and therefore a novelty. Anne Slowey, an editor of *Elle* magazine, and Lesley M.M. Blume, a fashion writer, were especially harsh in their comments.

For Gevinson, it was upsetting to have her work called into question like that. She defended herself by saying: "No one in my family helps me with my writing, outfits, videos, or pictures (they have offered now and then for the pictures but I guess it's kind of embarrassing for me so I refused)." Answering her critics in one of her blog posts, she said, "I will agree with the fact that I'm 12 shouldn't set me apart from other bloggers, and it definitely shouldn't play a part in how one might react to how I think or write or dress." She found the whole issue "really annoying" and commented that "People complain that my generation is stupid, but when I show that I have a brain, they call me a fake."

Gevinson continued to pursue and develop her interests in fashion and blogging despite her critics. She was getting plenty of positive publicity, too. For example, *Teen Vogue* published an interview with her and praised "her dead-on style observations and fearless fashion sense that puts even the most daring fashionistas to shame." The number of daily hits on her blog was climbing steadily, reaching about 30,000 hits a day.

Gevinson's Inspirations

To get inspiration for her blog, Gevinson visits other fashion blogs and Web sites from around the world. Even though she can't read all the languages, the visual nature of fashion makes that less important. Among her favorite designers are Rei Kawakubo, Yohji Yamamoto, Vivienne Westwood, Kate and Laura Mulleavy, Tao Kurihara, Alexander McQueen, and Luella Bartley.

She has also formed friendships with other like-minded bloggers. "It's pretty cool how global the fashion blogging community is," she noted. She likes to look at old and new fashion magazines, including *Sassy, Lula, Vogue, Numero,* and *Dazed and Confused.* Ideas also come from "photography (fashion and otherwise), movies, fine art, books, plays, street style, runway, music, hobos, celebrities … it changes a lot," she said. "Though I don't think I will ever tire of Japanese street style, the 70's, or evil fairy tale creatures."

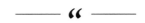

Ideas and inspiration come from "photography (fashion and otherwise), movies, fine art, books, plays, street style, runway, music, hobos, celebrities … it changes a lot," Gevinson remarked. "Though I don't think I will ever tire of Japanese street style, the 70's, or evil fairy tale creatures."

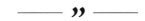

Small in stature, Gevinson has described herself as "a tiny 13-year-old dork that sits inside all day." She doesn't like to give her personal style a name. "It's still developing and evolving, and phrases and labels like 'hippie chic' bother me. I think giving it a description would tie me down too much, I'm still experimenting after all." Since becoming well-known, she has received gifts of clothing from many designers, but she also creates her outfits with items from her local thrift shop, hand-me-downs, and even the box of dress-up clothes she and her sisters played with when they were younger. She shops with money from her allowance and babysitting jobs. She doesn't sew, claiming that she might like to learn how but also admitting that she might not have the patience.

Fashion Connections and International Travel

The Internet has made it possible for Gevinson to reach millions of readers and to follow fashion trends in places far from her home, all without leaving her hometown in the Midwest. Her blog has also provided her with some incredible opportunities to travel the world. In September 2009, not long after she appeared on the cover of the trendy magazine *Pop* and was also featured in the fashion publication *Love*, Gevinson went to New York City with her father to attend a week of fashion events known as Fashion Week. There she was able to see the latest collections and meet some of her inspirations.

One such opportunity came from Kate and Laura Mulleavy, two sisters who design for the Rodarte fashion house. Once they discovered Gevinson's blog, they got in touch with her, even sending her a pair of hand-knitted tights from their collection. The relationship grew, and the sisters eventually gave Gevinson a personal invitation to one of their shows. Late in 2009, the Mulleavys launched a new clothing line in cooperation with the Target chain of stores. The pieces in the collection were inspired by Gevinson, who also starred in the promotional video shot for the line. "Tavi makes you think about things differently, makes you see things differently," said Kate Mulleavy.

Gevinson holds designer Rei Kawakubo of Comme des Garcons in such high esteem that in November 2008, she wrote a rap tribute to the designer and posted it on her blog and on the Web site Vimeo, where it got hundreds of hits. The following November, she was invited to Tokyo to be the guest of honor at the Comme des Garcons holiday party. Gevinson attended with her mother, and also had a series of photo shoots with Japanese magazines while she was there.

The following January, Gevinson and her father flew to Paris to see the spring fashion collections there, and in February they were in New York for more shows. She became the youngest person ever to contribute to *Harper's Bazaar* when she was asked to write up her impressions of some of the spring collections for the magazine's January 2010 issue. These travels led to more criticism for her family, as some columnists expressed the opinion that a girl of her age shouldn't be missing school to attend fashion events. Such comments irked Gevinson, who replied, "My parents and I are the ones who know my school's absences policy, how my teachers feel about my missing school, and what my grades look like—not anyone else."

A 2010 runway show featuring creations by Japanese designer Rei Kawakubo for Comme des Garcons, one of Gevinson's favorite designers.

Throughout her travels, Gevinson has continued to focus on her "Style Rookie" blog. Estimates of how many people regularly check in with her blog range from one to four million. Still, she says she simply does it because it is fun. She likes "getting dressed and taking pictures and rambling on about fantastic editorials and runway collections," but says she will give it up if it starts to have a negative impact on her grades at school. "I'm here to develop my style and be able to converse with other bloggers that share my love for fashion," she stated.

> "Wear what you want, write about things that you care about, and just have fun with it," Gevinson advised those interested in blogging. "It's easy to tell when someone is trying too hard to impress readers and get more comments, and it's kind of a turnoff." For those interested in creating their own personal style, she said, "Dress however you please and embrace rude stares. It means that what you're wearing isn't boring!"

Future Plans

Gevinson doesn't really see herself pursuing a career in fashion, but says she isn't sure yet what she will do with her future. She has lots of ideas. "I would like to go to school, then have a band, then have a magazine where I could photograph/art direct/write, then write and direct and maybe act in the movies, then write and direct and maybe act on stage, then be an elementary school teacher, then write again, then move to the woods."

To anyone who might be interested in blogging about fashion, Gevinson had this advice: "Wear what you want, write about things that you care about, and just have fun with it. It's easy to tell when someone is trying too hard to impress readers and get more comments, and it's kind of a turnoff." For those interested in creating their own personal style, she said: "Dress however you please and embrace rude stares. It means that what you're wearing isn't boring!"

HOME AND FAMILY

Gevinson said there wasn't anyone else in her family particularly interested in fashion, although her mother sometimes wears "strange things, like painted harem pants and purple tie-dye leggings. She likes dressing up but isn't into fashion like a blogger is, and still doesn't understand some of my outfits. My dad dresses like dads dress." In general, her parents don't

Gevinson at the Marc Jacobs Fall 2010 collection,
showing off her unique sense of style.

read her blog much, but they are "very supportive," she said. "Sometimes I'll show them a post or two especially if I'm proud of it or something. They think it's crazy, some of the things that have come out of it, but they're happy that I have fun with it."

FAVORITE BOOKS AND MUSIC

Gevinson's favorite musician is Bob Dylan. Her favorite band is Wilco. She also likes many other bands and artists, including Neutral Milk Hotel, Cat Power, Pete Seeger, Joni Mitchell, Frank Sinatra, Joan Baez, and Feist.

Some of her favorite books are *The Westing Game* by Ellen Raskin, *Arthur and the True Francine* by Marc Brown, *The Lorax* by Dr. Seuss, *The Five People You Meet in Heaven* by Mitch Albom, and *Walk Two Moons* by Sharon Creech.

HOBBIES AND OTHER INTERESTS

Gevinson enjoys sledding with her friends, reading, writing, playing guitar, riding her bike, singing, and acting. She has been in several musicals, including *Thoroughly Modern Millie, Beauty and the Beast, Seussical,* and *Once on This Island.*

FURTHER READING

Periodicals

Independent, Oct. 10, 2009, p.28
Times (London), Oct. 8, 2009, p. T2
Wall Street Journal, Sep. 11, 2009, p. W1

Online Articles

http://www.chicagotribune.com
   (Chicago Tribune, "Tavi Gevinson Earns Acclaim with Style Rookie Fashion Blog," Dec. 30, 2009)
http://www.dailymail.co.uk
   (Daily Mail, "Move over Geldof Girls: Meet Tavi, 13, the 'Tiny' Blogger with the Fashion Industry at Her Feet," Sep. 23, 2009)
http://thefashioninformer.typepad.com
   (Fashion Informer, "Random Questions for .... Tavi G," Feb. 4, 2010)
http://www.interviewmagazine.com
   (Interview, "Tavi Williams, Rookie of the Year," Mar. 13, 2009)
http://www.nytimes.com
   (New York Times, "Bloggers Crash Fashion's First Row," Dec. 24, 2009)

http://www.nytimes.com
   (New York Times Style Magazine, "Post Adolescents," Fall 2008)
http://www.teenvogue.com
   (Teen Vogue, "Tavi Gevinson defines Rodarte for Target," Nov. 11, 2009)
http://www.telegraph.co.uk
   (Telegraph, "Pre-Fall 2010 Heralds the Return of Classic Dressing,
   Brown Leather and Tavi Gevinson," Feb. 3, 2010)
http://www.timesonline.co.uk
   (The Times, "Tavi, the Tiny Fashion Blogger: Tavi Gevinson Is Fashion's
   New It Girl—and She's Only 13," Oct. 8, 2009)

ADDRESS

Tavi Gevinson
Biz 3 Publicity
1321 North Milwaukee Avenue #452
Chicago, IL 60642

WORLD WIDE WEB SITES

http://www.thestylerookie.com
http://tavi.thepop.com

Hugh Jackman 1968-

Australian Actor, Singer, and Dancer
Award-Winning Star of Movies and Musical Theater
Plays Wolverine in the *X-Men* Movie Series

BIRTH

Hugh Michael Jackman was born on October 12, 1968, in
Sydney, New South Wales, Australia. His mother, Grace Watson, and his father, Chris, were both British. The family moved
from England to Australia when Jackman's father, an accountant, accepted a job transfer a year before Jackman was born.
Jackman has two older sisters and two older brothers.

YOUTH

Jackman grew up in an upper-class suburb of Sydney, the largest city in Australia. He liked to spend time outdoors, and he went to the beach almost every day. His family often went on camping trips and traveled extensively throughout Australia. As a child, Jackman dreamed of visiting other countries and far-away places. "I used to spend nights looking at atlases," he recalled. "I decided I wanted to be a chef on a plane. Because I'd been on a plane and there was food on board, I presumed there was a chef. I thought that would be an ideal job." Jackman also liked to sing and dance in variety shows that he made up for his family.

> "It wasn't until I was 22 that I ever thought about my hobby being something I could make a living out of," Jackman commented. "As a boy, I'd always had an interest in theater. But the idea at my school was that drama and music were to round out the man. It wasn't what one did for a living. I got over that. I found the courage to stand up and say, 'I want to do it.'"

When Jackman was eight years old, his parents divorced and his mother moved back to England. She eventually married again and later gave birth to his half-sister. Jackman didn't see his mother very often after she left Australia, and he had almost no relationship with her for many years. His father did not remarry, and he raised Jackman and his brothers and sisters as a single father.

EDUCATION

Jackman attended an exclusive school for boys in Sydney. He liked to participate in musical productions at school, beginning when he was about five years old. His interest in theater continued into his teen years—although he has admitted that by that time he was partly motivated by the chance to meet girls. Jackman also played rugby on the school's team. (Rugby is a ball game that is roughly similar to American football, though the rules of play are different. Rugby involves a lot of physical contact, but players don't wear protective gear.)

After completing high school, Jackman began studying journalism at the University of Technology in Sydney. He planned to become either a television news reporter or a talk show host. While working on his journalism degree, Jackman decided on a whim to take a drama class at the Actors

Center in Sydney. He enjoyed it so much that he abandoned journalism and began to study acting full time. "It wasn't until I was 22 that I ever thought about my hobby being something I could make a living out of," Jackman explained. "As a boy, I'd always had an interest in theater. But the idea at my school was that drama and music were to round out the man. It wasn't what one did for a living. I got over that. I found the courage to stand up and say, 'I want to do it.'" He applied and was accepted to study acting at the prestigious Western Australian Academy of Performing Arts, one of Australia's premiere schools for the arts. Jackman graduated from the Academy in 1994.

CAREER HIGHLIGHTS

Jackman's career has been one of the most varied among current performers. He has been described as "a singer, a dancer, an actor, and an action figure" and "an absolute gentleman" by those who have worked with him over the years. Though he is perhaps best known for his portrayal of mutant superhero Wolverine in the *X-Men* movie series, Jackman has found success in stage plays, musical theater, television, and movies of almost all genres. He has hosted numerous performing arts award ceremonies, including the televised broadcasts of the Tonys and the Oscars. Though his projects are not always commercially successful, Jackman has earned critical acclaim and multiple awards and honors for his performances.

Getting Started as an Actor

Jackman has worked almost continuously as an actor since graduating from the Academy in 1994. In fact, on the night of his final Academy graduation performance, he got a phone call offering him a starring role on "Corrrelli," a 1995 Australian television crime drama. Jackman accepted the part. "I was technically unemployed for about 13 seconds," he later recalled. On "Correlli," his costar was Deborra-Lee Furness, a well-known Australian TV actress. The characters' on-screen romance soon developed into a real-life relationship for the two actors, ultimately leading to marriage. "Correlli" lasted only one season. Jackman said of his time on the show, "Meeting my wife was the greatest thing to come out of it."

After "Correlli," Jackman was cast in a 1996 production of the musical *Beauty and the Beast* in Melbourne, Australia, even though at that time he couldn't sing very well. "I guess they liked me enough to send me away for singing lessons," he speculated. "Either that or they were desperate to fill this role." The lessons paid off, and critics praised Jackman as one of the most promising newcomers in musical theater. His success in *Beauty and the Beast* led to more roles in musical theater. In 1998, Jackman won a star-

Jackman shows the ferocity and physicality of Wolverine.

ring role with the London National Theater in England, playing Curly in the musical *Oklahoma!* Jackman has said that being in *Oklahoma!* ranks among his all-time favorite performances. "I totally felt like it can't get any better than this. On some level that production will be one of the highlights of my career." He also had admitted that his success in musicals was completely unexpected. "Musical theater was something of a pleasant surprise for me. There was a musical theater school where I studied acting and I never took those classes."

After *Oklahoma!* Jackman decided to leave musical theater and focus on movie roles. He made his movie debut in the late 1990s, appearing in a few Australian films that were praised by critics but did not do well with audiences. None of them became a hit in the U.S.

Breakout Success: *X-Men*

Jackman's big break came when he was offered a part in the ensemble cast of *X-Men*, released in 2000. In *X-Men*, he was cast as Logan / Wolverine, a mutant superhero with unbreakable bones, the power to heal wounds quickly, and trademark razor-sharp metal claws. Wolverine was his breakout success, his biggest and perhaps best-known movie role—and it almost never happened.

When Jackman first auditioned for the part of Wolverine, he had never read any comic books. He had no idea that the *X-Men* comics were so

"I think we all feel like mutants and outsiders at some point. That's when I realized that this wasn't your average comic book. There was a reason it meant so much to the fans," Jackman acknowledged. "I didn't realize the extent of it, how big a thing it was. But now I meet people with full-color Wolverine tattoos on their backs.... It's the kind of challenge you relish as an actor."

successful or that the *X-Men* series ranked as one of the best-selling comics of all time. When another actor was cast as Wolverine, Jackman moved on to other projects. But then the original actor had to withdraw from the movie, and Jackman was offered the role. At first, he was going to turn it down. He wasn't sure he wanted to do a comic book movie after all. But something about the character of Wolverine had already left an impression on him. "I think we all feel like mutants and outsiders at some point. That's when I realized that this wasn't your average comic book.

A scene from X-Men:
Wolverine with Cyclops, Professor Xavier, Storm, and Jean Grey.

There was a reason it meant so much to the fans," Jackman said. "I didn't realize the extent of it, how big a thing it was. But now I meet people with full-color Wolverine tattoos on their backs.... It's the kind of challenge you relish as an actor; it's there whenever you step into any role that's well-known—Curly in *Oklahoma!*, or Hamlet."

The story of *X-Men* revolves around a group of mutant superheroes, each with a unique superpower that sets them apart from the human world they have sworn to protect. But the human world fears and hates mutants, and it seems that a war between humans and mutants is inevitable. Magneto, an evil mutant, has a plan to prevent this war by turning all humans into mutants. Led by Professor Charles Xavier, the X-Men must act together to stop Magneto before he destroys the human race.

Playing Wolverine

Bringing Wolverine to life turned out to be more challenging than Jackman originally thought. Wolverine had very little dialogue in the movie, but there was still a lot of emotion to convey. To figure out how to do that, Jackman watched Clint Eastwood in the *Dirty Harry* movies and Mel Gibson in *Road Warrior*. "Here were guys who had relatively little dialogue, like Wolverine had, but you knew and felt everything. I'm not normally one to copy, but I wanted to see how these guys achieved it." Meanwhile, the movie's director encouraged Jackman to make Wolverine appear angrier and meaner. Jackman decided to look further into the animal side of the character. "The battle between animal and human, I broke that down to be the most essential thing to focus on with this character," he explained. "We can all relate to that. Maybe not in the extreme level, but we wrestle every day with that argument between chaos and control and freedom and discipline."

Playing Wolverine was also a physically demanding role. Jackman insisted on performing some of his own stunts and worked hard to make Wolverine's fighting style seem realistic. "We worked a lot on the movement style of Wolverine, and I studied some martial arts. I watched a lot of Mike Tyson fights, especially his early fights. There's something about his style, the animal rage, that seemed right for Wolverine," Jackman recalled. "I kept saying to the writers, 'Don't give me long, choreographed fights for the sake of it. Don't make the fights pretty.'" And then there was the issue of Wolverine's lethal claws, which Jackman had to get used to wearing as naturally as Wolverine does. "Every day in my living room, I'd just walk around with those claws, to get used to them. I've got scars on one leg, punctures straight through the cheek, on my forehead. I'm a bit clumsy. I'm lucky I didn't tell them that when I auditioned."

Once the movie was released, Jackman was anxious to know what fans of the *X-Men* comics would think of his portrayal of Wolverine. Two days after the movie opened, Jackman went to a Manhattan movie theater to see the audience reactions for himself. When he got to the theater, he was surprised at the number of people waiting for the next showing of *X-Men*. "There was a huge queue [line] going around the corner. I'm thinking, 'I either have to go to the front and say who I am, but that's not really me, or wait at the end, but those people weren't going to get in anyway.' So I failed."

But Jackman didn't have to wait very long to find out what people thought of the movie. *X-Men* was a huge success with fans and became one of the biggest blockbuster hit movies of 2000, earning almost $300 million worldwide. A film critic for the *Los Angeles Times* called Jackman the star of the movie, saying that he brought a "necessary level of acting intensity" to the role. *Variety* said that Jackman "perfectly brought the comic-book character of Wolverine, a conflicted anti-hero, to vivid life, pleasing general moviegoers and hard core fans of the comic book." Jackman won a Saturn Award from the Academy of Science Fiction, Fantasy & Horror Films, and was nominated for two MTV Movie Awards and a Blockbuster Entertainment Award.

A scene from X2: X-Men United, *with (from left)*
Iceman, Wolverine, Pyro, and Rogue.

X2: X-Men United

After the runaway success of *X-Men*, Jackman went on to other projects. Then in 2003, he revived the character of Wolverine for the sequel *X2: X-Men United*. In *X2*, the story picks up just a few months after the events of *X-Men*. There's an assassination attempt on the U.S. president, and that sets off a war between humans and mutants. The X-Men team up with their former arch-enemy, Magneto, to try and stop the elimination of Earth's mutant population.

For Jackman, getting ready for the movie was a lot of work. Returning to the role of Wolverine required him to bulk up physically and to follow a strict weight-lifting routine. He also had to follow a low-fat, high-protein diet in order to gain enough weight. Jackman needed to weigh about 200 pounds for the role, and he struggled to reach that goal. His regimen demanded that he eat special meals every three hours, including waking up in the middle of night just to eat. Every day at four o'clock in the morning, Jackman would get out of bed to eat meals like egg whites and dry toast, or a whole chicken. Then he would go back to bed until it was time to go to the gym.

X2: X-Men United was a lot of fun, with the same types of humor and action sequences that made the first film so popular. But it also dealt with issues of identity, tolerance, and accepting those who are different. Stan Lee, who created the first *X-Men* comic book, has said that he wrote it during the civil rights movement. "I wanted to show the evils of bigotry," Lee once said. These more serious elements reverberated with Jackman also, who was attracted to the sequel so he could explore Wolverine's inner life. "There was one bit of the script where we flash back to Wolverine's origins, the experiments where they turn him into a killing machine. We see Wolverine come out of this laboratory, his body is in absolute agony, he's got blood all over him, he's just killed (his captors), he's got all these knives (coming out of his hands) but he doesn't know who he is, doesn't know anything except this horrific thing happened," he explained. "In that moment, he unleashes that sort of primal scream that you see on the screen and I thought, this is what has burned inside of Wolverine for 15 years. I wanted to make that moment as intense as possible because I felt, it's one of those crisis points in life where you either fold, or you're driven forward."

X2: X-Men United proved to be a huge hit with critics and fans alike, many of whom called it superior to the original film. *Entertainment Weekly* called it "a fun thrill ride that heroically surpasses the original." That view was echoed in the *Seattle Post-Intelligencer.* "On a purely visceral level, the movie is a doozy. Its action sequences and possibly thousands of special effects shots are all seamlessly choreographed to be an exhilarating thrill ride and total immersion in a comic-bookish future/gothic world. The cast of mutant characters with their various shape-shifting, telepathic, telekinetic, teleporting, pyromaniacal and other powers are great fun, and are portrayed with enough flashes of vulnerability and psychological

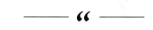

"*The battle between animal and human, I broke that down to be the most essential thing to focus on with this character," Jackman mused. "We can all relate to that. Maybe not in the extreme level, but we wrestle every day with that argument between chaos and control and freedom and discipline.*"

depth to emerge as recognizably human characters." The film ultimately earned over $400 million worldwide at the box office.

X-Men: The Last Stand

Jackman returned to the role of Woverine for the third time in *X-Men: The Last Stand*, released in 2006. In this installment of the *X-Men* series, the

Wolverine and Storm make an amazing discovery in
X-Men: The Last Stand—*Jean Grey, who they thought had died.*

war still rages between humans and mutants. Scientists have discovered a cure for mutation, which would permanently turn mutants into humans, taking away their powers and making them "normal." The mutant community becomes divided between those who want the cure and those fighting against it. Many of the mutants struggle with whether it is more important to fit in or to remain an individual. Others are more sure about themselves. "There's nothing to cure," declared the mutant Storm. "There's nothing wrong with any of us." Although the X-Men feel they are hated by the human world, they still believe mutants and humans should be able to live together in an integrated society. But the evil Magneto joins with former allies of the X-Men to build an army to fight the humans and destroy the cure. That leads to a battle between the mutants led by the evil Magneto and those led by the more idealistic Professor X, as the X-Men realize that to end the human-mutant war once and for all, they must once again stop Magneto from destroying humanity.

In *The Last Stand,* as in the earlier *X-Men* movies, many reviewers saw more than just the typical popcorn action flick. Many considered it an allegory on different social issues, viewing the anti-mutant discrimination as racism, anti-Semitism, homophobia, and other forms of hatred against others. For Jackman, though, the characters were the key element. "I wouldn't have gone back to do it if I didn't really like playing the role," he acknowledged. "Wolverine is a bit of a gift as a character because, in all the comic-book movies and action movies, there are not many roles that have this kind of complexity. It is a movie that is really about people. It is about their flaws as much as their abilities and that is what I like about it."

Still, reviews of the film were divided. While acknowledging that Jackman's performance "again steals the film," *People* complained that the movie was "crowded with so many superpower-endowed mutants ... that none of the characters show up long enough to make an impact." But other reviewers were more impressed. "It is action that aspires," wrote the *Globe and Mail.* "Things explode, and explode beautifully. There are deaths, operatic deaths, and the viewer is strangely moved. And at the heart of it is Wolverine, armed with fierce conviction." Reviewers may have been conflicted, but fans clearly were not: they turned out in droves to watch the new installment. The movie earned $120.1 million in its opening weekend alone, making it the largest Memorial Day weekend opening in box-office history and the fourth-largest opening weekend of all time. It went on to earn over $450 million worldwide.

"To me, he's one of the great screen archetypes," Jackman declared. "He's like, when I was growing up, Han Solo and Mad Max, or Dirty Harry. These were all the kind of roles I loved. And that's what Wolverine is. He's that reluctant hero. He is a good guy but he's not a nice guy. I think we all love that character. He's the guy you want on your side."

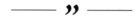

X-Men Origins: Wolverine

After appearing in a string of movies that were not as successful as the *X-Men* series, Jackman revisited the character of Wolverine for the fourth time in 2009 in *X-Men Origins: Wolverine.* This installment of the *X-Men* series capitalized on the popularity of Wolverine. The film serves as a prequel to the previous *X-Men* movies, telling the story of how Logan became the mutant Wolverine. The prologue, opening in 1845, establishes the story of two mutants, Logan (Jackman) and his brother Victor (Sabretooth), and their inhuman strength, agility, and ability to heal their own wounds. The movie goes on to show Logan's relationship with his brother, the beginning of his involvement with William Stryker, the source of his metal

A scene from X-Men Origins: Wolverine, *as he seeks revenge.*

claws, and his struggles between his human and his baser instincts as he seeks revenge.

By focusing on Wolverine's background, Jackman was able to give the character more depth. "Wolverine's fun and cool, but I wouldn't be down for my fourth time doing it if there wasn't something more interesting to it than just slicing and dicing and smoking a cigar and saying a few cool lines." Jackman seemed to have great respect for the character. "To me, he's one of the great screen archetypes. He's like, when I was growing up, Han Solo and Mad Max, or Dirty Harry. These were all the kind of roles I loved. And that's what Wolverine is. He's that reluctant hero. He is a good guy but he's not a nice guy. I think we all love that character. He's the guy you want on your side."

The movie received mixed reviews from critics. "For all its attempts to probe the physiological and psychological roots of its tortured antihero," wrote *Daily Variety,* "this brawny but none-too-brainy prequel sustains the rest mainly—if only fitfully—as a nonstop slice-and-dice vehicle for Hugh Jackman." *USA Today* observed that Jackman "artfully embodies a character who is both ferocious and humane ... compelling viewers to care about his metamorphosis." Despite such reviews, fans loved the movie, which earned over $370 million at the box office worldwide. Fans at the 2008

Comic-Con in San Diego, California, went wild when Jackman made a surprise appearance to promote the movie's upcoming release. Jackman earned a Teen Choice Movie Award for his performance.

Branching Out

Between filming movies in the *X-Men* series, Jackman kept busy working on other projects. To avoid being typecast in any one kind of role, he chose a variety of different parts in movies and on stage. From 2001 to 2008, Jackman had roles in serious dramas, romantic comedies, suspense thrillers, and musical theater, and he also did voice acting for animated movies. All of these different projects expanded his fan base and helped to draw new audiences to the *X-Men* movie series.

After the first *X-Men* movie, Jackman starred in the 2001 romantic comedy *Kate & Leopold*, playing the role of a time-travelling 19th-century gentleman. For this performance, he was nominated for two awards: the Golden Globe Award for best actor in a comedy or musical and the Hollywood Foreign Press Association Award for best performance by an actor in a motion picture musical or comedy. Then after making *X2*, Jackman returned to musical theater. He starred in the 2003 Broadway production of *The Boy from Oz*, the story of Peter Allen, a flamboyant Australian songwriter who died of AIDS-related cancer in 1992. Jackman won a Tony Award for best actor in a musical for his performance in that play. Jackman then appeared in the movie *Van Helsing*, released in 2004. He starred in the title role as the hero out to kill Dracula, the Wolf Man, and Frankenstein. *Van Helsing* was not a success at the box office or with critics. *People* called the movie "pretty darn dumb, with even the main characters so thinly drawn that one remains indifferent to their fates."

While working on *X-Men: The Last Stand*, Jackman was also providing character voices in two popular animated movies released in 2006. In *Happy Feet*, Jackman was the voice of Memphis, a member of a community of singing

> **"**
>
> *In the future, Jackman hopes to be able to play Wolverine and to perform in stage and movie musicals. "I love both. What I realize now is that I have to have the stage in my professional diet. It's a lot more tiring, particularly doing musicals, but it informs my movie-acting," Jackman said. "In the end, it's all about variety—mixing an action film with something lighter."*
>
> **"**

*Leaving Wolverine far behind,
Jackman did voice work on two
animated movies,* Happy Feet *(top)
and* Flushed Away *(bottom).*

penguins. Memphis's son Mumble cannot sing, but knows how to tap dance instead. The story unfolds as Mumble struggles with being different and ultimately teaches the penguin community that everyone doesn't have to be exactly the same. In *Flushed Away*, Jackman was the voice of Roddy, a cultured high-society rat who lands in the sewers of London after being flushed down the toilet. Roddy learns about the underground world of "real" rats as he undertakes an adventurous journey to get back home. "Roddy fancies himself as a James Bond character. See, I get to live out my fantasies through this movie," Jackman said. "I can see some of my facial expressions, and I can see some of my gestures and things like that because they filmed me in the studio the entire time." Jackman enjoyed voice acting and also appreciated the opportunity to play lighter roles in a family-oriented feature. "It is great to finally have something that my kids can see," he remarked.

Jackman's next big project after *X-Men: The Last Stand* was the World War II-era Western drama *Australia*, released in 2008. Jackman starred opposite Nicole Kidman in the role of the nameless Drover (cowboy) hired to drive a herd of cattle across the inhospitable Australian outback. "This is definitely the straight-down-the-line, classic, old-school leading-man role I've been waiting for," he remarked. To prepare for the role, he trained in horseback riding and wrangling cattle like a real cowboy. One scene of the film required Jackman to lasso a wild horse. His characteristic dedication and intensive practice helped him do it. "The horse went ballistic when I got that rope around his neck," he admitted. "My gloves ripped, the rope peeled skin off my hands. I just remember being so happy that I did it that I didn't care at all." Unfortunately, *Australia* was not well-received by critics, who generally dismissed it as unoriginal and clichéd. However, the *New York Times* credited Jackman's performance with giving the film "oomph." *Newsweek* called Jackman "gruff and hunky," while *USA Today* praised his performance as the "rough-hewn cattle driver."

Future Plans

Recognizing that *X-Men* gave him his big break as an actor, Jackman hopes to be able to play Wolverine in more films in the future. He is also interested in continuing to perform in stage productions and in movie versions of musicals. "I love both. What I realize now is that I have to have the stage in my professional diet. It's a lot more tiring, particularly doing musicals, but it informs my movie-acting," Jackman said. "In the end, it's all about variety—mixing an action film with something lighter."

Part of the appeal of such a diverse performing career is the variety of opportunities for reaching different audiences. Action movies and Broadway musicals seem to be on nearly opposite ends of the performing arts spectrum, but Jackman enjoys mixing up his roles to keep his performances fresh. "I'm the same as everyone else in the audience. I get sick of seeing the same faces after a while and I know that this amazing run of roles I've been getting will one day just grind to a halt and nobody will want to know me for ages." But for now, Jackman's popularity shows no sign of waning.

Jackman has often been compared to such other well-known Australian actors as Mel Gibson, Russell Crowe, and Heath Ledger. Jackman doesn't mind the comparisons, saying, "I watched Mel in all those *Road Warrior* movies and he was just brilliant. I thought if I could just be half as good." In fact, Jackman credits his versatility as a performer to his Australian roots. He believes that the relative isolation of the island continent requires people to develop diverse talents. "With a population of just 20 million, you can't be too fussy. You have to be able to do everything. That may be some of the reason Australian actors have done well. There's more versatility to what they can do. Plus, we have a saying here: Have a go. We don't like people who play things safe. It's not enough just to be successful. You have to take a bit of a risk," Jackman said. "Greater than my fear of failure—which we all have—is my fear of mediocrity and of being hemmed in by just the lack of courage to try something.… The worst thing is not to have a go."

MARRIAGE AND FAMILY

Jackman married Deborra-Lee Furness in 1996. They have two adopted children, a son, Oscar Maximilian, born in 2000, and a daughter, Ava Eliot, born in 2005.

HOBBIES AND OTHER INTERESTS

In his spare time, Jackman enjoys dancing, windsurfing, playing piano and guitar, and practicing yoga and meditation. He can juggle five balls at once, and he knows the score of every Rodgers and Hammerstein musical by heart. Whenever Jackman is shooting a movie, every Friday he brings a bag of lottery tickets to the set. He gives tickets to everyone working on the movie. "You know, ever since I started 'Lucky Friday,' I never get a Friday off," he joked. "I think people are hooked on those lottery tickets."

SELECTED CREDITS

"Correlli," 1995 (TV series)
Beauty and the Beast, 1996 (musical theater)
Sunset Boulevard, 1997 (musical theater)
Oklahoma!, 1998 (musical theater)

Erskinville Kings, 1999 (movie)
Paperback Hero, 1999 (movie)
X-Men, 2000 (movie)
Kate & Leopold, 2001 (movie)
Someone Like You, 2001 (movie)
The Boy from Oz, 2003 (musical theater)
X2: X-Men United, 2003 (movie)
Van Helsing, 2004 (movie)
The Fountain, 2006 (movie)
The Prestige, 2006 (movie)
Flushed Away, 2006 (movie)
Happy Feet, 2006 (movie)
X-Men: The Last Stand, 2006 (movie)
Australia, 2008 (movie)
X-Men Origins: Wolverine, 2009 (movie)
"A Steady Rain," 2009 (play)

HONORS AND AWARDS

Variety Club Award: 1998, for *Oklahoma!*
Saturn Award (Academy of Science Fiction, Fantasy & Horror Films): 2000, for *X-Men*
Tony Award: 2004, Best Actor in a Musical, for *The Boy from Oz*
Emmy Award: 2005, Outstanding Individual Performance in a Variety or Music Program, for hosting the 58th Annual Tony Awards
Teen Choice Movie Award: 2008, Choice Movie Actor in an Action Adventure, for *X-Men Origins: Wolverine*

FURTHER READING

Periodicals

Biography, May 2003, p.46
Current Biography Yearbook, 2003
Entertainment Weekly, Aug. 22, 2008; Apr. 24, 2009, p.26
Globe & Mail (Toronto, Canada), May 27, 2006, p.R14
Interview, Sep. 2003, p.171; May 2004, p.99; June 2006, p.38
New York Times, July 21, 2000, p.E18; Sep. 7, 2008, p.36
Newsweek, May 18, 2009, p.67
O, The Oprah Magazine, June 2006, p.242
People, Aug. 7, 2000, p. 81; May 14, 2001, p.95; May 24, 2004, p.24
Time, Oct. 20, 2003, p.72
USA Today, Oct. 17, 2007, p.D12; Apr. 27, 2009, p.D1

Online Articles

http://www.allmovie.com
   (AllMovie, "Hugh Jackman Biography," 2009)
http://www.variety.com
   (Variety, "Hugh Jackman: Biography," 2009)

ADDRESS

Hugh Jackman
The Endeavor Agency
9601 Wilshire Blvd., 3rd Floor
Beverly Hills, CA 90210

WORLD WIDE WEB SITES

http://marvel.com/movies/X-Men.X-Men_~op~2000~ep~
http://marvel.com/movies/X-Men.X2~colon~_X-Men_United
http://marvel.com/movies/X-Men.X3~colon~_The_Last_Stand
http://marvel.com/movies/X-Men.X-Men_Origins~colon~_Wolverine
http://marvel.com/universe/X-Men

Jesse James 1969-

American Motorcycle Customizer and Television Personality

Founder and CEO of West Coast Choppers

Host of "Monster Garage" and Star of "Jesse James Is a Dead Man"

BIRTH

Jesse Gregory James was born on April 19, 1969, in Lynwood, California. He grew up in the same area, in various homes around Compton and Long Beach. His father, Larry James, made his living selling antiques and used furniture at flea markets. His mother worked as a florist. He is named after Jesse James, the famous American bandit who was gunned down in 1882. James's great-great-grandfather was a cousin of the outlaw.

YOUTH

James's parents split up when he was five years old, and Jesse lived with his father after that. Larry James has said that even at a very young age, his son had the interests and skills that would eventually make him famous as a motorcycle customizer. "It didn't matter if it was Legos, a pile of Tonka trucks, or his bikes," his father once recalled, "you could always find Jesse with everything laid out on the floor, tearing things apart to see if he could make them better in some way."

> "It didn't matter if it was Legos, a pile of Tonka trucks, or his bikes," his father once recalled, "you could always find Jesse with everything laid out on the floor, tearing things apart to see if he could make them better in some way."

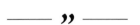

For a while, Larry James's shop was located next door to Performance Machine, owned by Perry Sands. The company made aftermarket accessories for motorcycles—special parts that owners of mass-produced bikes can add to their machines to give them some individual style. Performance Machine was filled with men and noisy equipment, changing pieces of metal into motorcycle parts. James loved to watch them. "My early, early memories are going next door and playing with all the metal chips, and seeing those guys," he recalled. "I don't even remember the inside of my dad's shop, but I can remember what it looked like inside Perry's shop."

James was seven years old when he got his first motorcycle, a Kawasaki 50 cc minibike that he rode every day. When he was about 12 years old, he began learning the art of welding and started his first serious customizing project. Taking an old, beat-up Schwinn bicycle from the 1940s, he cleaned it up, repaired it, and tricked it out with lots of chrome and a great-looking pinstripe paint job. His creation sold at a flea market for $850. The experience taught James that both personal satisfaction and financial rewards could come from working with his hands.

James showed a real flair for learning about machines and metal, but he also had a knack for getting into trouble. He was left on his own a lot, and he got involved in illegal activities, including car theft. On three occasions, he was taken into custody by the California Youth Authority, which deals with young lawbreakers. James eventually changed his ways when he realized that if he didn't, he would end up in the "big-boy jail," as he put it.

EARLY MEMORIES

James has been fascinated by motorcycles since he was very young. "I remember seeing a pack of [the motorcycle club] Hell's Angels blasting by our family car when I was about six, and they were all riding choppers," he recalled. "I remember all the noise and all the chrome. It was the coolest thing I ever saw. I knew then that I was going to be involved in motorcycles in some way."

EDUCATION

James didn't have an easy time at school. He played on the high school football team, but was frequently kicked out of practice for being too rough. A loner at school, he said that "I hated everybody and everybody hated me." Those feelings of being at odds with everything and everyone inspired his first major motorcycle project. He decided to build a "big, loud obnoxious bike … to make 'em hate me more." He had very little money to work with, but he succeeded in putting together a rigid-framed, stripped-down, no-frills chopper. His finished ride was definitely loud and fast, and he had done all the work on the frame, engine, and paint job himself.

After graduating from La Sierra High School in Long Beach, James began studying at University of California, Riverside, where he had been awarded a football scholarship. A knee injury ended his athletic career, however. He left college before completing his degree.

FIRST JOBS

After building that first chopper in high school, James continued working on new motorcycle projects, using a corner of his mom's garage as his shop. In 1988, when he was 19 years old, he came up with a name and logo for the business he dreamed of owning. It was "West Coast Choppers," with the name incorporated into a Maltese cross design. Even at that age, he was shrewd when it came to marketing. He knew it would be important to his success to have a brand with strong appeal. He printed up about ten T-shirts featuring the logo and tried to give them to his friends, saying: "Trust me, this is my shop." Their response, he recalled, was generally something like: "You don't have a shop. What are you talkin' about?" Most of them didn't even want the free shirt. Despite their skepticism, James said: "I always knew that West Coast Choppers was gonna be it.

A chopper designed and built by James and his team.

That was my dream." He continued to use his original logo as his business slowly took shape and prospered, and millions of people all over the world now wear West Coast Choppers T-shirts.

James knew it would take money to realize his dream of owning a motorcycle shop. He had matured into an imposing man, over six feet tall with lots of muscle. After taking some specialized training, he found work as a professional bodyguard. In that capacity, he provided security for musical acts ranging from the pop star Tiffany to heavy-metal bands like Slayer, Danzig, and Soundgarden. Working in security paid well, and when he wasn't on tour he was able to keep working on motorcycles. After about five years on the job, however, while working at a concert in Detroit, he suffered a dislocated elbow—a very painful injury. The incident helped him decide it was time to get out of the bodyguard business and pursue the West Coast Choppers dream full-time. In 1992, his shop was officially launched.

Working at Many Apprenticeships

James had some very clear ideas about how he wanted to do things at West Coast Choppers. He knew he didn't want to take out any loans; the business should pay for itself. He wanted everything from his shop to be a product of great design and craftsmanship. He hoped to eventually manufacture most of the parts for his motorcycles on-site, rather than buying parts elsewhere. James understood that he had a lot to learn before he could reach these goals and that it would take many hours of hard work to reach the level of quality he wanted. He set out on a series of apprenticeships under the masters of metalworking and machine-building.

James started at Performance Machine, the same shop that had fascinated him as a little kid. Owner Perry Sands first assigned him to the research and development department, and later allowed him to design and build the prototype Corbin Warbird body kit. Sands appreciated James's natural talent and his hard-working attitude. After about a year and a half, James moved on to work with Boyd Coddington, a legendary car customizer. Serving as a design and fabrication specialist at Coddington's shop, James improved his ability to transform ideas and sketches into working parts. He also mastered the operation of the computer numerical control (CNC) machine. The CNC can read any three-dimensional design programmed into it and then

"I remember seeing a pack of [the motorcycle club] Hell's Angels blasting by our family car when I was about six, and they were all riding choppers," James recalled. "I remember all the noise and all the chrome. It was the coolest thing I ever saw. I knew then that I was going to be involved in motorcycles in some way."

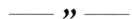

create that shape out of metal. The machine is very important in the world of custom cars and motorcycles, particularly for producing wheels. Leaving Coddington's shop, James next worked with Ron Simms, another well-known customizer in the San Francisco area, who taught him a lot about producing fenders and other sheet-metal accessories.

One thing James had noticed about many older choppers he'd worked on was the way their parts were fabricated with cheap materials and substandard techniques. Welds that separate and parts that break can cause accidents, and on a fast-moving chopper an accident can easily be fatal. James wanted his creations to be really rugged, able to hold up to the toughest conditions. His desire to learn the best possible working methods led him to the East Coast in 1999, where he studied with Fay Butler in Massachusetts. Butler is highly respected in the metalworking world because he is

James, an accomplished metalworker, shown welding in his shop.

one of only a handful of people who still know how to shape steel and other metals with early 20th-century tools, such as the Yoder power hammer and the English Wheel. These tools demand a high level of skill and can deliver finer results than mass-production techniques. Butler described James as "an extremely talented person with a great eye for design and style. He's one of the best welders I've ever come across."

CAREER HIGHLIGHTS

West Coast Choppers

James built several motorcycles in his little shop in Long Beach and sent pictures of them to biker magazines and design shops, hoping to get some attention. But for a few years, he was mostly ignored. The kind of motorcycles James liked building were very unfashionable when West Coast Choppers was starting out. Sedate, comfortable street bikes like the Harley-Davidson Fatboy were in style at that time. The rigid-frame, stripped-down choppers he created were considered a relic of the 1970s, favored only by outlaws and those out-of-touch with the times. James didn't care. As usual, he had his own vision and he stuck to it.

A West Coast Choppers bike is likely to include a lot of unusual features. For example, James likes to build bikes that have a foot clutch and a "jockey shifter," worked by hand—an old-fashioned setup that is difficult to handle but preferred by some chopper enthusiasts. He likes "ape hanger" handlebars, which require the rider to reach up and out, and long, stretched-out frames. He works the Maltese cross into his designs in many different ways, and many of his bikes have air filters fashioned to look like a spade from a deck of cards. On some of his choppers, he has adapted old cavalry swords for use as a functioning jockey shifter. One of his creations included special neon tubing for the spark plug wires, which glowed when powered up. Sections of metalwork that look like spiderwebs are frequently found on bikes from West Coast Choppers. Wild paint jobs, beautiful wheels, and clean, sweeping lines are also part of the West Coast Choppers aesthetic.

Jesse refuses to build bikes for people he doesn't like, and he spends long hours trying to figure out what makes a prospective owner tick. Then he tries to reflect that individual's special qualities in the design of their one-of-a-kind chopper. Once it is finished, James or one of his trusted assistants puts every motorcycle through hundreds of hours of riding under all conditions, making sure that there are no unexpected problems or bugs to be worked out. No formal warranty agreements are ever signed, but if anyone ever has a problem with their motorcycle, the West Coast Choppers crew will travel hundreds of miles to pick up the bike and bring it back to the shop in Long Beach to do whatever repairs might be needed.

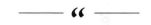

Respected metalworker Fay Butler described James as "an extremely talented person with a great eye for design and style. He's one of the best welders I've ever come across."

Celebrity Welder

Throughout the 1990s, James's reputation as a superb artist and craftsman slowly grew. The shop's location near Los Angeles, the heart of the entertainment industry, made it accessible for the many musicians and actors working there. The attention-getting looks and high-performance capabilities of West Coast Choppers had a lot of appeal for rock stars and high-profile actors and athletes. When such celebrities as Keanu Reeves, Kid Rock, and Shaquille O'Neal began buying choppers from James, the reputation of his shop quickly spread across the nation and, ultimately, the world. Soon there was a waiting list of the rich and famous who wanted to own a custom bike designed by Jesse James and built at West Coast Choppers. He expanded his shop and hired more employees, but even so, only about a dozen bikes are finished in a year. Each one takes about 400 to 1,000 hours of work and wil cost somewhere between $60,000 and $250,000.

One of James's customers was Thom Beers, a producer for the Discovery channel. He brought his motorcycle in for an overhaul at James's shop, and he was excited by the atmosphere there—the bright glare of the welding torches, the sound of engines being put through tests, metal being hammered, and over it all the blaring of the rap and acid rock music that's usually playing while the crews do their work. Beers decided the place was the perfect setting for a television special. With James's permission, Beers followed James and his workers for two weeks as they worked feverishly on several bikes they hoped to have ready in time for a rally at Daytona Beach, Florida.

> "Part of me really appreciates the attention," James said after the debut of his TV show, "but part of me thinks of all the metal guys, all the craftsmen who came before me, and all they did is work and punch a clock and no one gave them a TV show."

The finished show, called "Motorcycle Mania," aired in 2001, drawing the largest audience the Discovery channel had ever had. James's artistry and his no-nonsense persona translated well to the screen. Suddenly, the designer, builder, and self-proclaimed outlaw was as much a celebrity as many of his wealthy clients. James wasn't sure how he felt about his change in status. "Part of me really appreciates the attention," he said, "but part of me thinks of all the metal guys, all the craftsmen who came before me, and all they did is work and punch a clock and no one gave them a TV show." Despite his reservations, the show did so well that Discovery went on to produce "Motorcycle Mania II" in 2002 and "Motorcycle Mania III" in 2004. By that time, James had already started the show that would make him famous.

Boss of the "Monster Garage"

James's star status led the Discovery Channel to create "Monster Garage," a regular program built around the welder and his shop. "Monster Garage" first aired in 2002, and production continued until 2006. Each episode featured a different crew of five people with mechanical or metal-

*In this scene from "Monster Garage," James is working on a project to transform
a Mazda into a dune buggy.*

working experience who had applied to be on the program. With Jesse as
their boss, each team faced an assignment of transforming an ordinary vehicle into some sort of outrageous machine. They were given seven days to
work on their project. The first was for designing, the next five days were
for work, and the seventh day was set aside for testing the finished vehicle.
The entire project could not cost more than $3,000 (later raised to $5,000).
In theory, the end product was supposed to look like the original vehicle,
but in practice, this rule wasn't always followed.

Some of the more memorable "Monster Garage" transformations included a PT Cruiser that could become a wood chipper, a school bus that could
also function as a pontoon boat, a Mustang GT that became a high-speed
lawnmower, a Volkswagen that could float, and a police car that doubled as
a donut shop. One of James's particular favorites was a Ford ambulance
that was modified so that it could do impressive wheelies. Part of the appeal of "Monster Garage" came from the vehicles themselves, but another
element of its success was the way it showed the tensions and the cooperation between James and his crew members as they struggled to turn an
idea into a reality, in time to meet the deadline.

Not all the monsters were successes. Some were ranked as failures because the crew couldn't meet the budget and deadline. Others didn't work

properly when tested. Whatever the reason they were rejected, those projects deemed failures were destroyed in various ways devised by James. They were blown up, crushed, shot with handguns, smashed into walls, and torched with flamethrowers, among other things. The crazy concepts behind the monster vehicles and the spectacular ends they sometimes met made for winning entertainment. Episodes of "Monster Garage" were re-broadcast frequently and remained very popular on the Discovery channel. The show has been adapted as a video game, and models of the monster creations have been sold as toys.

James took the "Monster Garage" concept to Iraq with the special "Iraq Confidential with Jesse James," which aired in 2006. Besides taking a look at what conditions were like for military men and women in Iraq and visiting wounded soldiers in a hospital, James also worked with some of the troops to try transforming a bombed-out Humvee into a flying machine. The building project didn't work out as planned, but James found it a life-changing experience to enter a combat zone and see what soldiers go through on a daily basis. In yet another TV appearance, he was a contestant in the second season of "Celebrity Apprentice," a competition to see who would be selected for a demanding job. James remained in the running until the next to last episode of the second season in 2009.

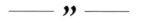

> Although James has filled many roles, he identifies himself primarily as a welder. "Metalworking is where my soul is," he has said.

Taking Risks in "Jesse James Is a Dead Man"

James began a new television series in 2009 with "Jesse James Is a Dead Man." Over two million viewers tuned in to see the show's debut on the Spike channel. It featured James in a new, risk-taking situation each week. The idea wasn't to have him take foolish chances doing pointless stunts; instead, each episode showed him learning a new skill or trying out a new experience. He was set on fire while wearing a fireproof suit, took a flight in a military jet to experience zero gravity, and rode a motorcycle through arctic conditions. He raced in a World War II fighter plane and rode a rocket-powered motorcycle. He even broke the world record for a hydrogen-powered vehicle, hitting 199.7 miles per hour at the El Mirage Dry Lake in California on June 23, 2009. Despite the show's title, James survived the first season, but he did suffer a possible concussion and break two ribs and a bone in his elbow.

James in a scene from "Jesse James Is a Dead Man," a Spike TV series in which he tries a variety of new experiences, all involving risk-taking situations.

Life has become more complicated for James since he became a celebrity, but he has continued to design and build choppers in his shop. Although he fills many roles, he identifies himself primarily as a welder. "Metalworking is where my soul is," he has said. Unquestionably a master welder and creator of machines, he has also proven himself to be an astute businessman. Despite the high price tag on every West Coast Chopper, so much work goes into every custom bike that the profit margin is small. The company's financial success comes from many other sources. Most of its profits come from merchandise bearing the West Coast Chopper logo—hundreds of items, from sunglasses and keychains to bandanas and T-shirts. The company produces specialized lines of clothing for women, industrial workers, and children. There are West Coast Choppers aftermarket accessories for motorcycles, such as fenders and wheels, and the Choppers for Life line of kit bikes, for those who want some of the Jesse James magic but can't afford a custom-designed chopper.

HOME AND FAMILY

James married his first wife, Karla, around the early 1990s. They had two children, a daughter, Chandler, and a son, Jesse Jr. Karla and Jesse Sr. divorced, and he married Janine Lindemulder. They had one daughter, Sunny, before divorcing in 2004.

In 2006, James married actress Sandra Bullock, whom he met when she brought her godson to tour the West Coast Choppers shop. In 2010, there were reports that James had had several affairs while married to Bullock. It became a very big story over the next several months, especially when it became known that James and Bullock had been in the process of adopting a baby at the time. James and Bullock were divorced later that year, and Bullock kept custody of the baby, Louis.

HOBBIES AND OTHER INTERESTS

James has a collection of about 50 motorcycles and custom cars and trucks. He has several dogs, some of them adopted from shelters. He likes taking in pets that might not otherwise find homes, due to disabilities or other problems. James also keeps pet sharks in a tank at the West Coast Choppers shop. He enjoys baking, with his specialty being almond tarts.

Because he believes strongly in improving industrial arts programs in schools, James established Jesse's Fund, a division of the Long Beach Education Foundation. This organization accepts donations of machinery and money for industrial-arts programs in the Long Beach area.

In addition to West Coast Choppers, James has started several other business ventures. In 2004, he began publishing *Garage,* a magazine about the custom car and motorcycle culture, and he also established his own TV production company, Payupsucker Productions. In addition, he owns a restaurant called Cisco Burger, named after one of his favorite dogs. Cisco Burger serves healthful food and makes use of solar power and other green technologies.

TELEVISION

"Motorcycle Mania I," 2001
"Motorcycle Mania II," 2002
"Motorcycle Mania III: Jesse James Rides Again," 2004
"Monster Garage," 2002-06
"Iraq Confidential with Jesse James," 2006
"Celebrity Apprentice," 2008-09 (contestant)
"Jesse James Is a Dead Man," 2009

HONORS AND AWARDS

Award for Contributions to Welding (American Welding Society): 2003

FURTHER READING

Books

Seate, Mike. *Jesse James: The Man and His Machines,* 2003

Periodicals

Autoweek, Aug. 18, 2003, p.16
Daily Variety, May 29, 2009, p.7
Los Angeles Times, May 24, 1009, p.D20
New York Times, Oct. 3, 2002, p.F1
People, Aug. 1, 2005, p.48; June 5, 2006, p.85; July 31, 2006, p.72
Popular Mechanics, Nov. 2007, p.90
USA Today, May 28, 2009, p.D7

ADDRESSES

Jesse James
The Discovery Channel
One Discovery Place
Silver Spring, MD 20910

Jesse James
West Coast Choppers
718 West Anaheim Street
Long Beach, CA 90813

WORLD WIDE WEB SITE

http://westcoastchoppers.com

LeBron James 1984-

American Professional Basketball Player with the Miami Heat
Winner of the NBA's Most Valuable Player Award in 2008-09 and 2009-10

BIRTH

LeBron James was born on December 30, 1984, in Akron, Ohio. He is the only child of Gloria James, who was 16 and single at the time of his birth. His biological father, Anthony McClelland, did not play a role in his upbringing. But LeBron developed a close relationship with one of his mother's boyfriends, Eddie Jackson, who lived with his family for a few years during his childhood. He has referred to Jackson as his father on several occasions.

YOUTH

LeBron first became interested in basketball in 1987, when he received a toy ball and adjustable hoop for Christmas. Although it was still a few days before he reached his third birthday, he loved running toward the hoop, jumping, and dunking the ball. He kept dunking even as the adults in the house raised the height of the basket. "All he would do is start back from the living room, run through the dining room, and he was still dunking the ball," Jackson recalled. "I was thinking, 'Man, this kid has some elevation for just being three years old.'"

James became interested in basketball when he received an adjustable hoop when he was almost three. He kept dunking the ball, and the adults kept raising the hoop. "All he would do is start back from the living room, run through the dining room, and he was still dunking the ball," Jackson recalled. "I was thinking, 'Man, this kid has some elevation for just being three years old.'"

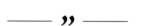

Up to this time, LeBron and his mother had been living with his grandmother, Freda James, in an old Victorian house in Akron. But when his grandmother died, Gloria James was unable to maintain the residence. She was forced to move into a public housing project in Akron and raise LeBron as a single mother. Although Gloria James worked at several jobs, she often struggled to put food on the table and provide a stable home environment for her son. In fact, LeBron lived in a dozen different places between the ages of five and eight. "I just grabbed my little backpack, which held all the possessions I needed, and said to myself what I always said to myself: 'It's time to roll,'" he remembered.

Despite his unsettled home life, LeBron somehow managed to stay out of trouble. "You had gunshots flying and cop cars driving around there all the time," he acknowledged. "As a young boy, it was scary, but I never got into none of that stuff. That just wasn't me. I knew it was wrong." Still, the frequent moves caused him to miss a lot of school, including more than half of the fourth grade. Once he started playing organized basketball at the age of nine, however, he gained some stability by living with the family of

In his book, Shooting Stars, *James recounts his early experiences playing basketball and the close friendships he developed with his teammates.*

his coach, Frankie Walker. It was in Walker's home that LeBron experienced structure and discipline for the first time. "It changed my life," he stated. "The next year I had perfect attendance and a B average."

Practically from the first time he walked onto a basketball court, LeBron dominated other players with his unusual size, strength, athleticism, ball-handling skills, and passing ability. He played on a youth basketball team called the Shooting Stars and developed close relationships with several of his teammates, including Dru Joyce Jr., Sian Cotton, and Willie McGee. The Shooting Stars won more than 200 games and claimed several Amateur Athletic Union (AAU) championships over the next few years.

In 2009 LeBron published a book called *Shooting Stars* about his youth basketball experiences and his friendships with his teammates. His early playing days also became the subject of a 2009 documentary film called *More Than a Game.* "I believe that everything happens for a reason, and my struggles here in [Akron] helped to make me who I am," he declared. "My teammates and I got to see the light at the end of the tunnel. We all loved basketball, we all had the same goal, and when you have six or seven guys with that much in common, all staying on the right track, you can accomplish a lot."

EDUCATION

By the time he reached high school age, James was recognized as one of the most talented young players in Akron. Several area coaches tried to lure him to their schools. Many people assumed that he would attend Buchtel, a public high school in West Akron that James described as "the school of choice for skilled black athletes." But James had made a pact with his three best friends, Joyce, Cotton, and McGee. "We called ourselves the Fab Four," he recalled. "We decided we'd all go to the same school together. We promised that nothing would break us up—girls, coaches, basketball. We'd hang together no matter what."

When it became clear that Joyce would not make the varsity basketball team at Buchtel, all four boys decided to attend St. Vincent-St. Mary, a private, all-boys Catholic high school in Akron. Their decision to attend this predominantly white school shocked and disappointed some local fans. "The four of us may have been brothers to each other," James acknowledged. "But to many in Akron's black community, we were now traitors who had sold out to the white establishment." James and his friends also faced a rough transition when they started classes at St. Vincent-St. Mary, with its strict dress code and high academic standards. But their success on the basketball court soon swept away any doubts they may have had.

With James and his friends leading the varsity team as freshmen, the St. Vincent-St. Mary Fighting Irish posted a perfect 27-0 record during the 1999-2000 season to win the Division III Ohio state championship. James contributed 18.0 points and 6.2 rebounds per game that year. As a sophomore in 2000-01, he increased his scoring average to 25.2 points per game while adding 7.2 rebounds, 5.8 assists, and 3.8 steals. The Fighting Irish posted an impressive 27-1 record and claimed a second straight state title. James became the first sophomore in history to be named Mr. Basketball for the state of Ohio.

To the surprise of many people, James also played varsity football during his second year at St. Vincent-St. Mary. His height and leaping ability made him a natural at wide receiver. He caught 42 passes for 820 yards and 7 touchdowns that year and earned all-state honors. As a junior, he caught 61 passes for 1,245 yards and 16 touchdowns and led his team to the semifinals of the state tournament. "Football is my first love," James declared. "I still like football more than basketball." Unfortunately, an injury prevented him from playing football again as a senior.

In high school, James made a pact with his three best friends, Dru Joyce Jr., Sian Cotton, and Willie McGee. "We called ourselves the Fab Four," he recalled. "We decided we'd all go to the same school together. We promised that nothing would break us up—girls, coaches, basketball. We'd hang together no matter what."

Becoming a National Phenomenon

By the time his junior-year basketball season got underway, James was widely considered to be among the best young players in the country. He had dazzled both college and National Basketball Association (NBA) scouts with his dominating performances at high-profile summer basketball camps. Although James showed great scoring ability, experts also praised his maturity and court vision, which had the effect of making his teammates better. Some observers even compared him to NBA Hall of Fame players like Magic Johnson and Michael Jordan.

During the 2001-02 season, when James was a junior, he averaged 29.0 points, 8.3 rebounds, 5.7 assists, and 3.3 steals per game and claimed his second straight Ohio Mr. Basketball award. His remarkable skills attracted

*James playing for St. Vincent-St. Mary High School in 2003, his senior year.
The crowds were so big that the team had to play at college facilities
to accommodate the spectators.*

national attention. In February 2002 the 17-year-old James appeared on
the cover of *Sports Illustrated* under the caption "The Chosen One." The
accompanying article described him as a "basketball genius" and predicted
that he would be the first player selected in the NBA draft. Los Angeles
Lakers star Shaquille O'Neal showed up to watch one of his high school
games and stuck around to talk with the young star afterward. "He said I

was going to be good, and to keep up the good work," James remembered. "As a junior in high school at the time, that sticks with you."

All the hype created a distraction for James and his teammates, however, and they fell short in their pursuit of a third consecutive state championship. "We didn't respect the game of basketball," he admitted. "When we got to the last game of the season, the championship, we got beat." But the heartbreaking loss helped them put things in perspective and get back on track for the following year. "We rededicated ourselves to the game, we approached the game the right way, and good karma came back to us," James noted.

During James's senior season in 2002-03, the Fighting Irish had to play their home games at the University of Akron in order to accommodate the crowds that wanted to see him play. Several St. Vincent-St. Mary games were nationally televised on cable sports network ESPN. "Now that I look back on it, I'm like, 'Wow, that was huge,'" James stated. "We were one of the first [high school teams] to start it all up, doing nationally televised games, traveling the U.S., taking planes to big tournaments." James lived up to the high expectations by averaging 31.6 points, 9.6 rebounds, 4.6 assists, and 3.4 steals per game. He led his team to a 25-1 record and another state title, as well as the *USA Today* National High School Championship.

James received a number of prestigious honors at the conclusion of his senior season. He claimed his third Mr. Basketball award, was named the national High School Player of the Year by *Parade Magazine* and *USA Today*, and was honored as a McDonald's High School All-American. Shortly before James graduated from St. Vincent-St. Mary in the spring of 2003, he announced that he would forego college basketball and make himself eligible for the NBA draft. Although few people doubted that he had the talent to play in the NBA, his decision generated a great deal of debate. Some people questioned the wisdom of NBA rules allowing young players to skip college and turn professional straight out of high school. They claimed that playing college basketball helped young players mature and gave them tools to make better decisions about their future.

To support this claim, critics pointed to some questionable decisions that had been made by James and his family. For example, Gloria James bought her son an $80,000 Hummer sport-utility vehicle—complete with built-in TV screens and a custom leather interior embossed with his nickname, "King James"—as an early graduation present. Since her struggles as a single mother were well known, many people wondered how she could afford such a lavish gift. Some speculated that James had violated the rules that prohibited amateur athletes from accepting money or gifts based on their potential future earnings and marketability. Following an investigation, the Ohio High School Athletic Association ruled the vehicle acceptable since Gloria James had obtained loans to purchase it. But the investigators suspended James for one game for improperly accepting two vintage jerseys worth an estimated $850 from a Cleveland store owner.

CAREER HIGHLIGHTS

NBA—The Cleveland Cavaliers

The controversy surrounding James's finances ended when he was selected as the top pick in the 2003 NBA draft by the Cleveland Cavaliers. He signed a four-year, $18.8 million contract with the team. He also arranged several major endorsement deals with large companies, including a seven-year, $90 million contract with Nike that was believed to be the most lucrative ever awarded to an athlete. At the age of 19, James was expected to resurrect the Cavaliers franchise—which had posted a dismal 17-65 record the previous year—and bring new fans and energy to the NBA. He remained calm under the intense pressure and expressed confidence in his ability to turn his hometown team into a contender. "This is going to be great," he stated. "We're finally going to get more life in this city."

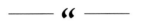

"I just wanted to be on the Olympic team and have the experience," James said after the 2004 Olympics. "Everything on the court I did not expect, but I think I'd do it again."

During his rookie season in 2003-04, James somehow managed to exceed the high expectations that had greeted his arrival in the NBA. He put the league on notice by scoring 25 points and handing out 9 assists in his first professional game. He went on to start 79 games that season and average 20.9 points, 5.5 rebounds, 5.9 assists, and 1.65 steals per game. During a game against the New Jersey Nets in March 2004, he scored 41 points to become the youngest player ever to score more than 40 in a game. James's strong performance helped the Cavs double their number of victories from the previous season to finish with a 35-47 record. Although Cleveland missed the playoffs by one game, James easily claimed the NBA Rookie of the Year award.

During the 2004 offseason, James became the youngest male basketball player ever to compete in the Summer Olympic Games. As a member of

Airborn in 2004, winding up for a breakaway dunk against the Los Angeles Lakers.

Team USA, he joined a group of fellow NBA stars that included Allen Iverson, Carmelo Anthony, and Tim Duncan. The American "Dream Team" arrived in Athens, Greece, as heavy favorites to win the gold medal. After all, Team USA had earned an impressive 109-2 record against international competition and won three Olympic gold medals since the United States first allowed professional basketball players to compete in 1992. Limited practice time and internal bickering made it difficult for the 2004 players to come together as a team, however, and the Americans had to settle for a bronze medal. "I just wanted to be on the Olympic team and have the experience," James said afterward. "Everything on the court I did not expect, but I think I'd do it again."

James continued to prove he belonged in the NBA during the 2004-05 season. He scored 56 points during a game against the Toronto Raptors to become the youngest player ever to score more than 50 in a game. He was also named a starter on the NBA All-Star Team. In just his second NBA season, James ranked third in the league in scoring with an average of 27.2 points per game, while adding 7.0 rebounds, 7.2 assists, and 2.21 steals. The Cavs started the season strong with a 31-21 record, but then spiraled downward to post an 11-19 record over the last 30 games. Although Cleveland achieved its first winning record since 1998 at 42-40, the Cavs failed to make the playoffs. Some observers argued that James needed to speak up and take more of a leadership role if he hoped to lead the Cavs into the postseason.

Leading His Team to the Playoffs

During the 2005-06 season James emerged as one of the most dominant players in the NBA. Appearing in just his second All-Star Game, he scored 29 points and became the youngest player ever to be named the contest's Most Valuable Player. He went on to post amazing season averages of 31.4 points, 7.0 rebounds, 6.6 assists, and 1.56 steals per game. With James leading the way, the Cavs posted an impressive 50-32 record to finish second in the Central Division of the Eastern Conference and earn a spot in the playoffs. The Cavs defeated the Washington Wizards in the first round, but lost a tough, seven-game series to the Detroit Pistons in the conference semifinals.

At the conclusion of the 2006 season, the 21-year-old James surprised many observers by firing his agent and forming his own company, LRMR Marketing, with three of his longtime friends. Although the foursome lacked business experience, they hired top-notch lawyers and accountants to assist them. James also made friends with billionaire investor Warren Buffett, who

James led his team to the 2007 Eastern Conference Finals, where they beat the Detroit Pistons in six games to reach the NBA Finals for the first time in franchise history. Here, James is pressured by Chris Webber (84) and Tayshaun Prince (22).

provided him with financial advice. James and his colleagues negotiated a three-year, $10.8 million contract extension with the Cavaliers. His NBA salary made up just a small portion of his overall earnings, however, which included more than $100 million in endorsement deals with Nike, Sprite, Powerade, Upper Deck, Bubblicious, and other companies.

In James's fourth pro season in 2006-07, he became the undisputed leader of his team, both on the court and in the locker room. He made his third consecutive appearance in the All-Star Game and scored 28 points for the Eastern Conference team. Posting season averages of 27.3 points, 6.7 rebounds, 6.0 assists, and 1.6 steals per game, James led the Cavs to another 50-32 record and second place finish in the division. Cleveland knocked out the Washington Wizards in the first round of the playoffs, then beat the New Jersey Nets in the second round to advance to the Eastern Conference Finals.

James and his teammates faced the Detroit Pistons, a tough, playoff-seasoned team full of talented veterans. Few people believed that the relatively inexperienced Cavs could prevail in a seven-game playoff series. The Pistons won the first two games, but Cleveland surprised many fans by coming back to win the next two. In Game 5, James turned in what broadcaster Marv Albert described as "one of the all-time performances in NBA history." He was an unstoppable force on the court, scoring 48 points—including 29 of his team's last 30—to lift the Cavs to victory in a double-overtime thriller. "That was the single best game I've ever seen at this level in this atmosphere, hands down," Cleveland Coach Mike Brown said afterward. The Cavaliers went on to eliminate the Pistons in six games to reach the NBA Finals for the first time in franchise history. James could not re-create the magic in the Finals, however, and the Cavs were swept in four games by the San Antonio Spurs.

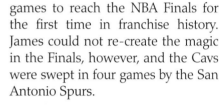

"It's hard for me to congratulate somebody after you just lose to them," James conceded. "I'm a winner. It's not being a poor sport or anything like that. If somebody beats you up, you're not going to congratulate them. That doesn't make sense to me. I'm a competitor."

James had another outstanding season in 2007-08. He became the youngest player in NBA history to score 10,000 career points, surpassed 10,389 points to become the Cavaliers' all-time leading scorer, and scored 27 points to be named Most Valuable Player of the All-Star Game. James also led the NBA in scoring average with 30.0 points per game, while adding 7.9 rebounds, 7.2 assists, and 1.8 steals. The Cavs struggled with injuries to key players for part of the season, then made a big trade in February to bring in such veteran players as Ben Wallace, Joe Smith, Wally Szczerbiak, and Delonte West. Although Cleveland finished the season with a 45-37 record, the Cavs seemed well-positioned to make some noise in the playoffs.

After eliminating the Washington Wizards in the first round, the Cavs faced the Boston Celtics in the Eastern Conference Semifinals. In a grueling playoff series, the two teams battled to a 3-3 tie. The deciding Game 7 turned into a scoring duel between James and Celtics veteran Paul Pierce. Although James outscored Pierce 45-41, the Celtics prevailed and went on to win the NBA title. "I did everything I could to get us over the hump," James said afterward. "Paul Pierce made some spectacular plays. He just willed his team to victory."

Although his fifth pro season ended in disappointment, James was determined to continue improving his game. "We had a great season, but I knew that I could get better, and I took it as a challenge to get better," he stated. "In the summer I dedicated myself to working hard so I could come in and be successful every night." Part of his summer workout regimen included playing in the 2008 Summer Olympic Games in Beijing, China. James joined an American team that had undergone major changes following the embarrassment of 2004. Team USA coaches took their time in selecting a roster of players who would work well together, then made sure that they got plenty of practice as a team. The changes paid off, as the American "Redeem Team" won all eight games in the Olympic tournament in convincing fashion to bring home a gold medal.

Earning MVP Honors

Over the course of the 2008-09 season, James "catapulted himself from among the elite of today's NBA players into the mix of all-time greats," according to Sean Deveney of *Sporting News.* He played in his fifth consecutive All-Star Game, shot a career high .489 from the field and .780 from the free-throw line, and led the NBA with seven triple-doubles (games in which he posted double-digit numbers in three statistical categories). James's stellar season averages of 28.4 points, 7.6 rebounds, 7.2 assists, and 1.69 steals per game helped him earn the NBA's Most Valuable Player Award.

James led the Cavaliers to a league-best 66-16 record to earn the top seed in the playoffs. Cleveland swept past the Detroit Pistons and the Atlanta Hawks in the first two rounds to reach the Eastern Conference Finals. Although James averaged an incredible 35.3 points per game throughout the playoffs, the Cavaliers lost a tough, six-game series to the Orlando Magic. At the conclusion of Game 6, a disgusted James walked off the court without shaking hands with his opponents or speaking with the media. "It's hard for me to congratulate somebody after you just lose to them," he explained later. "I'm a winner. It's not being a poor sport or anything like that. If somebody beats you up, you're not going to congratulate them. That doesn't make sense to me. I'm a competitor." Many basketball analysts, however, dismissed James's words as a poor excuse for unsportsmanlike behavior.

When the 2009-10 NBA season got underway, James continued to make his case for being the best player in the league. He averaged an amazing 29.7 points, 8.6 assists, and 7.3 rebounds per game during the regular season and made the All-Star Team for the sixth straight year. "He's incredible," said NBA Hall of Famer George Gervin. "The combination of speed

The Cavaliers made it to the Eastern Conference playoffs in 2010, but ultimately lost to the Boston Celtics in a crushing defeat that had James ripping off his shirt in frustration at the end of the final game.

and power and athleticism is something you just don't see." In recognition of his performance, James was named NBA Most Valuable Player for the second year in a row. He received 116 out of 123 possible first-place votes from a national panel of sportswriters and broadcasters.

James led the Cavaliers to a 61-21 record and the top seed in the Eastern Conference for the playoffs. Cleveland eliminated the Chicago Bulls in five games in the first round, then moved on to face the Boston Celtics in the conference semifinals. Cleveland fans were excited when the Cavs crushed Boston by 29 points on the road in Game 3 to take a 2-1 series lead. But the Cavs failed to keep the momentum going and lost the next two games in Cleveland. James struggled with a sore elbow that affected his jump shot, and critics claimed that he appeared disinterested at times.

Down 3-2 in the best-of-seven series, however, James turned in an MVP-caliber performance. He posted a triple-double with 27 points, 19 rebounds, and 10 assists. Unfortunately, it was not enough to save the Cavs from elimination. As the final seconds ticked off the clock of the disappointing Game 6 defeat, James ripped off his Cleveland jersey in frustration. "I guess you have to go through a lot of nightmares before you find your dream," he said afterward. Some analysts blamed the Cavs' unexpectedly early playoff exit on the lack of support James received from his teammates. "Anyone with an ounce of basketball knowledge can see the Cavaliers' playoff shortcomings for what they really are," Drew Sharp wrote in the *Detroit Free Press.* "It doesn't matter if you're the greatest player of the day, you're never going to win a best-of-seven playoff series if you're the best player on the floor, but the next three or four best are on the opposing team."

Looking to the Future

By the time James completed his seventh NBA season, he was still only 25 years old. Yet he has already scored more than 15,000 points and posted career averages of 27.8 points, 7.0 rebounds, 7.0 assists, and 1.7 steals per game. To the amazement of many analysts, James seems to keep improving his game with each passing year. He has addressed problems with his shooting mechanics, improved his defensive play, and grown more vocal on the court with his teammates and coaches.

In addition to his outstanding individual contributions, however, James has also shown a remarkable ability to elevate the play of his teammates. His court vision and intelligence enable him to consistently rank among the best playmakers in the league, even though he is also among the top scorers. "When I'm on fire, I can go for a lot of points," he acknowledged. "But getting my teammates involved is good for us in the long run. I can't do it by myself."

James's contract with the Cavaliers was set to expire on July 1, 2010. As that date approached, his future became the subject of intense speculation. Some observers believed that he would remain in Cleveland and try to bring an NBA title to his hometown. The Cavaliers had tried to surround him with talented players during the 2009-10 season—adding Shaquille

O'Neal and Antawn Jamison—in an effort to convince him that the franchise was serious about winning. Following the Cavs' disappointing exit from the playoffs, Cleveland owner Dan Gilbert promised to make whatever other changes were needed to capture an NBA championship.

But many observers believed that James would move on to a new team that plays in a bigger market, such as the New York Knicks, the New Jersey Nets, or the Miami Heat. These teams made roster moves in 2009-10 designed to free up salary room so that they could offer him a blockbuster contract. James insisted that he would choose a team based on where he would have the best chance of winning an NBA title. "The only reason I do what I do on the court is to compete for an NBA championship," he declared. "I understand that, until I win that, I won't go down as one of the greatest players to play this game. Individual accolades definitely come into account, but team is what it's all about. That's my only goal right now."

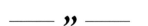

> *"The only reason I do what I do on the court is to compete for an NBA championship," James declared. "I understand that, until I win that, I won't go down as one of the greatest players to play this game. Individual accolades definitely come into account, but team is what it's all about. That's my only goal right now."*

Media speculation about his plans became intense in early summer, as sports commentators and fans wondered where James would choose to go. He ultimately announced that he would join the Miami Heat, along with Chris Bosh. The Heat also re-signed Dwyane Wade. Cleveland fans were devastated by the decision, but Miami fans were thrilled and eager to see what the new powerhouse team could accomplish. James made this announcement to fans on his web site: "Next year, I will be playing for the Miami Heat. I would like to thank all of my fans for supporting me and I am looking forward to seeing you guys next season as I chase the NBA Championship."

HOME AND FAMILY

James has two sons with his longtime girlfriend, Savannah Brinson. LeBron James Jr. was born in 2004, and Bryce Maximus James was born in 2007. The family lives in a luxurious home in the suburbs of Akron. "I love [fatherhood] and everything that comes with it," James declared. "The best

James with his family: his girlfriend, Savannah Brinson, left; his son, LeBron Jr.;
his mother, Gloria James; and his son, Bryce.

thing is they know who I am. My sons call me Daddy. I see them run around and smile and have fun. They live stress-free." He also remains close to his mother, Gloria, and sports a large tattoo in her honor. "My mother is my everything," he stated. "Always has been. Always will be."

HOBBIES AND OTHER INTERESTS

When he has time to relax, James can often be found playing video games. "I love video games. I'm a video game-aholic," he admitted. "All the guys I grew up with come to the house and every day, all day, we just play video games."

In addition to his remarkable talents on the basketball court, James is well known for the elaborate routines and rituals he performs before every game. During pre-game warm-ups, for instance, he always takes an underhand shot from half court and forms the numbers 3-3-0 with his fingers to symbolize Akron's area code. When James is introduced at the start of a game, he always shakes hands with a lifelong friend at courtside before he runs out onto the floor. Prior to tipoff, he always takes a handful of chalk from a bag near the bench and tosses it into the air before pointing to fans in the upper deck. Finally, he always takes the game ball from the referee and checks it over just before the game begins. "It gets me ready to get out and do what I do best," James explained of his pre-game rituals, "and that's to go out there and play basketball at a high level."

James is also active in volunteer work and community service in the Akron and Cleveland areas. He and his mother started a nonprofit organization called the James Family Foundation to help needy children and support youth programs. The foundation donates 1,000 backpacks full of school supplies each fall and also sponsors an annual fundraiser called the King for Kids Bike-a-thon.

WRITINGS

Shooting Stars, 2009 (with Buzz Bissinger)

HONORS AND AWARDS

Ohio Mr. Basketball (Associated Press): 2001-2003
Gatorade Player of the Year: 2002, 2003
High School Boys Basketball Player of the Year (*Parade Magazine*): 2002, 2003
High School Boys Basketball Player of the Year (*USA Today*): 2002, 2003
McDonald's High School Basketball All-American: 2003
NBA Rookie of the Year: 2004
Olympic Men's Basketball: 2004, bronze medal; 2008, gold medal (with Team USA)
NBA All-Star Team: 2005-2010
NBA All-Star Game Most Valuable Player: 2006, 2008
NBA Most Valuable Player: 2009, 2010
BET Sportsman of the Year Award (Black Entertainment Television): 2010

FURTHER READING

Books

Biography Today Sports, Vol. 12, 2004
Christopher, Matt. *On the Court with ... LeBron James,* 2008 (juvenile)
Freedman, Lew. *LeBron James: A Biography,* 2008 (juvenile)
Jacobs, L.R. *LeBron James: King of the Court,* 2009 (juvenile)
James, LeBron, and Buzz Bissinger. *Shooting Stars,* 2009
Morgan, David Lee. *The Rise of a Star: LeBron James,* 2003
Savage, Jeff. *Amazing Athletes: LeBron James,* 2005 (juvenile)

Periodicals

Current Biography Yearbook, 2005
Detroit Free Press, May 15, 2010, p.B1
Fortune, Dec. 10, 2007, p.100
New York Times, Feb. 12, 2010, p.B11; Mar. 4, 2010, p.B13
Sporting News, Dec. 20, 2004, p.18
Sports Illustrated, Feb. 18, 2002, p.62; Jan. 13, 2003, p.70; Feb. 25, 2005, p.64;
    Apr. 26, 2006, p.46; June 11, 2007, p.38; Nov. 2007, p.52; Feb. 2, 2009, p.34
Sports Illustrated Kids, Jan. 2004, p.27; Feb. 2005, p.18; June 2008, p.20; Nov.
    2009, p.34
Time, Aug. 4, 2008, p.44
USA Today, Feb. 13, 2008, p.C1; Feb. 11, 2010, p.D5

Online Articles

http://espn.go.com/magazine/vol5no26next.html
    (ESPN The Magazine, "Next: LeBron James," Dec. 10, 2002)
http://www.topics.nytimes.com
    (New York Times, "LeBron James," multiple articles, various dates)
http://www.sportsillustrated.cnn.com/vault/
    (Sports Illustrated, "LeBron James," multiple articles, various dates)

ADDRESS

LeBron James
Miami Heat
American Airlines Arena
601 Biscayne Boulevard
Miami, FL 33132

WORLD WIDE WEB SITES

http://www.lebronjames.com
http://www.nba.com/playerfile/lebron_james
http://www.nba.com/heat
http://www.basketball-reference.com

Taylor Lautner 1992-

American Actor
Star of "The Twilight Saga" Movies

BIRTH

Taylor Lautner was born on February 11, 1992, in Grand
Rapids, Michigan. His father, Dan, is a commercial airline
pilot, while his mother, Deb, is a project manager for a soft-
ware company. The oldest of two children, he has a sister,
Makena, who was born in 1999. He comes from a diverse eth-
nic background. "I'm French, Dutch, and German, and part
Native American," he explained. "My mom has some
Potawatomi and Ottawa Indian in her."

YOUTH

One of Lautner's earliest memories is when his family lost their house and all of their possessions in an electrical fire. He was just four years old. Luckily, his dad was away at work and he and his mom were spending the night at his aunt's house when the blaze broke out. "The police called and told us our house had burned down," recalled Lautner. "If my aunt hadn't invited us to sleep over ... well, wow." Afterward, members of his tight-knit community came to the family's aid with donations. "Everyone pulled together for us," he said.

> *When Lautner was just four years old, his house burned down, fortunately when the family was not at home. "The police called and told us our house had burned down. If my aunt hadn't invited us to sleep over ... well, wow."*

At age six, Lautner took an interest in martial arts and began studying karate. When he was seven, he traveled to Louisville, Kentucky, to participate in his first karate tournament. While there, he met a Thai-American martial arts coach named Mike Chaturantabut, commonly known as Mike Chat. Chat is the founder of Xtreme Martial Arts—a discipline that blends gymnastics and martial arts—and an actor best known for his role on the television show "Power Rangers: Lightspeed Rescue." Impressed by Lautner's abilities, Chat invited him to attend an Xtreme Martial Arts training camp. Lautner jumped at the chance. "I fell in love," he said. "By the end of the camp, I was doing aerial cartwheels with no hands." He continued to train with Chat for the next several years. By the time he was 12, he had won three junior championships while representing the United States in World Karate Association competitions around the world.

Lautner's self-confidence blossomed as a result of his accomplishments in the martial arts. At age seven, he was encouraged by Chat to audition for a part in a Burger King commercial, but he did not get the job. Nonetheless, he continued to audition for acting roles by periodically flying out to Los Angeles. "I'd go to an audition in the afternoon, take the red-eye back to Grand Rapids, then go to school," he remembered. "I heard 'no, no, no, no' so many times." His luck began to change when, at age 11, he landed a part in a television commercial for the movie *Rugrats* and a role in the 2001 film *Shadow Fury*. At that point his family decided to move to Hollywood. For the next few years, he worked on such TV shows as "The Bernie Mac

Show," "My Wife and Kids," and "Summerland." He also honed his skills as a voiceover artist on animated programs like "What's New, Scooby Doo?" and the TV special "He's a Bully, Charlie Brown."

EDUCATION

Lautner grew up in Hudsonville, Michigan, just outside of Grand Rapids, and attended Jamestown Elementary School. "He was very bright, very well-liked by his peers," recalled Principal Jack DeLeeuw in the *Detroit Free Press*. City of Hudsonville employee Patty Meyer was impressed by his athletic abilities when he walked across the entire stage on his hands during a school show. "He had such talent," Meyer said in the *Detroit Free Press*. "You could see it right away." After the family moved to southern California, Lautner attended Rio Norte Junior High School and Valencia High School. In 2008, due to his busy acting schedule, he began studying privately. He tested out of high school and started taking online college courses.

When he lived in Michigan, Lautner studied martial arts at Fabiano's Karate in Holland. Marcus Allen, an instructor who studied with him at the time, remembered that he would "practice for hours and hours." "He was very talented, but he had to work for it, just like everybody else has to," Allen told the *Detroit Free Press*. "He would come in on Sundays for at least four hours to practice." He was also active in baseball, which he started playing at age five, and football, which he took up at age eight.

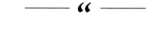

After the success of The Adventures of Sharkboy and Lavagirl 3-D, *Lautner began attracting the attention of fans. "Ten-year-old boys were the ones who first recognized me," he said. "I'd be in the store, and boys would whisper to their moms. Then moms would say, 'Excuse me, are you Sharkboy?'"*

CAREER HIGHLIGHTS

After moving to California, Lautner continued to audition for roles in TV shows and movies. His break came in 2005 when he nabbed the starring role in *The Adventures of Sharkboy and Lavagirl 3-D*. "Oh, we freaked out," he remembered. "My whole family couldn't sleep for, like, a week." He played Max, a boy who draws the adventures of two superheroes named

Lautner's role as Sharkboy was his first break as an actor.

Sharkboy (who was raised by sharks) and Lavagirl in his journal. One day, after being confronted by a bully, Max finds that he has turned into Sharkboy and that his sister has become Lavagirl. Together, the heroes battle Max's bully as well as a villain named Mr. Electric from the Planet Drool. The movie was a hit with young people, and Lautner began attracting the attention of fans. "Ten-year-old boys were the ones who first recognized me," he said. "I'd be in the store, and boys would whisper to their moms. Then moms would say,'Excuse me, are you Sharkboy?'"

In addition, Lautner was cast in a supporting role as actor Eugene Levy's son Eliot in the 2005 film *Cheaper by the Dozen 2,* starring comedian Steve Martin. Working with someone as famous as Martin was another turning point for the young actor. "That's when I stopped looking at movie stars as movie stars, and just looked at them as people," he said. In 2008 he played Christian Slater's son on the short-lived TV show "My Own Worst Enemy."

Twilight

Lautner's next big break came when he was up for the role of Jacob Black in the film *Twilight.* The movie was based on the young adult book of the same name by Stephenie Meyer, the first of four books that have become known as "The Twilight Saga." (For more information on Meyer, see *Biography Today,* April 2010.)

When Lautner auditioned for the role of Jacob Black, he was unaware that the books were so popular. Fans of the series, however, were anxiously anticipating the movie version, and he was right at the center of the whirlwind. "Suddenly, it was all over the Internet. I started hearing about all the hype, all the fans. I thought,'Oh my goodness. If I get this, it'll be huge.' I realized I really want this." Before long, he learned that he got the part. "I was sweating, I was so excited," he confessed.

Twilight is about a teenaged girl named Isabella "Bella" Swan who moves to Forks, Washington, and falls in love with a vampire named Edward Cullen. Bella meets Edward in one of her high school classes and becomes intrigued by his strange ways. When Edward saves her life by stopping an oncoming van with his bare hands, Bella asks her friend Jacob Black about the Cullen family. Jacob, a Quileute Indian, tells her about a local legend concerning vampires who live on animal blood instead of hurting humans. Bella becomes convinced that the Cullens are a family of vampires, and her suspicion proves true when they defend her from a rival vampire clan.

After getting the part of Jacob, Lautner had to become familiar with the books. "I was not a vampire or werewolf fan at all. I'd never even heard

Scenes from "The Twilight Saga": Lautner & Stewart in a scene from New Moon *(top); Lautner in* Twilight *(middle); director Chris Weitz and actors Ashley Greene, Stewart, and Lautner on the set of* New Moon *(bottom).*

of the series," he admitted. "I auditioned for the role, and as soon as I got it, I started reading the books. I'm not a reader, but I really did get hooked on them." In fact, Lautner said, "I actually wasn't much of a book reader at all before the 'Twilight' series. They just draw you in.... They're terrific books." In addition to poring over the novels for character insights, he also studied the cultural background of his character. "Before I went up to Portland [to start filming], I did some research on the Quileute tribe," he said. "I set up a meeting with some real Quileute tribal members in Portland and I got to meet and talk with them. To my surprise, I learned that they are just like me."

Twilight was a huge box office success, and Lautner, along with his co-stars Kristen Stewart (Bella) and Robert Pattinson (Edward), became instant celebrities. He now had to deal with a rapidly growing fan base and intense scrutiny from the media, but he kept it all in perspective. "I don't have time to breathe," he commented at the time. "But it's a lot of fun." At the 2010 People's Choice Awards, *Twilight* won Favorite Movie and Lautner was named Favorite Breakout Movie Actor. His family also became swept up in the *Twilight* enthusiasm. "All of my family lives in Michigan and every family member has read the books, I mean all four of my grandparents, aunts and uncles, everybody! It's just crazy cool that they love it so much!" (For more information on Stewart, see *Biography Today,* Jan. 2010; for more information on Pattinson, see *Biography Today,* Sep. 2009.)

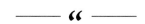

"I was not a vampire or werewolf fan at all. I'd never even heard of ['The Twilight Saga'] *Lautner admitted. "I auditioned for the role, and as soon as I got it, I started reading the books. I'm not a reader, but I really did get hooked on them."*

New Moon

Lautner's character Jacob plays a much larger role in the movie's sequel, *The Twilight Saga: New Moon,* which was released in 2009. In this film, Edward and his family leave Forks out of concern for Bella's safety. Distraught by the loss of Edward, Bella finds herself growing closer to Jacob. She soon learns that he descends from a family of wolves that were transformed into humans by a sorcerer. Jacob vows to protect her against Victoria, a vengeful vampire from a dangerous coven whose threats cause him to shape-shift into a huge werewolf. His transformation leads to a conflict between Edward and Jacob for Bella's affections and escalates the deep-rooted tension between vampires and werewolves in the town of Forks.

The character of Jacob goes through a lot of changes from the first story to the next. So even though Lautner played Jacob in the first film, he still had to prove his ability to tackle the the character's wider physical and emotional range in the sequel. At one point, the producers discussed replacing him because some thought he was too small to play an older version of Jacob. But the fans spoke up on his behalf. According to *Interview* magazine, one fan claimed, "If they don't put him in ... there will be a massive *Twilight* fan attack!" Fortunately, *New Moon* director Chris Weitz saw Lautner's potential. "It was a question of letting him hit his range, which included being angry, resentful, dangerous, and violent," Weitz recounted in *People*. In the end, the producers and director of *New Moon* kept him on board.

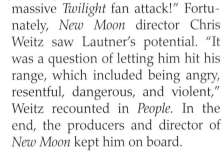

"When I was reading the books, I felt so bad for Jacob," Lautner revealed. "But now that I'm [playing] him, I feel way worse. Bella's toying with Jacob! One moment, she'll want to kiss him, and the next moment, she's ditching him for Edward."

To prepare for the physical demands of playing this chapter in Jacob's life, Lautner had to transform his body. "As soon as I finished filming *Twilight*," he explained, "I got myself a personal trainer, hit the gym five to six days a week, and ate at least 4,000 calories a day." All in all, he gained 30 pounds of muscle for *New Moon*. "At one point, I was going [to the gym] seven days straight. I had put on a lot of weight, and then I started losing it drastically, so I was worried," he stated. "It turned out I was overworking myself. My trainer told me that I couldn't break a sweat, because I was burning more calories than I was putting on." After taking his trainer's advice, he began to notice a difference. "I grew out of a lot of my clothes," he recalled. "I went from a men's small to a men's large."

The love triangle between Edward, Bella, and Jacob is one of the main attractions of the series, and Lautner was sympathetic to his character's situation. "When I was reading the books, I felt so bad for Jacob," he revealed. "But now that I'm [playing] him, I feel way worse. Bella's toying with Jacob! One moment, she'll want to kiss him, and the next moment, she's ditching him for Edward." In addition to portraying the sensitive underdog in the battle for Bella's affection, however, he found that he had to explore

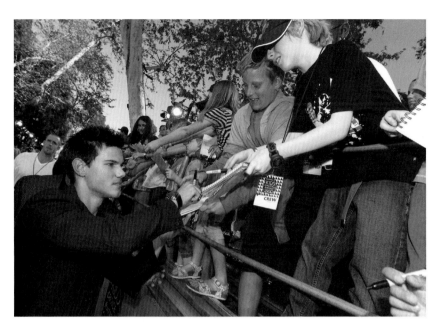

As Lautner's role expanded in New Moon, *he became a fan favorite, as* Twilight *fans pledged allegiance to Team Jacob or Team Edward.*

a complicated personality in the second installment of the series. "There are two sides to Jacob," he explained. "One is like me: friendly, outgoing, and just a nice kid. Then there's the werewolf side, when he's fierce and grumpy." He discovered that playing Jacob in the sequel was almost like playing two roles at the same time: "It's like I'm playing a split personality," he noted. "Which is tricky, because sometimes I've had to play pre- and post-transformation Jacob on the same day of filming."

Earning the Respect of Critics, Co-Stars, and Fans

New Moon was another major hit. Lautner proved himself a commanding screen presence, prompting Karen Levy from *InStyle* magazine to claim that his performance in the movie "makes him a leading man in his own right." His co-stars were likewise impressed with his demeanor on the set. "He's very honest, very open," claimed Kristen Stewart. "It definitely says something about him—he puts people at ease."

Lautner, Stewart, and Pattinson enjoy a close working relationship that Lautner feels has strengthened their on-camera chemistry. "[Jacob and Bella] can tell each other everything. So it was very important for me and Kristen to grow very close," he explained. "[We] can talk things through in rehearsals, and if we're out at dinner, we'll just randomly start talking about the scene we're shooting the next day.... If we weren't able to do those things, I don't know where we'd be." As the young actors continue to work together on the *Twilight* series, Lautner appreciates the positive vibe on set. "We're all really good friends now, so that's really cool," he said.

Lautner has admitted that the attention from *Twilight* fans can become overwhelming. "They are very intense, but it's cool that they're so dedicated and so passionate. They're the reason we're here doing this sequel. So I'm thankful for the fans. But, yeah, they're pretty intense." He has one request of "Team Jacob" supporters: "Please, don't ask me to growl," he begged. "Just wait for the movie." Even though he jokes around with his fans, Lautner remains grateful. "The fans would love anybody who played Jacob," he has insisted. "I'm just lucky to be the one who got the chance."

> *"There are two sides to Jacob," Lautner explained. "One is like me: friendly, outgoing, and just a nice kid. Then there's the werewolf side, when he's fierce and grumpy." Playing Jacob in the sequel was almost like playing two roles at the same time: "It's like I'm playing a split personality."*

Eclipse

In 2010, Lautner and his co-stars filmed the third part of the saga, *The Twilight Saga: Eclipse*. This installment is of personal interest to the actor, who has cited *Eclipse* as his favorite novel in the series. "You have Edward and Jacob teaming up to protect Bella. And then there's the love triangle among all three of them. I think that's the ultimate high point of the series," he said. In this film, Bella awaits high school graduation while grappling with the choice to become a vampire or remain mortal and commit to either Edward or Jacob. This choice is even more difficult because she knows that her decision will impact the course of the war between vampires and werewolves. The Cullens band together with their sworn enemies, the wolf pack, to protect Bella. And in the process, Edward and Jacob become allies as they fight against other vampires.

Reviews of the movie were mixed. Some called it a retread of the previous film, criticizing the dialogue, the acting, and the directing. Other critics praised it as the best film yet in the series, particularly the romantic scenes

Jacob and Bella grow closer in Eclipse, *and Bella faces a difficult choice.*

and the exciting action sequences. Critic Betsy Sharkey offered this praise in the *Los Angeles Times*. "*The Twilight Saga: Eclipse* is back with all the lethal and loving bite it was meant to have: The kiss of the vampire is cooler, the werewolf is hotter, the battles are bigger, and the choices are, as everyone with a pulse knows by now, life-changing." Reviewer David Germain from *AP* also recognized the film's appeal: "Meyer's millions of fans know what they want in a good *Twilight* movie, and they are going to love *Eclipse*." Indeed, the fans turned out en masse, with the film breaking all box-office records on its release.

Lautner will reprise his role as Jacob in two additional movies based on the final novel in the series, *Breaking Dawn*. Fans were thrilled to learn that this long novel would be made into two movies, rather than condensed into one. In this episode from the saga, Bella is married and pregnant with a unique, supernatural child. The two films adapted from *Breaking Dawn* are scheduled for release in 2011 and 2012.

Balancing His Professional and Personal Life

Although his role in the *Twilight* series made him a star, Lautner has said that his parents have helped him stay levelheaded. "Because of all that's happening for him, we want him to do normal things," Dan Lautner told the *Grand Rapids Press*. "We give him responsibilities at home—chores he has to do. He gets an allotted allowance and he has to budget it. We're trying to teach him things, so that when he goes out on his own, he'll be prepared." His parents often remind him, "You have no idea what's gonna happen tomorrow, so enjoy today. Have fun." Lautner has taken heed of his parents' advice. "It's important to maintain as much normalcy as possible," he said. "Staying true to yourself and spending time with the people you did before, your family and friends. But sometimes it's hard and you definitely have to make adjustments."

———— *"* ————

When he's not busy working on a film, Lautner spends his downtime playing football. "It's my indulgence," he admitted. "I've played it my whole life. I always need to have a football in my hand. Like, whenever I'm on set, I'm always holding a ball. If I get a break from shooting, I throw it around with somebody."

———— *"* ————

Lautner readily admits he is enjoying his success. "I'm having the time of my life," he said. "[The *Twilight*] franchise has allowed me to do what I want to do, meet new people and travel the world." At the same time, he acknowledges the pressures of being a celebrity. When he visited a bookstore near his hometown for the release of *Breaking Dawn* (the final book in the *Twilight* series), he thought he would just put in a brief appearance. Things did not go as planned, however; he ended up signing books for his female fans until 2:00 a.m. "I didn't realize 1,000 girls were gonna be there," he laughed. "I would feel miserable if I left and there were still 100 girls who had been waiting two hours to get my autograph."

Lautner found himself in the public eye once again when he took a supporting role in the 2010 romantic comedy *Valentine's Day*. The movie features a series of interconnected stories about love that all take place on Valentine's Day—some funny, some sad, some poignant, some uplifting. The star-studded cast included Jessica Alba, Jessica Biel, Bradley Cooper, Jamie Foxx, Jennifer Garner, Anne Hathaway, Ashton Kutcher, Queen Latifah, George Lopez, Julia Roberts, and Taylor Swift, among others. "I've only really done one comedy before … and that's why I wanted to be a part of this," Lautner explained. "I wanted to challenge myself to something new, and there's not a better way to do that than with [director] Garry Marshall." Lautner played Willy—the star athlete

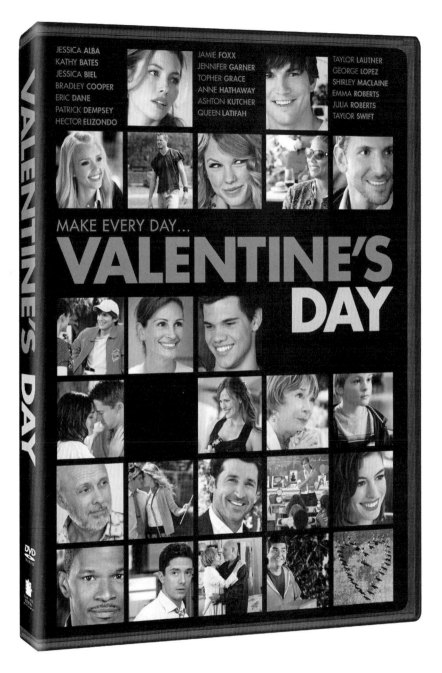

Lautner was part of an all-star cast in the romantic comedy Valentine's Day, *in which he appeared opposite Taylor Swift.*

on the high school track team—opposite country music sensation Taylor Swift—who played his girlfriend. Their scenes were some of the funniest parts of the movie. Although speculation swirled regarding the pair's brief off-screen romance, Lautner refused to discuss his private life, saying only that Swift is "an amazing girl." When asked what kind of girl he likes to hang out with, he said, "Someone who can be a dork. I don't want anybody too uptight and trying to impress me. If they're outgoing and fun, then that works for me." He also commented, "I'm definitely more for the girl who can smile and laugh all the time and just have a good time!"

HOME AND FAMILY

As his career continues to grow, Lautner remains close to his sister, Makena. "[She] looks up to me, but I also look up to her in a way.… I'm probably going to be one of those brothers who are watching her with boys, which she's probably not going to like too much," he admitted.

Even though he spends most of his time away from his home and family in Michigan, Lautner goes back whenever he has the chance. "I miss the seasons, the green, the lakes. But I miss Hudsonville ice cream the most," he said, referring to the popular brand made in his hometown. "I've looked into getting it shipped to me, but I don't know how they'd do it." He also speaks fondly of the attitude of the people in Michigan, saying that "people are way more down-to-earth."

HOBBIES AND OTHER INTERESTS

When he's not busy working on a film, Lautner spends his downtime playing football. "It's my indulgence," he admitted. "I've played it my whole life. I always need to have a football in my hand. Like, whenever I'm on set, I'm always holding a ball. If I get a break from shooting, I throw it around with somebody." Lautner is a fan of the University of Michigan Wolverines football team and the Detroit Lions, citing Barry Sanders of Detroit Lions fame as one of his all-time favorite players. He is also a hockey fan. In June 2009, he was spotted attending the Stanley Cup finals and rooting for the Detroit Red Wings.

Lautner has confessed to a hearty appreciation of simple food. "I love my steak—no sushi, blue cheese, coconut or beets for me. My trainer actually gets on me, saying, 'You need to start eating chicken; stop eating that red meat!' But I can't help it. I am a steak-and-burger kind of guy." He also loves Mexican and Chinese cuisine.

SELECTED CREDITS

"The Twilight Saga"

Twilight, 2008
The Twilight Saga: New Moon, 2009
The Twilight Saga: Eclipse, 2010

Other Films

The Adventures of Sharkboy and Lavagirl 3-D, 2005
Cheaper by the Dozen 2, 2005
Valentine's Day, 2010

HONORS AND AWARDS

Teen Choice Awards: 2009, Choice Movie Fresh Face Male, for *Twilight;*
    2010 (four awards), Choice Movie Actor: Fantasy, Choice Male Hottie,
    Choice Red Carpet Fashion Icon—Male, Choice Smile
People's Choice Awards: 2010 (two awards), Favorite Breakout Movie
    Actor and Favorite On-Screen Team (with Kristen Stewart and Robert
    Pattinson), for *Twilight*
Nickelodeon Kids' Choice Awards: 2010 (two awards), Favorite Movie
    Actor and Cutest Couple (with Kristen Stewart), for *The Twilight Saga:
    New Moon*

FURTHER READING

Books

Leavitt, Amie Jane. *Taylor Lautner,* 2010 (juvenile)
Ryals, Lexi. *Taylor Lautner, Breaking Star: An Unauthorized Biography,* 2009
    (juvenile)

Periodicals

Entertainment Weekly, Aug. 21, 2009, p.34; Nov. 20, 2009, p.30; Mar. 12,
    2010, p.14; July 2, 2010, p.30
Girl's Life, Dec. 2009, p.42
InStyle, Dec. 2009, p.157
Interview, Aug. 2009, p.62
People, Nov. 30, 2009, p.35
Teen Vogue, Oct. 2009, p.130

Online Articles

http://www.mediablvd.com
    (MediaBlvd Magazine, "Taylor Lautner & Edi Gathegi Discuss Their
    Roles in *Twilight,*" Oct. 20, 2008)

http://www.mtv.com
(MTV, "*Twilight* Actor Taylor Lautner Is Eager To Deliver 'Naked' Line, Master Driving," May 20, 2008)
http://www.people.com/people/taylor_lautner
(People, "Top 25 Celebs: Taylor Lautner," multiple articles, various dates)
http://www.people.com
(People, "Taylor Lautner Growing (Literally) with the *Twilight* Franchise," June 1, 2009)
http://www.seattlepi.com
(Seattle Post-Intelligencer, "Taylor Lautner Talks *New Moon* and *Valentine's Day*," Nov. 19, 2009)
http://movies.yahoo.com
(Yahoo, "Taylor Lautner," no date)

ADDRESSES

Taylor Lautner
William Morris Agency
One William Morris Place
Beverly Hills, CA 90212

Taylor Lautner
Luber Roklin Entertainment
8530 Wilshire Blvd., 5th Floor
Beverly Hills, CA 90211

WORLD WIDE WEB SITES

http://www.twilightthemovie.com
http://www.stepheniemeyer.com/twilightseries.html

Chuck Liddell 1969-

American Mixed Martial Arts Fighter
Former UFC Light Heavyweight World Champion,
known as "The Iceman"

BIRTH

Chuck Liddell was born in Santa Barbara, California, on December 17, 1969. His mother was Charlene Liddell Fisher, a single mom who worked for the county social services office but frequently took odd jobs to help support her family: Chuck, his older sister Laura, and his two younger brothers, Sean and Dan. Liddell's parents divorced when he was young and his father was not around while Chuck was growing up.

Instead, he found a male role model in his maternal grandfather and namesake, Charles Liddell. Chuck's grandparents helped their daughter raise their grandchildren after the high cost of living forced his mother to move the family in with her parents.

YOUTH

Liddell was a determined person even when he was very young. When he was a toddler, he began collapsing while walking and sometimes while standing; a doctor diagnosed faulty hip joints that couldn't keep his leg bones in their sockets. Although the doctor suggested braces as a treatment, they would have immobilized the toddler's legs, leaving him unable to walk for a time. Liddell's mother was afraid this would damage her young son's development and elected to give him physical therapy instead. For a year and a half she gave young Chuck two sessions of therapy almost every day. Although these sessions were very painful, by the time Liddell was three he could move around normally, except for a slight hitch in his gait.

Liddell enjoyed growing up with his grandma and "Pops" around. His grandfather taught him and his siblings to box when they were young, believing they should know how to defend themselves. His extended family also challenged the kids to learn, giving them regular vocabulary words and discussing politics around the dinner table. Liddell became a good student at school, involved in Boy Scouts and the chess club as well as athletics.

At the age of 12, Liddell discovered martial arts through the television show "Kung Fu Theatre." "They had demonstrations on every show and it got me really interested," he recalled. "I'd go to the library and look at all the books." His mother finally enrolled him at the dojo (a karate studio or school) of Jack Sabat, where Liddell studied the Koei-Kan style of karate. The school emphasized effective combat techniques, including striking methods and pressure points. Liddell loved learning and perfecting moves. "For me, it was never about getting the next level of belt," he said. "I just wanted to learn." He especially loved sparring and started out fighting with protective gear. He considered himself a "gym rat" and spent a lot of time analyzing which techniques were effective. At age 14, as a green belt, he came in second at a national

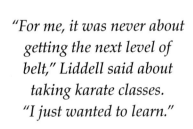

"For me, it was never about getting the next level of belt," Liddell said about taking karate classes. "I just wanted to learn."

karate competition. He loved competing and at his dojo he would fight anyone, no matter how much older or bigger they were. As he remembered, "the bigger and more painful the challenge, the more I wanted to do it."

EDUCATION

Liddell attended San Marcos High School in Santa Barbara, California, where he was a standout athlete and excellent student. He was a starter on the school's football team all four years; although he was "small and scrawny" until he filled out between the ages of 15 and 16, he didn't let anyone out-

Liddell while a wrestler at Cal Poly.

work him in practice or outplay him on the field. He played both center and linebacker on the football team, and in many games he was on the field for every play except for punts. His coach wanted him to take up another sport to keep in shape during the off-season, so Liddell chose wrestling. He was a natural at the sport, finishing third in a state tournament his junior year, mainly because of his superior conditioning. He also continued to study karate during high school. He was judged ready to test for black belt at 16, but he held off until he was an adult at his mother's request.

Liddell graduated from San Marcos High in 1988. He earned wrestling scholarships to several schools, but wanted to play football as well. When he was offered the chance to walk on the football team at California Polytechnic State University in San Luis Obispo, he decided to enroll there. He played football for a year, then decided to focus on wrestling so he wouldn't have to keep adjusting his weight for the different sports. He wrestled for four years and majored in accounting, eventually earning his Bachelor of Arts (BA) degree from Cal Poly in 1995. The university inducted him into their Athletics Hall of Fame in 2009.

CAREER HIGHLIGHTS

From Kickboxing to Mixed Martial Arts

As a graduation present to himself, Liddell got his scalp tattooed with the Japanese characters for Koei-Kan, which means "house of peace and prosperity" and is the name of the style of karate he practices. He got his scalp tattooed because he figured he could cover it with hair when he needed to apply for a regular job, but he didn't look for accounting work after graduation. He had worked as a bartender and bouncer during his college years and continued those jobs while he considered what he really wanted to do. He loved to fight and was good at it; he had gotten into fights on the street since high school, and he usually came away the winner. "I didn't start anything," he noted. "But I never made it too easy for a guy to back away." Still, he wasn't sure how he could make a living at fighting, besides teaching the occasional class at local dojos. After a college wrestling buddy went to Las Vegas to try professional kickboxing, Liddell eventually joined him at the gym of former champion Nick Blomgren.

Liddell began studying the Muay Thai style of fighting, which allows strikes from the elbows and knees, and started competing professionally. He made a steady living fighting on the weekends and bartending and teaching karate during the week. Then he met trainer John Hackleman, a former kickboxing champion who also had experience in judo and had created his own style of karate, which he called Hawaiian Kempo. Liddell began training at Hackelman's gym in San Luis Obispo, called The Pit, where he focused on conditioning as well as martial arts techniques. His workouts at the Pit taught Liddell that "being mentally tough is not a sometimes thing," he explained. "You don't turn it on and off. If you're not mentally tough in the gym while you are training, then when you're challenged in a fight, you will fold."

Liddell was having success as a professional kickboxer; he eventually ended up with an overall win-loss record of 20-2. This included championships from the United States Muay Thai Association and the World Kickboxing Association, as well as a U.S. title through the International Kickboxing Federation. Liddell was a good draw, bringing in a big audience to his fights, but he rarely earned more than $500 for a fight. His trainer Blomgren thought he should consider competing in the Ultimate Fighting Championship (UFC), a new mixed martial arts (MMA) league. It brought together fighters from different disciplines—including karate, judo, jiujitsu, and wrestling—to fight using both striking and grappling techniques. With its no-holds-barred style, the UFC was gaining fans through pay-per-view broadcasts. To prepare Liddell for MMA fighting, Blomgren sent him to train with John Lewis, a martial arts expert with particular expertise in Brazilian jiu-jitsu. Because of his wrestling experience, Liddell was hard to take down and keep down, but he needed more experience with the wide range of martial arts moves he might encounter in a mixed martial arts match. With Lewis's help, Liddell learned about administering and guarding against submission moves such as joint locks and improved his ability to fight while on the ground.

Starting with the UFC

Although Lewis had connections with the UFC, Liddell couldn't immediately break into the league. He competed in an MMA fight organized by Blomgren, knocking out his opponent with head kicks in the first round. Eventually he found a couple of managers who sent footage of that fight, as well as his kickboxing matches and training sessions, that helped secure him his first UFC fight. In 1998 Liddell debuted at UFC 17 as part of the undercard—an opening act, not the main draw—and was matched against fighter Noe Hernandez. The fight went the full 12 minutes with no knock-outs, and the judges unanimously declared Liddell the winner. Just as important as the victory was the show Liddell put on: he fought aggressively, entertaining the crowd and making him someone to watch in the league.

Liddell couldn't get another UFC fight right away, however, as the league was having trouble finding state athletic organizations that would officially sanction their no-holds-barred style of fighting. In the meantime, the fighter headed to Brazil in August 1998, where he competed in the sixth International Vale Tudo Championship. Not only were the rules looser in Vale Tudo, a MMA-style competition with a long history in Brazil, but a fight going the distance would last a full 30 minutes. Liddell's opponent had won 13 of 15 fights, all by knockout, but the American held his ground and won another unanimous decision. He returned

Working out at the gym taught Liddell that "being mentally tough is not a sometimes thing. You don't turn it on and off. If you're not mentally tough in the gym while you are training, then when you're challenged in a fight, you will fold."

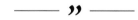

home to San Luis Obispo and in January 1999 opened SLO Kickboxing with Scott Adams, a college wrestling buddy. The gym became successful enough that Liddell was able to quit bartending jobs and focus solely on teaching and training in mixed martial arts.

Liddell returned to fight in UFC 19 against Jeremy Horn, and ended up losing when he encountered a choke hold he didn't know how to counter. But Liddell—who by now had earned the nickname "The Iceman" from his trainer because he never got nervous before a match—wasn't crushed by

Liddell (left) and Tito Ortiz square off at the UFC 47 fight in 2004,
when Liddell knocked out Ortiz in the second round.

his first MMA defeat. "I don't crawl into a shell after a loss," he revealed. "What's the point? I knew I'd get another fight. I knew I'd get better. I knew I'd find a way to win the next time." After the loss to Horn in early 1999, Liddell racked up 10 consecutive MMA victories, seven of them in the UFC. The league had turned a corner in 2001, when it was purchased by Liddell's former manager, Dana White, and brothers Frank and Lorenzo Fertitta. They introduced rules and regulations, standardized equipment, and established a scoring system and medical safeguards. The changes made the sport more acceptable to state athletic commissions, and the UFC was soon able to appear in more venues. They created a crowd-pleasing atmosphere and got the fights returned to cable pay-per-view systems.

Becoming a Title Contender

By this time Liddell was considered a genuine title contender in the UFC light heavyweight division. His upset technical knockout (TKO) of former

NCAA wrestling and UFC champ Kevin Randleman in 2001 gave him the qualifications to take on the then-current UFC champ, Tito Ortiz. It also allowed him to negotiate a new contract that guaranteed him between $25,000 and $45,000 per fight, with the chance to double the money if he won. While waiting for Ortiz to agree to a title shot, he knocked out contender Guy Mezger in a Pride tournament in Japan and earned a TKO against Renaldo Sobral in UFC 40. By mid-2003 Ortiz still hadn't granted him a title fight, so the UFC set up an "interim title" bout between Liddell and Randy Couture, a former UFC champ in both the heavyweight and light heavyweight divisions. Six weeks beforehand Liddell tore a ligament in his knee and had to change his training routine to avoid sharp lateral movements. In UFC 43 Liddell couldn't counter the experienced Couture's wrestling moves and lost by TKO in the third round.

There was only one way for Liddell to get back into title contention: keep fighting. He fought twice more in 2003 on the Pride circuit, winning by knockout against Alistair Overeem and losing by TKO to Quentin "Rampage" Jackson. He attributed the loss to poor training, and decided that in the future he would stick to training at The Pit. "I like being in one gym," he said. "I fight my way. I go to other gyms and train and learn from other places but when I'm training for a fight I train my way and train to fight the way I fight. If I lose I don't blame my camp." The loss to Jackson had one positive, however: it made Tito Ortiz, who had lost a title bout to Couture, finally agree to fight him. The fight, scheduled for UFC 47, would be one of the UFC's highest pay-per-view sellers to that date, and Liddell upped his training workouts in preparation. The work paid off, and Liddell knocked Ortiz out with a series of punches shortly after the start of the second round.

> *"Fighting is like chess, and boxing is like checkers,"* Liddell suggested. *"You have to defend against guys who are coming at you with all sorts of new tactics, new martial arts. You must be aware on different levels."*

By the end of 2004, Liddell was not only one of the top light heavyweight contenders in the UFC, he was one of its most popular stars. UFC president Dana White was still trying to expand the league's audience, however, so he put together a reality show that would bring together 16 potential UFC fighters to battle for a professional contract. The contestants would be split into two teams, and Liddell agreed to coach one of them. Although Liddell and White believed that "The Ultimate Fighter" had great potential, they had difficulty convincing any networks to buy into the program. Finally Spike TV agreed to broadcast the show, although the UFC had to secure advertisers. When TUF debuted in January 2005, nearly 2 million viewers tuned in to the show, a huge number for a cable program. Not only did the show broaden the audience for the UFC, by showing the training that mixed martial arts fighting required, it demonstrated that the sport was more than brawling—it involved skill and strategy. "Fighting is like chess, and boxing is like checkers," Liddell suggested. "You have to defend against guys who are coming at you with all sorts of new tactics, new martial arts. You must be aware on different levels." When the final episode of the series aired, it brought Spike TV its highest ratings ever, over three million viewers.

Claiming the UFC Title

A week after "The Ultimate Fighter" finale scored with audiences, Liddell got another shot at the UFC light heavyweight title in a rematch against Randy Couture. The Iceman trained hard for the match, focusing on strength and stamina and studying their previous bout to come up with a better strategy. At UFC 52 on April 16, 2005, Liddell finally claimed the UFC title by knocking out Couture two minutes into the first round. Over the next two years he successfully defended the title four times, each time by TKO. These victories included one over Jeremy Horn—one of the only three men who had ever beaten him, and a fighter who had never before lost by knockout—as well as rematches against Couture, Sobral, and Ortiz.

The wins were a product of hard work. Liddell's typical training schedule involved workouts three times a day, five times a week, with one extra day off per month to let off steam and party. "If I'm feeling burned out, I go out and get loose and have a good time," he related. "Then I take the day off Sunday and come back on Monday ready to train."

Liddell finally lost his UFC title in May 2007, in a rematch against Quinton "Rampage" Jackson in UFC 71. He attributed the loss to a mistake in technique, not a loss of confidence. "Like both of the other guys I went back and avenged, I think I should have beaten him the first time," Liddell explained. "Afterward, I thought I messed up. I should go out there and be able to beat him." He lost his next match as well, in a split decision against Keith Jardine in UFC 76 in September 2007, before winning a unanimous decision against former Pride league champ Wanderlei Silva in UFC 79 in December 2007. He then lost his next two matches, in UFC 88 to Rashad Evans in September 2008 and in UFC 97 to Mauricio Rua in April 2009, both by knockout. About the 2008 loss to Evans, he noted: "I got a little

Liddell (left) fights Keith Jardine at UFC 76 in 2007.

impatient. I got in a bad position and got caught. I don't think it's because I'm predictable. You know I'm going to come and try to knock you out. But I don't think it's that simple." He planned to change up his strategies and techniques for future matches, a challenge he found interesting: "Discovery is still a draw for me, in the same way it made me want to keep going in karate when I was a teenager," he said. "Fighting is as much about the internal challenge as it is the external battle."

The Face of the Sport

After winning the UFC title in 2004, Liddell's public recognition and celebrity continued to increase. Even after losing the title in 2007, he was still the most recognizable figure in the league, the face of the UFC. He began making appearances as himself in films and on television. He had an extended role in 2007 on an episode of the television series "Entourage," and voiced his own character on "The Simpsons" in 2009. He also tried minor acting roles: in the 2006 television pilot of "Blade: The Series," he made an appearance as a tattoo artist, and in the 2007 film *The Death and Life of Bobby Z*, he played a tough prison inmate named Mad Dog.

Liddell's biggest challenge, however, was appearing on the reality show "Dancing with the Stars" on ABC, taking advantage of a long break between fights. He planned to "go out and be myself and show what kind of people we do have in this sport," he remarked. "I'm sure the reaction will be mixed. My friends are [going to] be excited and I'll never hear the end of it because they'll make fun of me, but it should be fun and I think everyone will like it." Liddell and his dancing partner Anna Trebunskaya lasted four episodes before being voted off the show.

Liddell has spent much of his time traveling and promoting the UFC, but he continues to find celebrity a difficult adjustment. "Even after all this time, I still don't know how to take it," he remarked. "I almost feel like saying, 'sorry.' I love the fact that people appreciate the sport and how tough it is, but it's still strange to be a celebrity." He is known for taking time with his fans, however, especially kids and those in the military and emergency services. "Those fans were there for me when I started, I got involved with them. I appreciate it.... I get to do what I love for a living. If taking a few minutes out of my time is part of the price, great. I try to remember, even when it gets hard, I remember this is the first time this guy gets to meet me. He's excited. I try to give enthusiasm back."

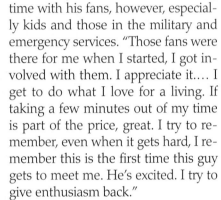

"All I've been doing my whole life is training to compete. It's a hard thing to give up for an athlete. It's hard to stop competing after so many years," Liddell observed. "I'm going to fight as long as my body's working.... I enjoy it that much."

In 2009, as Liddell was inducted into the UFC Hall of Fame, it was announced that he would face off against Tito Ortiz one more time, as opposing coaches on season 11 of "The Ultimate Fighter." He spent six weeks working with other mixed martial artists on the reality TV show. In June 2010, Liddell faced Rich Franklin in UFC 115. It was his first bout since losing to Rua 14 months earlier. In the interim, Liddell had faced criticism that he was no longer willing to work hard at training and that he wasn't showing the self-discipline of an athlete. For UFC 115, though, Liddell was in great shape, with a ripped physique and a better variety of strikes. He appeared to be doing well at the opening, but he was knocked unconscious by a right hook to the face just before the end of the first round and lost by a knockout.

In recent years, some observers have suggested that it was time for Liddell to retire. He has said that he still had enthusiasm for fighting and wasn't ready to retire. "All I've been doing my whole life is training to compete,"

Liddell with dancing partner Anna Trebunskaya on "Dancing with the Stars."

he observed. "It's a hard thing to give up for an athlete. It's hard to stop competing after so many years." He hoped to continue fighting for the foreseeable future. "I'm going to fight as long as my body's working," he noted. "I keep saying another two to four years. And I hope in two years I can say it's still two to four years. I enjoy it that much." For the future, Liddell has suggested that he might become a trainer. "I like the personal interaction. I like working on the finer points, improving the little things that can make a big difference that the younger fighters don't always know about." Whenever he decides to officially retire from fighting, he will likely stay with the UFC in some capacity. "I don't think you could get me away from it," he noted. "I love this sport."

HOME AND FAMILY

Although Liddell has never married, he is the proud father of two children, both born to former girlfriends. Daughter Trista was born in September 1997 to Casey Noland, while son Cade was born in October 1998 to Lori Geyer. Liddell loves spending time with his kids, and has been known to fly in for a single day just to visit. He still lives in San Luis Obispo, where he has a comfortable home that has been profiled on MTV's "Cribs."

HOBBIES AND OTHER INTERESTS

Liddell enjoys the perks of the celebrity lifestyle, particularly the nightlife. He likes to go out to dance or sing karaoke, usually with a group of buddies that has been with him since college. He likes driving fast cars, especially the Ferrari F430 Spider that UFC President White gave to him as a bonus. He is also known for his love of pedicures and likes to paint his toenails, especially in black or even pink.

Liddell makes frequent appearances for various charities. He signed a prototype toy of himself to be auctioned for Special Olympics and was the first mixed martial artist to participate in the charity golf tournament that supports the Lance Armstrong Foundation. The Iceman has also attended Celebrity Fight Night, which helps support the Muhammad Ali Parkinson Center and other charities, and has worked with groups that assist low-income and at-risk youth through martial arts. He is also known to take time to visit young fans with special needs and military veterans.

HONORS AND AWARDS

North American Heavyweight Champion (United States Muay Thai Association): approx. 1996-97

Amateur International Rules U.S. Super Heavyweight Champion (International Kickboxing Federation): 1996-97
World Light Heavyweight Champion (Ultimate Fighting Championship): 2004-07
Guys Choice Awards (Spike TV): 2007, for Most Dangerous Man
Hall of Fame (Ultimate Fighting Championship): 2009

FURTHER READING

Books

Liddell, Chuck, with Chad Millman. *Iceman: My Fighting Life,* 2008

Periodicals

Atlanta Journal-Constitution, Sep. 6, 2008, p.D1
ESPN The Magazine, May 21, 2007
Fight! Magazine, Sep. 2008, p.40
Las Vegas Review-Journal, Aug. 18, 2009
Men's Fitness, Apr. 2007, p.94
Miami Herald, May 24, 2007
MMA United, June 2009, p.28
TapouT Magazine, issue 26, 2008, p.41
USA Today, Sep. 8, 2008, p. C2; Apr. 17, 2009, p.C10; June 11, 2010, p.C15

Online Articles

http://www.mmafighting.com
 (MMA Fighting, "Chuck Liddell: 'Hard for an Athlete to Quit What He's Done His Whole Life,'" Aug. 13, 2009)
http://content.usatoday.com/topics/topic/People/Athletes
 (USA Today, "Chuck Liddell," multiple articles, various dates)

ADDRESS

Chuck Liddell
Zinkin Entertainment
5 River Park Place West, Suite 203
Fresno, CA 93720

WORLD WIDE WEB SITE

http://www.icemanmma.com

MARY MARY
Erica Campbell 1974?-
Tina Campbell 1975?-
American Gospel Singers
Grammy Award-Winning Creators of the Hit
Albums *Thankful* and *The Sound*

EARLY YEARS

Mary Mary is the gospel singing duo of sisters Erica Campbell and Tina Campbell. Although their exact birth dates are not publicized, most sources indicate that Erica Monique Atkins was born in 1974, and Trecina "Tina" Evette Atkins was born in 1975. Later, they both married men with the last name Campbell, though their husbands are not related to each other. Their father, Eddie Atkins, was a postal worker, youth minister, and church choir director before he became a Pentecostal pastor. Their mother, Thomasina Atkins, was a homemaker and church piano player. Erica and Tina have five sisters and one brother.

Erica and Tina grew up in Inglewood, California, a suburb of Los Angeles. Their family was poor and sometimes struggled financially. "We lived on faith," Tina recalled. "Looking back, it's hard to see how we didn't become homeless. Each year our parents were $7,000 short of what was needed and just had to trust God. We ate noodles every day, so we never went hungry. We didn't know we were poor because we had so much love and faith. We had a lot of fun, too. The church was our recreational center." One Christmas was particularly memorable, according to Tina: "Since it's the thought that counts, we gave one another thoughts for Christmas." Erica explained, "What we did is take a piece of paper, and we all wrote down individually what we thought of each sister and the cousins and my mom and dad. Some were funny, and some of them were touching. But we had so much fun, and I don't think we will ever forget that."

>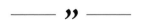
>
> "We lived on faith," Tina recalled. "Looking back, it's hard to see how we didn't become homeless. Each year our parents were $7,000 short of what was needed and just had to trust God. We ate noodles every day, so we never went hungry. We didn't know we were poor because we had so much love and faith. We had a lot of fun, too. The church was our recreational center."

Their parents were strict and kept a close watch over their children's activities. The family was very involved in the church community and attended the Evangelistic Church of God in Christ. As the children of a church choir director and later pastor, the Erica and Tina spent a lot of time at church, basically seven days a week, and gospel music was a constant presence in their life. The Atkins children first sang in their church choir and later went along with their father to sing during his ministry visits to what Erica called "seemingly godforsaken parts of the inner city." The Atkins children were forbidden to listen to any non-gospel music at home, although Erica and Tina were exposed to other kinds of music, including hip-hop and R&B, while at school and in their neighborhood. "We were born and raised in urban communities," Tina explained. "And so what happened in the community was that the sound of the community, the look, the lingo, all of those things—we were exposed to that."

CAREER HIGHLIGHTS

Erica and Tina began their singing careers working separately. They each performed as backup singers with such R&B artists as Brian McKnight, Brandy, Eric Benet, and Kenny Lattimore. Touring with these performers gave them each a chance to develop their talents as well as their independence. In 1995, Erica and Tina both went on tour with the traveling gospel music show *Mama I'm Sorry*. Later, they toured together again with the gospel show *Sneaky*. With these productions, the sisters performed up to eight shows each week.

During these years, Erica and Tina learned a lot about the business side of the music industry. They were able to observe all of the off-stage activities and responsibilities held by performers, including media appearances, interviews, and working with producers and agents. This experience helped Erica and Tina to gain a better understanding of the business. Tina said of these early years, "I won't say that it was our ministry to go sing background with different R&B artists that were singing, you know, about different things [that are] not necessarily Christian, but I do think that that was part of God's plan for us."

Erica and Tina formed the group Mary Mary in 1996. The name Mary Mary is taken from the two women named Mary in the Bible. "It's inspired by the two Marys: Christ's mother, who many people think of as perfect, and Mary Magdalene, who, well, isn't," Tina clarified. "But meeting Jesus caused Mary Magdalene to change her life and become one of his strongest followers. So we tell people it doesn't matter who you are or where you're from, we all can be changed by God's love."

Mary Mary first got a music contract as songwriters. They created songs that were recorded by other performers, including gospel star Yolanda Adams and gospel group 702. Their first big break came in 1998, when their original song "Let Go, Let God" was included on the *Prince of Egypt* movie soundtrack. Their song "Dance" was included on the soundtrack for the movie *Dr. Doolittle* in that same year. Then their next big success came when Yolanda Adams recorded two of their songs, and the album went platinum. These successes lead to a recording contract for Mary Mary in 1999, and Erica and Tina began to work on songs for their own record release.

Mary Mary's debut album, Thankful, *was enjoyed by both Christian and mainstream audiences.*

Thankful

Mary Mary's debut album, *Thankful,* was released in 2000. *Thankful* included mostly original songs written by Erica and Tina, along with versions of the gospel classics "What a Friend We Have in Jesus" and "Wade in the Water." The record blended gospel, R&B, hip-hop, and dance rhythms in a surprising combination that appealed to both Christian and mainstream audiences. Erica described their approach to creating the record, saying, "We wanted to do something different, kind of innovative. We wanted to give the world the gospel according to Mary Mary, which is different from how others have done."

The breakout first single "Shackles (Praise You)" featured a dance beat that propelled it to the top of the Billboard music charts. The song became a Top 10 hit in the U.S., United Kingdom, France, the Netherlands, and Australia.

The video for "Shackles (Praise You)" went into heavy rotation on MTV. A music critic for *People* magazine praised Mary Mary for their "funky hip-hop beats and lush harmonies worthy of Destiny's Child." *Ebony* magazine said that Mary Mary's "voices are [steeped] in soulful intensity, and the songs they sing thump with a thunderous bass that makes you want to let loose and dance." *Thankful* won a Grammy Award for Best Contemporary Gospel Album.

Incredible

Mary Mary's second record, *Incredible,* was released in 2002. With *Incredible,* Mary Mary once again used R&B and hip-hop beats to draw a younger generation of listeners to gospel music. "Gospel tells you about what

"Gospel tells you about what God can do, it tells you the good news of Jesus," Erica remarked. "Because our music is so hip-hop and has an urban feel, a lot of people think, 'Oh, it's inspiriational, it's contemporary.' It can be. But listen to what we're saying in our songs which tell the message of Christ specifically."

God can do, it tells you the good news of Jesus," Erica remarked. "Because our music is so hip-hop and has an urban feel, a lot of people think, 'Oh, it's inspirational, it's contemporary.' It can be. But listen to what we're saying in our songs which tell the message of Christ specifically."

Incredible was a huge hit for Mary Mary, capturing the No. 1 spot on Billboard's Top Christian Album and Top Gospel Album charts at the same time. The record was both a commercial and critical success, earning praise from critics. *Essence* magazine congratulated Mary Mary for their ability to "combine traditional gospel concepts with hip-hop rhythms and R&B balladry to deliver straightforward messages of God's love through every soul-stirring song." A music critic for the *Baltimore Sun* noted that *Incredible* "sounds like an R&B album that just happens to mention Jesus a lot."

After the release of *Incredible,* Mary Mary took a three-year break from recording new music. During this time, Erica and Tina wrote their autobiography, *Transparent,* which was published in 2002. They also appeared in the 2003 musical comedy *The Fighting Temptations.*

Mary Mary and A Mary Mary Christmas

The duo's self-titled third record *Mary Mary* was released in 2005 and debuted in the No. 1 position on the Billboard Gospel Album sales chart.

Mary Mary produced the hit single "Heaven" and once again drew critical acclaim. *People* magazine praised *Mary Mary* for its "decidedly contemporary style that blurs the lines between sacred and secular music." *Ebony* called the record "jubilant" with "enhanced emotional depth, earthy soul, and stronger faith." *Mary Mary* won an American Music Award for Favorite Inspirational/Christian Contemporary Artist, and was nominated for a Grammy Award as Best Contemporary Soul Gospel Album.

Mary Mary's fourth record, *A Mary Mary Christmas*, was released in 2006. This collection includes versions of holiday standards, hymns, and original new Christmas songs written by Mary Mary. As Tina observed, "The CD captures the holiday spirit and the true reason for Christmas. The spirit of it all. All the elements of the season." *A Mary Mary Christmas* was generally well received and praised for its introduction of new contemporary Christmas songs.

The Sound

In 2008, Mary Mary released *The Sound*, their fifth record. *The Sound* became an instant success, reaching No. 1 on Billboard's Gospel chart. It was also Mary Mary's first big crossover hit, rising to the No. 2 spot on Billboard's R&B/Hip-Hop chart. The popularity of *The Sound* with R&B and hip-hop audiences as well as gospel music lovers proved that Mary Mary had a growing fan base. A music reviewer for SoulTracks.com noted that this release was surprising because "Mary Mary can sound so new—and maybe even better—five records into their career." Tina explained, "We try to make sure everything we put out there represents what we represent, that is true to us first—lyrically, creatively, sonically. We want it to be banging, on point. We want it to be respected across the board."

The Sound earned Mary Mary many awards in 2009: they won an NAACP Image Award and a BET Award, both for Best Gospel Artist, and the song "Get Up" won a Grammy Award for Best Gospel Performance and a Dove Award for Urban Recorded Song of the Year. "That song embodies what the whole album is about, Erica revealed. "It asks people 'Why are you waiting? Why do you care what other people think?' It reminds us that your beginning can be whatever you want it to be."

But not everyone was pleased with Mary Mary's performance on *The Sound*. The song "God in Me" caused some controversy among gospel music fans because of its secular subject matter. The lyrics refer to owning flashy cars and designer clothes, unusual topics for a gospel song. And at first, Mary Mary wasn't even sure they wanted to record "God in Me,"

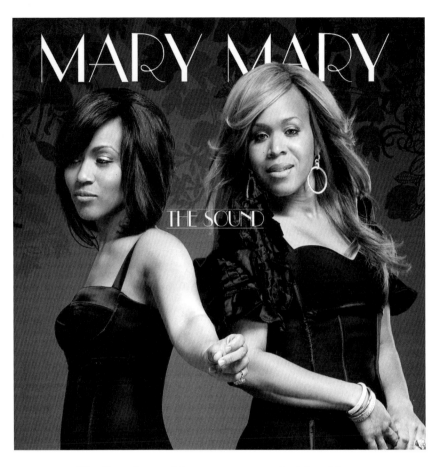

The Sound *was a big crossover success for Mary Mary,*
reaching No. 2 on the Billboard R&B/Hip Hop chart.

Erica recalled. "But when I started paying attention to what it was saying
… this is how, this is why, this is what has enabled me, I was like, 'You got
me!'" Erica said. Ultimately, the song won a lot of admirers: Mary Mary
won the 2010 Grammy Award for Best Gospel Song, a songwriting award,
for "God in Me."

Despite this controversy, *The Sound* has ultimately been received as an uplifting, empowering, and inspirational contribution to contemporary
gospel music. SoulTracks.com called *The Sound* a "treat from beginning to
end and a great reminder that effective praise comes in all forms—and
maybe is even more effective when it simply sounds this good." Tina explained, "The album is about overcoming and thriving. I think this record

is kind of a perfect soundtrack for where America is right now, for what we're going through with the economy and other challenges. We need strong faith in our sovereign God."

Responding to Criticism

Mary Mary's success has drawn some additional criticism over the years. Some people in the gospel music community feel that their music is not true gospel because of their use of secular musical styles. The sisters generally take this criticism in stride and remain confident in their talents. "It's all good; you just have to brush that dirt off your shoulder," Tina remarked. "When we go into the studio we are very true to ourselves. Yes, we are aware of the trends, but we don't force things or try to become something else. We write from our hearts and sing about what we believe in and stay true to who we are."

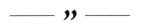

> "Sometimes people think we're a little bit sexy. I don't have a problem with that," Tina said. "Some people in church unfortunately are not aware that we are not supposed to just be there. We're supposed to go out and reach people. And you can't go out with a long white dress on and think they're going to pay attention to you."

Erica and Tina have also been criticized for appearing on stage and in photos wearing form-fitting clothing. "Sometimes people think we're a little bit sexy. I don't have a problem with that," Tina said. "Some people in church unfortunately are not aware that we are not supposed to just be there. We're supposed to go out and reach people. And you can't go out with a long white dress on and think they're going to pay attention to you."

In fact, Erica and Tina use their music to talk about God and Christianity. "We want to encourage people to expect big things of God," Erica stressed. "A lot of people just want a healthy family or to pay their bills, and don't really expect great things from God. We don't want to live just-average Christian lives because we don't serve an average God. He's extraordinary. Of course, we can't just sit back and expect great things; we need to do great things." Tina added, "We represent a great, big God who is excellent, so we like to think that our work represents that, too. God's blessings are new every day. He's blowing our minds every day. We should be able to speak to a new day in a new way."

Erica Campbell (left) and Tina Campbell (right) at the 2009 Grammy Awards, after winning Best Gospel Performance for "Get Up."

Mary Mary has helped to create an updated sound and image for gospel music with their unique combination of traditional gospel themes and elements of R&B, urban, hip-hop, electronica, and dance music. This mix of diverse musical styles has helped Mary Mary bring gospel music to a new audience. "There's always someone who has music that will reach an unchurched audience," Erica commented. "That's definitely the position Mary Mary holds. Growing up, we didn't look at people who didn't go to church any differently from those who did. When it comes to our music, our music is for everyone. Everyone needs to know that God loves them."

Future Plans

Mary Mary has many plans for the future, both in and out of the recording studio. "We don't want to limit ourselves to just singing. All the gifts and all the talents and all the great entrepreneurial ideas that God has given us, we want to use them," Tina said. "I don't care if you're making a statement in fashion, doing movies that reflect who you are, whatever it is that you decide to do outside of just one thing—if God has gifted you, you should do it all to bring Him glory."

Mary Mary has released a bath and beauty line called Be U and plans to develop a clothing line and a series of books, music, and interactive computer games for children. Erica and Tina are also executive producers and featured judges on the BET cable network series "Sunday Best," an "American Idol"-style competition for gospel singers. "We consider ourselves to be unpredictable," Tina said. "We like to think that we're innovative and original so you cannot figure out what our next move is and you can't really define our ability or what you think the expectations are."

MARRIAGE AND FAMILY

In 2000, Tina married Teddy Campbell, a musician and drummer in the "American Idol" band. They have three daughters, Cierra, Laiah, Meela, and one son, TJ. Erica married Warryn Campbell, who is Mary Mary's music producer, in 2001. They have one daughter, Krista. Teddy Campbell and Warryn Campbell share a last name, but they are not related.

Balancing their careers and families is the highest priority for both Erica and Tina. "We try not to be gone more than four or five days at a time," Tina said. "We've got to be there to put our kids to bed, pray with them, and go over homework with them. Parenting is hands-on, and you can't do that through the phone or text messages." Erica added, "If Tina and I are going to be gone for more than four or five days, we bring our families with us. If I'm a public success and a private failure at home, then I've failed. We have to make sure we succeed at home and the only way to do that is love." Erica explained that the support of their families is critical to Mary Mary's success. "Real success starts with all the love you have in your heart. It's about family and having the emotional support of those you love." Tina added, "It can inspire you and catapult you in so many amazing ways. All the money in the world can't help you do that."

RECORDINGS

Thankful, 2000
Incredible, 2002
Mary Mary, 2005
A Mary Mary Christmas, 2006
The Sound, 2008

HONORS AND AWARDS

Dove Awards (Gospel Music Channel): 2001, Urban Album of the Year, for *Thankful* and Urban Recorded Song of the Year, for "Shackles (Praise You)"; 2002, Urban Recorded Song of the Year, for "Thank You"; 2003, Contemporary Gospel Recorded Song of the Year, for "In the Morning"; 2004, Urban Recorded Song of the Year, for "Dance, Dance, Dance"; 2006, Contemporary Gospel Album of the Year, for *Mary Mary*; 2009, Urban Recorded Song of the Year, for "Get Up"

Grammy Awards (Recording Academy): 2001, Best Contemporary Soul Gospel Album, for *Thankful*; 2009, Best Gospel Performance, for "Get Up"; 2010, Best Gospel Song, for "God in Me" (with Warryn Campbell)

Soul Train Music Awards: 2001, Best Gospel Album, for *Thankful*

Stellar Awards (Gospel Music Channel): 2001, Group/Duo of the Year, Contemporary Group/Duo of the Year, New Artist of the Year and Contemporary CD of the Year, for *Thankful*

American Music Awards: 2005, Favorite Contemporary Inspirational Music Artist; 2009, Favorite Contemporary Inspirational Music Artist

BET Awards: 2009, Best Gospel Artist

NAACP Image Awards: 2009, Best Gospel Artist; 2010, Best Song, for "God in Me"

FURTHER READING

Periodicals

Ebony, Sep. 2000, p.100; Dec. 2006, p.50; Jan. 2007, p.86
Essence, Feb. 2004, p.120; Nov. 2008, p.68; Nov. 2009, p.20
Jet, Sep. 23, 2002, p.19; May 11, 2009, p.36
Today's Christian Woman, Mar.-Apr. 2009, p.22

Online Articles

http://www.mtv.com/music/artist/mary_mary/artist.jhtml (MTV, "Mary Mary," undated)
http://www.npr.org/templates/story/story.php?storyId=102868367 (NPR Music, "Mary Mary: Pop-Gospel Disciples," Apr. 10, 2009)

http://www.soultracks.com/mary_mary.htm
  (Soul Tracks, "Mary Mary," undated)
http://www.vh1.com/artists/az/mary_mary/artist.jhtml
  (VH1, "Mary Mary," undated)
http://new.music.yahoo.com/mary-mary
  (Yahoo Music, "Mary Mary," undated)

ADDRESS

Mary Mary
Columbia Records
550 Madison Avenue
New York, NY 10022

WORLD WIDE WEB SITE

http://www.mary-mary.com

Christianne Meneses Jacobs 1971-
Nicaraguan-Born American Writer and Teacher
Creator of Spanish-Language Children's Magazines
Iguana and *¡Yo Sé!*

BIRTH

Christianne Meneses Jacobs was born Christianne Marcelle Meneses Palma on March 28, 1971, in Managua, Nicaragua, a country in Central America located just north of the equator. In Nicaragua, her father, Enrique Meneses Peña, was a lawyer and politician, while her mother, Thelma A. Meneses, worked as a legal secretary. After moving to the United States, both of her parents had jobs checking luggage at the Los Angeles International Airport. She has one younger brother, Enrique M. Meneses.

YOUTH AND EDUCATION

As a young girl growing up in Nicaragua, Meneses Jacobs enjoyed a comfortable life. Her grandfather, Dr. Ildefonso Palma Martinez, was a highly respected lawyer, law professor, and a justice on the Nicaraguan Supreme Court. Her father was a lawyer and the vice-president of the National Liberal Party, which at that time was one of Nicaragua's large political organizations. Meneses Jacobs has described her childhood years as privileged. "I attended private school and ballet lessons. We had domestic servants that performed several jobs: nannies, cook, chauffer, gardener, cleaning, laundry, and ironing." Her whole family, including aunts, uncles, and cousins, took vacations together at the beach, swimming and collecting shells. Iguanas (large tropical lizards) lived in her backyard, and every day around noon they came out to bathe in the hot sun.

> "
>
> *Meneses Jacobs has described her childhood years as privileged. "I attended private school and ballet lessons. We had domestic servants that performed several jobs: nannies, cook, chauffer, gardener, cleaning, laundry, and ironing."*
>
> "

But Meneses Jacobs's childhood experiences were also closely tied to the political situation in Nicaragua during that time. After years of economic instability and accusations of government corruption, civil war broke out in the late 1970s. Meneses Jacobs recalled, "The Sandinista revolution occurred when I was eight years old. I remember the civil war and the attacks on the small towns." The Sandinista National Liberation Front, known as the Sandinistas, fought against the existing government for control of Nicaragua. Fighting quickly spread to towns and cities throughout the country, and many people died.

The existing government was eventually overthrown by the Sandinistas, but this did not end the war. Some Nicaraguans did not support the Sandinistas and thought they should not be allowed to run the government. An opposing army known as the Contras (short for "Contrarrevolución Nacional," meaning National Counter-Revolution) fought against the Sandinistas. The Contras were supported by some of the former Nicaraguan leaders, who fled Nicaragua when the Sandinistas took over the government.

The Contras were also supported by the U.S. government, which opposed the Sandinistas, partly because of their ties to Communist countries like Cuba. All of this created a complicated political situation involving many countries in Central America, Europe, and the Middle East. During this time, life for many Nicaraguans was dangerous and difficult. Fighting was still going on, and widespread food shortages affected everyone.

Leaving Nicaragua

Trouble soon came to Meneses Jacobs's father and their family, in part because he worked as an attorney. "My father was on the defense team for an American pilot whose plane was shot down by the Sandinista artillery at the border of Nicaragua and Costa Rica in December of 1997," she stated. "The American pilot was accused of being a CIA agent." At this time, the Sandinistas suspected the U.S. Central Intelligence Agency (CIA) of spying in order to help the Contras. It was very dangerous for Meneses Jacobs's father to defend the American pilot, but he did. The pilot was eventually freed by the Sandinistas and allowed to return to the U.S. By then, it was no longer safe for Meneses Jacobs's family to stay in Nicaragua. "Three months later we left Nicaragua," she recalled. "The Sandinista government had threatened my father's life and he realized that the country was unsafe. I left March 19, 1988. My parents and brother arrived a week later in Los Angeles."

Meneses Jacobs was 17 years old when she and her family relocated to Los Angeles. When they left Nicaragua, the family was allowed to take only $500 with them. "One day you are rich and you are affluent … and you have maids, cooks, a driver, and nannies," she remembered. "And the next day, you come to this country and you are poor and you have nothing." Although in Nicaragua her parents were highly educated professionals with careers, in the United States they could only find work checking luggage at the Los Angeles International Airport. "It was pretty hard for them to support me and my brother on less than $20,000 a year," Meneses Jacobs said. Looking back on that time, she realized that the sacrifices her parents made then allowed her and her brother "[to] finally enjoy the opportunities of freedom [and] taught us to speak up when there is injustice."

Adjusting to Life in the U.S.

Life in the U.S. turned out to be very different from life in Nicaragua. One of the first differences that struck Meneses Jacobs was the abundance of food and the attitude of most Americans. "I was particularly surprised (and continue to be surprised) by the amount of food that is wasted in this country," she observed. "We had a food rationing card in Nicaragua and

Meneses Jacobs with her magazine's namesake.

had to pick up one pound of rice, one pound of beans, one pound of sugar, and one quart of oil per person in the household for a two-week period."

Language was another big difference. When she first arrived in the U.S., Meneses Jacobs had trouble with English. This made going to Los Angeles High School difficult. "The most challenging part was that I was a senior in high school in Nicaragua but I was placed in the 10th grade at L.A. High because I did not speak English well," she revealed. "It was also challenging that although I had studied English in Nicaragua I could not understand it in the U.S. That lasted for my first four months and was very frustrating." Meneses Jacobs refused to allow the language barrier to become a permanent setback. She worked hard to improve her English and quickly overcame that challenge. She credits her high school teachers for helping her succeed. "They encouraged me every day to rise above expectations. I will always be grateful to them for I would not be who I am now without their nurturing and encouragement."

While in high school, Meneses Jacobs was also inspired by local television news anchor Carla Aragon. "One of my role models was anchorwoman Carla Aragon (who is now in Albuquerque). I met her in high school and established a friendship with her for several years while we lived in L.A. She once called me 'a diamond in the rough waiting to be discovered.' She was my role model for an educated, professional, and successful Latina."

Meneses Jacobs was a serious student who excelled in all of her classes and became the Editor-in-Chief of both the Spanish and English school newspapers. "I adapted to the American school system fairly quickly," she recalled. "At the beginning, I thought it was so strange that we all had to move classrooms and run to different floors of the school building. I was very confused. In Nicaragua, the teachers rotate and the students stay in the same classroom."

Meneses Jacobs faced many challenges adjusting to her new life, but she also said, "I am glad I moved when I was 17 years old. I had a strong educational foundation and a sense of who I was. As a result, I was not an easy target for peer pressure." There were also some things she liked about life in the U.S. "As I began to understand the American way of life, I began to like the idea of meritocracy [a system in which individuals are rewarded for their achievements]. I admired Americans that worked hard and became successful in their careers. I believe that one's dreams are possible when one has the motivation and willingness to work hard."

> ―― **"** ――
>
> *"One day you are rich and you are affluent … and you have maids, cooks, a driver, and nannies," Meneses Jacobs said about her experience before and after her family immigrated to the U.S. "And the next day, you come to this country and you are poor and you have nothing."*
>
> ―― **"** ――

Meneses Jacobs graduated from Los Angeles High School when she was 20 years old. She received a scholarship to attend Wesleyan University in Middletown, Connecticut. At Wesleyan, Meneses Jacobs studied government and international relations. She earned a Bachelor's Degree from Wesleyan in 1995. She later went on to earn a Master's Degree in education in 2001 and a Reading Specialist Certification in 2005.

CAREER HIGHLIGHTS

Meneses Jacobs originally planned a career in the entertainment industry, working with Latino filmmakers. But by the time she graduated college in 1995, she realized that teaching children would be a better choice for her. She had returned to Los Angeles after graduation, and a friend mentioned that the public school system was looking for bilingual teachers. Meneses Jacobs called to find out about possible job openings, and was asked if she could come in right away. She began teaching second grade that same day.

Supporting Bilingualism

In 1998, Meneses Jacobs was married to Marc Jacobs who was not a native Spanish speaker. They had their first daughter in 2001. Before their daughter was born, they had already decided to raise their children in a bilingual (two language) family. They strongly believed in the importance of exposing their children to the Spanish language and Latin American heritage. When their daughter was born, they decided that Meneses Jacobs would speak only Spanish at home and her husband would speak only English. In this way, they hoped their daughter would naturally learn both languages.

> "
>
> *"My advice to bilingual children is to continue learning more about their chosen language," Meneses Jacobs said. "We are living in a global economy and parents need to help their children understand that being bilingual, or multilingual, is an asset to them. Being bilingual in this country is a necessity, not just a cultural pride. Anyone who wants to be successful needs to learn a second language."*
>
> "

This worked well except in the case of reading together, or finding books to begin teaching their daughter to read. Almost everything was in English. The Spanish books that were available for children were poorly translated versions of English books. "When my oldest daughter was two she became more interested in words and books," Meneses Jacobs explained. "As a teacher, I knew that it was important to expose her to Spanish through reading. I searched for books and magazines in Spanish that were not translations of English-language works. However, I discovered that it was difficult to find quality literature written in Spanish."

When she couldn't find the books that she wanted for her daughter, Meneses Jacobs started thinking about creating a new source of Spanish-language stories for children. She thought that a magazine could provide a mix of entertaining and educational stories that would be interesting to children and their parents. "My husband and I realized that a magazine could deliver a variety of original Spanish-language materials for parents. We researched the idea for over a year." As her idea began to take shape, Meneses Jacobs had the complete support of her husband. "He believed in my idea from the very beginning and has not stopped supporting and en-

The Spanish-language magazine Iguana *contains fiction, biographies, and fun activities for kids.*

couraging me," Meneses Jacobs said. "My husband and I initially used our own savings and personally financed the launch of the magazine."

Iguana

In 2005, Meneses Jacobs published the first issue of her new magazine, *Iguana*. It is the first Spanish-language magazine created especially for readers aged seven to 12. The magazine's goal is to encourage young people to be proud of their native language and culture. As she remarked, "I want kids to learn about our people, take ownership about who they are and what they can aspire to be." Meneses Jacobs is the editor, and her husband is the art director. They create *Iguana* with contributions from Spanish-speaking writers around the world. Each issue includes fictional stories, biographies, interviews with people who have influenced the lives of Latinos in America, true stories about children around the world, recipes, crafts, puzzles, and artwork and poetry from readers.

As the first publication of its kind, *Iguana* received a tremendously positive response. The magazine has been universally praised by experts in children's literature, who have called it "snappy," "readable," and "light-hearted." As Meneses Jacobs pointed out, "We have received a very enthusiastic response from teachers, especially those in bilingual and dual-language schools. Parents are delighted that they can pick up the magazine and read to and with their children. Librarians are the most enthusiastic because they see its educational value and they can offer an alternative for their Hispanic patrons." The education community recognized *Iguana*'s importance with the 2009 Multicultural Children's Publication Award from the National Association for Multicultural Education.

In addition, the magazine has been welcomed by Spanish speakers in the U.S. and abroad. After placing an Internet advertisement to find contributing writers, Meneses Jacobs was overwhelmed by responses from Venezuela, Mexico, Argentina, Puerto Rico and the U.S. *Iguana* has also been a hit with non-native speakers of Spanish. "It surprised us to learn that many Anglo families are discovering *Iguana* and subscribing for their children who attend Spanish-immersion schools or dual-language programs. We also receive many subscriptions from adults who are learning Spanish."

¡Yo Sé!

The success of *Iguana* inspired Meneses Jacobs to create a second Spanish-language publication for young people. ¡*Yo Sé!* (meaning "I know!") was launched in 2009 as a kids' page in more than 40 different Spanish-language newspapers. Each ¡*Yo Sé!* page includes short articles about popular culture, celebrities, upcoming movies and television shows, biographies, interviews with Latino personalities, features on young Latinos who are making a difference in the world, comics, and more. Meneses Jacobs created ¡*Yo Sé!* to help parents and children preserve the Spanish language together. "This is my literacy campaign. I'm on a quest to teach Latino parents they have to read to their children every night." In the future, Meneses Jacobs hopes to expand *¡Yo Sé!* into a small magazine that can be included as a weekly newspaper insert.

Meneses Jacobs firmly believes in the importance of bilingualism, particularly in Spanish. "The Hispanic community continues to grow at a high rate," she asserted. "As the population grows in importance so does the Spanish language. Because of that growth, the Spanish language has positioned itself as the second language of this country. The Spanish language will continue to grow and will not die because millions of immigrants will continue to keep it alive." She especially believes in the importance of bilingualism in the schools. "It is a shame that many individuals are so narrow minded that they help pass legislation against the use of any language other than English. It is a shame that many Hispanic children are not given the opportunity to learn their own language because of the elimination of bilingual education programs. I have seen the rise of dual language programs at public schools that are offered to non-Spanish speaking children. The opportunity for Hispanic children to participate in this kind of programs is taken away from them. As a result, many Hispanic children are growing up not knowing how to read or write in their own language. By taking their language away, the school system is robbing these children of their culture and heritage."

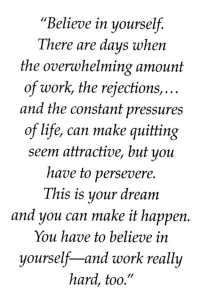

"Believe in yourself. There are days when the overwhelming amount of work, the rejections,… and the constant pressures of life, can make quitting seem attractive, but you have to persevere. This is your dream and you can make it happen. You have to believe in yourself—and work really hard, too."

Meneses Jacobs hopes that resources like *Iguana* and *¡Yo Sé!* will help preserve the Spanish language and Latino cultures while preparing young people for their futures in a changing world. "My advice to bilingual children is to continue learning more about their chosen language," she said. "Learning to speak the language is not enough, children must learn to read and write like native speakers. We are living in a global economy and parents need to help their children understand that being bilingual, or multilingual, is an asset to them. Being bilingual in this country is a necessity, not just a cultural pride. Anyone who wants to be successful needs to learn a second language."

Meneses Jacobs after winning the Anna Maria Arias Memorial Business Fund Award, recognized for her innovation, achievement, and community service.

Future Plans

Meneses Jacobs still works as a teacher and plans to continue publishing *Iguana*. Eventually, she would like *Iguana* to be distributed internationally, to reach Spanish-speaking children everywhere. For now, though, cost is the biggest obstacle in the way of that goal. "The biggest challenge was to find funding," she acknowledged. "My husband and I started *Iguana* by using our personal savings. *Iguana* is an educational magazine. Therefore, it does not contain advertising. The magazine sustains itself with subscriptions. It has also been a challenge to market and distribute the magazine due to a limited budget."

Meneses Jacobs is committed to meeting any challenges that the future may hold. "Life's journey is like an obstacle course," she observed. "Our job is to reach the finish line with our dreams intact. Some of those obstacles might be hard to overcome but the key is to never lose sight of the dream. We must achieve that dream with perseverance. All is lost if we give up. We will live a frustrated life if we don't try to overcome those obstacles." For Meneses Jacobs, perseverance, hard work, and belief in self are the tools to succeed. "Believe in yourself. There are days when the overwhelming amount of work, the rejections,… and the constant pressures of life, can make quitting seem attractive, but you have to persevere. This is your dream and you can make it happen. You have to believe in yourself—and work really hard, too."

MARRIAGE AND FAMILY

Meneses Jacobs married Marc Jacobs, a graphic artist, in October 1998. They live in Scottsdale, Arizona, and have two daughters, Isabelle Selene (born in 2001) and Katherine Celeste (born in 2005).

Meneses Jacobs was raised Catholic but converted to Judaism after graduating college. "When I met my (future) husband, Marc Jacobs, I asked if he was Jewish, but I didn't tell him I was studying Judaism," she revealed.

"After graduation, I moved back to Los Angeles and studied with a rabbi for three more years. In March 1998, I converted. It was very emotional. I felt I was detaching from my parents, but my father gave me a big hug and said in Spanish, 'God of any religion is a good God.' In May of that year, my husband proposed, and we got married in October."

HONORS AND AWARDS

Anna Maria Arias Memorial Business Fund Award (*Latina Style* magazine): 2007
Multicultural Children's Publication Award (National Association for Multicultural Education): 2009, for *Iguana*

FURTHER READING

Periodicals

Arizona Republic, Apr. 18, 2005, p.D5; Sep. 27, 2007
Criticas, June 15, 2008
Jewish News of Greater Phoenix, Spring 2008, p.8
NEA Today, Apr. 2006

Online Articles

http://www.criticasmagazine.com/article/ca6560349.html
    (Criticas, "Spanish-Speaking Iguana Turns Three," June 15, 2008)
http://www.latinopm.com
    (Latino Perspectives, "A Happy Niche," June 2006)

ADDRESS

Christianne Meneses Jacobs
Iguana Magazine
NicaGal, LLC
PO Box 26432
Scottsdale AZ 85255

WORLD WIDE WEB SITES

http://www.iguanamagazine.com
http://www.nicagal.com

Melinda Merck 1963-

American Forensic Veterinarian
Animal Crime Scene Investigation Expert

BIRTH

Melinda Denise Merck was born on December 22, 1963, in Tucson, Arizona. Her father, Jerry Merck, served in the U.S. Air Force and later worked for IBM. Her mother, Glenda Crowe, was a homemaker when Merck was young. She returned to college to earn a nursing degree when Merck was in high school, and later worked as a nurse. Merck's parents divorced in 1984. She has one younger sister named Melanie.

YOUTH

Merck's family moved around a lot when she was young, depending on where her father was transferred for work. She grew up living in different cities in Texas, Ohio, and Michigan. No matter where she lived, Merck tried to save any injured birds or chipmunks that she found. "I was one of those kids who always had a shoebox with an injured bird or turtle," she recalled. She learned that approach from her grandfather, who lived on a farm and was always taking in stray animals. He was a big influence on her and helped shape her ideas about caring for animals that needed help. By the time she was in kindergarten, Merck already knew that she wanted to become a veterinarian. Then when she was eight years old, she saw a puppy get hit by a car, and this made a big impact on her. She knew that she also wanted to make a difference helping animals and to prevent people from mistreating them.

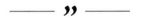

> *As a child, Merck tried to save any injured birds or chipmunks that she found. "I was one of those kids who always had a shoebox with an injured bird or turtle," she recalled.*

As a young girl, Merck was greatly inspired by the 1966 movie *Born Free*, which told the true story of George and Joy Adamson and their work with lions in Kenya. The story focuses on how the couple came to adopt and raise three lion cubs and how they developed a special attachment to a female cub they named Elsa. When Elsa reached maturity, the Adamsons were determined to help her return to life in the wild, rather than sending her to a zoo. After seeing this movie, Merck said, "I wanted to be Joy Adamson—join the Peace Corps and travel the world saving all the lions and other big cats."

EDUCATION

Merck was a good student who excelled in school. Her favorite subjects were science and biology. She got bored very quickly in her classes and always wanted to learn more, which challenged her teachers to find extra assignments for her. She also loved reading, especially mysteries like the Nancy Drew series. In high school, Merck enjoyed playing team sports like softball, basketball, and volleyball. When she began thinking about college, a high school counselor told her that women didn't become doctors or veterinarians and advised her to choose a different career. But Merck was very stubborn, and that advice only made her more determined to follow her dream.

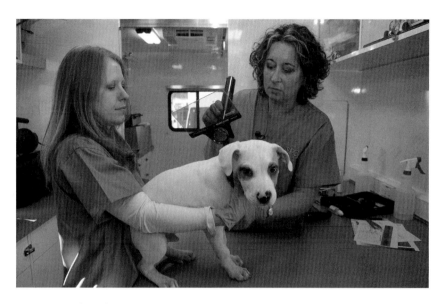

Merck and veterinary assistant Felicia Early doing an examination.

Merck enrolled in the pre-veterinary program at Michigan State University. Although she had graduated at the top of her class in high school, she quickly found that she was unprepared for course work at the college level. She struggled with challenging classes during her first semester, and had to work hard to adjust to college life. By the end of her first year, she had achieved a perfect 4.0 grade point average. In her second year of college, Merck took a test for admission into Michigan State University's school of veterinary medicine. She scored so high on the test that she was offered early admission, a privilege given to only eight students each year.

Merck did well in veterinary school, although the coursework was increasingly difficult. During her second year, she struggled with classes that were exceptionally tough. For the first time in her life, Merck questioned her conviction to become a veterinarian. She transferred to Michigan State University's medical school and began to study radiology. After one semester, however, she realized that she really didn't want to work with people and that she belonged in veterinary school after all. She was allowed to transfer back to the veterinary program and graduated with honors in 1988. She earned her DVM degree, or Doctor of Veterinary Medicine.

CAREER HIGHLIGHTS

In 1990, Merck opened The Cat Clinic, her own veterinary practice in Roswell, Georgia. She explained that her decision to specialize in treating cats was due in part to her childhood love of the movie *Born Free*. But she also felt that cat medicine was a frontier where she could make a difference. Merck felt that cats were the one species that was neglected in veterinary school. At that time, classes were very focused on treating dogs and not much time was given to the study of cats. Diagnosing and treating cats was something of a mystery, and this also interested Merck. "In vet school, cats really got the short end of the stick," she explained. "Dogs are easy to treat. A dog will practically check himself into the hospital and tell you exactly where it hurts. Cats will just curl up and stop eating no matter what's wrong."

> *Merck felt that cats were neglected in veterinary school: classes focused on treating dogs, and treating cats was considered something of a mystery. "In vet school, cats really got the short end of the stick," she explained. "Dogs are easy to treat. A dog will practically check himself into the hospital and tell you exactly where it hurts. Cats will just curl up and stop eating no matter what's wrong."*

At The Cat Clinic, Merck treated animals regardless of whether their owners could pay for treatment. She was sometimes criticized by people who thought she was crazy to work for free, but Merck had a different opinion. "If I can fix the animal, I'm going to fix the animal. It's the right thing to do," she emphasized. "If you do things for the right reasons, eventually it pays off. It really does. It works. It may take several years to see the benefit, but it pays off. What goes around comes around."

Treating Animal Cruelty Cases

Merck began seeing cases of animal cruelty in her first year of practice. She reported her first case of suspected abuse when a kitten's injuries didn't seem to match its owners' story. "[A] couple brought in a two-pound, eight-week-old Persian kitten that was in a coma with bleeding in the lungs," she reported. "Their reaction was blasé, and their story just didn't add up. So I called the police. The officer had never had a vet report cruelty before. The boyfriend confessed to throwing the kitten against the wall, charges were brought, and the couple fled the state. Being right about that gave me the confidence to pursue other leads." Merck was surprised that no other veterinarians had ever reported suspected abuse to the police. Soon after, she started working with various rescue groups and local animal control agencies.

In 2000, after some particularly bad animal cruelty cases in Atlanta, Georgia, the state passed the Animal Protection Act, making animal cruelty a felony crime (meaning that convictions could result in harsher sentencing than other types of crimes). Merck knew the law would be no good unless people knew how to enforce it. She joined the Georgia Legal Professional for Animals organization and began working to educate people about how to investigate and prosecute animal cruelty cases. Her first task for the organization was to determine how to process a crime scene involving animal cruelty. At that time, Merck could find no information about veterinary forensics, so she turned to experts in human forensics.

Moving into Veterinary Forensics

To learn about forensic techniques and practices, Merck studied human forensics textbooks and worked with local medical examiners and crime scene investigators. She learned how to collect and preserve evidence, such as fluids and fibers, and how to interpret crime scene information, such as bullet trajectories and blood spatter. She then determined how the practices of human forensic investigations could be applied to animal cases. Merck combined the techniques of human forensic science with the specialized knowledge of veterinary medicine. "Forensic veterinary medicine is the application of veterinary medical knowledge to legal matters," she observed. "Evidence associated with any crime has to be analyzed and interpreted in the proper context. In order to properly identify evidence, analyze it, and interpret the findings, you have to know animals and animal behavior. This is what I do and what I bring to a crime scene."

> "Forensic veterinary medicine is the application of veterinary medical knowledge to legal matters," Merck observed. "Evidence associated with any crime has to be analyzed and interpreted in the proper context. In order to properly identify evidence, analyze it, and interpret the findings, you have to know animals and animal behavior. This is what I do and what I bring to a crime scene."

Merck soon began giving seminars on veterinary forensic investigations for law enforcement and veterinarians. "Veterinarians are naturally the experts on what an animal's response to fear and pain would be," she explained. In her seminars, Merck covered such topics as how to interpret claw marks

Merck with some of her veterinary forensics tools outside of the Mobile Animal CSI unit, part of the ASPCA (American Society for the Prevention of Cruelty to Animals). The tools include an evidence collection kit, an evidence tagging kit, a UV light, an x-ray machine, and a photography kit for identifying evidence at the scene.

at a crime scene and how the marks might indicate a struggle with a perpetrator. She reminded investigators that evidence at a scene would be different: for example, gravesites could be as small as one foot long, not human sized. She pointed out how animal cases differ from human cases, including examples such as animal bleeding patterns, which explained why crime scene photos might lack evidence of the bloody paw prints investigators expected to see.

Within a few years, Merck was spending more time assisting with animal cruelty investigations than she was at her private practice. She helped local law enforcement and animal control officers with crime scene investigations as well as with the examination of live and deceased animal victims. She assisted on cases including animal neglect, hoarding, torture, and dog fighting. Merck traveled the country speaking at veterinary and law enforcement conferences, taught an online course in forensics for veterinarians, and lectured at several university veterinary schools. She spoke on topics related to veterinary forensics and crime scene investigations from a veterinarian's perspective for the Georgia State Bar Association (a professional licensing organization for attorneys). Although it took time away from her private practice, Merck saw tremendous value in the time she spent educating others. "Every time I lecture, whether to vet students, police, or prosecutors both in the U.S. and abroad, there is a ripple effect—they go out and do more for animals."

Finally, in 2006, Merck sold her private practice so that she could devote all of her time to teaching and practicing veterinary forensics. In 2007, she took a full-time position working with the ASPCA (American Society for the Prevention of Cruelty to Animals). In this position, Merck serves as a national and international consultant and expert witness on animal cruelty cases and animal control investigations. It was through the ASPCA that she became involved in one of the most high-profile cases of animal abuse in recent times.

The Michael Vick Dog Fighting Case

In 2007, rising NFL star and Atlanta Falcons quarterback Michael Vick was accused of animal abuse and running a dog fighting ring. Law enforcement authorities were trying to build their case against Vick, but they weren't sure how to prove that he engaged in dog fighting and abuse. They turned to Merck, who conducted a crime scene investigation at property owned by Vick. She located and excavated the graves of many pit bulls and analyzed their remains. In this process, Merck was able to piece together the details of their lives and deaths. Her expert testimony helped put Vick in prison and brought more attention to veterinary forensics as an important tool in law enforcement. "I think the high-profile nature of this case has had a positive impact on animal welfare and cruelty investigations," she observed. "It raised the public's awareness of not only dog fighting but all types of cruelty. It also has had an impact on law enforcement in demonstrating the link between animal cruelty and other types of crimes." Vick was sentenced to 23 months in prison. "It's not about punishment or getting people put into jail," Merck argued. "It's about protecting the animals. If we're not the voice for that animal, who is?"

During this time, Merck also compiled her knowledge and experience processing crime scenes in the book *Veterinary Forensics: Animal Cruelty Investigations*, published in 2007. The book was well received and widely praised. The Veterinary Information Network recommended it as "a book that should be in every clinic." A reviewer for *Veterinary Pathology* said the book "helps fill the void in the forensic veterinary medical literature. Nobody could argue with Dr. Merck's enthusiasm and zeal to make us aware of an important topic that we would prefer to ignore, but should not." *Midwest Book Review* praised the book as a "resource essential for

Merck excavating a grave site during an animal cruelty investigation.

animal cruelty investigators." Merck also co-wrote a second book, *Veteri-nary Forensic Investigation of Animal Cruelty: A Guide for Veterinarians and Law Enforcement.*

In 2008, Merck helped found the International Veterinary Forensic Sciences Association. This professional organization works to continue developing veterinary forensics and educate the animal welfare community, law enforcement agencies, courts, and veterinarians on the importance of veterinary forensics. Merck was honored in 2009 with the U.S. Department of Justice Outstanding Investigation or Case Award for her work on the Michael Vick trial. It was the first time that an animal-related case had received such an award.

Around this time Merck also helped design and launch the nation's first formal veterinary forensic sciences program at the University of Florida. As part of the veterinary master's degree program, the veterinary forensics certificate gives veterinarians the training to recognize crime against animals and the tools to do something about it. She explained the need for the program by saying, "A problem is that once [a vet] becomes suspicious, they may not have been taught what to do next." Merck currently teaches at the University of Florida while continuing to investigate cases for the ASPCA.

Handling Difficult Cases

During her investigations, Merck has seen horrific cases of animal torture, neglect, and other forms of abuse. She is often asked how she can work in a field that requires her to closely examine and document the details of such cases. "It is certainly difficult to work with these cases because they represent the ultimate breakdown of the human-animal bond," she acknowledged. "I think my work as a veterinarian has helped me because you learn to compartmentalize in order to do your job—you cannot succumb to emotion while working on an animal or case. For cruelty, I turn it into a puzzle that I have to solve. My goal is to gather evidence to find and successfully prosecute the offender. I realize that what's done is done and I have to work toward justice. It is very hard because of my empathy for animals, but the best thing I can do for them is be their voice."

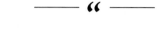

"It's not about punishment or getting people put into jail," Merck said about investigating and prosecuting animal cruelty cases. "It's about protecting the animals. If we're not the voice for that animal, who is?"

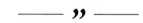

Merck channels her feelings about a case into positive action, focusing on being objective and seeking justice for the animal victims. She works hard to try to determine what really happened to them, gathering evidence and bringing it into a legal case that can be prosecuted. It also helps Merck to remember that she works as part of a team, and that the entire outcome of each case does not rest completely on her shoulders. She believes that people with special skills or knowledge have an obligation to use those talents for the benefit of society. In this way, she puts her work into perspective. "In every case we make a difference. Even if the animal has died, we can prevent it from happening again."

Merck also recognizes the importance of her own recuperation time after a particularly difficult case. She makes sure to spend time between cases with her own pets. She recharges and relaxes by reading and watching television. She also finds it particularly rewarding to see how well the animals she has rescued are doing in their new homes. Merck is committed to placing animals rescued during cruelty cases into foster homes, special rehabilitation shelters, or permanent homes.

Despite the emotional strain of some cases, Merck has said that the part of her work that she enjoys most is investigating animal cruelty. "It is challenging to figure out these puzzles, each case is different. And working with the investigators and prosecutors is always interesting. The casework is satisfying because I am giving the animal a voice," she commented. "The best part of the job is when we succeed—this can mean a conviction, successful intervention or when the animal is now protected from future harm. I work with a group of investigators and prosecutors who support going after the criminals who commit cruelty—that continually validates what I am doing and keeps me motivated."

HOME AND FAMILY

Merck lives in Gainesville, Florida, with an ever-changing assortment of dogs and cats, nearly all rescued from bad situations.

HONORS AND AWARDS

Outstanding Investigation or Case Award (U.S. Department of Justice): 2009, for her work in the investigation of the Michael Vick case

FURTHER READING

Periodicals

Atlanta Journal-Constitution, Mar. 17, 2005, p.JF2
Kansas City (MO) Star, Aug. 5, 2009
People, Mar. 26, 2007, p.113
St. Petersburg Times, June 28, 2009, p.E1
USA Today, Oct. 9, 2007

Online Articles

http://veterinarynews.dvm360.com/dvm/article/articleDetail.jsp?id=622205
  (dvm360, "The New Welfare War," Sep. 1, 2009)
http://veterinarynews.dvm360.com/dvm/article/articleDetail.jsp?id=501366
  (dvm360, "Reporting Suspected Animal Abuse Getting Easier, Experts Say," Mar. 1, 2008)
http://veterinarymedicine.dvm360.com/vetmed/Medicine/ArticleStandard
  /Article/detail/491398
  (dvm360, "The Veterinary Medicine Interview: Dr. Melinda D. Merck," Feb. 1, 2008)
http://www.veterinarypracticenews.com/vet-industry-people/profiles-in
  -medicine/voice-for-justice.aspx
  (Veterinary Practice News, "Voice for Justice: Melinda Merck, DVM," Oct. 2009)

ADDRESS

Melinda Merck, DVM
ASPCA
424 East 92nd Street
New York, NY 10128

WORLD WIDE WEB SITES

http://www.veterinaryforensics.com
http://www.aspca.org

Stephenie Meyer 1973-

American Author
Creator of the Bestselling Novel Series, "The Twilight Saga"

BIRTH

Stephenie Meyer was born Stephenie Morgan on December 24, 1973, in Hartford, Connecticut. She was the second of six children born to Stephen and Candy Morgan; her siblings are Emily, Heidi, Paul, Seth, and Jacob. The unusual form of her first name is the result of her father's decision to add "ie" to the end of his name rather than using the conventional spelling, "Stephanie."

YOUTH

When Meyer was four years old, her family moved to Phoenix, Arizona, where her father began working as the chief financial officer at a contracting company. Growing up in a large family was good for her as a writer, she has said. It helped her understand many different personality types and the way people interact. "My siblings sometimes crop up as characters in my stories," she commented. Her father enjoyed reading to his children—not from books written for kids, but from whatever he was interested in at the time. Because of her father's influence, Meyer never really read much children's literature, even when she was young. Instead, her favorites included classics like *Jane Eyre* by Charlotte Bronte and *Pride and Prejudice* by Jane Austen.

EDUCATION

Meyer attended Chaparral High School in Scottsdale, Arizona. It was an affluent school, "the kind of place where every fall a few girls would come back to school with new noses," she commented, "and there were Porsches in the student lot." She graduated from high school in 1992. Meyer won a National Merit Scholarship and selected Brigham Young University in Provo, Utah. Meyer was raised as a member of the Church of Jesus Christ of Latter-Day Saints (commonly known as the Mormon church), and BYU is run by the Mormon church. The atmosphere there is quiet and conservative, which was fine with her. "On the list of the biggest party schools in the country," she remarked, "BYU consistently and proudly finishes dead last." In 1997, she graduated with a Bachelor of Arts (BA) degree in English.

CAREER HIGHLIGHTS

Even though she was an avid reader and had studied literature in college, Meyer never had any ambition of making her living as a writer. She considered going to law school, but her plans changed after she became involved with Christiaan "Pancho" Meyer. The two had known each other casually since childhood, and they attended the same church. It wasn't until the summer before her senior year of college, however, that they got to know each other well. The relationship took off, and they married the year she graduated from college. After that, she worked as a receptionist briefly, and even made a couple of starts at writing some stories. She gave up working outside the home, however, when she became pregnant with her first child, Gabe. Two more sons, Seth and Eli, soon followed. Any interest Meyer had in writing was sidetracked by the demands of taking care of three small boys.

Meyer was glad to stay at home with her children, but their early years were a challenging time. Her sons were fussy babies, sleeping very little and crying a lot. Up with them at all hours of the night, Meyer became sleep-deprived herself. At times she felt she was merely going through the motions, walking through life like a zombie. On June 2, 2003, however, a dramatic transformation began in her life. On that morning, she had a very vivid dream. It concerned two teenagers conversing in a beautiful meadow, brightly lit by sunlight but situated deep within a forest. Despite the beauty of the scene, there was a sense of danger in the air. The boy and the girl were having an intense discussion about the problems they faced because the girl was human and the boy was a vampire, and they were in love.

> *Meyer attended Brigham Young University, where the atmosphere is quiet and conservative. That was fine with her. "On the list of the biggest party schools in the country," she remarked, "BYU consistently and proudly finishes dead last."*

From Dream to Multi-Book Contract

This dream was so powerful and so interesting that Meyer didn't want to get out of bed after she woke up. She knew she had many things to do that day, but she lay there for a while, savoring every detail of the dream. She continued to think of it after she got up and began her daily routine. As soon as she could find a spare moment, she wrote down everything at she could remember. The pages she wrote that day eventually became Chapter 13 of the book *Twilight.*

From that day onward, Meyer's life changed. The characters she had dreamed continued to dominate her thoughts. As she went about her business, running errands, changing diapers, taking children to swim lessons and other activities, she was thinking about the boy and the girl, hearing them converse in her mind. Whenever an opportunity presented itself, she hurried to the computer to type out all she had been thinking, fleshing out the story that had started with her dream and grown from there. First of all, she continued from the scene in the forest clearing and wrote until she reached the end of the story. Then, she backed up and started at the beginning, writing up to Chapter 13. She kept a notebook by her bedside so she could write down any ideas that struck in the middle of the night.

Meyer started writing Twilight
after being inspired by a dream about Bella and Edward.

Meyer was a little alarmed by her obsession, especially because she'd never had the slightest interest in vampires before that summer. Despite a wide range of reading interests, horror was the one genre that she had never enjoyed. At first, she was too embarrassed even to tell her husband what was going on, and he wondered why she rarely seemed to sleep or let him use the family computer. For a while, only her older sister Emily knew about the story. She urged Meyer to continue working on it. Once Meyer let her husband in on her secret, he also encouraged her to keep writing.

Meyer wanted to set her story somewhere with abundant rainfall. Her research showed her that the rainiest place in the United States is the Olympic Peninsula, in the state of Washington. Looking at more detailed maps, she noticed the small town of Forks, surrounded by forest and situated close to the La Push Reservation of the Quileute Tribe of Native Americans. The Quileute mythology gave Meyer still more inspiration for her story. She decided to use Forks as her setting, not even changing the name of the town. In fact, "Forks" was her original title for the book, one she says she still likes.

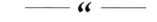

"It certainly wasn't belief in my fabulous talent that made me push forward," Meyer said about trying to get her first book published. "I think it was just that I loved my characters so much, and they were so real to me, that I wanted other people to know them, too."

By August 2003, Meyer had finished her story—130,000 words of it, written just for fun. After reading the whole thing, however, her sister Emily urged her to look into having it published. Meyer didn't know anything about the book business, and once she started investigating, she felt quite intimidated. "It certainly wasn't belief in my fabulous talent that made me push forward," she said. "I think it was just that I loved my characters so much, and they were so real to me, that I wanted other people to know them, too."

Meyer sent about 15 queries to publishing houses and authors' agents she had located by searching the Internet. Some didn't answer at all, several sent rejection letters, but one—an assistant at the Writers House literary agency—responded enthusiastically. Soon Meyer got a phone call from Jodi Reamer, an agent at Writers House. Reamer saw the great potential in Meyer's work and wanted to represent her. The two of them worked together to polish the manuscript for a couple of weeks. At Reamer's suggestion, they gave it a new, more marketable title: *Twilight*. On the Wednesday before Thanksgiving, Reamer sent the manuscript to editors at several publishing houses.

The following Monday, Reamer called Meyer to say that an editor at the Little, Brown publishing house had made an offer of $300,000 for *Twilight*. Meyer could hardly believe this incredible news, but she was even more shocked when Reamer said she'd turned down the offer, holding out for more money. It seemed crazy to Meyer, but Reamer knew what she was doing. In the end, eight publishers bid against each other for the rights to *Twilight*, and Meyer ended up with a $750,000, three-book contract from Little, Brown, as well as selling the film rights to her first book. Her road from dream to six-figure, multi-book deal had unfolded within a matter of six months, an almost unbelievable success story.

Twilight, a Vampire Romance

Twilight proved to be every bit as popular as Meyer's agent or publisher could have hoped. There was a lot of excitement and publicity about the book even before it reached the public. Within five weeks of its release in October 2005, *Twilight* was on the *New York Times* bestseller list. Entering at the No. 5 position, it soon reached the top and stayed there for many weeks. Sales remained strong years after its initial publication, spurred by the popularity of sequels and the movie adaptations.

Twilight is narrated by Bella Swan, a 17-year-old girl. As the story begins, she is leaving Phoenix, where she has lived with her mother, to move to the town of Forks, Washington, where her father is the police chief. On the first day in her new school, she notices a strange, pale, beautiful boy staring intently at her. He is Edward Cullen, and what Bella doesn't realize is that he is a vampire who appears as the 17-year-old he was when he became immortal, about 100 years earlier.

Edward is intensely attracted to Bella. With the wisdom gained over 100 years of life, he recognizes her as his great love. In addition to his feelings of pure love, however, he also has a ravenous desire to taste her blood. He resists this, as he resists all such temptations. Edward and his family are part of a coven of vampires that choose not to take human life. Instead, they have disciplined themselves to feed only on the blood of animals, hunting at night, as they never need to sleep. There are other covens, however, that make no attempt to resist their thirst for human blood. Tension in the story comes both from the dangerous nature of Edward's love for Bella and from the threat of vampire covens that prey on humans. A re-

The movie Twilight *proved to be as popular as the book—if not more so.*

viewer for *Publishers Weekly* called *Twilight* a "riveting first novel, propelled by suspense and romance in equal parts."

Meyer has insisted that she writes stories, not messages. When asked about the main theme running through *Twilight,* however, she noted that one important idea is that we all have free will. That concept is demonstrated by the Cullens' decision not to take human life, even though they are vampires. "It doesn't matter where you're stuck in life or what you think you have to do; you can always choose something else. There's always a different path," she said.

With her story, Meyer touched on feelings that many teenagers could understand—of being different, feeling like an outcast, and trying to control powerful impulses. She also offered a unique depiction of vampires. The author had never read any of the classic or contemporary works of vampire literature, such as Bram Stoker's *Dracula* or the novels of Anne Rice. Her characters don't share the traits often associated with vampires. In addition to being able to choose not to drink human blood, they are able to venture out in daylight without risking their lives—although they will give off a peculiar sparkling effect in sunlight. They can't fly, don't transform into bats, and don't rest in coffins. Though *Twilight* is intense, it is ultimately a romance, not a horror story; there are no graphic, violent scenes. "I do like to say it's a vampire book for people who don't like vampire books," Meyer commented.

A Series Emerges: "The Twilight Saga"

When Meyer had finished her original story, she still couldn't stop thinking about her characters. She wrote three different epilogues to the story, each more than 100 pages long. Realizing there was more she wanted to say about Edward and Bella, Meyer began to expand one of her epilogues into a full-length sequel, which she called "Forever Dawn." At that point, her first novel *Twilight* was still "Forks," a private work that only a handful of people had read. Meyer intended "Forever Dawn" as a birthday present for her sister Emily. When she was about 300 pages into writing "Forever Dawn," however, her life was turned upside down by the news of her book deal and the impending publication of *Twilight.*

> **"**
>
> *"Let me say that I do believe in true love. But I also deeply believe in the complexity, variety, and downright insanity of love. A lucky person loves hundreds of people in their lives, all in different ways.... The bottom line is that you have to choose who you're going to commit to—that's the foundation of love, not a lack of other options."*
>
> **"**

Little, Brown wanted at least two sequels to *Twilight,* but there was a problem: *Twilight* was being marketed as a young-adult book, and "Forever Dawn" didn't fit into the young-adult formula. In "Forever Dawn," Meyer had skipped past the conclusion of Bella's high-school years and written about a later part of her life. She knew she'd have to write a completely different story for Little, Brown—one that picked up directly after the conclusion of *Twilight.* She finished "Forever Dawn" and gave it to her sister as planned, then plunged into work on the official sequel, called *New Moon.* With the publication of *New Moon* and the following sequels, *Eclipse* and *Breaking Dawn,* the series became known as "The Twilight Saga."

New Moon

Writing the first book had been an act of pure joy, fun, and personal satisfaction for the author. Writing *New Moon* was an entirely different experience. "I knew enough about the editing process to know that there were painful changes ahead; the parts I loved now might not make the final cut," Meyer explained. "I was going to have to rethink and revise and rework. This made it very hard to put the words down, and I had a horrible feeling much like stage fright the whole time I was writing." Although the process of creating a sequel awaited by millions of eager readers was very difficult, Meyer felt it helped her to grow as a writer. It also provided an opportunity for her to give more depth to her characters.

Edward is absent from much of *New Moon*. Fearing that his presence brings too much danger to his beloved Bella, he has traveled far from her, at great risk to himself. Bella is devastated by his disappearance. The title of the book refers to the darkest point in the moon's cycle, a symbolic reference to this, the darkest period in Bella's life. With Edward lost to her, Bella develops a friendship with Jacob Black, a classmate who is part of the Quileute tribe. He tells Bella the tribe's legends, which say that its people descend-

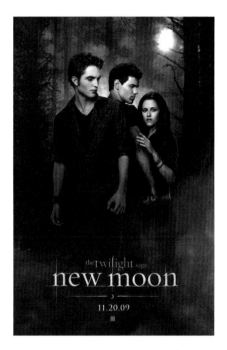

New Moon *built on the success of* Twilight, *bringing more fans to the work.*

ed from wolves that were transformed into humans by a sorcerer. Jacob becomes Bella's protector when she is menaced by a vampire from a dangerous coven, whose presence causes Jacob to shape-shift into a huge werewolf. Released in September 2006, *New Moon* spent more than 25 weeks at the top of the *New York Times* bestseller list.

Eclipse

The publication of *Eclipse*, the third installment of the series, was eagerly awaited by the ever-growing ranks of "Twilight Saga" fans. Published in August 2007, the book sold 150,000 copies on the first day it was released. In *Eclipse*, Bella's high school graduation is approaching. While most students her age are concerned with choices about colleges or careers, Bella must make vital decisions on matters that may influence the course of a war between vampires and werewolves. Her choices will involve life and death and whether to remain human or become a vampire. Ultimately, she must choose between Edward and Jacob, which places them in competition, but the two rivals work together to try to save Bella when she is placed in harm's way.

A scene from the movie Eclipse, *released in 2010,*
to be followed by Breaking Dawn *in 2011.*

Some fans were dismayed by the growing relationship between Bella and Jacob. Bella had been portrayed as deeply in love with Edward, and fans disliked the idea that Bella could even consider a relationship with Jacob. But Meyer defended Bella: "First of all, let me say that I do believe in true love. But I also deeply believe in the complexity, variety, and downright insanity of love. A lucky person loves hundreds of people in their lives, all in different ways, family love, friendship love, romantic love, all in so many shades and depths. I don't think you lose your ability—or right—to have true love by loving more than one person.... The bottom line is that you have to choose who you're going to commit to—that's the foundation of love, not a lack of other options."

Reviewer Janis Flint-Ferguson wrote in *Kliatt* that *Eclipse,* like Meyer's first two books, "is hard to put down as it draws the reader into heart-pounding gothic romance tinged with mythic horror." Another reviewer, Anne Rouyer, commented in *School Library Journal* that "Meyer knows what her fans want: thrills, chills, and a lot of romance, and she delivers on all counts."

Breaking Dawn

Meyer's original deal with Little, Brown had been for three books, but with "The Twilight Saga" such a runaway success, the publisher was happy to extend the series with a fourth volume. At 12:01 a.m. on August 2, 2008, *Breaking Dawn* was released. Midnight parties were held at bookstores, with excited fans standing in line for hours to be able to get their hands on a copy of the book the instant it was available. Approximately 1.3 million copies were sold on the very first day *Breaking Dawn* came out.

The plot of *Breaking Dawn* sees Bella married. She soon becomes pregnant with a very unique, supernatural child, but the pregnancy is extremely dangerous to her. With this kind of storyline, *Breaking Dawn* is "darker and more mature than the previous titles" in "The Twilight Saga," according to Cara von Wrangel in a review for *School Library Journal.* Some fans weren't pleased with the plot, but as Meyer pointed out, any book with such a large, passionate audience would draw some negative response along with the positive.

Commenting on her decision to write a story about marriage and child-birth—subjects that might seem less appealing to her readers than high-

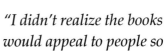

"I didn't realize the books would appeal to people so broadly," Meyer remarked. "I think some of it's because Bella is an everygirl. She's not a hero.... She doesn't always have to be cool, or wear the coolest clothes ever. She's normal. And there aren't a lot of girls in literature that are normal."

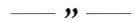

school romance—Meyer said the following: "To me, the story was realistic. Things do change, you do grow up, and the world changes," she explained. "I wanted to see reality, and the reality is that things don't fade to black when you get married." *Breaking Dawn* provided closure to Bella's story, but the plot also left possibilities for new stories set in "The Twilight Saga" universe.

Throughout the creation of "The Twilight Saga," Meyer's busy imagination had driven her to begin rewriting the events from Edward's perspective, instead of Bella's. Initially, she only meant to do one chapter in this way, just as an exercise, but as usual, her imagination carried her further. She called the Edward-narrated story "Midnight Sun" and considered publishing it someday. Late in August 2008, Meyer was horrified to learn that a rough draft of "Midnight Sun" was being widely posted on the Internet. She had never intended the pages to be seen by the general public and was very upset. She responded by putting the draft up on her own Web site so that curious fans could read it there instead of on sites that had violated copyright laws by posting it. She also made a statement that she was putting the "Midnight Sun" project on hold indefinitely.

There was more excitement to come in 2008, when the film version of *Twilight* was released. Directed by Catherine Hardwicke, it featured Robert Pattinson as Edward, Kristen Stewart as Bella, and Taylor Lautner as Jacob (for more information on Pattinson, see *Biography Today,* 2009; for more information on Stewart and Lautner, see *Biography Today*, 2010). Meyer even appeared in the film, in a non-speaking role as a customer in a Forks diner. Fans flocked to see the movie, many of them dressing like their favorite characters for the occasion and returning for multiple viewings. *Twilight* was the No. 1 movie at the box office when it was released, with nearly $70 million in ticket sales on that weekend alone. It earned more than $392 million in box-office receipts during its run in theaters worldwide.

Excitement was just as high for the film sequels. *New Moon*, released in 2009, shattered the record for most money earned by a movie on its opening day, bringing in $72.7 million on opening day, more than $142 million over the opening weekend, and more than $710 million worldwide. *Eclipse*, released in 2010, was also a huge hit. After bringing in more than $64.8 million its opening weekend, it went on to earn more than $689 million worldwide. Fans are eagerly awaiting the movie versions of *Breaking Dawn*, the longest book in "The Twilight Saga" series. Filmmakers have announced plans to divide the book and make it into two movies, currently scheduled for release in 2011 and 2012. In another re-creation of this world, Meyer republished the original book in the series as *Twilight: The Graphic Novel, Volume 1*, with drawings by illustrator Young Kim.

"Twilight Saga" Mania

"The Twilight Saga" books appeal to fans of all ages and both genders, but younger teenage girls form the core of its fans. Often referring to themselves as "Twilighters," the vampire-obsessed girls are passionately interested in everything to do with "The Twilight Saga" books, movies, and author. They often define themselves as members of "Team Edward" or "Team Jacob" to show which character they're more devoted to. They have waited for hours in lines to get copies of the books on the day of their release, to have books signed by Meyer, or to be among the first to see the movie versions. They write their own fan-fiction based on the characters and listen to "Twilight Saga"-themed music. When special "Twilight Saga" prom parties were held with Meyer in attendance, tickets sold out within an hour after going on sale. "The Twilight Saga" books have sold some 70 million copies in total, and have been translated into more than 30 languages.

Meyer at the 2009 premiere of New Moon *with some of her dedicated fans.*

Meyer is very appreciative of all the fans who are so loyal to her work. "They have the best questions, and they're so into the stories," she said. "You really can't write for a better audience. I say to all other authors: if you're not writing for teenage girls, you're missing out on a lot of love." Little, Brown has sent Meyer out on many tours to promote her work, and she has tried her best to keep in contact with her readers. Although the huge volume of mail she receives makes it impossible for her to answer every letter personally, she uses her Web site to provide fans with up-to-date information about what's going on with her and her work.

Meyer does have some detractors who find fault with her writing style. To such criticism, she responded: "I don't think I'm a writer; I think I'm a story-teller. The words aren't always perfect." Reflecting on the popularity of "The Twilight Saga," Meyer said: "I didn't realize the books would appeal to people so broadly. I think some of it's because Bella is an everygirl. She's not a hero.… She doesn't always have to be cool, or wear the coolest clothes ever. She's normal. And there aren't a lot of girls in literature that are normal."

Meyer is a quiet person who was happy with her life before she became a publishing celebrity. After a few whirlwind years of appearances at book-stores, special parties, concerts, and on national television programs to support "The Twilight Saga," she announced she would be stepping away from the media limelight for a while. She hoped to recapture some of her privacy and to get time to work on new writing projects. "Look, I'm not just a vampire girl," she said. "I can do other worlds."

Beyond "The Twilight Saga"

Meyer's first book outside "The Twilight Saga" was *The Host,* a science-fiction novel released in 2008. *The Host* is not considered a young-adult book, but Meyer's fans of all ages were eager to read it. It debuted at the top of the *New York Times* bestseller list and remained on the list for 26 weeks. *The Host* concerns a time when most of Earth has been taken over by alien invaders, called Souls, who inhabit human bodies. The host humans appear to go about their daily routines as usual, but once a Soul takes over, their human personalities cease to exist and their minds no longer function. The Souls have resolved many global problems, but there are still some renegade humans who want control of the planet.

—— " ——

"If you love to write, then write. Don't let your goal be having a novel published, let your goal be enjoying your stories. However, if you finish your story and you want to share it, be brave about it. Don't doubt your story's appeal.... If I would have realized that the stories in my head would be as intriguing to others as they were to me, I would probably have started writing sooner. Believe in your own taste."

—— " ——

A showdown of sorts takes place within the body of Melanie Stryder, a human who is still without a Soul. She is what the aliens consider a rare, "wild" human, and as such, she is hunted down and taken into captivity. Her body is assigned to an experienced Soul called Wanderer, but when Wanderer inhabits Melanie's form, she finds that Melanie will not relinquish control of her mind. Instead, Melanie starts to exert control over Wanderer, filling the Soul's mind with thoughts of Jared, the man she loves. Jared is in hiding, and it is Wanderer's job to track him down. With Melanie's influence, however, Wanderer begins to have difficulty with her assignment. Things become even more complicated when Wanderer becomes attracted to Ian, another rebel human. Reviewing the book for *Library Journal,* Jane Jorgenson said Meyer succeeded in "blending science fiction and romance in a way that has never worked so well."

When asked by young writers how to achieve success, Meyer has given this advice: "If you love to write, then write. Don't let your goal be having a novel published, let your goal be enjoying your stories. However, if you finish your story and you want to share it, be brave about it. Don't doubt your story's appeal. If you are a good reader, and you know what is interesting, and your story is interesting to you, then trust in that. If I would have realized that the stories in my head would be as intriguing to others as they were to me, I would probably have started writing sooner. Believe in your own taste."

HOME AND FAMILY

Meyer and her family live in Cave Creek, Arizona, not far from where she grew up. Her parents still live nearby. Her husband formerly worked as an auditor at an accounting firm, but after Meyer became so busy touring and making appearances to support *Twilight* and its sequels, he quit his job so that one of them could be home to take care of their sons. The boys, Gabe, Seth, and Eli, were born in 1997, 2000, and 2002, respectively. Meyer is still a member of the Mormon church, which she calls "a huge influence on who I am and my perspective on the world."

FAVORITE BOOKS AND MUSIC

Meyer is an avid reader of all kinds of fiction, but she has named science fiction author Orson Scott Card and fantasy writer Terry Brooks as two of her favorite modern novelists. She likes all kinds of music, and a couple of her favorite groups are Linkin Park and Muse.

WRITINGS

The Host, 2008
Twilight: The Graphic Novel, Volume 1, 2010

"The Twilight Saga"

Twilight, 2005
New Moon, 2006
Eclipse, 2007
Breaking Dawn, 2008

HONORS AND AWARDS

Editor's Choice Selection (*New York Times*): 2005, for *Twilight*
Top Ten Best Books for Young Adults (American Library Association): 2005, for *Twilight*

Top Ten Books for Reluctant Readers (American Library Association): 2005,
  for *Twilight*
Most Promising New Authors of the Year (*Publishers Weekly*): 2005
Best Books of the Year (*Publishers Weekly*): 2005, for *Twilight*
Teen Choice Book of the Year Award: 2009, for *Breaking Dawn*
Children's Choice Author of the Year Award: 2009

FURTHER READING

Periodicals

Current Biography Yearbook, 2008
Entertainment Weekly, July 18, 2008, pp.22, 28
New York Times, Aug. 2, 2008, p.B7
New York Times Book Review, Aug. 12, 2007, p.19
Newsweek, Aug. 4, 2008, p.63
Publishers Weekly, July 18, 2005, p.207
School Library Journal, Oct. 2005, pp.37, 166; Oct. 2007, p.160; Oct. 2008,
  p.154
Time, May 5, 2008, p.49; Sep.1, 2008, p.4
USA Today, May 6, 2008, p.D7; July 31, 2008, p.D1

ADDRESS

Stephenie Meyer
Author Mail
Little, Brown and Company
237 Park Avenue
New York, NY 10017

WORLD WIDE WEB SITE

http://www.stepheniemeyer.com

Orianthi 1985-

Australian Singer and Guitarist
Guitarist for Michael Jackson and Singer of
"According to You"

BIRTH

Orianthi Panagaris, known professionally as Orianthi, was born on January 22, 1985, in Adelaide, the largest city in South Australia. Her unusual first name came from her Greek grandmother and is pronounced "Or-ee-AN-thee." She was the first child of Peter Panagaris, a musician, and his wife Susanne; they had a second daughter, Tina, 11 months after Orianthi was born.

YOUTH

With a father in the business, Orianthi grew up surrounded by a wide variety of music. Through her father's extensive collection of records, she heard classic rock from the 1960s and 1970s, which featured such guitarists as Jimi Hendrix, Eric Clapton, and Carlos Santana. At the same time, she listened to hard rock guitar bands like Van Halen and Def Leppard on the radio.

Orianthi also started playing music at a young age. Her father kept plenty of instruments around the house, and she started playing piano when she was only three. At six she picked up her first guitar, an acoustic model that she learned to play in classical style. She began playing the guitar all the time, at home and at school. At age 10 she was playing guitar in the pit orchestra for an Adelaide University Theatre production of the musical "Oklahoma."

Orianthi was 11 when her life changed after hearing Carlos Santana in concert. The Mexican-American guitarist had produced the hit singles "Black Magic Woman" and "Oye Como Va" with his group Santana in the early 1970s and was known for the blistering guitar solos that highlighted his band's Latin-flavored rock. After the show, "I begged my dad to get me a second-hand electric guitar so I could be like Carlos, and that was it, no more acoustic," she remembered. "After that, I would buy all of Carlos's videos—on VHS!—which I kept rewinding to try and learn his solos. I totally wore out the tapes."

> **"**
>
> *After Orianthi saw Carlos Santana performing live for the first time, "I begged my dad to get me a second-hand electric guitar so I could be like Carlos, and that was it, no more acoustic," she remembered. "After that, I would buy all of Carlos's videos—on VHS!—which I kept rewinding to try and learn his solos. I totally wore out the tapes."*
>
> **"**

Orianthi worked hard to perfect her guitar skills, practicing as much as five or six hours a day. As a teenager she played with two cover bands that performed popular Top 40 songs in pubs, clubs, and talent shows. Her father helped her record a demo CD, *Under the Influence,* on which she paid tribute to the great guitarists who had inspired her. She mailed the CD with a letter to guitar companies, music magazines, and music managers all over the world. She was only 14 years old, but her hard work eventually paid off with her first management deal.

Orianthi recorded her first CD at age 14 and has been playing professionally ever since.

EDUCATION

Growing up in Adelaide, Orianthi attended several schools, where her focus on the guitar sometimes made her the target of bullies. "I was called a freak because I was so engrossed in music," she noted. At lunchtime at school, if she'd left her guitar at home, she would make one from a milk carton and some rubber bands. She changed primary school at least five times, once so she could play soccer, another favorite activity. She finally ended up at Cabra Dominican College, a private high school in Adelaide, where she found friends who supported her. Nevertheless, by age 15 she was missing so many classes because of her music that she started home schooling instead. She continued with this distance learning program for another year before leaving to concentrate on music. "It was so hard to keep focused on history and math when all I wanted was to be a guitarist," she said.

CAREER HIGHLIGHTS

Pursuing Her Musical Dreams

Orianthi spent most of her teenage years developing her musical talents, and the hard work paid off with some impressive gigs supporting international artists during their Australian tours. At age 15 she opened for one of her idols, Grammy-winning guitarist Steve Vai, who got his start working with rock icons like Frank Zappa, David Lee Roth, and the band Whitesnake. At age 16 she played as the opening act for ZZ Top, the noted blues-rock trio and members of the Rock and Roll Hall of Fame. At the same time she continued playing with cover bands. She loved guitar so much that "I would put guitar solos in the songs, even though they weren't there." But she also began working with a vocal coach so she could sing with the group. At first she was shy about singing, "but as we rehearsed more I became more comfortable with it," she said. "I think once you start singing, you can connect with more people." By age 18 she was fronting her own band, DropD, singing and playing guitar at clubs around Adelaide.

> *After Santana listened to her demo CD, he invited Orianthi to his sound check. "We wound up jamming, and then he invited me to join him onstage that night," she recalled. She ended up playing for 45 minutes in front of 15,000 fans, even getting her own solo. "It was nerve-wracking but once I was up there it was fantastic," she said.*

That same year Carlos Santana played another important role in the aspiring rocker's musical development. He had returned to Australia for another tour, but this time Orianthi didn't watch from the audience. Santana had heard her demo CD and invited her to his pre-concert sound check in Adelaide. "We wound up jamming, and then he invited me to join him onstage that night," she recalled. She ended up playing for 45 minutes in front of 15,000 fans, even getting her own solo. "It was nerve-wracking but once I was up there it was fantastic," she said. Even more important, Santana took a video of the concert back to his guitar manufacturer, Paul Reed Smith Guitars. In 2004 PRS Guitars invited her to Los Angeles to play at NAMM, one of the world's largest music product trade shows. Eventually PRS Guitars became her sponsor, providing her with guitars and contacts in the music industry.

Orianthi kept playing at trade shows around the world and increasing her exposure. While bystanders may have wondered whether she earned stage time because of her good looks, music insiders knew better. In 2005, her idol Carlos Santana was interviewed on Australian television about her skill. "It's not cute any more. It's seriously [awesome]," he said. "If I was going to pass the baton to somebody, she would be my first choice." While playing at another NAMM show she met record executives at Geffen, who signed her to an international recording contract in late 2006.

Orianthi began working on her first full-length CD, *Violet Journey*, which she released in 2007. On this collection of original material, she wrote the songs, sang, played guitar, and also played almost all of the other instruments, including bass, drums, and percussion. She also produced the entire album, engineering and mixing the tracks herself. *Violet Journey* was distributed by a minor label and didn't make much of a splash.

Still, Orianthi kept working to advance her career. She wrote and performed the song "Now or Never" for the 2007 movie *Bratz,* a film targeting the young girls she hoped to inspire with her music. That same year she worked with two great guitarists: she served as the opening act for Steve Vai's international tour and she was invited to participate in Eric Clapton's Crossroads Guitar Festival in 2007. Clapton is the legendary guitarist who is the only person to have been inducted into the Rock and Roll Hall of Fame three times: with the groups Cream and the Yardbirds, and as a solo artist. He founded the Crossroads Festival, which features some of the world's greatest guitar players in concert, to benefit the Crossroads addiction rehab center. At the 2007 festival in Chicago, Orianthi played some of her own songs on stage and also had the chance to meet some of her guitar idols, including Clapton and blues legend B. B. King.

Working with Michael Jackson

In 2009 Orianthi started getting worldwide attention for her talents. It began in February, when she was invited to perform at the Grammy Awards with country superstar Carrie Underwood. "I was so nervous, looking out into the audience and seeing people like [U2's singer] Bono and Paul McCartney!" she noted. Nevertheless, her blistering solo on Underwood's "Last Name" brought her lots of attention. When someone saw the video of her performance and contacted her via MySpace to audition for singer Michael Jackson's upcoming tour, she thought it was a joke. The audition was real, however, and soon she was performing the guitar solo in "Beat It" for the superstar. "He started walking me up and down the stage," she remembered. "And he asked, 'Can you play that solo for me when walking at this pace?' And I said, 'Totally.' It was an amazing moment." She was soon signed for Jackson's tour, which was scheduled to play 50 concerts at the O2 Arena in London, England.

The tour was to launch a comeback for Jackson, whose 1982 album *Thriller* was the biggest selling record of all time. Orianthi and a huge cast of

Orianthi worked with Michael Jackson preparing for a series of comeback concerts in London in 2009. Jackson died suddenly before the concerts took place, but the rehearsals, which were filmed and produced in the film This Is It, *prominently featured Orianthi's guitar work.*

singers, musicians, and dancers rehearsed with Jackson six days a week for three months. "Rehearsals were intense," she noted. "[Jackson] was really particular. He wanted to be sure everything was perfect for his fans." She found herself learning not just about showmanship, but more about playing rhythm guitar in a group. "Going into it, I thought it would be all about playing guitar solos," she noted. "But the majority of it was playing chords and funky rhythms." The rehearsals were thrilling and intensive, but Jackson seemed up to the challenge. Orianthi was stunned when he suffered a heart attack and died in June 2009, less than three weeks before the tour was due to begin. Instead of performing in concert with Jackson, she sang and played at his memorial tribute, which was televised to millions of viewers around the world. "I wish he was still around," she shared. "He made me believe in myself more, and I learned so much."

The outpouring of public grief at Jackson's death, as well as curiosity about his final tour, led to a film that documented the show's rehearsals. *This Is It* was released in October 2009, and Orianthi's rocking guitar solos were featured prominently. The film showed "the whole process of putting together what would have been the biggest show on Earth," she revealed. "You can just see how excited he was about it. It was his vision." Although the film was only in theaters a few weeks, it earned $260 million worldwide and introduced Orianthi to a wider audience.

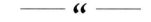

When Orianthi auditioned for Michael Jackson, she performed the guitar solo in "Beat It." "He started walking me up and down the stage," she remembered. "And he asked, 'Can you play that solo for me when walking at this pace?' And I said, 'Totally.' It was an amazing moment."

Becoming an All-Star Musician

Orianthi's record company capitalized on the publicity by moving up the release of her first major-label album, *Believe,* to October 2009. She co-wrote eight of the album's 11 tracks, all of which included a guitar solo. "It's bringing the '80s back, in a way. I just love that music," she said of the album. "I hope [listeners] want to put it in their car and not want to change it." Many critics observed that the artist achieved a power pop feel to the recording, and compared her to artists like Avril Lavigne, Kelly Clarkson, and the group Paramore. In *Billboard,* Lars Brandle called *Believe*

Orianthi's fame has grown as she has appeared with different musicians. In 2010 she made several appearances on "American Idol," including this collaboration with Mary J. Blige.

"essentially a conventional pop album with an utterly unconventional guitar solo on each track." Its first single, "According to You," hit the top 20 of *Billboard's* Hot 100 chart and peaked at No. 4 on the pop chart. To prove she hadn't lost any of her rock edge, she also released a video for the instrumental number "Highly Strung," which she wrote and recorded with Steve Vai. Both tunes received a lot of attention, and the album itself hit No. 1 on the *Billboard* New Artist and Heatseekers charts.

Through late 2009 and early 2010, Orianthi kept building momentum with several appearances on television. Besides several talk shows, she also played at an NFL game in Miami in December 2009 and performed her single "According to You" live on "American Idol" in 2010. She became part of two all-star recordings, contributing guitar and backing vocals to the 2010 remake of "We Are the World," which benefited victims of the Haiti earthquake. She and Steve Vai contributed guitar solos to R&B diva Mary J. Blige's version of the Led Zeppelin classic "Stairway to Heaven," and the all-star group performed the song live on the "American Idol Gives Back" special. Throughout the spring and summer of 2010 she appeared as a supporting act for Daughtry, John Mayer, Adam Lambert, and Kid Rock. "I don't consider these opportunities stepping stones, I consider them honors," she said of these chances to play with music stars.

As a female rock guitarist, Orianthi has often encountered skepticism when playing her guitar on stage. "It's like you have to prove yourself to them. Hopefully, I can change that a little bit so more guys can look at women playing the guitar and take them seriously. Anyone can do anything if they really have a passion for it."

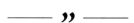

Although the life of a rock star is full of potential pitfalls, Orianthi plans to focus on the music, not the lifestyle. "It's a crazy industry," she commented. "I'm not into the partying, I'm a pretty healthy person. I don't like drinking or doing drugs but it does happen and I hear it's insane. But once you go off the rails like that, you can't really take the craft that seriously—that becomes your life. I've seen young musicians and actresses go down that self-destructive path. I'll probably overdose on spinach before any of that." Her future career plans include more pop-rock music and an all-instrumental album, as well as further partnerships with other musicians and singers. "I love fronting my own band and singing and playing my own material," she said, but she stressed that "I also love collaborating and just being the guitar player. I get the same rush from doing both."

Orianthi also wants to inspire her listeners to share her love of music and playing. In 2010 Paul Reed Smith Guitars brought out the Orianthi signature model, a relatively affordable electric guitar which she hoped would bring more girls to the field. "Being a female guitar player is not easy. It's kind of like being a male ballerina," she said, drawing a parallel to another gender stereotype. "It's a guy thing. And I accept that. But I love it as much as they love it." Early in her career, she often encountered skepticism when playing her guitar on stage. "It's like you have to prove yourself to them. Hopefully, I can change that a little bit so more guys can look at women playing the guitar and take them seriously. Anyone can do anything if they really have a passion for it." Her attitude is to ignore the naysayers and concentrate on making the best music she can. "My outlook on life is to keep looking up," she remarked. "If you're looking down, you don't see the light. For me, it's all about embracing that and thinking positively."

HOME AND FAMILY

Orianthi moved from Australia to Los Angeles in 2006 to pursue her dream of a musical career. The musician, who is single, said she has adjusted to living in a new country, although she misses her family and all the animals on their suburban Adelaide home. She often has her sister Tina for company, both in Los Angeles and on the road. She also has two small dogs, Pumba and Harriett.

FAVORITE MUSIC

Although Orianthi loves all kinds of music, including pop and country, she considers rock and blues guitarists her most important influences. She has been lucky to play with her two idols, Carlos Santana and Steve Vai, and cites several others as favorites. These include British rocker Eric Clapton, American blues man B. B. King ("he can hit one note and move you"), and the late American blues rocker Stevie Ray Vaughan, who "played with such fire [and] attitude." She also once played with the funk-rock singer and guitarist Prince, who called her up and invited her to jam with his band after seeing videos of her performances.

HOBBIES AND OTHER INTERESTS

When she isn't on the road, the mostly vegetarian Orianthi loves cooking and baking for her family and friends. When she's touring she relaxes by watching TV, walking, and going to the gym. She also has a very strong love for animals; she grew up with the usual cats and dogs, but also had rabbits, pigeons, doves, mice, and fish at various times during her childhood. Some of her favorite pets were ducks; at one point her family had seven of them on their property.

CREDITS

Violet Journey, 2007
"Now or Never," on *Bratz,* 2007 (movie soundtrack)
Believe, 2009
This Is It, 2009 (movie)

FURTHER READING

Periodicals

The Age (Melbourne, Australia), July 7, 2007
Billboard, Nov. 7, 2009, p.27; Jan. 30, 2010, p.35
Boston Herald, Oct. 26, 2009, p.E3
Entertainment Weekly, Oct. 16, 2009, p.58; Oct. 30, 2009, p.58
Guitar Edge Magazine, Nov. 23, 2009; Jan. 24, 2010
Houston Chronicle, Oct. 28, 2009, p.1
Los Angeles Times, Oct. 30, 2009
Sunday Mail (Adelaide, Australia), Oct. 11, 2009, p.15; Feb. 28, 2010, p.4
USA Today, Oct. 26, 2009, p.2D

Online Articles

http://www.mtv.com
(MTV, "Michael Jackson Guitarist Orianthi Is 'Bringing the '80s Back' with Debut," Oct. 26, 2009)
http://www.musicsa.com.au
(Music SA, "Orianthi Autobiography," 2006)
http://www.prsguitars.com
(Paul Reed Smith Guitars, "Orianthi," Feb. 26, 2010)
http://www.rollingstone.com
(Rolling Stone, "Breaking: Orianthi," Dec. 16, 2009)
http://www.teenmusic.com
(Teen Music, "Exclusive Interview! At the Hard Rock with Orianthi!," Feb. 6, 2009)
http://www.truthinshredding.com
(Truth in Shredding, "Orianthi: Truth in Shredding Exclusive Interview," Nov. 12, 2009)

ADDRESS

Orianthi
Interscope Geffen A&M Records
2220 Colorado Avenue
Santa Monica, CA 90404

Orianthi
19 Entertainment
8560 West Sunset Blvd.
West Hollywood, CA 90069

WORLD WIDE WEB SITE

http://www.orianthi.com

Alexander Ovechkin 1985-

Russian Professional Hockey Player with the
Washington Capitals
Winner of the Hart Trophy as the NHL's Most
Valuable Player in 2008 and 2009

BIRTH

Alexander Ovechkin, known as Alex or Ovi to his friends, was
born on September 17, 1985, in Moscow, Russia. At that time,
Russia was part of the Union of Soviet Socialist Republics
(USSR), or the Soviet Union. His mother, Tatiana Nikolaevna
Ovechkina, was one of Russia's greatest female basketball
players. She won Olympic gold medals in 1976 and 1980 as

Ovechkin (center) after leading the Russian team to the gold medal at the 2003 World Junior Hockey Championships.

the starting point guard for the Soviet national women's team. After her athletic career ended, she became president of the Dynamo Moscow women's professional basketball team. Alex's father, Mikhail Ovechkin, was a professional soccer player until his career was cut short by a leg injury. He later worked as a taxi driver and as a director for his wife's basketball team. Alex had two older brothers, Sergei and Mikhail. Sadly, Sergei died in a car accident when Alex was 10.

YOUTH

Ovechkin became fascinated with the sport of hockey at a very young age. When he was just two years old, he picked up a hockey stick and helmet in a sporting-goods store and refused to put them down. His interest grew when he saw his first hockey game on television. "When he was about four years old, the first time he saw hockey on TV, his jaw just dropped and he froze," his father remembered. "That was the only thing he wanted to watch." Before long, Ovechkin had started a collection of National Hockey League (NHL) trading cards that eventually totaled around 2,000 cards.

By the time Ovechkin joined a youth hockey league at the age of eight, however, he discovered that some of the other boys had already been skating for several years. Determined to catch up with his peers, Ovechkin worked hard to improve his skills. He woke up early in the morning to practice before school, and he stayed late after team practices. "He would skate there until his legs fell off," his father recalled. "He'd come home every evening just completely exhausted. He would drop in the hallway, and we'd pick him up and just carry him to his room."

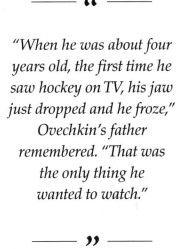

"When he was about four years old, the first time he saw hockey on TV, his jaw just dropped and he froze," Ovechkin's father remembered. *"That was the only thing he wanted to watch."*

Ovechkin's hard work paid off, though, as he quickly emerged as one of Russia's top young hockey players. He started playing professionally at the age of 16 for the Dynamo Moscow hockey team in the Russian Superleague. He scored 8 goals and made 8 assists in 40 games as a teenaged rookie playing against much older and more experienced men. Ovechkin played with the Dynamo for the next three seasons as well. By the time he left the team he had scored 36 goals and tallied 32 assists in 152 career games.

Ovechkin also represented Russia in international hockey tournaments throughout his teen years. In 2002 he played for the Russian team at the International Ice Hockey Federation (IIHF) World Under-18 Junior Championships. He led the team to a gold medal by scoring 14 goals in 8 games. The following year he moved up to the World Under-20 Junior Championships. Ovechkin led the tournament with 6 goals to help Russia claim another gold medal. In 2004 he earned a silver medal at the Junior Worlds and also became the youngest player ever to play for the Russian national men's ice hockey team at the IIHF World Championships.

EDUCATION

Ovechkin attended the Military Institute in Moscow during his early hockey career. His studies there fulfilled the mandatory military service requirement that Russia imposed on all of its young male citizens.

CAREER HIGHLIGHTS

NHL—The Washington Capitals

Ovechkin's outstanding performance in the Russian professional league and in international competition brought him to the attention of NHL scouts. Ever since he had started collecting hockey cards as a kid, he had dreamed of playing in the NHL someday. "It's the best hockey there is and I think I'm ready to play there," he declared. "It has always been my dream to play in North America and in the NHL."

As soon as Ovechkin turned 18 and became eligible for the NHL, it became clear that he would be the top player selected in the 2004 entry draft. The Washington Capitals won the first pick in the league's draft lottery because the team had finished 28th out of 30 NHL teams during the previous season (2003-04). "We were all excited," Capitals General Manager George McPhee related. "I called our chief amateur scout. I said, 'If you had to pick today, who would you take?' He said, 'It's got to be Ovechkin.' We just felt like Alex's character and his physical playing really separated him from any other player we could see."

Ovechkin was thrilled to be chosen first overall in the draft, and he expressed great excitement about joining the Capitals. The start of his NHL career was delayed, however, by a labor-management dispute between the NHL Players Association and team owners. They held lengthy negotiations but failed to reach an agreement on several important issues. Since both sides refused to play without a new contract, the entire 2004-05 NHL season was canceled. It marked the first time in the history of American professional sports that a whole season was lost to a labor dispute. The situation, which became known as the NHL lockout, made many hockey fans angry. They felt that greed and selfishness had overtaken the sport.

Ovechkin returned to Dynamo Moscow during the NHL lockout. "There are still things that I can work on with the Dynamo," he explained. "I'd rather be playing there than not playing at all. I always want to be playing hockey. It's what I love. Hockey, hockey, hockey." When the NHL team owners and players' union finally reached an agreement in July 2005, Ovechkin immediately signed a contract with the Capitals and joined the team in Washington DC.

Making Waves as NHL Rookie of the Year

Ovechkin made his NHL debut on October 5, 2005, and immediately established himself as one of the most promising young players in the league. Wearing jersey number 8, which had been his mother's number

Ovechkin celebrates after scoring his first goal in the second period of his first game in the NHL, 2005.

when she played basketball in the Olympics, the young left wing scored two goals in his first NHL game to lead his team to a 3-2 victory over the Columbus Blue Jackets. He went on to score a point in each of his first seven games (in hockey, a player receives a point for scoring a goal or assisting on a goal by a teammate). "He has exceeded expectations," McPhee acknowledged. "We were hoping that he would just hold down a regular shift and contribute in his first year."

As the season progressed, Ovechkin impressed hockey fans with his unique combination of speed, scoring ability, physical play, and obvious enthusiasm for the game. He also made a number of amazing plays that showed up on TV sports highlight reels and Internet video sites. One memorable example came on January 16, 2006, during the third period of a game against the Phoenix Coyotes. Ovechkin sped toward the Coyotes' goal and got knocked off his feet as he prepared to fire a backhand shot. While sliding on his back across the ice, he somehow managed to extend his stick over his head and knock the puck into the goal. "We all lost our minds on the bench," recalled Capitals goalie Ollie Kolzig. "A talent like his only comes along once in a lifetime."

In February 2006 the NHL suspended play for two weeks to allow its best skaters to play in the Winter Olympic Games in Turin, Italy. Ovechkin led

―――― " ――――

"We were all excited,"
Washington Capitals
General Manager George
McPhee said when they
drafted Ovechkin. "I called
our chief amateur scout. I
said, 'If you had to pick
today, who would you take?'
He said, 'It's got to be
Ovechkin.' We just felt like
Alex's character and his
physical playing really
separated him from any
other player we could see."

―――― " ――――

the Russian national team with five goals and was named to the all-tournament team. Although Russia finished fourth and failed to win a medal, Ovechkin enjoyed his Olympic experience. "It was the coolest time in my life to play in the Olympics," he said. "In Russia you know we have a [proud Olympic] history and also my family has a history."

After returning to the Capitals, Ovechkin put the finishing touches on a great rookie season. He set a team record by scoring 52 goals and added 54 assists for a total of 106 points. He thus became the first player in NHL history to register more than 50 goals and 100 points in his rookie season. Ovechkin also became the first rookie to be named to the NHL All-Star Team in 15 years, earned the Kharlamov Trophy as the best Russian player in the league, and easily won the Calder Memorial Trophy as the NHL's Rookie of the Year. Although the Capitals only won 29 games and failed to make the playoffs, Ovechkin felt confident that his team would soon become a contender. "Right now our team is starting out. We will play better and better and better," he predicted. "I look forward to playing many years with the Washington Capitals, and my goal is to win Stanley Cup."

Winning Hearts and the Hart Trophy

Ovechkin's dynamic play continued in the 2006-07 NHL season, during which he tallied 46 goals and 92 points. "He's all over the place," said Capitals captain Chris Clark. "He's not just hitting guys, he's running over guys. If he's not shooting the puck on net, he's driving to the net. He's making something happen on every shift." Ovechkin was voted into the starting lineup for the NHL All-Star Game and received his second consecutive Kharlamov Trophy. Despite his efforts, however, the Capitals only managed to win 28 games and failed to make the playoffs once again. "We have not seen the limits of what Alex can do," said McPhee. "He is one of the most creative players we have seen in a long time. He's only going to

Here Ovechkin shoots the puck past Philadelphia Flyer goalie Martin Biron in Game 6 of the 2008 Eastern Conference playoffs, but the Capitals ultimately lost the playoff series to the Flyers.

improve, and we're going to see how good he can be. If we make the club better, people will see a lot more of him."

As the 2007-08 NHL season got underway, Ovechkin was determined to lead his team into the playoffs. The Capitals struggled early, though, and sat in last place with the worst record in the league at the end of November. Desperate to salvage the season, team management hired a new head coach, Bruce Boudreau. The move had its desired effect. Under Boudreau's guidance, Ovechkin and his teammates improved significantly. In fact, the Capitals made the largest single-season comeback in NHL history. Washington won 11 of the last 12 games on its way to 43 victories and a coveted spot in the playoffs.

The excitement surrounding the young team spread quickly throughout Washington DC and the surrounding area. The Capitals started selling out home games for the first time in franchise history. "Now we bring the fans

341

and the crowd is very good. When it's full, it's unbelievable," Ovechkin stated. "Everybody has to understand, one player cannot bring a good team. It's a whole team. We just have a great team right now, a young team, and everybody does what they can try to do to win."

As in his previous two seasons, Ovechkin remained the undisputed star of the team. He scored a franchise-record 65 goals during the regular season. He thus became the first NHL player in a decade to break 60 goals—and one of only a dozen players ever to score 65 or more. Ovechkin also contributed 47 assists to lead the league in points with 112. His outstanding play continued in the playoffs, where he notched 4 goals and 5 assists, but the Capitals lost a tough seven-game series to the Philadelphia Flyers in the first round.

Ovechkin's remarkable season was recognized with a slew of prestigious postseason awards. He received the Hart Memorial Trophy as the league's most valuable player, the Lester B. Pearson Award for outstanding player as voted by peers, the Maurice Richard Trophy as the NHL's leading goal scorer, and the Art Ross Trophy as the league leader in points. He became the first player ever to capture all four major awards in a single season. "I think I'm the happiest 22-year-old guy on the planet," he said afterward. "I wanted to win everything. Maybe next year the Stanley Cup."

Ovechkin capped off his great year in 2008 by helping the Russian national ice hockey team win a gold medal at the World Championships. He led the team with 6 goals and 6 assists in 9 tournament games. Russia's strong performance made it one of the medal favorites for the 2010 Winter Olympic Games, scheduled to be held in February 2010 in Vancouver, Canada.

A Stellar Season

Prior to the start of the 2008-09 season, Ovechkin signed a 13-year, $124 million contract extension with the Capitals, making him the highest-paid player in NHL history. As the season got underway, Ovechkin proved that management's faith in him was justified. With the young Russian star leading the way, the Capitals competed for the best record in the entire Eastern Conference. "He's playing more of a team game. I think he has a better surrounding cast on the whole, but it's not all about scoring goals. It's about playing to win," Coach Boudreau explained. "There's just nobody that does what Ovechkin does. He shoots the puck harder, crashes into the net. He does what he needs to do to win. He plays hard all the time. We've got a good team, but we'd be nowhere without Alex."

In February 2009 Ovechkin scored his 200th career goal, becoming only the fourth player in league history to accomplish this feat in four NHL seasons. The following month he scored his 50th goal of the season—and one of the most controversial goals of his career—during a game against the Tampa Bay Lightning. He celebrated the goal by dropping his stick on the ice in front of the opposing goaltender, warming his hands over it as if it were on fire, and then pretending that the stick was too hot to pick up.

Many people criticized Ovechkin's behavior as unsportsmanlike. Although the NHL does not penalize excessive celebrations, critics claimed that he broke a longstanding tradition by rubbing his goal in the face of his opponents. "To do that, especially on our ice, I took it as an insult," said Lightning wing Ryan Malone. "It's embarrassing. This isn't football."

On the other hand, some people appreciated Ovechkin's showmanship. Supporters found his exuberance entertaining and claimed that he attracted new fans to the sport. They noted, for example, that the Capitals' 2008-09 TV ratings were 65 percent higher than the previous season—and 182 percent higher than they had been during Ovechkin's rookie year.

According to the Washington Capitals head coach, Bruce Boudreau, "There's just nobody that does what Ovechkin does. He shoots the puck harder, crashes into the net. He does what he needs to do to win. He plays hard all the time. We've got a good team, but we'd be nowhere without Alex."

Ovechkin finished the regular season with 56 goals and 54 assists for 110 points. He earned a second consecutive Richard Trophy as the league leader in goals scored, and he finished second in points for the season. He also led the NHL with an amazing 528 shots on goal—156 more than any other player. Ovechkin's outstanding performance was honored with a second straight Hart Trophy and Pearson Award as the NHL's most valuable player.

Reaching for a Stanley Cup

Ovechkin and his teammates entered the 2008-09 postseason in a confident mood. After all, the Capitals had won 50 games to claim first place in the Southeast Division of the Eastern Conference. In the first round of the playoffs, Washington defeated the New York Rangers in a tense 7-game series. The Capitals thus advanced to face the Pittsburgh Penguins in the Conference semifinals. The highly anticipated series featured a matchup between Ovechkin and Penguins star Sidney Crosby, who had entered the

Ovechkin faces off against Sidney Crosby of the Pittsburgh Penguins in game 1 of the 2009 conference semifinals, a highly anticipated matchup between the two players that many consider the league's best young players.

league the same year. (For more information on Crosby, see *Biography Today Sports,* Vol. 14.) The young rivals had teamed up in the NHL All-Star Game, but their head-to-head meetings during the season were marked by verbal exchanges and shoving matches. "There's more to stars meeting here, great hockey players meeting, there's great personalities, strong personalities, there's faces of the league that are clashing," said Penguins Coach Dan Bylsma. "That's great for the league, great for the postseason."

In the end, Crosby and the Penguins beat Ovechkin and the Capitals in a hotly contested 7-game series. Ovechkin shone in the playoffs once again, contributing 11 goals and 10 assists for 21 points in 14 games. He hoped that the additional playoff experience would help to prepare his team to reach the Stanley Cup finals in 2009-10. "It's time for us," Ovechkin declared. "The organization, the guys understand that if we make the playoffs, it's not [enough]. Now we have to move forward."

By the end of the regular 2009-10 season, the Caps had won 54 games and earned 121 points for the season, and Ovechkin had scored 50 goals and 59 assists. The Caps won the Presidents' Trophy, which is awarded each year by the NHL to the team that finishes the regular season with the best overall record. The Caps started the playoffs as the top-seeded team, but lost to the Montreal Canadiens, the eighth-seeded team, in the first round. According to Scott Burnside for ESPN, "[This was] a collapse of historic proportions. Defying all logic, the NHL's best regular-season team by a country mile folded in spectacular fashion, losing Game 7 of its conference quarterfinals series 2-1 and becoming the first No. 1 seed to blow a 3-1 series lead in the playoffs to an 8-seed." For the Caps and their fans, it was a tremendous disappointment after a great season, and many pointed to the difference in the team's play between the regular season and the postseason. "I think everyone wants to win not regular season, we want to win the Cup," he said. "We all played great in season, but in the playoffs something missed. We just have to concentrate more on playoffs.... We just have to be ready for the playoffs and be ready for that kind of pressure."

Small consolation came to Ovechkin in the form of two awards. He became the first player in NHL history voted a First Team All-Star in each of his first five seasons. In addition, he was the inaugural recipient of the 2009-10 Ted Lindsay Award, presented annually to the Most Outstanding Player in the NHL as voted by fellow members of the NHL Players' Association. Ted Lindsay was on hand to present the award as part of the 2010 NHL Awards.

Many hockey analysts believe that Ovechkin, who has been described in the *New York Times* as "the league's best as well as its most exciting and charismatic player," stands ready to lead his team to a championship. Some observers claim that his remarkable skills and pure love of hockey have already changed the face of the game. "If there was ever an athlete who you'd pay to see no matter what his team did, he'd be the guy," said

Columbus Blue Jackets Coach Ken Hitchcock. "I'd watch him in the warmup. He transcends. I think he's the evolution of our game—a young, reckless, skilled player."

HOME AND FAMILY

Ovechkin owns a home near Arlington, Virginia, that he often shares with his brother and parents. He spends his summers in Moscow.

HOBBIES AND OTHER INTERESTS

In his spare time, Ovechkin likes to relax by playing cards, watching movies, and playing video games. He gives back to the community through a program called Ovi's Crazy Eights. He purchases eight tickets to every Capitals home game and donates them to needy children or U.S. soldiers and their families. The group sits in a special section and receives free souvenirs, and Ovechkin pays them a personal visit after the game. The Ovi's Crazy Eights program also donates money to Russian orphanages and to Right to Play, an international charity that uses sports to help disadvantaged children.

HONORS AND AWARDS

Calder Memorial Trophy (NHL Rookie of the Year): 2006
NHL All-Star Team: 2006, 2007, 2008, 2009, 2010
Kharlamov Trophy (Best Russian Player in the NHL): 2006, 2007, 2008, 2009
Hart Trophy (NHL Most Valuable Player): 2008, 2009
Lester B. Pearson Award (outstanding NHL player as voted by peers): 2008, 2009
Maurice "Rocket" Richard Trophy (most goals in NHL season): 2008, 2009
Art Ross Trophy (most points in NHL season): 2008
Ted Lindsay Award (NHL Players' Association): 2010, for Most Outstanding Player in the NHL

FURTHER READING

Periodicals

Current Biography Yearbook, 2008
Hamilton Spectator (Ontario, Canada), Apr. 8, 2008, p.SP10
New York Times, Oct. 1, 2006; Feb. 13, 2008; Feb. 22, 2009
Sporting News, Sep. 29, 2006, p.14; Sep. 29, 2008, p.50; Mar. 16, 2009, p.62; May 25, 2009, p.10
Tampa Tribune, Mar. 27, 2008, p.1

USA Today, Oct. 18, 2005, p.C10; Dec. 7, 2005, p.C1; Feb. 3, 2006, p.C13
Washington Post, June 13, 2008, p.E1; Apr. 30, 2010

Online Articles

http://www.canada.com
(Canada.com, "Ovechkin: NHL Fans' Plan B," Apr. 12, 2008)
http://sports.espn.go.com
(ESPN, "Ovechkin Confident of His Arrival," May 30, 2004; "This Wasn't
a Loss; This Was a Collapse," Apr. 28, 2010)
http://www.nytimes.com/2010/04/11/magazine/11Ovechkin-t.html
(New York Times, "Alexander Ovechkin, the Mad Russian," Apr. 9, 2010)
http://www.nhl.com
(NHL, "Cheers, Jeers for Ovechkin Celebration," Mar. 20, 2009)
http://sportsillustrated.cnn.com
(Sports Illustrated, "Q&A: Alexander Ovechkin," Feb. 16, 2007; "Shooting for 60 Goals: Being the First to Hit that Scoring Milestone since 1996
Would Place Alexander Ovechkin in the Company of Greats. Would It
Also Be a Sign of an Offensive Renaissance in the NHL?" Mar. 18, 2008)
http://www.washingtonpost.com
(Washington Post, "The Great Ones Get It," May 6, 2009)
http://www.washingtonpost.com/wp-srv/special/sports/ovechkin
(Washington Post, "Alex Ovechkin: A Look at the Capitals Star's Ca-
reer," no date)

ADDRESS

Alexander Ovechkin
Washington Capitals
627 North Glebe Road, Ste. 850
Arlington, VA 22203

WORLD WIDE WEB SITES

http://www.alexovechkin8.com
http://capitals.nhl.com
http://www.nhl.com

Brad Paisley 1972-

American Country Singer, Songwriter, and Guitarist
Named Top Male Vocalist by the Country Music
Association and the Academy of Country Music

BIRTH

Brad Douglas Paisley was born October 28, 1972, in the small
town of Glen Dale, West Virginia, located on the Ohio River.
He was the only child of Doug Paisley, who worked for the
West Virginia Department of Transportation, and Sandy Jarvis
Paisley, a teacher.

YOUTH

Paisley had a very close bond with his maternal grandfather, Warren Jarvis, who lived nearby. Jarvis was a railroad employee who worked the night shift. Because he was home in the afternoons, his grandson spent a lot of time at his house. "He was the best friend I ever had," Paisley has said. Jarvis was an enthusiastic guitar player who loved traditional country music. He often sat for hours on his porch, playing one song after another.

When Paisley was eight years old, his grandfather gave him a Sears Danelectro Silvertone guitar and began teaching him how to play. Learning can be difficult at first, as it requires holding the hands in some uncomfortable positions. "I kind of fought it for a while,'cause at eight you'd rather play sports or do anything other than something that hurts your hand," Paisley recalled. "But the thing that kept me going was knowing how bad he wanted me to do that. I think he enjoyed it so much he wanted me to be able to have that in my life. He changed my life in a way no one ever will again."

> **When Paisley was eight years old, his grandfather began teaching him how to play guitar. "I kind of fought it for a while, 'cause at eight you'd rather play sports or do anything other than something that hurts your hand," Paisley recalled. "But the thing that kept me going was knowing how bad he wanted me to do that. I think he enjoyed it so much he wanted me to be able to have that in my life. He changed my life in a way no one ever will again."**

Paisley gave his first public performance when he was 10 years old, singing at church. His hometown audience was very supportive of the young musician. "Pretty soon, I was performing at every Christmas party and Mother's Day event," he remembered. "The neat thing about a small town is that when you want to be an artist, by golly, they'll make you one." At the age of 12, Paisley wrote his first composition, "Born on Christmas Day." By that time, he had started taking lessons with a local guitarist, Clarence "Hank" Goddard. Recognizing Paisley's great potential, Goddard gave his student a lot of encouragement, and a thorough grounding in the basics. By the time Paisley was 13 years old, he and Goddard had formed a band called Brad Paisley and the C-Notes. Two of Goddard's other friends, both seasoned, adult musicians, filled out the group.

Regular on Radio

When Paisley was in junior high school, his principal heard him perform "Born on Christmas Day" and invited him to play at a meeting of the local Rotary Club. At that meeting was Tom Miller, the program director at a radio station in nearby Wheeling, West Virginia. Miller asked Paisley if he'd like to be a guest on "Jamboree USA," a program that aired on Saturday nights. The show was legendary in the area, and Paisley was thrilled to accept. "I ran through the house screaming, 'I'm going to play the Jamboree!'" he said. "My grandfather was just super-proud. All of a sudden, he was seeing this guitar he'd given to me become my life."

After his first appearance, Paisley was asked to become a member of the show's weekly lineup. For the next eight years, he opened the show for some of the biggest acts in country music. He eventually became the youngest person ever inducted into the Jamboree USA Hall of Fame. He was also part of the regular lineup at Jamboree in the Hills, a famous outdoor music festival held near Wheeling. His experiences on the radio show and at the festival were invaluable in learning about both the artistic side and the business side of music. About two months before his grandfather died, Paisley was asked to go on tour with the Judds, one of the most popular acts in country music. "He got to see that," Paisley said of his grandfather. "It was like giving Moses a look at the Promised Land. He knew that guitar was the best gift I ever received."

EDUCATION

By the time he started high school, Paisley had an extensive background in traditional gospel and country music and was performing regularly with world-famous entertainers. Still, he was able to pick up more musical knowledge at John Marshall High School in Glen Dale. Playing in the school's jazz band exposed him to a kind of music he never heard at home, and listening to music with his friends introduced him to rock bands that were new to him, like Pink Floyd and U2. He'd listen to the different kinds of music, then try to play what he heard. These influences gave depth to his developing musicianship.

After graduating from high school in 1991, Paisley started classes at West Liberty State College, about 20 miles from his home town. He went there for two years before transferring to Belmont University in Nashville, Tennessee. Nashville is the capital of country music, and Paisley's time there was valuable not only for what he learned in his courses, but also for the friends and business contacts he made. He had internships at ASCAP (the American Society of Composers, Authors & Publishers), Atlantic Records,

Paisley's first album, Who Needs Pictures, *featured a traditional country sound.*

and the Fitzgerald-Hartley management firm. He also made friends with other young people who would become his partners in writing and producing many albums—Frank Rogers, Chris DuBois, and Kelley Lovelace, among others. In 1995, Paisley graduated from Belmont with a bachelor's degree in music business.

CAREER HIGHLIGHTS

Within a week of his college graduation, Paisley had signed a deal with EMI to work as a songwriter. Songwriters frequently record demos of their compositions for vocalists to preview, and Paisley turned out many of these. His first hit was "Another You," as recorded by David Kersh. Before long, the strength of Paisley's demos led executives at Arista Records to offer him his own contract as a recording artist. Paisley was only 26 years old, but he had years of experience behind him and an excellent grasp of what elements were needed for success in the music business. "Brad came to the table with very concrete, very well-thought ideas of what should be done at every level," recalled Mike Dungan, a senior vice-president and general manager at Arista. "I'm not talking about an uneducated kid here. I'm talking about somebody who came to the table with really great ideas."

Who Needs Pictures

Paisley had never recorded an album before, yet he had enough confidence to do things his own way. He insisted on using his own band and on playing all the guitar tracks himself, rather than using studio musicians as is usual for recording sessions. Instead of hiring an experienced producer, he hired his friend from college, Frank Rogers. While Rogers was inexperienced, Paisley had faith in his talent and in their ability to work together. Drawing from their large backlog of compositions, they began work on Paisley's album in 1998.

On June 1, 1999, *Who Needs Pictures* was released. Featuring a traditional country sound, impressive guitar work, and strong lyrics, *Who Needs Pictures* was an immediate success. The album yielded two chart-topping country singles, the romantic "We Danced" and "He Didn't Have to Be." The lyrics of "He Didn't Have to Be," co-written with Kelley Lovelace and telling the story of a man who cares enough to be a good father to a child who isn't his own, were inspired by the relationship between Lovelace and his stepson. "He Didn't Have to Be" spent two weeks at the top of the country singles charts and was nominated as Song of the Year and Single of the Year by the Country Music Association. Both awards ended up going to other artists, but it was significant even to be nominated. Strong sales of *Who Needs Pictures* continued long after its initial release. By February 2001, it was certified platinum, meaning it had sold more than one million copies.

When Paisley was in junior high school, he was asked to be a guest on "Jamboree USA," a program that aired on Saturday nights and was legendary in the area. "I ran through the house screaming, 'I'm going to play the Jamboree!'" he said. "My grandfather was just super-proud. All of a sudden, he was seeing this guitar he'd given to me become my life."

Paisley humbly receives the Grand Ole Opry Member Award after being inducted into the Opry in 2001.

Youngest Member of the Grand Ole Opry

On May 28, 1999, just before the release of *Who Needs Pictures,* Paisley was asked to make an appearance at the Grand Ole Opry, a weekly concert and radio broadcast originating from Nashville, Tennessee. First broadcast on the Nashville radio station WSM in 1925, the Grand Ole Opry has long been an important institution in country music, showcasing classic acts alongside rising stars. After making about 40 appearances on the show, Paisley was invited to become a member of the Opry on February 17, 2001. This invitation is a great honor, given only to those who represent the best in country music. If accepted, artists must keep their membership active by making numerous appearances at the Opry throughout the year. Paisley was 28 years old when he accepted the invitation, making him the youngest member of the Opry.

Paisley's close association with the Opry showed his dedication to country music's roots. His story songs and humorous numbers were very tradition-al, yet his music also featured a strong guitar sound that was fresh and ap-pealing. The Grand Ole Opry had lost some of its influence over the years, as more and more crossover artists came to dominate the country music scene. Traditionalists were thrilled to have one of country's hottest young stars become a member of the Opry. When the CBS television network produced a special in honor of the Opry's 75th anniversary, Paisley and

Chely Wright performed a duet called "Hard to Be a Husband, Hard to Be a Wife," written especially for the show. Released in 2000 on the album *Backstage at the Opry,* the duet was nominated for the Vocal Event of the Year award at 2001 Country Music Association Awards.

Part II

Recording artists sometimes have a tough time following up a sensational debut like *Who Needs Pictures,* but Paisley had no such problem. In fact, he visualized his second album as the sequel, and the title, *Part II,* reflected this. To emphasize the continuity between the two albums, *Part II* even begins with fiddle music that was the last sound heard on *Who Needs Pictures.* Released in 2001, *Part II* was on the *Billboard* country albums charts for more than 70 weeks and was certified platinum in August of that year. Paisley supported the album by touring as the opening act for Lonestar, a popular modern country group, and by performing at fairs and summer music festivals around the country.

Part II had two singles reach the top of the country charts, "I Wish You'd Stay" and "I'm Gonna Miss Her (The Fishin' Song)." Two other singles, "Wrapped Around" and "Two People Fell in Love," also charted in the country Top 10. The No. 1 singles showed Paisley's diversity: "I Wish You'd Stay" was a wistful number about saying good-bye to a loved one, while "I'm Gonna Miss Her" is a tongue-in-cheek song about a man whose girlfriend tells him she'll leave him if he doesn't stop spending so much time fishing. As he sits in his boat waiting for a nibble on his line, he reflects that she will be missed. "I'm Gonna Miss Her" became one of Paisley's signature songs, and it also had special significance in his personal life. While casting the video for the song, Paisley thought of Kimberly Williams, an actress he'd seen some years before in the movie *Father of the Bride.* He asked her to play the part of the girlfriend in the video, and she and Paisley began dating in real life. They were married in 2003.

Mainstream Success and Multiple Awards

Paisley's third album, *Mud on the Tires,* came out in 2003. It topped the *Billboard* country album charts and was certified double platinum, meaning it sold more than two million copies. *Mud on the Tires* was Paisley's first album to make it into the Top 10 of the general album charts as well. "I'm Gonna Miss Her" had firmly established Paisley as a funny singer in many peoples' minds. While he appreciated the success of his song, he didn't like being pigeonholed. "It's sort of an insult," he remarked. "To me, part of entertaining is trying to capture all the various experiences. I'm a big fan of

In concert, Paisley offers an elaborate stage show to create a memorable experience for concert-goers.

... [artists] like the Beatles—from single to single, you didn't know where they were going next. Nothing makes me want to go do a really dark album more than the people who say, 'You're all about funny.'"

One of the most popular tunes from *Mud on the Tires* showed Paisley's darker side. "Whiskey Lullaby," written by Jon Randall and Bill Anderson, told a grim tale of a love gone wrong and the man and woman who drink themselves to death over it. Paisley recorded it as a duet with Alison Krauss, an acclaimed bluegrass vocalist. The song and the dramatic video made for it got a lot of attention. The album brought Paisley more Grammy nominations than any other male artist that year, but he still didn't win, in any category.

That changed after the release of his fourth album, *Time Well Wasted,* which came out in 2005. *Time Well Wasted* again demonstrated Paisley's range, containing both funny and serious songs. One standout from the album was "When I Get Where I'm Going," an uplifting gospel duet with Dolly Parton, one of country's most respected female stars. A completely different tone was struck with "Alcohol," which was nominated for a Grammy Award. "Whiskey Lullaby" had portrayed the tragic and fatal effects of drinking, but "Alcohol" was more lighthearted, while still pointing out alcohol's negative effects. The lyrics are written from the point of view of the alcohol itself, including

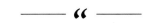

"With each song I choose, I have to visualize the people in the front rows of my shows enjoying it as we perform it," Paisley said. "If I can see them singing along, smiling and laughing, or holding up a lighter or cell phone, then the song is a keeper."

the line, "You had some of the best times you'll never remember with me, alcohol." *Time Well Wasted* eventually went double platinum and was awarded Album of the Year honors by both the Academy of Country Music and the Country Music Association.

As his popularity continued to increase, Paisley remained down-to-earth, giving lots of credit for his success to his songwriting collaborators, his backing musicians, and his recording crew. After winning the Country Music Association's Album of the Year award for *Time Well Wasted,* he brought the trophy into the recording studio to share with everyone there. "We gave each other a round of applause, and I told everybody, 'Congratulations, this is yours. Now, let's do even better.' That's the mindset we had," he recalled. "I didn't mean that we expect to win it again. What I meant was, 'Let's see if we can top it.' We wanted to aim at pushing ourselves and at doing something we felt moved the music forward."

Moving ahead in High Gear

Paisley's next major album was *5th Gear,* released in 2007. The title is not only a reference to it being his fifth major album, but also to the fifth gear used in driving. Fifth gear "is something you reach when you're on a long, good stretch and you're really rolling," he said. "This album, and this time in my career, feels like that. We are pushing things further in every way—musically, lyrically, and in our concerts."

5th Gear reached No. 1 on the country charts and No. 3 on the general album charts. It yielded five No. 1 country singles: "Ticks," "Online," "Letter to Me," "I'm Still a Guy," and "Throttleneck," a hard-driving instrumental that won Paisley his first Grammy Award. In "Letter to Me," the lyrics reflect on the singer's younger self, a theme that runs through the entire project. "Online" was a funny number about the way people misrepresent themselves when chatting online. "Ticks" was another humorous song, about a guy trying to charm a girl by inviting her to take a romantic walk in the woods, reassuring her that he'll make sure she hasn't been bitten by any ticks when they're done walking. "If you think this song is gross, you're missing the point," he said. "It's not about bloodsucking bugs. It's about a guy flirting with a girl, and, in trying to tell her he's interested in her, he's using a term that's about as country as can be."

In 2007, Paisley was recognized with Male Vocalist of the Year honors from both the Country Music Association and the Academy of Country Music. That year he produced a more expensive and elaborate stage show that featured the music from *5th Gear.* Paisley loves to use cutting-edge technology to create a memorable experience for concert-goers. He always keeps his live shows in mind during the process of writing and selecting songs for albums. "With each song I choose, I have to visualize the people in the front rows of my shows enjoying it as we perform it," he said. "If I can see them singing along, smiling and laughing, or holding up a lighter or cell phone, then the song is a keeper." The tour ran from April 2007 through February 2008, stopping in 94 cities and attracting more than one million fans.

In 2008, Paisley followed *5th Gear* with *Play,* an album of mostly instrumental music. He had earned a reputation as one of the best guitarists in country music, but Paisley knew that instrumental albums are rarely

Paisley's most recent release, American Saturday Night, *includes "Welcome to the Future," the song that he says is his personal favorite.*

as popular as vocal music. He didn't mind. "Many of my fans have probably never bought a jazz album or a true blues album," he said, "so it was a challenge to make something that's not a complete disaster to them. I wanted *Play* to be something that people who never bought an instrumental record of any kind before would have a good time listening to." *Play* featured duets with Keith Urban and Vince Gill, two other country artists known for their guitar skills, as well as the legendary blues musician B.B. King and other top musicians. The result was a "risky, thrilling" album, according to *Guitar Player* reviewer Jude Gold. It was also another hit with Paisley's audience, debuting at the top of the country album charts.

American Saturday Night

After taking an instrumental break on *Play,* Paisley geared up for his next album, *American Saturday Night.* As usual, it was a group effort. "I rely on these guys that I trust like Chris [DuBois], Frank [Rogers] and Tim Owens, Kelley Lovelace, Ashley Gorley, and Bill Anderson—all these guys that throughout the years have become family," he said. "It's truly just a team now." *American Saturday Night* was released in 2009, at a time when many Americans were struggling with the effects of global economic problems. The overall tone of the album expressed hope and gratitude, even in the face of tough times. The first single released, a ballad called "Then," became Paisley's 14th No. 1 country hit, and his 10th No. 1 single in a row.

> *Paisley remains humble about his talent and his success. "I've really not been good at much else," he remarked. "Thankfully I was able to do this for a living because ... I did not have anything to fall back on, that's for sure."*

The title track evoked a picture of Americans working hard through the week and looking forward to a bit of freedom on the weekends. "Water" celebrated summer fun, and "The Pants" was a wry look at relationships. "Welcome to the Future," which Paisley wrote with Bill Anderson, is the songwriter's personal favorite and the one he feels is the most important. It was inspired by the 2008 election of Barack Obama as president of the United States. Paisley was very moved that, after years of racism, the country was ready to accept an African American as its leader. The lyrics express wonder at how quickly things can change, referring to rapid advancements in technology, shifting relationships between countries, and improvements in civil rights.

On July 21, 2009, Paisley was one of a group of entertainers invited to be part of the White House Music Series launched by First Lady Michelle Obama. The series was designed to encourage the arts and arts education, and included a music workshop with the invited performers. Alison Krauss, Paisley's partner on the "Whiskey Lullaby" duet, was another of the musicians who took part. The artists later had the opportunity to perform for President Barack Obama, Michelle Obama, the White House staff, and members of Congress.

Paisley was honored to be part of a group of performers invited to perform at the White House by First Lady Michelle Obama.

Despite selling millions of albums, touring the world, and being invited to perform at the White House, Paisley remains humble about his talent and his success. "I've really not been good at much else," he remarked. "Thankfully I was able to do this for a living because … I did not have anything to fall back on, that's for sure."

HOME AND FAMILY

Paisley lives with his wife, Kimberly Williams-Paisley, and their two sons, William Huckleberry and Jasper Warren. William Huckleberry's middle name was taken from Mark Twain's classic American novel *Huckleberry Finn,* and his parents call him by his nickname, "Huck." Jasper Warren's name honors Paisley's guitar-playing grandfather.

The family has two homes. Williams-Paisley is a co-star of the television comedy "According to Jim," which is taped in Los Angeles, California, where they have a home. Paisley prefers to spend time at their other residence, which is a big log home on 87 acres in Franklin, Tennessee. There they do some farming and keep horses and other animals, including a Cavalier King Charles Spaniel named Holler.

HOBBIES AND OTHER INTERESTS

Paisley has a large collection of exotic and vintage guitars. He enjoys matching the various sounds they produce to the songs he's working on.

His favorite guitar is a 1968 Fender Telecaster. The fret board is made of maple wood, and it's decorated with a paisley design. He loves gadgets and new technology and has taught himself to use animation software and other tools to create videos that enhance his stage shows. He likes many outdoor activities, including horseback riding, fishing, and hunting with bow and rifle.

From 2003 until 2005, Paisley was on the national board of advisors of Mothers Against Drunk Driving (MADD). He formed the Brad Paisley Foundation to benefit charities such as the Children's Miracle Network, St. Jude's Research Hospital, the Opry Trust Fund, and the American Cancer Society.

RECORDINGS

Who Needs Pictures, 1999
Backstage at the Opry, 2000 (contributor)
Part II, 2001
Mud on the Tires, 2003
Time Well Wasted, 2005
Brad Paisley Christmas, 2006
Cars, 2006 (contributor to soundtrack)
5th Gear, 2007
Play, 2008
American Saturday Night, 2009

SELECTED HONORS AND AWARDS

Academy of Country Music Awards: 2000, Top New Male Vocalist of the Year; 2005 (2 awards), Vocal Event of the Year and Video of the Year, both for "Whiskey Lullaby" (with Alison Krauss); 2006 (3 awards), Album of the Year, for *Time Well Wasted*, and Vocal Event of the Year and Video Event of the Year, both for "When I Get Where I'm Going" (with Dolly Parton); 2007, Top Male Vocalist of the Year; 2008 (2 awards), Top Male Vocalist of the Year, and Video of the Year, for "Online"; 2009 (2 awards), Video of the Year, for "Waitin' on a Woman," and Vocal Event of the Year, for "Start a Band" (with Keith Urban); 2010, Top Male Vocalist of the Year
Country Music Association Awards: 2000, Horizon Award; 2001, Vocal Event of the Year, for "Too Country" (with Buck Owens, George Jones, and Bill Anderson); 2002, Music Video of the Year, for "I'm Gonna Miss Her (The Fishin' Song)"; 2004 (2 awards), Music Video of the Year and Musical Event of the Year, both for "Whiskey Lullaby" (with Alison Krauss); 2006 (2 awards), Album of the Year, for *Time Well Wasted*, and Musical Event of the Year, for "When I Get Where I'm Going" (with

Dolly Parton); 2007 (2 awards), Male Vocalist of the Year and Music Video of the Year, for "Online"; 2008 (2 awards), Male Vocalist of the Year and Music Video of the Year, for "Waitin' on a Woman"

Orville H. Gibson Guitar Award for Best Country Guitarist (Male): 2002

Nashville Songwriters Association International Award for Song-writer/Artist of the Year: 2002, 2005

CMT/Flameworthy Music Awards: 2002, Flameworthy Concept Video of the Year, for "I'm Gonna Miss Her (The Fishin' Song)"; 2005, CMT Music Award for Collaborative Video of the Year, for "Whiskey Lullaby" (with Alison Krauss); 2006, CMT Award for Most Inspiring Video of the Year, for "When I Get Where I'm Going" (with Dolly Parton); 2008, Comedy Video of the Year, for "Online"; 2009 (3 awards), Male Video of the Year, for "Waitin' on a Woman," Collaborative Video of the Year, for "Start a Band" (with Keith Urban), and CMT Performance of the Year, for "Country Boy"

ASCAP Country Music Award: 2004, Songwriter/Artist of the Year

Grammy Awards (The Recording Academy): 2008, Best Country Instru-mental Performance, for "Throttleneck"; 2009 (2 awards), Best Country Instrumental Performance, for "Cluster Pluck" (with James Burton, Vince Gill, Albert Lee, John Jorgenson, Brent Mason, Redd Volkaert, and Steve Wariner) and Best Male Country Vocal Performance, for "Letter to Me"

American Music Award: 2008, Favorite Country Male Artist

FURTHER READING

Periodicals

Billboard, Aug. 16, 2003, p.31; June 2, 2007, p.28; May 16, 2009, p.17

Boston Globe, July 5, 2009, p.N5

Entertainment Weekly, Aug. 24, 2007, p.27

Good Housekeeping, Jan. 2008, p.122

Guitar Player, Dec. 2007, p.78; Mar. 2009, p.74

New Yorker, Aug. 2, 2010, p.30

USA Today, Aug. 8, 2007, p.D8

Online Articles

http://www.cmt.com/artists
    (CMT, "Brad Paisley," no date)

http://www.people.com/people/brad_paisley
    (People, "Celebrity Central: Brad Paisley," no date)

http://www.washingtonpost.com
    (Washington Post, "White House Goes a Little Bit Country," July 21, 2009)

ADDRESS

Brad Paisley
Arista Nashville
1400 18th Ave. South
Nashville, TN 37212

WORLD WIDE WEB SITE

http://www.bradpaisley.com

Keke Palmer 1993-
American Actress and Singer
Star of the Film *Akeelah and the Bee* and the
Television Show "True Jackson, VP"

BIRTH

Lauren Keyana "Keke" Palmer was born on August 26, 1993,
in Robbins, Illinois, a suburb of Chicago. Her father,
Lawrence, worked for a plastics manufacturing company, and
her mother, Sharon, worked with autistic high-school students. Both of her parents were professional actors earlier in
life. She has an older sister, Loreal, who came up with the
nickname "Keke" when they were children. "[Loreal] had an

imaginary friend named Keke when she was four and wanted that to be my name," explained Palmer. She also has a younger sister and brother, Lawrencia and Lawrence, who are twins.

YOUTH

Palmer showed early promise as an entertainer. At the age of five, she impressed her church choir by singing an impassioned rendition of the traditional hymn "Jesus Loves Me." "I probably wasn't really, really in the choir," she later clarified. "I would just be sitting there dancing or singing or something, and ... they made me a little robe to fit in with the choir.... I knew I wanted to entertain." Palmer credits both her church and her parents with providing valuable support. "I think [my talent] comes from the encouragement my parents and my church gave me to follow my dreams and [their] telling me that I could achieve anything," she confided. "So, I've always felt confident and secure, and was able to be myself and to have a good time."

"I think [my talent] comes from the encouragement my parents and my church gave me to follow my dreams and [their] telling me that I could achieve anything," Palmer confided. "So, I've always felt confident and secure, and was able to be myself and to have a good time."

Palmer started acting when she was nine years old. "It was kind of spur of the moment. My dad was reading in the paper about *Lion King* auditions and asked me if I wanted to go," she recalled. "I auditioned and out of 400 kids ... I made it down to the top 15. And then I was out. ... I definitely got bit by the acting bug." In 2004 she made her film debut in *Barbershop 2: Back in Business,* the sequel to the hit 2002 comedy *Barbershop* starring rapper Ice Cube. The producers were so impressed with Palmer that they suggested she move to Los Angeles to be closer to the major film studios. Convinced of their daughter's chances at success in the entertainment industry, Palmer's parents moved the family to Duarte, a suburb of Los Angeles.

EDUCATION

Before moving to California, Palmer attended St. Benedict Catholic Elementary School in Blue Island, a suburb south of Chicago. "When I was in kindergarten all the way up to third grade, I was kind of an introvert," she disclosed. "I was a little bit more quiet in school than I was outside of

Palmer as Nikki Grady in Madea's Family Reunion, *shown with Tyler Perry as Madea.*

school." In third grade, she placed second in the spelling bee, but lost when she spelled the word "gorilla" with two R's and one L. "I'm not afraid, you know, to do good in school," she said. "[But] my friends back in Chicago ... some of them were afraid to be smart and do good in school because people might think they're nerds.... I didn't struggle with anything like that."

Since becoming an actress, Palmer has studied independently and has attended school on the sets of her films and television shows. "I go to school Tuesdays and Thursdays, so all of those days in between I work and do the school work that they give me. And then I turn it in to my teacher and they make me take a test to make sure that no one did my schoolwork for me. After that, I'm done with that subject," she explained. Her favorite subject is English, and her least favorite is math. She plans to attend college in the future. "I'm thinking about going to Howard University and getting my master's at Yale. If acting doesn't work out, maybe I'll be an anesthesiologist.... All I have to do is get a little bit better in math and science."

CAREER HIGHLIGHTS

Palmer began auditioning for acting roles in Los Angeles, and within weeks she found herself in a Kmart commercial as well as episodes of the television dramas "Strong Medicine" and "Cold Case." She was also given a chance to shoot a pilot episode of a show called "Keke & Jamal" for the Disney Channel. The show was about a cranky old man who finds himself taking care of his two grandchildren, but Disney decided not to air the program. Little did Palmer realize that she would later have her own successful series.

Landing a Major Role

Palmer first gained widespread recognition with her performance in *The Wool Cap,* a Turner Network Television movie that premiered in 2004. Starring opposite esteemed actor William H. Macy, Palmer played Lou, the daughter of a drug addict living in a neglected New York City apartment building. Macy played Charlie Gigot, the manager of the building. After Lou's mom leaves her in Charlie's care and never returns, both characters end up helping each other grow as individuals. She earned a nomination for Outstanding Performance by a Female Actor from the Screen Actors Guild for the movie, becoming the youngest-ever nominee in that category. The honor came as a total surprise to 12-year-old Palmer: "I couldn't believe it at first. When my mom came to tell me, I was just sitting there [thinking], 'She's kidding me.'"

"I was doubtful at first about doing some of the acting jobs because they were so big," Palmer confessed. *"But as I got to another level I kind of realized, well, I've gotten this far. Maybe I am good enough. And that's what Akeelah thought when she got to the regional bee."*

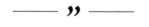

Over the next couple of years, Palmer appeared in a number of other television projects, including the hit shows "ER" and "Law & Order: Special Victims Unit." She also had a supporting role in filmmaker Tyler Perry's popular 2006 comedy *Madea's Family Reunion.* Palmer played Nikki Grady, a rebellious teenage runaway who has been in foster care most of her life and who joins Madea's family when the court orders Madea to take care of her.

Akeelah and the Bee

Palmer's major commercial and critical breakthrough came in 2006, when she starred in the acclaimed film *Akeelah and the Bee.* The plot concerns Akeelah Anderson, a middle-school student from an inner-city neighbor-

A scene from Akeelah and the Bee, *with Tanya, Akeelah's mother (Angela Bassett), Mr. Welch (Curtis Armstrong), Dr. Larabee (Laurence Fishburne), and Akeelah (Keke Palmer).*

hood in Los Angeles. When Akeelah wins the school's spelling bee, an English teacher named Dr. Joshua Larabee (played by Laurence Fishburne) suggests that she compete in the Scripps National Spelling Bee in Washington DC. Her widowed mother (played by actress Angela Bassett) is initially hesitant to let her participate, but she eventually agrees. In the end, Akeelah shares first prize with her former rival, a Chinese American boy named Dylan.

Palmer has remarked on the challenges of preparing for the role. "The script had words I didn't even know were real," she said with a laugh. She has related her own experiences as an actress to Akeelah's decision to compete at a national level. "I was doubtful at first about doing some of the acting jobs because they were so big," she confessed. "But as I got to another level I kind of realized, well, I've gotten this far. Maybe I am good enough. And that's what Akeelah thought when she got to the regional bee."

Akeelah and the Bee was a critical success, and Palmer was widely praised for her performance. "Palmer takes what could have been a conventional part in a feel-good movie to a higher level," raved Claudia Puig in *USA Today*. In *Variety*, critic Justin Chang argued that Palmer "movingly illuminates the pressures facing a girl caught between the ordinary and extraordinary." Palmer was honored with a Black Movie Award, a Black Reel Award, an NAACP Image Award, and a Young Artist Award for the role. At ShoWest, a prestigious tradeshow for owners of movie theaters, the judges created a special new award, the Rising Star of the Year Award, just for her.

Branching Out to Music

Akeelah and the Bee also afforded Palmer the opportunity to demonstrate her skills as a singer, featuring her vocal performance of the song "All My Girlz" on its soundtrack. Atlantic Records took note of her musical talent and offered her a record deal. Her debut album, *So Uncool,* was released in 2007. It contains four songs written by Palmer, including "Skin Deep," which addresses the importance of inner beauty rather than physical appearance. "I wrote that song for those people who are truly beautiful, but they just don't see it," she explained. Atlantic Records has described the songs on the album as "ranging from up-tempo R&B tracks to inspirational songs to youthful, fun material that kids can relate to." To promote *So Uncool,* Palmer toured with the WNBA and performed songs from the album at halftime.

Also in 2007, Palmer starred in the Disney Channel original movie *Jump In!* A musically oriented feature in the tradition of *High School Musical, Jump In!* is the story of Mary (played by Palmer) who convinces her male friend Izzy (played by Corbin Bleu) to join her competitive jump-rope team. Izzy discovers that he is a natural at jump rope, but worries what his father and friends will think when they find out. With 8.2 million viewers tuning in, *Jump In!* set a Disney Channel record for largest audience for an original television movie premiere. The movie's soundtrack was also a hit, and featured two new songs sung by Palmer.

The Longshots

In 2008 Palmer got the chance to portray a genuine trailblazer when she landed the lead role opposite Ice Cube in *The Longshots,* a movie directed by Fred Durst of the band Limp Bizkit. *The Longshots* is the true story of Jasmine Plummer (played by Palmer), an Illinois teenager who became the first female quarterback to play in a Pop Warner football tournament. The Pop Warner Little Scholars is the country's biggest youth football and cheerleading organization, and Jasmine Plummer led the Harvey Colts of Illinois to the Pop Warner Super Bowl in 2003. The movie was well received, with *Variety* critic Joe Leydon claiming, "Cube and Palmer show engaging sincerity and impeccable professionalism.... And the climax provides a welcome touch of realism that recalls the original *Rocky.*"

*Jasmine (Palmer) with Curtis Plummer (Ice Cube, center)
in a scene from* The Longshots.

Ironically, Plummer lived about five minutes from Palmer's suburban Chicago home when the events in the movie took place. The two girls got a chance to meet during filming, and Palmer was drawn to the positive message of Plummer's story. "What mainly interested me in the role was that it was so inspirational," she stated. "I thought it would really motivate young girls to pursue their dreams." Although she had no previous experience playing football, she learned how to handle the ball onscreen. "I practiced for about four months, getting my arm ready, and then learning the footwork," she said. "I was even better than some of the boys."

"True Jackson, VP"

Palmer's most high-profile role came in 2008 when the Nickelodeon Network hired her to star in her own television series, "True Jackson, VP." The show revolves around a teenage girl named True Jackson who becomes vice president of a billion-dollar fashion company. As she gets to know the fashion world, she realizes that it is a lot like high school. The show was a major success right from the start, becoming the largest debut in Nickelodeon's history. Palmer felt like she really connected with the role and the audience. "I really wanted to get [this part]," she admitted. "I do a lot of movies that are drama related and wanted [this] so my own peers could

True Jackson (Palmer) with Lulu Johnson (Ashley Argota) and Ryan Laserbeam (Matt Shively) in a scene from "True Jackson, VP."

see me as someone just like them. They could maybe understand me a little bit better, and I could be closer to them." Her work on the show impressed her bosses as much as her fans. "Keke is totally natural," Nickelodeon's Marjorie Cohn told *USA Today.* "She's bubbly, she's self-confident, but she's not conceited.... She's a real kid and a really nice person, and I think that just comes across on camera."

The success of "True Jackson, VP" led to the launching of a clothing line based on the show. Designed by Jane Siskin and sold at Walmart, the Mad Style by True Jackson line consists of a wide range of clothing and accessories for young girls. Although Siskin was the official designer, Palmer had plenty of input. "They showed me the first samples and I was able to say what I liked and what I didn't like," she explained. Commenting on her own personal sense of style, she declared: "I like to be edgy but I also make sure the look is still sweet and young."

Recent Work

In addition to her hit television series, Palmer appeared in *Madea Goes to Jail,* the 2009 Tyler Perry film. She again appeared as Nikki Grady, whom Madea has taken in as a foster child. She also appeared in the 2009 film *Shrink,* a dark comedy starring Academy Award-winner Kevin Spacey. He plays Henry Carter, a depressed psychiatrist attempting to solve his own issues while tending to his patients. One of these patients is Jemma (played by Palmer), a troubled teen who loves films. Although *Shrink* got mixed reviews, critics lauded her skills as an actress. "Keke Palmer's performance as a high school-age film nut provides some welcome grounding in reality," claimed John Anderson of *Variety*.

HOME AND FAMILY

Palmer has a close relationship with her older sister, Loreal, who co-wrote some of the tracks on *So Uncool* and also provided background vocals, along with her younger twin siblings. The family also has a pet dog, a lhasa apso named Rusty. She has cited her parents as the most inspirational people in her life. "They travel with me wherever I go and they are a huge blessing. They have truly inspired me to be the best I can be and have helped me to become a strong person."

"Keke is totally natural," raved Nickelodeon's Marjorie Cohn. "She's bubbly, she's self-confident, but she's not conceited.... She's a real kid and a really nice person, and I think that just comes across on camera."

HOBBIES AND OTHER INTERESTS

Palmer is active in several charitable causes, including the Girl Scouts and the mentor program It's Cool to Be Smart. "I try to tell the students to never give up on your dreams," she stated. In her spare time, she enjoys reading. "One of my favorite books is *A Wrinkle in Time* by Madeleine L'Engle," she said. "When you finish reading a book, you feel like you've accomplished a great thing." In addition, she likes going to the movies, talking on the phone, playing video games, and window-shopping with her friends. Her favorite foods include Chicago-style pizza and bacon cheeseburgers.

SELECTED CREDITS

Television and Movies

Barbershop 2: Back in Business, 2004
The Wool Cap, 2004 (TV movie)
Akeelah and the Bee, 2006

Madea's Family Reunion, 2006
Jump In! 2007 (TV movie)
The Longshots, 2008
"True Jackson, VP," 2008- (TV series)
Madea Goes to Jail, 2009
Shrink, 2009

Recordings

So Uncool, 2007

HONORS AND AWARDS

Black Movie Award (Film Life): 2006, Outstanding Performance by an Actress in a Leading Role, for *Akeelah and the Bee*
Special Award (ShoWest Convention, USA): 2006, Rising Star of the Year
Black Reel Award (Foundation for the Advancement of African-Americans in Film): 2007, Best Actress, for *Akeelah and the Bee*
Image Award (NAACP): 2007, Outstanding Actress in a Motion Picture, for *Akeelah and the Bee*; 2009, Outstanding Performance in a Youth/Children's Program—Series or Special, for "True Jackson, VP"
Young Artist Award (Young Artist Foundation): 2007, Best Performance in a Feature Film—Leading Young Actress, for *Akeelah and the Bee*
BET YoungStars Award (Black Entertainment Television): 2010

FURTHER READING

Books

Bloom, Ronny. *Keke Palmer: A True Star; An Unauthorized Biography,* 2009 (juvenile)
Brooks, Riley. *All Access: Keke Palmer; Unauthorized Bio,* 2009 (juvenile)

Periodicals

Cosmo Girl, Aug. 2008, p.67
Ebony, Dec. 2007, p.42
Jet, May 1, 2006, p.58; Apr. 26, 2009
Sports Illustrated, Mar. 17, 2008, p.22
Teen Vogue, Aug. 2009, p.46
TV Guide, Jan. 19, 2009
USA Today, Apr. 27, 2006, p.D5; May 5, 2009, p.D2

Online Articles

http://www.atlanticrecords.com/kekepalmer
    (Atlantic Records, "Keke Palmer," undated)

http://www.ew.com
  (Entertainment Weekly, "Keke Palmer: The Next Big Thing," Nov. 28, 2008)
http://www.mtv.com/movies/person/382096/personmain.jhtml
  (MTV, "Keke Palmer," undated)
http://www.people.com
  (People, "Nickelodeon's Keke Palmer Celebrates Sweet 16," Aug. 26, 2009, articles archive)

ADDRESS

Keke Palmer
Nickelodeon Network
1515 Broadway
New York, NY 10036

WORLD WIDE WEB SITES

http://www.kekepalmer.com
http://www.nick.com/shows/truejacksonvp
http://www.myspace.com/therealkekepalmer

PARAMORE
Jeremy Davis 1985-
Josh Farro 1987-
Zac Farro 1990-
Hayley Williams 1988-
Taylor York 1989-
American Punk-Pop-Rock Band
Creators of *RIOT!* and *brand new eyes*

EARLY YEARS

The Tennessee-based rock band Paramore, whose music has
been described as alternative rock, punk-pop, and emo, con-

sists of five members: vocalist Hayley Williams, guitarist Joshua Farro, drummer Zachary Farro, bassist Jeremy Davis, and rhythm guitarist Taylor York. Most of the band members were still in their teens when the group recorded their first album, and many of their fans fall into the same age group. As the group has matured, however, they have expanded their appeal as well as their success.

———— **"** ————

When they were just starting out, the members of Paramore shared their love of music. "Back then, I guess we were all thinking, after school we'll go to the house and practice," Williams recalled. "It was what we loved to do for fun, and still do! I don't think any of us really knew this would turn out to be what it's become."

———— **"** ————

Lead singer Hayley Nichole Williams was born on December 27, 1988. She moved from Meridian, Mississippi, to Franklin, Tennessee, in her early teens after her parents divorced. When she had trouble fitting in at a local public school, she enrolled at a private school, where she met fellow music lovers Josh and Zac Farro. They formed Paramore while she was still in high school. Because of the band's touring schedule, she finished her high school diploma through an internet home schooling program.

Guitarist Joshua Neil Farro was born on September 29, 1987, and grew up in Franklin, Tennessee. The second of five children, he learned to play guitar by watching his father teach his older brother. His next youngest sibling, drummer Zachary Wayne Farro, was born on June 4, 1990. Like Williams, he was still in school when the band formed—in fact, he was only 12. As its youngest member, he also completed his high school education through the same internet home schooling program as Williams.

Less is known about the childhoods of the other members of Paramore, although they also grew up around Franklin, Tennessee. Bassist Jeremy Clayton Davis was born on February 8, 1985. He is the oldest member of Paramore by a couple of years, and he had more experience as a musician before joining the band. He had even played as a session musician in Nashville studios. Guitarist Taylor Benjamin York was born on December 17, 1989. Although York was not an original member of Paramore, he had been involved with the band from its early days, co-writing the occasional song and performing live with the group on tour. He joined Paramore's official lineup in June 2009.

FORMING THE BAND

An early version of Paramore was formed around 2002 in Franklin, Tennessee. Brothers Zac and Josh Farro formed a band and asked Williams, the new girl at their school, if she would like to join. "They were the first people I met who were as passionate about music as I was," Williams recalled, and the three met to play together and listen to bands. Williams soon brought in bassist Davis, with whom she had played in a funk cover band. Davis, an experienced musician, was startled to arrive at the first rehearsal and discover that the drummer was only 12 years old. "I had very, very, very little faith in everyone in the band because of their age," he admitted. He already knew Williams had vocal potential, however, so he stuck around and was amazed by his new band mates' creative abilities. "I remember thinking, 'This is not going to work because this kid is way too young,' but that first day of practice was amazing. I knew we were onto something."

The band, now composed of the two Farro brothers, Williams, and Davis, later added a rhythm guitarist, Jason Bynum. They soon began playing high school talent shows and local rock clubs. By 2004 they were known as Paramore and had begun touring the southeast, often driven around by Williams's parents. "Back then, I guess we were all thinking, after school we'll go to the house and practice," Williams noted. "It was what we loved to do for fun, and still do! I don't think any of us really knew this would turn out to be what it's become."

It wasn't long before the group was attracting industry notice. The Agency Group, a music management company, signed them when Williams was just 14. "I was impressed by her raw talent at that young age," booking agent Ken Fermaglieli told *Billboard* magazine. "I knew when I met her that there was a star there. She knew exactly what she was doing, how she wanted to do it, and she had a plan." The company helped Paramore book gigs all around the southeast region. While performing in Florida, they were seen by independent label Fueled By Ramen and signed in April 2005. The label had also broken such punk-flavored acts as Jimmy Eat World, Fall Out Boy, Gym Class Heroes, and Panic! At the Disco, and they thought Paramore was a natural fit. "Even though they were very young, I could see there was something special there," label president John Janick told *Billboard*, "and I could look down the road and see them playing much bigger venues." Their deal with the label—known as a "360-degree" deal—meant they would share touring and merchandise revenue with their label in exchange for extra promotional support and time to grow a fan base on the road.

Paramore's debut album, All We Know Is Falling.

CAREER HIGHLIGHTS

Developing an Audience

Paramore recorded its first album, *All We Know Is Falling,* and released it in late summer 2005. Williams and Josh Farro co-wrote all of the album's songs, most of which dealt with relationships. Davis had left the band for a short period after they began recording—he returned shortly after the album was released—and his departure inspired the song "All We Know." Williams noted that the single "Emergency" was inspired by the failure of her parents' marriage and that although the band was young, they could still write meaningful songs. "I know we are a lot younger than even a lot of our fans, and it's a constant fight to get people to take us seriously," the singer said. "I grew up with my parents fighting a lot and the guys in the band grew up with similar situations and anyone can see what love isn't, no matter what their age."

With songs that combined mid-tempo verses with fast-paced power choruses, *All We Know Is Falling* found an audience of mostly younger fans. The group's pop-punk sensibilities and Williams's powerhouse vocals drew comparisons to such hard-driving popular artists as Evanescence and Avril Lavigne. The album drew some favorable notices from critics, including comments from a *New York Times* writer that Williams's "impressive" vocals made her "a potential star." Although the group made videos for singles "Pressure," "Emergency," and "All We Know," the record had only modest sales, not enough to make the Billboard 200 Album chart.

Their label wasn't alarmed. Their plan was to grow a fan base through live shows, and Paramore set out on tour in summer 2005. They appeared at New Jersey's Bamboozle Festival as well as several dates on the Vans Warped Tour. They were on a side stage that focused on female-fronted groups; the band had to help assemble the stage and only played before 40 or 50 people, but soon their high-energy performances began to draw in bigger audiences. Bynum left the group that year, replaced by Hunter Lamb on rhythm guitar, and still the group continued to tour. In 2006 they began playing some headlining dates at small venues around the United States, including New York City.

> "
>
> *"Paramore realizes the punk-pop formula with such guileless fervor that it becomes entertaining in itself," a reviewer for* **Stylus Magazine** *observed, adding that "as punk more extravagantly flirts with pop and pop explores short, sharp rock songs, Paramore finds a comfortable place between the two."*
>
> "

Paramore rejoined the Vans Warped Tour in 2006, this time on a bigger stage. They also began touring internationally. The time away from home was challenging for the young performers, but the band felt the experience and exposure was worth it. "We all miss home sometimes and wonder what we'd be doing if we weren't sitting in a van traveling to the next venue," Williams noted, "but at the same time, some kid might be sitting in class wondering how it would be to be sitting in a van traveling to the next venue. We are all doing what we love and don't regret any of it." By fall 2006, *All We Know Is Falling* made an appearance on Billboard's Heatseekers Album chart.

Breaking out with *RIOT!*

In early 2007, only a few months before their second album was due to be released, Lamb left the group to get married. Paramore announced the band would continue as quartet for the near future, even as they prepared to support their new CD. *RIOT!* was produced by David Bendeth and covered many of the same themes as their first album, although the group branched out a bit musically. "For us, the title *RIOT!* literally means an unbridled outburst of emotions," Williams explained. "When we were writing, it seemed our thought and emotions were coming out so fast that we couldn't control them. It felt like there was a riot within us. So the album takes our passion to a new level; it's just all raw energy." The CD produced several successful singles that charted on the Billboard Hot 100, including "Misery Business," "crushcrushcrush," and "That's What You Get." The album received positive attention from critics, too. "Paramore realizes the punk-pop formula with such guileless fervor that it becomes entertaining in itself," a reviewer for *Stylus Magazine* observed, adding that "as punk more extravagantly flirts with pop and pop explores short, sharp rock songs, Paramore finds a comfortable place between the two."

Paramore continued touring to support the album, this time playing the main stage on some 2007 Vans Warped dates. Their videos began to get airplay on MTV, and a partnership with retailer Hot Topic led to Paramore T-shirt/download bundles being featured in the store. People were beginning to take notice of the group, helped along by Williams's powerful vocals, colorful hairstyles (usually involving some bright shade of orange or red), and sense of style. Having a female singer front the band helped them stand out among all the other punk-inspired rock groups, something that inspired Williams. "I don't think so much about the fact I'm a girl fronting the band; it's just there's not a lot of girls fronting bands in our genre," she explained. "It's just how it is. It's really motivating to me." In summer 2007 *Entertainment Weekly* named Paramore one of the Ten Most Exciting Artists of the year, and *RIOT!* was well on its way to gaining platinum (million-selling) status.

The year 2008 provided other milestones for the group. They kept touring, including two months as co-headliners with their idols Jimmy Eat World. *RIOT!* officially earned platinum status in July, and the group earned a Grammy nomination for best new artist (they lost to singer Amy Winehouse). They performed at the 2008 MTV Video Awards, where "crushcrushcrush" was nominated for Best Rock Video and also won the 2008 MTVu Woodie of the Year Award. They picked up two Teen Choice Awards, for choice Rock Group and Rock Song for "crushcrushcrush." They were also nominated for Breakthrough Artist at the 2008 American Music Awards.

Paramore in about 2007, when RIOT! *was released.*

Their increased visibility also brought out skeptics who wondered whether the young band was really in control of their music or whether they were manufactured, like some other teen performers. Band members were quick to defend themselves. Zac Farro disputed that idea by recalling his childhood pudginess, since outgrown. "Would a label put us together if I was 11 years old and weighed, like, 400 pounds?" he asked. "They wouldn't be like, 'Let's get that guy!'" Davis added that youth had nothing to do with talent. "Some of the ideas that come out of Josh and Zac and Hayley's heads—it astounds me at times, because I remember how young they are," the bassist said. "I just feel like they're super-creative." Williams noted that one advantage Paramore had was that they wrote all their own songs. "It's really important for an artist to believe what they're talking about," the singer remarked. "I've gone through everything I wrote about, and I hope that gives people an emotional connection to the music."

Working through Growing Pains

With the increased media attention came increased pressure. Rumors surfaced that Paramore was breaking up after they cancelled some tour dates in Europe in early 2008, citing "internal issues" that needed to be resolved within the band. While some observers speculated that there was friction because Williams was getting more media attention than the rest of the band, the singer explained to MTV that the group was merely exhausted after more than a year on the road. "Touring really got to us. We still love it with all our hearts, but it takes a toll mentally and physically. But we just needed time with our friends and family, and just [to relax] and basically refuel." The break made them eager to keep working together. As bassist Davis commented afterward, "things haven't been this good in a very long time as far as our relationships with each other." "All of us are looking forward to getting back in the studio," Williams added. "That will be amazing for us—therapeutic, even. It will be great to have time set aside to just be a band, apart from the hype and insanity."

It wasn't long before Paramore was back on the road, making occasional appearances on the Vans Warped Tour and headlining several dates, including a performance at Central Park in New York City. Reviewing the concert on *The Blender.com*, Ryan Dombal called the band "stupendously tight and anything but amateur live." While the band received a lot of press for their

Paramore performing live in Hollywood in 2008.

youth, Dombal added that *RIOT!* "is one of the best mainstream rock albums of the decade" and that Paramore is "making vital music that their young followers can grow into naturally." The live CD/DVD of the tour, *Final RIOT!*, appeared in late 2008 and sold 500,000 copies within four months to be certified gold. The DVD captured the energy of the band's live shows, where the charismatic Williams commanded the stage despite her petite frame. Her youthful appeal led to some acting offers, but Williams turned them down. "I love the stage, the sweaty sickness, dancing and screaming," she said. "I'm not sure I'd fit on the big screen."

Nevertheless, Paramore found a way to get involved with one of the biggest films of 2008. They recorded two songs for the soundtrack to *Twilight,* the vampire love story based on the bestselling book of the same name by Stephenie Meyer (for more information on Meyer, see p. 77 of this issue). Williams had fallen in love with the *Twilight* books while on tour, and she asked Paramore's management to arrange for the band to contribute music to the movie. "We kinda fought tooth and nail to make sure we could be part of the soundtrack," Williams said. Featuring two Paramore songs, "Decode" and "I Caught Myself," the *Twilight* soundtrack album was No. 1 in its first week of release with over 165,000 copies sold and eventually sold more than two million copies. "Decode" was the lead single from the CD and became the group's first Top 40 single, hitting No. 33. The video for "Decode" earned a MTV Video Music Award nomination for best rock video, as well as an MTV Movie Award nomination for best song from a movie. The single also brought the group its second Grammy nomination: a songwriters' award for Williams, York, and Josh Farro, for Best Song Written for Motion Picture, Television, or Other Visual Media.

The band went through more personnel changes in June 2009. Guitarist Taylor York, who had frequently worked with the band as a songwriter and touring performer since its founding in 2004, was announced as an official member and joined band members for their next recording session. They went into the studio with producer Rob Cavallo, who had worked with such superstars as Green Day, Kid Rock, and Avril Lavigne. He helped Paramore expand the group's sound. As Zac Farro noted, "Our heavier songs are a lot bigger. I really think they capture that live sound. Our ballads are a lot more mature. I think we took a slight risk." Many of Williams's lyrics dealt with the group's conflicts, so she was a bit leery to share them with the band. "I was kind of embarrassed and didn't know how they would take it," she revealed. "But once all those words were out on the table, it gave us the opportunity to hash through our problems and internal struggles that we had been facing." She added that "once that was done, it was back to the old us and back to the old reasons why we started a band and why we wanted to play music together." If you listen closely to the album, the singer suggested, "you can hear the progression of songs go from angry and spiteful to super-hopeful and positive."

brand new eyes

While the group members hoped their expanded sound would appeal to a wider audience, even they were surprised by the performance of *brand new eyes* when it debuted in October 2009. It sold over 175,000 copies in its first week alone and entered the Billboard 200 chart at No. 2, behind Barbra

brand new eyes *features the band's current lineup: Jeremy Davis, Josh Farro, Zac Farro, Hayley Williams, and Taylor York.*

Streisand but ahead of new albums by Mariah Carey, Alice in Chains, and Madonna. The album charted at No. 1 in Ireland, Australia, New Zealand, and the United Kingdom, and the band sold out England's famous Wembley Stadium in eight hours. Fans weren't the only ones to take notice of the new album. Evan Lucy noted in *Billboard* that the album showed a "newfound maturity that makes for a compelling set of songs," while a *New York Times* contributor noted that the new album "broadened the band's dynamics without sacrificing momentum." The album produced the singles "Ignorance" and "Brick by Boring Brick." The video for the latter track was a special effects-laden, story-driven piece with no scenes of the band performing—a first for the group.

The year 2009 had other triumphs for the group. They were chosen by supergroup No Doubt to open for them on their 2009 comeback tour, a thrill for longtime fan Williams. She considered singer Gwen Stefani one of the few female role models in her genre, and Williams and Davis had covered the reggae-influenced group when they were in a funk cover band. In the fall of 2009 the group recorded an episode of "MTV Unplugged," bringing high energy to their set with only acoustic instruments. Headlining a show in Boston, the group "looked and sounded like a unified force, spring-loaded to deliver the kind of boisterous pop that defines summer soundtracks," Jonathan Perry remarked in the *Boston Globe.* The group also headlined MTV's first Ulalume Music Festival in the fall and was selected to co-headline New Jersey's Bamboozle Festival in 2010.

> ——— **"** ———
>
> *"Our faith is very important to us," Josh Farro remarked. "It's obviously going to come out in our music because if someone believes something then their worldview is going to come out in anything they do. But we're not out here to preach to kids, we're out here because we love music. We do believe that God has blessed us with an opportunity to be in a band and tour the world and we're going to use this gift to the full potential."*
>
> ——— **"** ———

As awards season rolled around, Paramore found themselves in contention once again. They repeated as Teen Choice Award winners, taking home the 2009 awards for Choice Rock Group and for Choice Rock Track, for "Decode." They also won the 2010 People's Choice Award for Favorite Rock Band. Band members attributed their success to a lot of hard work. "It took a lot of sacrifice and years of touring and working our way from the ground up to get to this point," Williams stressed. "And even if it was all taken away from us tomorrow, every bit of it was worth it." They were also ready for any further successes that might come: "Maybe this record [*brand new eyes*] will be the one that has paparazzi following us around," the singer remarked. "But if there's anything I know more than anything else in the world, it's that I'm not gonna change for anyone. I just don't see the point."

The band credits their ability to avoid the usual pitfalls of musical stardom to their strong Christian beliefs. "Our faith is very important to us," Josh Farro remarked. "It's obviously going to come out in our music because if someone believes something then their worldview is going to come out in anything they do. But we're not out here to preach to kids, we're out here because we love music." He added, "We do believe that God has blessed us with an opportunity to be in a band and tour the world and we're going to use this gift to the full potential." While out on the road, the band avoids partying and enjoys watching movies and sightseeing instead, but they don't believe this makes them better than anyone else. As Williams explained, "I try to talk about struggles and imperfections and even questioning your faith at times. I don't have anything figured out that the next kid doesn't. It's the people who shove their faith down people's throats who create the stigma against artists with religious backgrounds."

Many people have asked Williams about her future plans, but she has no plans to go solo. "I love being in a band. I can't see myself singing alone and just being Hayley, you know. That would feel so weird." In fact, many attribute Paramore's success to the band members' ability to work together as a group to create their songs. Josh Farro comes up with music, sometimes a lyric or vocal line. He brings it to Williams, who builds lyrics and adds melodies. Then the rest of band fleshes out the arrangements and transitions. "There's something Hayley is able to draw out of me that I can't seem to do with anyone else," Josh Farro said about his songwriting partner. As long as the band keeps exploring music together, he added, "I don't really care how many records we sell." Williams expressed a similar sentiment: "I just want to feel like this is my band, this is awesome, I'm living the dream. If we can accomplish that together, there's nothing more that we can ask for." They'll keep making music together as long as they have devoted fans, many of whom correspond with the band on their web site and find comfort in Paramore's music. As Davis concluded, "I feel like, if we were ever to break up, we would be letting down all those kids. That's never even an option."

HOME AND FAMILY

As a popular band on tour, the members of Paramore get little time to spend at home. When they get a chance, however, they enjoy being with their families and friends back in Franklin, Tennessee. All of the band members are single and plan on devoting their time to the band in the near future.

FAVORITE MUSIC

Although the band has a variety of influences, they cite several groups as their favorites, including Jimmy Eat World, Death Cab for Cutie, Radiohead, mewithoutYou, Mum, Sigur Ros, and sunny day real estate.

HOBBIES AND OTHER INTERESTS

When the band gets a chance to enjoy some rare free time, their interests are pretty typical of young adults. They all enjoy hanging out with friends and family, and Josh and Jeremy enjoy movies. Taylor cites bicycling as a favorite activity, while Zac likes bowling. Hayley likes fashion, especially playing with hair and make-up; she has said that if she hadn't become a musician she would gone to cosmetology school.

RECORDINGS

All We Know Is Falling, 2005
RIOT!, 2007
The Final RIOT!, 2008 (live CD/DVD)
Twilight: Original Motion Picture Soundtrack, 2008 (contributor)
brand new eyes, 2009

HONORS AND AWARDS

Woodie Award (MTVu): 2008, for Woodie of the Year
Teen Choice Awards: 2008, for Choice Rock Group, and for Choice Rock Track, for "crushcrushcrush"; 2009, for Choice Rock Group, and for Choice Rock Track, for "Decode"
People's Choice Award: 2010, for Favorite Rock Band

FURTHER READING

Periodicals

Alternative Press, Oct. 11, 2007; Mar. 27, 2008; Oct. 13, 2009
Billboard, Oct. 6, 2007, p.18; Sep. 27, 2008, p.21; July 18, 2009, p.13; Sep. 18, 2009, p.36
Boston Globe, Oct. 18, 2009; Oct. 21, 2009
Houston Chronicle, May 30, 2009
Los Angeles Times, June 28, 2007, p.E4; May 10, 2009, p.E13
New York Times, Dec. 22, 2005, p.E1; Nov. 30, 2007, p.E23; Sep. 28, 2009, p.C3
Rolling Stone, Mar. 6, 2008, p.20; May 28, 2009, p.19; Oct. 1, 2009, p.34
San Jose Mercury News, Apr. 6, 2008
USA Today, Aug. 31, 2007, p.E10
Washington Post, Nov. 23, 2008, p.M2

Online Articles

http://www.theagencygroup.com
(The Agency Group Ltd., "Paramore," Oct. 2, 2009)

http://newsvote.bbc.co.uk
   (BBC News, "Talking Shop: Paramore," Feb. 6, 2008)
http://www.blender.com
   (The Blender, "Live: Paramore Are the Future," Sep. 1, 2008; "Collect
   Call from Paramore," Dec. 15, 2008)
http://www.fueledbyramen.com
   (Fueled by Ramen, "Paramore," Sep. 3, 2009)
http://www.mtv.com
   (MTV, "Paramore Exclusive: Band Addresses Breakup Rumors, 'Internal
   Issues,'" Mar. 14, 2008; "Paramore Battle Doubt, Each Other to Make
   New Album," May 19, 2009)
http://www.shockhound.com
   (Shockhound.com, "Paramore: Group Therapy," July 15, 2009)
http://www.soundthesirens.com
   (Sound the Sirens Magazine, "Paramore: Youth Gone Wild," Oct. 17,
   2005)
http://www.stylusmagazine.com
   (Stylus Magazine, "Paramore: Riot!," Aug. 13, 2007)

ADDRESSES

Paramore
Fueled By Ramen
PO Box 1803
Tampa, FL 33601

Paramore
The Official Paramore Fan Club
853 Broadway, 3rd Floor
New York, NY 10003

WORLD WIDE WEB SITE

http://www.paramore.net

Candace Parker 1986-
American Professional Basketball Player with the
Los Angeles Sparks
WNBA Rookie of the Year and Most Valuable Player
in 2008

BIRTH

Candace Nicole Parker was born on April 19, 1986, in St.
Louis, Missouri. Her father, Larry Parker, is in the insurance
business. Her mother, Sara Parker, works in the front office for
the WNBA's Chicago Sky. Candace is the youngest of three
children in her family. Her brother Anthony, who is 11 years
older, plays guard for the NBA's Toronto Raptors. Her brother
Marcus, who is eight years older, is a doctor.

YOUTH

Candace grew up in Naperville, Illinois, about 25 miles southwest of Chicago. Her whole family loved basketball, so she learned about the game from an early age. Her father played at the University of Iowa in the 1970s, and her brother Anthony was a standout player at the high school, college, and professional levels. Candace first attended one of her brother's games when she was just two weeks old.

> "If me and my dad went to a park and he didn't think I was practicing hard enough, he'd just get in the car and leave," Parker remembered. "And I'd have to run home. I mean run home. Once I figured that out, I'd always try to go to close-by parks."

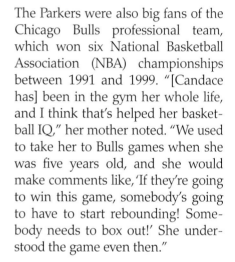

The Parkers were also big fans of the Chicago Bulls professional team, which won six National Basketball Association (NBA) championships between 1991 and 1999. "[Candace has] been in the gym her whole life, and I think that's helped her basketball IQ," her mother noted. "We used to take her to Bulls games when she was five years old, and she would make comments like, 'If they're going to win this game, somebody's going to have to start rebounding! Somebody needs to box out!' She understood the game even then."

Although Candace understood basketball, she was initially reluctant to play the game. She worried that she would always be compared to her father and brother. This concern led her to focus her athletic talents on soccer until she reached the eighth grade. By that time, however, she had grown so tall that her parents encouraged her to switch sports. As soon as she started playing organized basketball, Candace proved to be a natural on the court. She also worked hard to improve her skills and often tested herself by playing against her bigger, stronger brothers.

Candace's father became her coach, as well as her toughest critic. "He did things to make me mad, to challenge me, because I was so much more athletic and had so much more knowledge of the game than everyone else that sometimes I just coasted," Candace recalled. Her father always pushed her to do her best, even in practice. They spent countless hours at local parks doing rigorous drills to improve her shooting, ball handling, and passing skills. "If me and my dad went to a park and he didn't think I was practicing hard enough, he'd just get in the car and leave," she remembered. "And I'd have to run home. I mean run home. Once I figured that out, I'd always try to go to close-by parks."

EDUCATION

Parker attended Naperville Central High School, where she became the star player on the powerful Lady Redhawks basketball team. During her sophomore year, she came to national attention by becoming the first female high-school player—and only the fifth woman at any level—to dunk a basketball during a sanctioned game. "The first two times I tried it in games I failed. Embarrassing," Parker recalled. "The third time was a charm, and then cameras and reporters were everywhere—everyone wanted to talk about dunking."

Parker won the slam dunk contest at the 2004 McDonald's High School All-American Game, the first girl ever to win that event.

In March 2004, during her senior year of high school, Parker became the first girl ever to win the slam-dunk contest at the annual McDonald's High School All-American Game. She defeated some of the top male players in the country, including two future NBA first-round draft picks. "It was special, but that's not what I want to be known for," she said. "Eventually the hype about my dunks will die down because more women players will do it."

Parker proved herself to be an outstanding all-around player throughout her high-school career. She averaged 22.9 points and 13.2 rebounds per game and led her team to consecutive Class AA Illinois state championships in 2003 and 2004. She received several major national awards following both her junior and senior seasons, including the Naismith Prep Player of the Year, Gatorade High School Player of the Year, and *USA Today* Player of the Year awards. By the time she graduated in 2004 with a 3.7 grade-point average, Parker was the most highly recruited player in the country. When she signed a letter of intent to play college basketball for the University of Tennessee Lady Volunteers, the signing ceremony was broadcast live on ESPN.

University of Tennessee Lady Volunteers

Parker was thrilled to go to Nashville and play for legendary Tennessee basketball coach Pat Summitt, who had won more games than any other National Collegiate Athletic Association (NCAA) Division I coach in history. (For more information on Summitt, see *Biography Today Sports,* Vol. 3.) Shortly before the start of her freshman year, however, Parker underwent surgery to repair an injured left knee. After several unsuccessful attempts to come back from the surgery, she reluctantly agreed to sit out the 2004-05 season. "In my head I knew I shouldn't play, but my heart wanted to," she admitted. Parker received a special status called a "redshirt," which meant that she still retained four years of eligibility to play college basketball. Although she felt deeply disappointed about missing the season, Parker worked hard at knee rehabilitation and other training exercises. She added 10 pounds of muscle to her six foot, five inch frame and increased her vertical leap to an impressive 27 inches.

———— **"** ————

"She's the toughest matchup in the game," said University of Mississippi Coach Carol Ross. "On many nights, she's the best guard on the floor, the best post on the floor, the best rebounder on the floor, the best passer on the floor and, let's not forget, the best scorer on the floor. She's got the strut of a competitor and the stuff of a champion."

———— **"** ————

Parker made her long-awaited college debut during the 2005-06 season. Although she was listed as a forward on the team roster, she also played center and guard. From the beginning, opposing coaches struggled to find a way to defend against her. "She's the toughest matchup in the game," said University of Mississippi Coach Carol Ross. "On many nights, she's the best guard on the floor, the best post on the floor, the best rebounder on the floor, the best passer on the floor and, let's not forget, the best scorer on the floor. She's got the strut of a competitor and the stuff of a champion." On March 19, 2006, Parker made history once again by becoming the first woman ever to dunk twice in an NCAA game.

During her second season (2006-07), Parker led the Lady Vols to their first NCAA championship since 1998. Parker's strong performance earned her

Parker, a three-time All-American and 2008 Naismith Player of the Year, helped the Lady Vols to National Championships in 2007 and 2008 before becoming the number one draft pick in the WNBA. She holds the school record with seven career dunks.

Most Valuable Player honors in the NCAA tournament, as well as the John R. Wooden Award as the nation's top female college player. She came back in 2007-08 to help Tennessee claim a second consecutive national title. In addition to earning tournament MVP honors for the second straight year, Parker also claimed the Naismith Player of the Year Award and won the prestigious Honda-Broderick Cup as the Collegiate Female Athlete of the Year.

In February 2008 Parker announced that she planned to give up her fourth year of college eligibility to play professionally in the Women's National Basketball Association (WNBA). "My experience here at Tennessee has been great. I look back at my growth, not only as a player but also just as a person, and I feel like it's been the best four years of my life. I wouldn't change anything," she stated. "It was a difficult decision for me to forego my senior year, but I just felt like it was the right decision to make going out as a champion." Parker completed her time at Tennessee with career averages of 19.4 points, 8.8 rebounds, and 2.2 blocks per game—and a college diploma as well. A two-time Academic All-American, she earned a bachelor's degree in sports management in May 2008.

CAREER HIGHLIGHTS

WNBA: The Los Angeles Sparks

Parker was selected first overall in the 2008 WNBA draft by the Los Angeles Sparks. The Sparks had a proud history—they won back-to-back WNBA championships in 2001 and 2002. But the team had posted a league-worst 10-24 record in 2007. The Sparks' star player, veteran center Lisa Leslie, had given birth to her first child and missed the entire season. In her absence, Los Angeles failed to make the playoffs for the first time in nine years.

Parker made her professional debut for the Sparks on May 17, 2008. Playing against the defending WNBA champion Phoenix Mercury, she scored 34 points, grabbed 12 rebounds, and dished out 8 assists. She set a new record for points scored by a WNBA rookie in her very first game. "It obviously was better than I expected," she acknowledged. "Coming out, I just wanted to play hard. I was a little nervous, and I think my teammates did a good job of just keeping me in it mentally and not allowing me to get frustrated."

Another highlight of Parker's rookie season came on June 22, when she became the second player ever to dunk in a WNBA game (the first was her teammate Lisa Leslie in 2002). "When I caught the ball and there was an open lane, it was a good opportunity," she recalled. "I'm happy that I was able to do it in Los Angeles in front of the home fans."

In August the WNBA suspended play for a few weeks to allow some of the league's star players to join the U.S. national women's basketball team at the 2008 Summer Olympic Games in Beijing, China. Parker was delighted to be invited to represent the United States in the Olympics. She and her teammates breezed through the Olympic basketball tournament, winning eight straight games by an average margin of 38.8 points. Team USA defeated Australia by a score of 92-65 to win the gold medal. Parker averaged 9.4 points per game in the Olympic tournament and contributed 14 points in the gold medal game.

After returning to the Sparks, Parker resumed her fantastic rookie season. She led her team to a 20-14 record and a spot in the playoffs. The Sparks beat the Seattle Storm in the Western Conference semifinals, but lost to the San Antonio Silver Stars in the conference finals. Parker's season averages of 18.5 points and 9.5 rebounds per game made her an easy choice for WNBA Rookie of the Year honors. She also earned the league's Most Valuable Player Award, thus becoming the first player in WNBA history to win both awards in the same season.

Parker has expressed confidence that she can balance her career and her family life. "There's room for basketball, there's room for Lailaa," she explained. "I have, from a young age, said I wanted both. I want a career and I want a family and I wasn't going to have to choose. Right now I'm living my dream because I have the best of both worlds. I go to basketball and I love it and I play and then I come home and there's that joy."

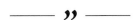

To cap off one of the greatest individual years in the history of women's basketball, Parker was named Female Athlete of the Year by the Associated Press. "She enjoyed an incredible run," Coach Summitt said of Parker's 2008 NCAA title, Olympic gold medal, and prestigious awards. "It was an exceptional year for an exceptional athlete and person."

Balancing Career and Family

Parker's remarkable season drew the attention of basketball fans across the country. The Sparks attracted huge crowds wherever they played, and the WNBA's TV ratings increased by 19 percent for the 2008 season. Parker quickly established herself as one of the most popular players in the league, and her number 3 Sparks jersey became the WNBA's top seller.

"When I see little girls wearing them it reminds me of when I was little at Bulls games and I wanted Ron Harper's jersey and autograph," she said. "To think someone feels that way about me is so flattering. It means the women's game is growing and it's a great time for me to be involved in the evolution of the game." In recognition of her appeal to fans, Parker received lucrative endorsement deals with Adidas and Gatorade.

In January 2009 Parker's personal life became the center of public attention. She announced that she and her husband of two months, Boston Celtics center Shelden Williams, were expecting a baby in the spring. Although they had not planned to start a family so soon, they looked forward to welcoming the new baby. "I was surprised," Parker admitted. "But everything happens for a reason. It will be exciting to have my child share my career and to remember what I was like when I was young."

The news of Parker's pregnancy came as a shock to her teammates, sponsors, and fans. Some critics questioned her commitment to her basketball career. Others called her careless or selfish. But WNBA commissioner Donna Orender defended Parker's right to make her own decisions. "It's the miracle of life, and it doesn't always happen on your time schedule," she said. "That's how it goes, you know? Parker will come back—and we'll have one more fan." Parker gave birth to a daughter, Lailaa, in May 2009. She missed the first eight games of the 2009 WNBA season.

After Parker took time off to have a baby, some people have questioned whether motherhood would limit her basketball career. But Parker has expressed confidence that she can balance her career and her family life. "There's room for basketball, there's room for Lailaa," she explained. "I have, from a young age, said I wanted both. I want a career and I want a family and I wasn't going to have to choose. Right now I'm living my dream because I have the best of both worlds. I go to basketball and I love it and I play and then I come home and there's that joy."

Parker also hopes to set a good example for her daughter, as well as for her many young fans. "Now everything I do is for my daughter," she noted. "She's going to be watching and I take that mindset with me. I want to be a good role model for her, show her girls can do anything guys can do."

Returning to the Court

While Parker was absent at the beginning of the 2009 season, the Sparks posted a 3-5 record. She returned to the court just seven weeks after giving birth and quickly regained her old form. By season's end she had regis-

Parker goes up against Phoenix Mercury guard Diana Taurasi during the 2009 WNBA Western Conference finals, which the Mercury ultimately won.

tered 13.1 points, 9.8 rebounds, and 2.6 assists per game. Her contributions helped boost the Sparks to an 18-16 record and a spot in the playoffs. But the Sparks' hopes of capturing the WNBA title ended in disappointment. Parker and her teammates defeated the Seattle Storm in the Western Conference semifinals, but they lost to the Phoenix Mercury in the conference finals. In addition, Lisa Leslie retired from the WNBA at the end of the season. Leslie, the team leader, had been with the team since its inception. Everyone knew that the three-time MVP would be missed, and many looked to Parker to pick up her game. (For more information on Leslie, see *Biography Today*, January 2004.)

After the season ended, Parker went to Yekaterinburg, Russia, to play for the UMMC Ekaterinburg in the women's EuroLeague. Parker felt that the experience of playing in Russia toughened her up a bit. "You're allowed to get away with more defensively," she said about their style of play. "You're allowed to push a little bit more. The refs give you some leeway when posting up. . . . Here, when you put your hand on somebody, it's immediately a foul. Overseas, they give you three or four times to put your hands on somebody, and if you displace them, then it's a foul." With the loss of Leslie, that type of physical play was exactly what the Sparks would need.

Unfortunately, Parker didn't get much time to try out this new style of play. The team got off to a rough start in 2010, with a 1-6 record that was the worst in team history. But Parker was playing well, leading the WNBA in scoring and rebounding. Then in June, she suffered an injury during a game against the Minnesota Lynx. After pulling down a defensive rebound, she left the game in pain holding her left shoulder, which was dislocated and required surgery. Parker was expected to be out for four to six months, and she missed the remainder of the season.

MARRIAGE AND FAMILY

Parker first met her husband, NBA player Shelden Williams, when she made an official recruiting visit to Duke University during high school. Williams was a sophomore at Duke and a star player on the Blue Devils men's basketball team at the time. They started dating two years later, when Parker and the Lady Volunteers came to Duke to play a game. They got married on November 13, 2008. "When I was getting ready to propose," Williams remembered, "she kept jamming her finger, and I could never get her actual ring size. So I got a special ring with a clasp at the bottom that allows her to open it and put it over her finger, so that no matter what happens to her knuckle, it'll always fit." Their daughter, Lailaa, was born on May 13, 2009.

HOBBIES AND OTHER INTERESTS

In her spare time, Parker likes to relax by walking her two dogs. She also enjoys watching old TV comedies like "Full House" and "The Cosby Show." Parker has performed community service work with a number of organizations, including D.A.R.E., Loaves and Fishes, and the Ronald McDonald House.

HONORS AND AWARDS

Illinois Miss Basketball: 2002, 2003, 2004
Gatorade High School Player of the Year: 2003, 2004
Naismith Prep Player of the Year: 2003, 2004
USA Today High School Player of the Year: 2003, 2004
Southeastern Conference Rookie of the Year: 2006
Kodak All-American: 2006, 2007, 2008
John R. Wooden Player of the Year: 2007, 2008
NCAA Women's Basketball Tournament Most Outstanding Player: 2007, 2008
Academic All-American: 2008
Naismith Player of the Year: 2008
Honda-Broderick Cup: 2008
Olympic Women's Basketball: 2008, gold medal
WNBA Rookie of the Year: 2008
WNBA Most Valuable Player: 2008
Female Athlete of the Year (Associated Press): 2008

FURTHER READING

Books

Ross, Alan. *Second to None: The National Championship Teams of the Tennessee Lady Vols,* 2009

Periodicals

ESPN The Magazine, Mar. 23, 2009 (cover story)
Jet, Oct. 20, 2003, p.54; Apr. 28, 2008, p.48
Los Angeles Times, May 11, 2010; June 18, 2010
New York Times, Jan. 23, 2004; Apr. 1, 2004; Apr. 4, 2007; Aug. 18, 2008
Sports Illustrated, Nov. 21, 2005, p.76; Feb. 12, 2007, p.32; Apr. 12, 2007, p.54; Apr. 17, 2008, p.50
Sports Illustrated for Kids, Mar. 1, 2006, p.44; July 2008, p.28
Time, Oct. 24, 2005, p.89
USA Today, Nov. 17, 2005, p.C1; Mar. 16, 2007, p.C1; Apr. 9, 2008, p.C11; June 20, 2008, p.C9

Online Articles

http://sports.espn.go.com
(ESPN, "Parker: First-Rate Game and a First-Rate Life," Dec. 4, 2007)
http://awards.honda.com
(Honda, "Collegiate Woman Athlete of the Year: Candace Parker," 2008)

http://www.nytimes.com
  (New York Times, "Candace Parker Is Balancing Career and Family," Jan. 24, 2009)
http://sportsillustrated.cnn.com
  (Sports Illustrated, "Parker Finding Balance between Motherhood, Basketball," July 6, 2009)
http://www.wnba.com
  (WNBA, "Candace Parker Dishes on Her Award Haul, Her Winter Plans, and Her Father's Motivation," Oct. 4, 2008)

ADDRESS

Candace Parker
Los Angeles Sparks
888 South Figueroa Street, Ste. 2010
Los Angeles, CA 90017

WORLD WIDE WEB SITES

http://www.wnba.com/sparks
http://www.utladyvols.com
http://www.wnba.com/playerfile/candace_parker/index.html

David Protess 1946-
American Educator, Legal Activist, and Journalist
Director of the Medill Innocence Project

BIRTH

David Protess was born on April 7, 1946, in the borough of Brooklyn in New York City. His father, Sidney Protess, was in business, and his mother, Beverly Gordon Protess, was a homemaker.

YOUTH

Growing up in the Sheepshead Bay neighborhood of Brooklyn, David Protess developed an early interest in social issues

——— " ———

Protess was deeply upset by the executions of convicted spies Julius and Ethel Rosenberg, especially by a newspaper headline that proclaimed "Rosenbergs Fried." "I can still recall standing there and seeing that," Protess remembered. "It seemed so unjust, and I'm not taking a position about whether they were guilty or not. What was unjust was that the state orphaned two young boys."

——— " ———

due to his mother's involvement in various causes. At age seven, an incident took place that focused his attention on one topic in particular. Julius and Ethel Rosenberg, a husband and wife, were convicted of spying for the Soviet Union and were sentenced to death. On June 19, 1953, they were put to death in the electric chair despite a worldwide campaign to stop their executions.

This highly publicized event had a lasting effect on Protess. He had been inspired by the efforts to spare the couple's lives, and his interest was heightened because he was the same age as one of the Rosenbergs' two sons. When the executions went ahead, Protess was deeply upset, and he grew angrier after reading a newspaper headline that proclaimed "Rosenbergs Fried." "I can still recall standing there and seeing that," he remembered. "It seemed so unjust, and I'm not taking a position about whether they were guilty or not. What was unjust was that the state orphaned two young boys." Decades later, Protess would return to the issues of crime and capital punishment—the execution of convicted criminals—which would become the center of his professional life.

EDUCATION

After graduating from high school, Protess moved to Chicago to attend Roosevelt University, where he earned a bachelor's degree in 1968. He went on to attend graduate school at the University of Chicago, earning a master's degree in 1970 and then a PhD (doctorate) in public policy in 1974 from the university's School of Social Service Administration.

CAREER HIGHLIGHTS

When his studies were completed, Protess took a job as a professor of political science at Loyola University in Chicago. He spent two years in that job, but he was also fascinated by another calling—investigative journalism. His interest was inspired by the Watergate scandal of the early 1970s. Watergate is the name of a hotel and office complex in Washington DC. In 1972, a group of people linked to President Richard M. Nixon were arrested while committing a burglary at the Watergate offices of the Democratic Party. After the failed burglary, Nixon and his aides created a massive cover-up to conceal any links between the burglars and the White House. But their efforts were unsuccessful. Over the course of the next two years, the involvement of the President and his aides in the burglary and the cover-up was revealed by many journalists and other investigators, but especially by two reporters at the *Washington Post,* Carl Bernstein and Bob Woodward. From that time on, the term "Watergate" became synonymous with the national scandal and the constitutional crisis that brought an end to Nixon's presidency and led to his decision to resign from office.

Protess was impressed by the work of the reporters who uncovered Watergate, and he realized that he wanted to devote himself to a similar type of work that would probe and publicize important issues. His wish came true in 1976, when he became the research director for the Better Government Association. An independent "watchdog" group based in Chicago, the association works to expose corruption and inefficiency in government. The job allowed Protess to demonstrate his skill in investigating the actions of public officials and employees. He also focused on writing newspaper stories during this period, and two articles that he authored for the *Chicago Sun Times* were named as finalists for the prestigious Pulitzer Prize.

As a journalist and in his investigative work for the Better Government Association, Protess carried on the tradition of the "muckrakers"—reporters who specialize in highlighting problems with the larger goal of changing public opinion and public policy on specific social issues. Muckraking writers had first become prominent during the progressive era of the late 1800s and early 1900s, and that style of crusading journalism enjoyed a resurgence beginning in the 1960s. "I just believe that the higher calling of journalism is that after you find the truth, you can in fact right the wrong," Protess explained.

A Professor with a Mission

In 1981, Protess once again took up the duties of a college professor, joining the faculty of the Medill School of Journalism at Northwestern University in Evanston, Illinois, near Chicago. Meanwhile, he continued to author investigative stories in his spare time, becoming a contributing editor and staff writer for *Chicago Lawyer* in 1986. In his work for that publication, Protess

Protess meeting with students while working on a case together in 1999.

specialized in sorting through the evidence in criminal cases and exposing instances where he believed there had been a miscarriage of justice.

By pursuing these stories, Protess was attempting to correct problems that he perceived within the criminal justice system. He noted that certain issues came up time and again in the cases he explored. In his opinion, police and prosecutors often made errors—sometimes by accident or carelessness and sometimes on purpose in order to attain a conviction. As a result, innocent people were jailed while the actual criminals went unpunished. In addition, he found that many defendants received poor legal representation, particularly those who had to rely on court-appointed lawyers because they could not afford to hire an attorney. These problems have been especially distressing for Protess when a wrongly convicted person has been sentenced to death. "No rational person would want to see an innocent person on death row or put to death," he noted. "And that's what's happening in … many cases."

Protess ultimately developed the idea of combining his teaching with his journalism projects. He began allowing students in his investigative reporting class to assist in his probes of questionable criminal cases, with their work counting toward their final grade in the course. This was a novel approach to teaching journalism, and it has proven to be very popular with students. At the beginning of each term, Protess presents the class with several cases in which there is a possibility that a person has been wrongly convicted. Students choose which case they want to explore and work in teams to pour through the facts.

Protess's students spend long hours reviewing court and police records, and they also "hit the street" to question people who may have knowledge about the crime, with the interviews frequently taking place in poor, inner-city neighborhoods in the Chicago area. Protess tries to prepare the class members for this difficult task by having them take part in role-playing exercises. In addition, a private investigator or Protess himself often accompanies the students on the real interviews, particularly those of crucial importance. While the work requires dedication and long hours, most members of the class become deeply devoted to their investigations. "You learn so much more from hands-on experience, talking to sources, digging for documents, getting information," explained Tom McCann, who took the class in the late 1990s. "That kind of investigative reporting fills you with so much adrenaline that you can't imagine doing anything else with your life."

"You learn so much more from hands-on experience, talking to sources, digging for documents, getting information," explained Tom McCann, one of Protess's students. "That kind of investigative reporting fills you with so much adrenaline that you can't imagine doing anything else with your life."

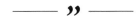

Success and Disappointment

One of the early cases that Protess and his students tackled involved the murder of a seven-year-old girl, Jaclyn Dowaliby, who went missing from her home in the Chicago suburb of Midlothian and was later found dead. Her parents, Cynthia and David Dowaliby, were accused of the crime. Charges were later dismissed against the mother, but in 1990, David Dowaliby was convicted of murder and sentenced to 45 years in prison. After covering the case for the *Chicago Tribune*, Protess continued to scrutinize the facts, calling on the assistance of his students and Rob Warden, the former publisher of *Chicago Lawyer*, who often collaborates with Protess.

Protess with the Ford Heights Four—(left to right) Willie Rainge, Kenny Adams, Dennis Williams, and Verneal Jimerson—who spent time in prison for a crime they didn't commit.

Because of the group's work, new evidence was discovered, and the main witness against Dowaliby recanted his court testimony. These developments helped to convince the Illinois Appellate Court to reverse the verdict, freeing David Dowaliby after more than a year in prison. In 1993, Protess and Warden published *Gone in the Night: The Dowaliby Family's Encounter with Murder and the Law*, which detailed their findings and their criticism of the official investigation and prosecution. It was the fifth book authored by Protess, who had previously written works on the subjects of social policy, citizen watchdog groups, and journalism. *Gone in the Night* was made into a made-for-TV movie that was broadcast in 1996.

While the Dowaliby case had been an encouraging experience for Protess, the project he and his students undertook in the early 1990s involving the case of Girvies Davis proved far less positive. In 1979, Davis had been convicted of murder and received the death sentence. Prosecutors had based their case on a written confession that Davis had given to police. But the suspect later maintained that officers had forced him to sign the document and had threatened to shoot him if he didn't admit that he was guilty of the crime. Moreover, Davis was illiterate, so it was impossible for him to read the confession he signed. Unfortunately for Davis, his court-appointed lawyer had never raised that important point during the trial.

After spending more than 15 years on death row, Davis was scheduled to be executed in 1995. Protess and his students spent six months attempting to get the authorities to reconsider the prisoner's guilt and to delay or cancel the execution, but in the early hours of May 17, 1995, Davis was put to death by lethal injection. Protess and the students who had worked on the project were devastated by the news, and a grief counselor was brought in to help them deal with the loss. While the prisoner's death was a heavy blow, it also provided Protess with a way forward. In the hours before he died, Davis had phoned Protess and his students, thanking them for their efforts on his behalf and asking them to assist a fellow prisoner on death row named Dennis Williams. Protess had agreed with the request, and when he convened his next investigative reporting class, students began looking into the facts surrounding the Williams conviction.

Four Innocent Men

On May 11, 1978, a young couple, Larry Lionberg and Carol Schmal, had been kidnapped during a gas station robbery in Homewood, Illinois. Their abductors took them to an abandoned house in the town of Ford Heights, where Schmal was raped and both she and Lionberg were shot to death. The brutal killings were front-page news, and several days later, four men were charged with the crime: Kenny Adams, Verneal Jimerson, Willie Rainge, and Dennis Williams. All four were black while the victims were white, adding a volatile racial element to the incident.

Police and prosecutors based their case largely on the testimony of Paula Gray, the girlfriend of Kenny Adams, who said she was present when the crime was committed. But Gray suffered from mental illness and an extremely low IQ, and her account of events changed dramatically over time. She initially said that the four had committed the crime, then recanted and said that police had forced her to implicate the men. Later, she once more reverted to her original story. Despite the inconsistency of Gray's statements, the accused men, who became known as the "Ford Heights Four," were found guilty and sent to prison. The questionable evidence and the shoddy work of defense lawyers led to numerous appeals, and the legal developments in the case stretched over many years. By the time that Protess and his investigative journalism class took up the case in January 1996, Adams and Rainge were still serving lengthy prison terms, and Williams was awaiting execution. Verneal Jimerson had gained his freedom in 1995, when the Illinois Supreme Court overturned his conviction.

Three college seniors in the class—Stephanie Goldstein, Stacey Delo, and Laura Sullivan—chose to investigate the charges against the Ford Heights

Four. In the months that followed, vital assistance was also supplied by René Brown, a private investigator who had worked on the case for a number of years, as well as several lawyers who agreed to contribute their services for no charge. By digging into the official files on the case, the students made an important discovery: the police had turned up evidence shortly after the murders took place that implicated four other men in the crime, but detectives had never followed up on the leads.

After an extensive amount of footwork, Protess, the students, and Brown were able to locate three of the four men who had been linked to the crime—one of whom was already in prison for another murder. In a stunning turn of events, two of the suspects confessed to the crime. Soon after, DNA testing confirmed that they had raped Carol Schmal and further proved that Williams, Adams, Rainge, and Jimerson were innocent. By July 1996, the charges against them had been officially dropped, and they were free men after an ordeal that marred 18 years of their lives. "We are victims of this crime, too," said Kenny Adams on the day that he was released from custody. "I want people to know that this could happen to anybody—and that's a crime."

> "We are victims of this crime, too," said exonerated prisoner Kenny Adams on the day that he was released from custody. "I want people to know that this could happen to anybody—and that's a crime."

In the Spotlight

The exoneration of the four men generated a tremendous number of media stories about the work of Protess and the students. The professor used the attention to emphasize his belief that police and prosecutors had knowingly ignored key evidence in the case in order to gain a quick conviction against the suspects they had initially arrested. "What we had here was a conspiracy to railroad four men," Protess said in *People*. "I've never seen anything this bad."

Some of the interest in the story had to do with the unusual circumstances of the investigation: young college students entering the dangerous streets of the inner city in order to win the freedom of innocent men. It sounded like the plot of a TV show or movie, so it was hardly surprising when the Walt Disney Company made a million-dollar offer for exclusive rights to the story, proposing to divide the money between the main participants, including Protess, the three students, and the Ford Heights Four. The deal ended up creating a rift between the professor and the students because

Protess with Kenny Adams after his release from prison.
A member of the Ford Heights Four, Adams spent 18 years in prison before
Protess and his students proved he was innocent.

Protess felt that all of the money should go to the former prisoners. "I do not intend to profit at the expense of these men," he stated. The students disagreed, and other players in the investigation, such as René Brown, were upset that they received little from the Disney offer. Ultimately, most of the money was divided five ways, with one share to the students and the rest to the former prisoners. In 1999, the wrongly convicted men won further compensation when they accepted a $36 million settlement in a civil suit they had filed against Cook County.

The book that addressed the case, *A Promise of Justice*, was authored by Protess and Rob Warden and was published in 1998 to mixed reviews. Some critics faulted the work for problems with the writing, including its unemotional, "just-the-facts" style, but *Booklist* found *A Promise of Justice* to be "an eloquent reminder of the justice system's flaws." The Disney film depiction of the Ford Heights case has yet to appear, but the work of Protess and his class members seems to have been the inspiration for a short-lived television series in the early 2000s. "Deadline" concerned a fictional college journalism professor who probes crimes with his students, but Protess had no involvement in the show. At one point, he even asked the producers of "Deadline" to confirm that fact publicly so that he wouldn't be mistakenly associated with the series.

413

A Last-Minute Cry for Help

Having gained a reputation for freeing the innocent, Protess was besieged with requests to help other prisoners. "My home number is scribbled on every death row in the country," he noted in *Newsweek*. In September 1998, a call came from an attorney who represented Anthony Porter, who was scheduled to be executed in Illinois just a few weeks later. Protess told the lawyer that he was unable to help because the prisoner would be put to death before his class could begin work on the case. Porter's chances looked dim, but just 48 hours before he was scheduled to die, he was granted a temporary stay of execution. The delay provided Protess's class with the time they needed, and a group of students began analyzing a crime that had occurred 16 years earlier.

> "I'm not a critic of the legal system. I believe it works, and I think most people in prison are guilty," Protess explained. "But the more mail I received [about wrongly convicted prisoners], the more I began to question whether we had a serious problem on our hands."

On a late summer evening in August of 1982, pistol shots rang out near a swimming pool in Washington Park in Chicago. The gunfire killed two teenagers, 18-year-old Jerry Hillard and his girlfriend, 19-year-old Marilyn Green. Two days later, Anthony Porter—a gang member who had previously been convicted of armed robbery—was charged with the crime. He was found guilty and assigned a cell on death row.

Prosecutors had relied heavily on a lead witness, William Taylor, who testified that he saw Porter shoot Hillard and Green. The students who took up the case began by checking Taylor's account of the crime. They staged a reenactment in the park, placing themselves in the positions that had been occupied by the victims, shooter, and the witness, and they realized that there was no way that the witness could have positively identified the killer in the nighttime darkness. "We couldn't make out our faces in the middle of the day," explained Shawn Armbrust, one of the class members probing the case. They also noted that the witness said that the killer fired the gun with his left hand, while Porter is right-handed.

These facts cast substantial doubt on the witness's account, so Protess and the students tracked down Taylor and interviewed him. He recanted his testimony, admitting that he had not seen the shooting. Instead, he said that police had "threatened, harassed, and intimidated" him until he

Former death row inmate Anthony Porter exuberantly hugs Protess after being released from prison due to the work of Protess and his students.

agreed to testify against Porter. Following another lead, the class members looked into the actions of two people who had been seen with Marilyn Green on the day of the murders—Alstory Simon and his wife at the time, Margaret Inez Jackson. Simon initially denied that he had anything to do with the killing, but when the students were finally able to find his ex-wife, she told a different story. The woman declared that Simon was the killer. Confronted with Jackson's videotaped statement, Simon confessed that he had shot Hillard and Green after he and Hillard had argued about money. On February 5, 1999, Anthony Porter walked out of prison after 16 years on death row and promptly hugged Protess and each of the students who had worked on his case.

Questioning Capital Punishment

The Porter case furthered Protess's reputation as a highly skilled investigator, but he has consistently downplayed his abilities as well as those of his students and other collaborators. Instead, he has stressed that his team's accomplishments are proof of the poor job that was done by police and

415

prosecutors in the initial investigations. "It's not that we are so good," he argued. "Any kind of diligent effort in these cases could do what we did.... Which is what is so outrageous about a college professor and his students solving these crimes. They were there to be solved from the start."

Protess's success in achieving justice for wrongly convicted individuals has made him a focal point in the debate over alleged problems with the law enforcement and the courts. While he often denounces miscarriages of justice, Protess does not think the system is fundamentally flawed. "I'm not a critic of the legal system. I believe it works, and I think most people in prison are guilty," he explained. "But the more mail I received [about wrongly convicted prisoners], the more I began to question whether we had a serious problem on our hands."

Protess's views on capital punishment are much more firm. "I think that when it comes to the death penalty system in our country, the system is broken and can't be fixed." A primary complaint made by Protess and other critics is that many innocent people have been sentenced to death, and unless executions are ended, innocent people are going to be killed by the state. As proof of the problem, opponents of capital punishment cite the large number of individuals who have won their freedom while awaiting execution. According to the figures compiled by the Death Penalty Information Center, 139 death row inmates in the United States were exonerated of their crimes between 1973 and 2009. Commenting in 2004 on the national yearly averages of death row inmates winning their freedom, Protess noted that "for every seven people we put to death, one is exonerated. That error rate in a matter with life and death stakes is intolerably high."

The state of Illinois had a particularly poor record in this regard, with 13 inmates being released from death row between 1977 and 2000. The work of Protess and his students made a significant contribution to that number, and the publicity surrounding the Ford Heights and Anthony Porter cases helped focus public attention on the subject. In January 2000, Governor George Ryan responded to the situation by halting all executions in the state, and he directly mentioned the achievements of Protess's journalism class as a reason for his decision. Before leaving office in 2003, the governor went further, granting clemency to the 167 inmates then on death row, exempting them from ever being executed.

A Growing Movement

In 1999, Protess's investigative work with Northwestern students was organized under the name of the Medill Innocence Project, with the profes-

Protess leading a group of students in an Innocence Project meeting at Northwestern University, 2009.

sor serving as the institution's director. The new name reflected the fact that Protess and his colleagues were linked with similar groups around the country that seek to correct miscarriages of justice, many of which use the title "Innocence Project." Protess has been a leading figure in this movement, and in 2000, he became a founding member of the Innocence Network. This group includes journalism and law schools throughout the United States that are following the model established by Protess of involving students in the investigation of questionable legal proceedings.

In addition to correcting miscarriages of justice, Protess has turned his attention to helping freed prisoners adjust to life on the outside. In the early 2000s, he established a program to help the former inmates find employment and receive adequate health care and psychological treatment, naming it in memory of Dennis Williams of the Ford Heights Four, who died in 2003. This initiative got an important boost when Protess received the Puffin/Nation Prize for Creative Citizenship in 2003 and used part of the $100,000 prize money to fund the program.

Despite his other responsibilities, Protess continues to teach the investigative journalism course. As of 2009, the investigations carried out by the class have helped win the freedom of 11 innocent people, five of whom had been on death row. In addition, other investigations are in the works, one of which has been the subject of great media interest.

> *Protess's devotion to certain cases can become obsessive. "I go a little further than investigative reporters," he explained. "Once I feel I've reached a firm conclusion that someone is innocent, I can't think of something I wouldn't do to help them except break the law."*

The case involves the conviction of Anthony McKinney for murdering a security guard in 1978 in the town of Harvey. It shares many of the elements that had figured in other Protess investigations. McKinney, who was 18 years old at the time of the crime, had signed a confession during questioning, but he later claimed that he did so only because he was beaten by police. An alleged eyewitness testified that he saw the teenager shoot the guard, but that witness later recanted his testimony and said that he, too, was brutalized by officers until he agreed to implicate McKinney. The investigation carried out by Protess's journalism students turned up other suspects, one of whom was in prison for a different murder. That man, Anthony Drake, admitted that he had been present when the security guard was shot and that McKinney was not involved in the crime.

Based on that information, a circuit court judge is considering a petition for a new trial for McKinney. But Cook County prosecutors are opposed to retrying the case, and they have tried to cast doubt on the work of Protess and his students. First, they subpoenaed grades, e-mail messages, and other information related to the students who investigated the case, in effect suggesting that the students' work is untrustworthy. A more sensa-

Flanked by the students whose records were subpoenaed, Protess speaks to reporters after a Cook County court hearing in Chicago, 2009.

tional development came in November 2009, when prosecutors accused the students of paying one of the witnesses in the case to provide a video statement to bolster McKinney's claims of innocence. Protess has strongly denied that charge. In addition, he has opposed the subpoena of information about his students, claiming that they were acting as journalists and deserve the protection of journalists' shield laws. These laws prevent law enforcement officials from requiring journalists to divulge their sources, since confidentiality is often crucial in getting sources to talk. Protess has suggested that Cook County prosecutors have ulterior motives for their approach. "Legally, what I take from it is that the prosecutors are on a fishing expedition," he said. "Practically, I think they have an interest in paying [us] back for years of embarrassment—and paying forward to deter us." The judge will conduct further hearings on the case in 2010.

A Controversial Crusader

Yet the McKinney case is not the first time that the work of Protess and his students has been scrutinized. A recurring charge against Protess is that he is more of an advocate for prisoners than a journalist. A journalist maintains his or her impartiality and detachment and tries to find the truth in an objective manner. But Protess, according to his critics, begins with the belief that convicts are innocent and tries to find evidence to support that belief. These critics have also argued that this bias could be reflected in the way the class is conducted, so that, for instance, students who uncover misdeeds by police or prosecutors receive higher grades than those who do not. Protess has maintained that he evaluates students on the quality of their work, regardless of their ultimate findings. Moreover, he has stressed that the majority of class investigations end up supporting the conviction. "In some cases, the truth was the guy was guilty, and those students [who made that determination] got an A."

Protess has admitted that he can become deeply involved in the subjects he investigates and that his devotion to certain cases can become obsessive. "I go a little further than investigative reporters," he explained. "Once I feel I've reached a firm conclusion that someone is innocent, I can't think of something I wouldn't do to help them except break the law." Not surprisingly, he has tried to instill a similar sense of commitment among the people who take his class. "I want to train students to think of their profession in broad terms," he said, "and not be afraid to shed their objectivity and get their hands dirty."

Though his job is demanding and often places him at the center of controversy, Protess has remained committed to his twin goals of freeing the innocent while also mentoring students who may go on to continue and expand that mission. "This is my life's work," he explained. "Sure, there are countless miscarriages of justice. I just hope I can be part of correcting them."

MARRIAGE AND FAMILY

Protess married Marianne Kreitman in 1969. The couple had one son, Daniel, and divorced in 1977. He wed Joan Perry in 1980 and has a second son, Benjamin, from that marriage.

WRITINGS

Community Power and Social Policy, 1974
Establishing a Citizens' Watchdog Group, 1979 (with Peter Manikas)
Uncovering Race: Press Coverage of Racial Issues in Chicago, 1989 (with James Ettema)
Agenda Setting: Readings on Media, Public Opinion, and Policymaking, 1991 (editor, with Maxwell McCombs)

Journalism of Outrage: Investigative Reporting and Agenda-Building in America, 1991 (with others)

Gone in the Night: The Dowaliby Family's Encounter with Murder and the Law, 1994 (with Robert Warden)

A Promise of Justice: The Eighteen-Year Fight to Save Four Innocent Men, 1998 (with Robert Warden)

HONORS AND AWARDS

National Teaching Award for Excellence in the Teaching of Journalism Ethics (Poynter Institute for Media Studies): 1986

Best Book of 1993 (Investigative Reporters and Editors): 1993, for *Gone in the Night*

Human Rights Award (National Alliance against Racist and Political Oppression): 1996

Person of the Week (ABC Network News): 1996

Champion of Justice Award (National Association of Criminal Defense Lawyers): 1997

Hal Lipset Truth in Action Award (World Association of Detectives): 1999

James McGuire Award (American Civil Liberties Union): 1999

H. Councill Trenholm Memorial Award (National Education Association): 2002

Clarence Darrow Award (Darrow Commemorative Committee): 2003

Herb Block Award (Newspaper Guild/Communication Workers of America): 2003

Puffin/Nation Prize for Creative Citizenship: 2003

National Intellectual Freedom Award (National Council of Teachers of English): 2010

Media Spotlight Award (Amnesty International)

FURTHER READING

Periodicals

American Journalism Review, June 1997, p.38

Biography, May 2000, p.100

Current Biography Yearbook, 1999

New York Times, Feb. 5, 1999, p.16; Mar. 6, 1999, p.7; Nov. 11, 2009, p.A20

Newsweek, May 31, 1999, p.32

People, July 29, 1996, p.44

Rolling Stone, Oct. 14, 1999, p.91

Online Articles

http://archives.chicagotribune.com/2009/oct/19/health/chi-nu-subpoena
-19-oct19
(Chicago Tribune.com, "Northwestern University's Medill Innocence
Project Is in a Standoff with Cook County Prosecutors," Oct. 19, 2009)
http://www.deathpenaltyinfo.org/innocence-list-those-freed-death-row
(Death Penalty Information Center, "The Innocence List," Nov. 3, 2009)
http://www.chron.org/tools/viewarticle.php?artid=677
(Northwestern Chronicle, "The Chronicle Interview: David Protess,"
Oct. 16, 2003)

ADDRESS

David Protess
Medill Innocence Project
1845 Sheridan Road
Evanston, IL 60208

WORLD WIDE WEB SITE

http://www.medillinnocenceproject.org

Albert Pujols 1980-

Dominican-Born American Professional Baseball
Player with the St. Louis Cardinals
National League Most Valuable Player in 2005, 2008,
and 2009

BIRTH

Jose Alberto Pujols (pronounced *POO-hoals*), known as Albert, was born on January 16, 1980, in Santo Domingo, Dominican Republic. The Dominican Republic is an island nation
located in the Caribbean Sea. Santo Domingo, its capital city,
lies on the southern coast.

Albert's mother left the family when he was three years old. His father, Bienvenido Pujols, was a painter who traveled frequently in search of work. As a result, Albert was raised primarily by his paternal grandmother, America Pujols, along with his father's 10 brothers and sisters. As an only child, Albert thought of his older aunts and uncles as siblings. He moved to the United States with his family in 1996, at the age of 16, and became an American citizen in 2007.

YOUTH

Albert grew up in a poor but close-knit family. During most of his childhood, he lived in run-down houses with dirt floors and no running water. His main interest was baseball, which he started playing at a young age. "I used to play catch with a lime," he remembered. "We made gloves out of cardboard milk boxes. Sticks were bats." He also watched American Major League Baseball (MLB) games on television whenever he had the chance and dreamed of playing professionally someday.

> *Growing up in the Dominican Republic, Pujol's main interest was baseball, which he started playing at a young age. "I used to play catch with a lime," he remembered. "We made gloves out of cardboard milk boxes. Sticks were bats."*

In the mid-1990s several members of the Pujols family decided to leave the Dominican Republic. They immigrated to the United States in hopes of building a better life for themselves. Albert and his father and grandmother joined them in 1996. After a brief stop in New York City, they settled in Independence, Missouri, where they joined a community of about 2,000 Dominican immigrants.

The Pujols family faced a difficult adjustment to life in the United States. They started out very poor, and it took a while for the older family members to find jobs. But Albert's grandmother made sure that he and the others were well cared for. "She gave me everything I needed," he recalled. "She supported me 100 percent. How they treated me and took care of me, that's where I learned everything." Albert's family even supported his dream of becoming a professional baseball player. "No one ever told me I couldn't be a big-league ballplayer," he noted. "They told me to keep working hard, that anyone who got there didn't get there easy."

EDUCATION

Pujols completed his early education in Santo Domingo. After moving to the United States in 1996, he entered Fort Osage High School in Independence as a sophomore. He spoke only Spanish at that time, so he struggled to fit in at school and keep up with his studies. He worked with a tutor, though, and learned to speak conversational English within a year. In spring 1997 Pujols tried out for the Fort Osage varsity baseball team. His incredible talent was obvious from the first time he took batting practice. "Every time he swung, the bat was just going crack, crack, crack," recalled his high school coach, Dave Fry. "I felt like the baseball gods had smiled down on me."

Pujols, shown here batting for the Prince William Cannons in 2000, played just one season in the minor leagues.

Pujols lived up to his early promise and had a remarkable high-school baseball career. He earned all-state honors as a sophomore with a .500 batting average and 11 home runs. During his junior year in 1998, he led Fort Osage to the Missouri state baseball championship and earned all-state honors for a second time. In only 33 at-bats, Pujols posted an outstanding .600 average and smacked 8 home runs as a junior—including a monster 450-footer that landed on top of a building located well beyond the fence of an opposing team's field. He actually came up to the plate a total of 88 times that season, but he also earned 55 walks (for statistical purposes, walks do not count as at-bats) because opposing teams were not willing to give him any good pitches to hit.

In January 1999, Pujols decided to forego his senior season of high school baseball and graduate early. Since opposing high school teams refused to pitch to him, he felt he could receive a better evaluation from professional baseball scouts by moving on to play college baseball. Pujols accepted a baseball scholarship to attend Maple Woods Community College in Kansas City. In his very first junior college game, he hit a grand slam and turned an unassisted triple play at shortstop.

Playing for Maple Woods, Pujols went on to bat .461 with 22 home runs and 80 runs batted in (RBIs). He left college that June, after completing only one semester, in order to pursue his dream of playing in the major leagues. Still, his single season of college baseball was quite memorable. "Coaches still talk about tape-measure shots Albert hit," recalled Maple Woods coach Marty Kilgore. "A ball he hit into somebody's backyard, over somebody's house, they're still fresh in the mind."

CAREER HIGHLIGHTS

Major League Baseball—The St. Louis Cardinals

Pujols had only played one season of college baseball, but he impressed professional baseball scouts enough to be selected in the 13th round of the 1999 MLB draft by the St. Louis Cardinals. He signed a contract for $10,000 and entered the Cardinals' minor league system in the spring of 2000. Pujols rocketed through the minor league ranks within a single season, turning in strong performances and earning repeated promotions to higher levels. During that one season, he played with the Class A Peoria Chiefs, the Class AA Potomac Cannons, and the Class AAA Memphis Redbirds. His accomplishments in the minor league system impressed the Cardinals' coaches, who invited him to join the big-league team for spring training in February 2001.

———— " ————

Pujols played four different positions during his rookie season—first base, third base, left field, and right field—but that didn't bother him.
"I want to be in the lineup every day," he explained. "Playing anywhere is better than playing the bench."

———— " ————

When the Cardinals' coaching staff invited Pujols to attend spring training camp, they did not intend to give him a permanent slot on the roster. St. Louis had won the National League Central Division championship the year before, so the club did not desperately need young players. The coaches simply planned to give him a taste of the big leagues, then send him back to the minors to develop his skills for another year or two. As spring training progressed, however, Pujols played so well that the Cardinals had no choice but to keep him on the major league roster. "Each week when we had our cut meetings, there we were, figuring he had to go back to the minors at some point, and

During his rookie season, shown here, Pujols batted .329 with 37 home runs and 130 RBIs.

each week he kept impressing us more and more," recalled Cardinals General Manager Walt Jocketty. "It got to the final week and we just said, 'Look, we're really a better club with him,' the way he was playing."

Pujols first played in the major leagues on April 2, 2001, and he quickly became a vital member of the St. Louis lineup. His performance at the plate remained consistent even as the Cards struggled to find a defensive position for him. In fact, as his rookie season progressed, Pujols played in four different spots on the field—first base, third base, left field, and right field. But he claimed that shuffling around from infield to outfield did not bother him. "I want to be in the lineup every day," he explained. "Playing anywhere is better than playing the bench."

Pujols had one of the best rookie seasons in major league history. He batted .329 with 37 home runs, while walking 69 times and striking out only 93 times. He finished fifth in the National League in RBIs (with 130), hits (194), and doubles (47), and sixth in batting average and extra-base hits (88). His remarkable performance earned him National League Rookie of the Year honors. Pujols also provided the spark that helped the Cardinals successfully defend their Central Division championship with a 93-69 record, although St. Louis was defeated in the divisional playoff series by the Arizona Diamondbacks.

Pujols at first base in 2005, the year he won his first MVP award.

Working Hard to Prove Himself

Over the course of the 2002 season, Pujols established himself as one of the best young players in the league. He batted .314 with 34 home runs and 127 RBIs, while walking 72 times and reducing his strikeout total to 69. Thanks to his impressive performance, the young star finished second to Barry Bonds in the voting for the National League Most Valuable Player (MVP) award. Pujols's terrific season helped steer the Cardinals to a 97-65 record and their third straight National League Central Division crown. St.

Louis then swept the Diamondbacks in three straight games to advance to the National League Championship Series (NLCS). But the team fell short in its bid for a World Series appearance, losing to the San Francisco Giants in five games.

Throughout his first two seasons in the majors, Pujols demonstrated a remarkable combination of power, versatility, and consistency at the plate. He attributed his success as a hitter to his ability to recall pitchers' tendencies, recognize pitches, and make adjustments to his stance and swing as needed. "The main thing is I can read a pitcher. I can make adjustments," he noted. "That's how you become a good hitter, when you can tell yourself what you're doing wrong and correct it the next at-bat."

Even after making it to the majors, Pujols worked hard to develop his skills as a ball player. His preparation and desire to improve impressed his Cardinals teammates and coaches. He watched hours of videotape of different pitchers in order to study their movements. He also warmed up before each game by doing a long series of hitting drills, including some that were recommended to him by New York Yankees star Alex Rodriguez. Pujols's hard work and focus contributed to his success, and his natural ability was undoubtedly an important factor as well. "He's rare," said Cardinals' hitting coach Mitchell Page. "You look at that and you think of names like [Ted] Williams, [Rod] Carew, and [George] Brett, guys with beautiful, pure swings. Swings like his don't happen very often. It's a gift."

> "The main thing is I can read a pitcher. I can make adjustments," Pujols noted. "That's how you become a good hitter, when you can tell yourself what you're doing wrong and correct it the next at-bat."

Winning the National League Batting Title

Pujols played exceptionally well during his first two major league seasons—then set a new standard for himself in 2003. While the Cardinals fell short in their bid for a fourth consecutive divisional championship, St. Louis fans witnessed the emergence of a superstar. Pujols posted a league-leading .359 batting average to claim the National League batting title. He also led the league in runs scored (137), hits (212), and total bases (394). He added an impressive 43 home runs and 124 RBIs while also reducing his strikeout total to an amazing 65 in 591 at-bats. In honor of his achievements, Pujols was voted Player of the Year by his peers in the MLB Players Association. He fell short of claiming the National League MVP, however, finishing behind Bonds for the second straight year.

> "He's rare," said Cardinals' hitting coach Mitchell Page. "You look at that and you think of names like [Ted] Williams, [Rod] Carew, and [George] Brett, guys with beautiful, pure swings. Swings like his don't happen very often. It's a gift."

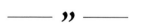

In early 2004, the Cardinals signed Pujols to a seven-year, $100 million contract—making him the highest-paid player in team history. "His accomplishments in his first three seasons are unmatched in the history of the game," said team co-owner Bill DeWitt. "Albert Pujols will serve as a cornerstone for the Cardinals for many years to come." The Cardinals also announced that Pujols would play a single position in the field for the first time in his major league career: first base. His coaches felt that this defensive position, which is considered less physically demanding than most others, would reduce his chance of injury and allow him to focus on his hitting.

As the 2004 season got underway, Pujols started out slowly. He struggled with chronic injuries to his heel and elbow for much of the year. As a result, he endured the first hitting slump of his career, which caused his batting average to dip below .300 at the end of May. But then his wife—an avid softball player—watched some videotapes of his swing and suggested that he narrow his batting stance. Pujols made the adjustment and immediately went on an offensive tear, hitting six home runs in the next nine games.

Pujols ended the 2004 season batting .331 with 46 home runs and 123 RBIs. St. Louis won an impressive 105 games to return to the top of the National League Central Division. The Cardinals swept the Los Angeles Dodgers in the divisional series, then defeated the Houston Astros in a tough seven-game NLCS to reach the World Series. Pujols was named the NLCS MVP, with a .500 batting average, 5 home runs, and 11 RBIs. Unfortunately for Pujols and his teammates, however, the promising season ended in disappointing fashion. The Cardinals lost the World Series to the Boston Red Sox in a four-game sweep. "It was great to be there," Pujols noted, "but it's too bad the way we played. You look at our season and you think, 'There's no way these guys are going to get swept.' But that's how this game is. We just have to forget about what happened and get ready for this year."

Claiming a World Series Championship

During the 2005 season Pujols turned in one of the best performances of his young career, batting .330 with 41 home runs and 117 RBIs. With rival Barry Bonds sidelined for most of the season with a knee injury, Pujols finally claimed his first National League MVP Award. Although he was pleased to receive the prestigious award, he insisted that the team's success was more important than individual honors. "I don't think about that stuff," he said. "I don't worry about winning the MVP, the batting title, or home runs. I just want to help my team out. If I do that, my numbers are going to be there."

Pujols and his teammates dominated their division in 2005 and finished the year with the best record in baseball at 100-62. With Pujols batting .556 in the playoffs, the heavily favored Cardinals swept the San Diego Padres in the National League Division Series. But the Cards fell short in their bid for a return trip to the World Series. Despite a dramatic game-winning homer by Pujols in Game 5, St. Louis was eliminated in the NLCS by the Houston Astros.

As the 2006 season got underway, Pujols was determined to achieve his dream of winning a World Series title. He got off to the hottest start in the history of baseball, hitting 19 home runs in the first 38 games of the season. He even tied an MLB record by hitting home runs in four consecutive at-bats. Yet he still insisted that he did not consider himself to be a home-run hitter. "[Mark] McGwire's a home run hitter, Bonds is a home run hitter," he explained. "I'm a line-drive hitter with power, and that's it. All I try to do is just hit for average, and hopefully if I put a good swing on it the ball's going to go out of the park."

Although he was nagged by injuries later in the 2006 season, Pujols still managed to post a career-high 49 home runs and 137 RBIs to go with his .331 batting average. After squeaking out a division title with 83 victories, the Cardinals defeated the San Diego Padres in the divisional playoff series. Then St. Louis survived a dramatic, seven-game NLCS against the New York Mets to earn a trip back to the World Series, facing the Detroit Tigers.

Pujols did not play his best during the series, batting only .200 with one homer. Still, the Cardinals managed to defeat the Tigers in five games to claim the World Series championship. "Now I can say I have a World Series ring in my trophy case," Pujols said afterward. "And that's what you play for. It doesn't matter how much money you make or what kind of numbers you put up in the big leagues. If you walk out of this game and you don't have a ring, you haven't accomplished everything." Although he

Pujols celebrating with teammates after the St. Louis Cardinals
defeated the Detroit Tigers to win the 2006 World Series.

was disappointed to finish second to Ryan Howard in the 2006 National League MVP race, Pujols was delighted to be honored for his defensive play by winning his first Rawlings Gold Glove Award.

Earning Back-to-Back MVP Awards

The Cardinals followed up their World Series title with a disappointing season in 2007. Pujols struggled with a torn ligament and bone spurs in his right elbow for much of the year. He still managed to hit .327 with 32 home runs and 103 RBIs, but the Cardinals finished six games below .500 and failed to make the playoffs. But Pujols accomplished an important personal triumph during the offseason: he scored 100 percent on his citizenship test and officially became a U.S. citizen.

The Cardinals continued to struggle in 2008, winning only 86 games to finish 11 1/2 games out of first place in the division. But Pujols overcame his elbow problems to post one of the greatest individual seasons in baseball history. After starting the season with a 42-game hitting streak, he finished second in the race for the batting title with a .357 average, while adding 37 home runs and 116 RBIs. Pujols was named Player of the Year by the MLB Players Association and also claimed the second National League MVP Award of his career. "I have to thank my teammates," he said afterward. "Obviously this is not an award that you win by yourself. My teammates were involved every day, day in and day out, supporting me, getting on base and driving me in. These kind of numbers, you can't do it by yourself." Following the 2008 season, Pujols had surgery to repair nerve damage in his elbow.

After the surgery, Pujols returned to top form in 2009. He batted .330 with 47 home runs and 134 RBIs to soar to his second straight MVP Award—and the third of his illustrious career. His strong performance helped St. Louis become the first to clinch the top spot in its division. Pujols and his teammates entered the 2009 playoffs with high hopes, only to see them dashed in the first round. The Cardinals failed to win a single playoff game, losing the divisional series to the Los Angeles Dodgers in three games. "I don't like the stigma of our club getting swept," St. Louis manager Tony LaRussa said afterward. "We're a better club than that, and the series was more competitive than that. But that's what it is."

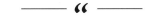

"Now I can say I have a World Series ring in my trophy case," Pujols said. "And that's what you play for. It doesn't matter how much money you make or what kind of numbers you put up in the big leagues. If you walk out of this game and you don't have a ring, you haven't accomplished everything."

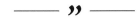

As the Cardinals entered the 2010 season, Pujols continued his superlative play. He got off to a slow start, and his batting was a bit inconsistent. But by the All-Star Break, the half-way point in the season, Pujols had 21 home runs, 60 RBIs, and was batting .308. Despite the early inconsistencies, he was confident about the season. "This is going to be the best year because I've never been in a situation where I've had to go through a first half like this and still have these numbers."

Emerging as the Best Hitter in Baseball

Pujols is widely considered to be among the best hitters in baseball history. His 2009 career batting average of .334 ranked the highest among all active

Pujols is widely considered one of the best hitters in the history of baseball.

players, and he also contributed a total of 366 home runs and 1,112 RBIs. He was the first player ever to hit .300 or better with at least 30 home runs and 100 RBI in each of his first nine MLB seasons. "If you define an effective hitter simply in terms of the runs he produces, Pujols is just the best in the game—a tremendous power hitter who seldom strikes out," baseball analyst Caleb Peiffer declared. "He might be the best right-handed hitter in baseball history." At the conclusion of the 2009 season, *Sporting News* named Pujols as Major League Baseball's Athlete of the Decade. Among St. Louis fans, he is known simply as El Hombre, which means "the man" in Spanish.

Perhaps the most remarkable thing about Pujols is that, by all accounts, he has achieved his success by working hard rather than by cheating. Unlike many other big hitters, he has never tested positive for performance-enhancing drugs or been implicated in any investigations of illegal steroid use. "After a decade of dirtiness and suspicion regarding some of the game's premier sluggers using steroids or being accused of such indiscretion," wrote Jon Saraceno in *USA Today,* "Pujols makes fans feel good again." In fact, Pujols has offered to undergo frequent, voluntary drug testing and promised to return every penny of his salary if the results are ever positive. "He isn't colorful and he isn't controversial," said LaRussa. "He's just great."

Pujols has said that hard work and dedication are the secrets to his long-term success. "One of the mistakes a lot of young players make is that once they get to the big leagues, they think, 'That's it,' and they don't work that hard," he explained. "But you have to work extra hard to get better. The older you get, the more you have to work to get better. I'm still working hard every day."

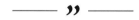

Among the Cardinals' top priorities for the 2010 season is to sign Pujols to another long-term contract. His existing deal is scheduled to end following the 2011 season, and he almost certainly stands to earn more money by changing teams. When asked about the contract situation in interviews, he indicated that he wants to remain in St. Louis, but only if Cardinals management continues to demonstrate a commitment to building a winning team. "It's not about the money all the time," he stated. "It's about being in a place to win and being in a position to win."

Despite all the praise and awards he has received, Pujols has remained humble and continued to work hard to improve his game. "He works harder than any hitter I've ever seen and studies the tendencies pitchers use to work him," said teammate Ryan Ludwick. "It's rare for a pitcher to get him out the same way. He adjusts so well, rarely gets fooled, and is never outmatched." Pujols has said that hard work and dedication are the secrets to his long-term success. "One of the mistakes a lot of young players make is that once they get to the big leagues, they think, 'That's it,' and they don't work that hard," he explained. "But you have to work extra hard to get better. The older you get, the more you have to work to get better. I'm still working hard every day."

MARRIAGE AND FAMILY

Pujols met his wife, Deidre Corona (known as Dee Dee), at a Latin dance club in Kansas City. He was 18 and still in high school at the time, while she was 21 and a college graduate. She had recently given birth to a daughter, Isabella, with Down Syndrome (a genetic disorder that occurs in one of every 800 births and results in various physical problems and moderate mental retardation). Despite the difference in their ages and situations, the couple began dating and soon fell in love.

Pujols married Dee Dee on New Year's Day in 2000, and he adopted Isabella a short time later. They had a son, Alberto Jose (known as A.J.), in January 2001, shortly before Pujols's stellar rookie year with the Cardinals. They added another daughter, Sophia, to their family in November 2005, around the time Albert won his first MVP. The Pujols live in the comfortable St. Louis suburb of Creve Coeur. Pujols takes every available opportunity to emphasize the importance of family in his life. "Dee Dee is the best wife. She's my cheerleader," he stated. "My kids are the best thing that ever happened to me. God and my family are why I do everything."

HOBBIES AND OTHER INTERESTS

Pujols says that he does not have time for hobbies. "I spend time with my family," he noted. "That's my hobby. That's it. Family and baseball." But he ranks among the most generous MLB players when it comes to charity work. He and his wife founded the Pujols Family Foundation in 2005 to help people with Down Syndrome and to support impoverished families in the Dominican Republic. In 2009 the foundation donated $70,000 to St. Luke's Hospital in St. Louis to open a wellness center for adults with Down Syndrome. Pujols also took a team of volunteer doctors and dentists to the Dominican Republic to provide health care to poor children.

Pujols received the prestigious Roberto Clemente Award in 2009 as the MLB player who best combined excellence on the field with service to the community. "I don't want to be remembered as the best baseball player ever," he stated. "I want to be remembered as a great guy who loved the Lord, loved to serve the community, and who gave back. That's the guy I want to be remembered as when I'm done wearing this uniform. That's from the bottom of my heart."

AWARDS AND HONORS

National League Rookie of the Year (Baseball Writers' Association of
America): 2001

National League All-Star Team: 2001, 2003-2009
National League Batting Champion: 2003
National League Player of the Year (MLB Players Association): 2003, 2008, 2009
National League Most Valuable Player: 2005, 2008, 2009
World Series championship: 2006, with St. Louis Cardinals
Gold Glove Award: 2006
Roberto Clemente Award: 2008
Major League Baseball Athlete of the Decade (*Sporting News*): 2009

FURTHER READING

Books

Abrams, Dennis. *Baseball Superstars: Albert Pujols,* 2008 (juvenile)
Christopher, Matt. *On the Field with ... Albert Pujols,* 2009 (juvenile)
Needham, Tom. *Albert Pujols: MVP on and off the Field,* 2009 (juvenile)
Rains, Rob. *Albert Pujols: Simply the Best,* 2009 (juvenile)

Periodicals

Baseball Digest, Dec. 2001, p.46; Nov. 2002, p.48; Oct. 2003, p.22; Feb. 2004, p.38; Aug. 2005, p.50; Jan.-Feb. 2009, p.38
Current Biography Yearbook, 2004
Kansas City (MO) Star, Oct. 9, 2001, p.C1; June 27, 2004, p.C1
New York Times, Nov. 18, 2008, p.B18
St. Louis Post-Dispatch, May 20, 2001, p.D1; Mar. 30, 2003, p.4; Feb. 21, 2004, p.3
Sports Illustrated, Apr. 16, 2001, p.48; Oct. 1, 2001, p.44; June 30, 2003, p.32; May 22, 2006, p.58; Nov. 8, 2006, p.48; Mar. 16, 2009, p.28
USA Today, May 22, 2001, p.C1; May 15, 2006, p.C6; May 23, 2006, p.C1; Mar. 31, 2009, p.C1; July 13, 2009, p.C1

ADDRESS

Albert Pujols
St. Louis Cardinals
250 Stadium Plaza
St. Louis, MO 63102

WORLD WIDE WEB SITES

http://stlouis.cardinals.mlb.com
http://www.pujolsfamilyfoundation.org

Zoë Saldana 1978-

American Actress
Star of the Hit Movies *Avatar* and *Star Trek*

BIRTH

Zoë Yadira Zaldaña Nazario was born on June 19, 1978, in New Jersey. Her father was from the Dominican Republic, and her mother was from Puerto Rico. Saldana has two sisters, Mariel and Cisely, one older and one younger. She also has one step-brother. Saldana changed the spelling of her last name when she started acting, to make it easy for people to pronounce. "I wanted to make it easier for everyone," she claimed. "Zaldaña is too complicated for everyone else. I would love to have kept my original name."

YOUTH AND EDUCATION

Saldana grew up in the Queens borough of New York. When she was 10 years old, her father died in a car accident. "My parents were a good team at raising us, they were very good friends, and my mom never expected to have to raise us without my father," she recalled. "It was a shock for all of us, for my mom having to become the father and the mother, and we did lose a lot of innocence and have to mature quickly." After her father's death, her mother sent Saldana and her sisters to live with relatives in the Dominican Republic. She lived there from about the age of 10 to 17. While there, she studied dance at the Espacio de Danza Dance Academy. There she learned ballet as well as other forms of dance and dreamed of becoming a ballerina.

> "My parents were a good team at raising us, they were very good friends, and my mom never expected to have to raise us without my father," Saldana said about her father's death. "It was a shock for all of us, for my mom having to become the father and the mother, and we did lose a lot of innocence and have to mature quickly."

When she was 17 years old, Saldana and her sisters moved back to New York to live with their mother. Saldana loved dancing, but she also developed a new interest in theater. She began performing with the Faces theater group, which put on improvised plays with positive messages for teens. Faces performed in schools and community centers and dealt with such real-life issues as substance abuse, violence, suicide, and HIV/AIDS. Faces gave Saldana valuable acting experience, and she also enjoyed helping young people deal with important issues. Around the same time, she was also performing with the New York Youth Theater, where she appeared in a production of the musical *Joseph and the Amazing Technicolor Dream Coat.* Her performance caught the attention of a talent scout, and Saldana was recruited by a talent agency. This helped her land her first movie role.

CAREER HIGHLIGHTS

Saldana made her movie debut in the role of Eva Rodriguez in the 2000 movie *Center Stage.* This movie followed the progress of a group of young

Drawing on her dance training, Saldana played a young gifted ballet dancer in Center Stage.

ballet dancers enrolled in the fictional American Ballet Academy. Saldana's dance background helped her land the role, in which she played a rebellious young woman who must learn to take dancing more seriously if she wants to succeed. For Saldana, the role was bittersweet, because she had already decided to leave dancing behind in order to pursue an acting career. The movie received lukewarm reviews, with most critics acknowledging that it was clearly a movie made for teen audiences. However, *Center Stage* gathered fans among younger viewers who enjoyed the movie for its coming-of-age story and its view into the drama of a competitive ballet school.

Center Stage led to more roles in teen movies. Saldana had a minor part in the 2001 musical romantic comedy *Get Over It,* a story about a high school jock who gets dumped by his girlfriend and then tries to win her back by signing up for the school play, the Shakespeare comedy *A Midsummer Night's Dream.* She went on to win a co-starring role alongside Britney Spears in the 2002 movie *Crossroads.* This movie tells the story of three childhood friends who decide to travel from their small Georgia hometown to Los Angeles, where one of the three has an audition for a record contract. Neither of these movies was commercially successful, although *Crossroads* became popular mainly among Spears's fans. In these roles, Saldana gained more acting experience and was offered more movie parts as a result.

In the 2002 movie *Drumline,* Saldana played the role of Laila, a college cheerleader who develops a romantic relationship with the movie's star, played by Nick Cannon. *Drumline* tells the story of a talented but untrained young drummer who is recruited to join the ranks of a prestigious Southern university marching band. As the story unfolds, tension grows between the young newcomer and the drum section leader as the band prepares for an important national competition. *Drumline* did not do particularly well in theaters, but the movie found an enthusiastic audience among young viewers who were drawn in by the story and the performance scenes with the marching band drum section. Saldana and Cannon shared a nomination for that year's MTV Movie Award for best kiss in a love scene.

Transitioning from Teen Roles

Saldana successfully moved away from teen movies with her appearance in *Pirates of the Caribbean: The Curse of the Black Pearl,* released in 2003. She played Anamaria, the lone female pirate who casts a spell on Captain Jack Sparrow. Though her role was small, she was credited with creating one of the movie's best comic scenes with Johnny Depp.

In 2004, Saldana appeared in *The Terminal*, a movie starring Tom Hanks as Viktor Navorski, an Eastern European tourist stranded in New York City's JFK airport. While Navorski is in flight, the government of his home country is overthrown and the U.S. refuses to recognize the new government. He can't enter the U.S. because his passport is viewed as invalid, but he also can't return home because all flights in and out of his home country have been suspended. Stuck between two countries, he is forced to take up residence in the airport terminal. The story unfolds as Navorski tries to get home, making friends with various airport employees and building a life for himself in the terminal in the meantime. Saldana plays Dolores Torres, an immigration agent working in the terminal where Navorski is stranded. Her performance earned her a Young Hollywood One to Watch Award from *Movieline* magazine.

> ―――― **"** ――――
>
> *"I don't feel that there are enough roles that resemble the American women nowadays in Hollywood,"* Saldana argued. *"It's almost an insult when you read scripts and you see that the guy's the hero."*
>
> ―――― **"** ――――

In 2005, Saldana starred in *Guess Who?*, a romantic comedy remake of the 1967 critically acclaimed drama *Guess Who's Coming to Dinner*. In the remake, Saldana played a young black woman who brings her white fiancé, played by Ashton Kutcher, home to meet her family, much to the distress of her father, played by Bernie Mac. Although *Guess Who?* was not very successful either with critics or at the box office, Saldana earned praise for her performance. She was nominated for best actress at the NAACP Image Awards, the Black Movie Awards, and the Black Reel Awards.

Star Trek

Saldana's breakout role was in the highly anticipated 2009 *Star Trek* movie, in which she played communications specialist Uhura. This movie is a prequel to the groundbreaking original 1966 "Star Trek" television show, which began a science fiction storytelling legacy that has grown to include five additional TV series, 10 other movies, and countless books. Many of these productions featured the same characters at different points in their lives, building a long continuing story that developed over more than 30 years. In the 2009 *Star Trek* movie, new actors were cast to portray the same characters shown in the original 1966 series, but in an earlier time period when they were young Starfleet Academy students being trained as spaceship crew

Saldana as Uhura, right, with fellow Star Trek *cast members Anton Yelchin (Chekov), Chris Pine (James T. Kirk), an unnamed cast member, Karl Urban (Dr. Leonard "Bones" McCoy), and John Cho (Sulu). Not shown: Zachary Quinto as Spock.*

members. In this movie, an emergency finds the group of young cadets suddenly assigned as crew members on the new starship *Enterprise*. A complicated and adventure-filled story unfolds, involving personality conflicts, space battles, an evil enemy determined to destroy Earth and the planet Vulcan, time travel, and a series of events that change the future for everyone.

Before making the movie, Saldana had only seen a couple of episodes of the original "Star Trek" TV series. She was excited to take on the role, however. "I'm very proud to say I am a geek," she boasted. "But I'm kind of a cool geek. I grew up in a very sci-fi home so I've seen a lot of sci-fi movies, from *Dune* to *Alien, 2001, ET, Batteries Not Included....* All these films I go crazy for. But never *Star Trek*." Among the episodes of the original series that Saldana did watch was a pivotal one in which William Shatner as Captain James T. Kirk and Nichelle Nichols as Uhura share a kiss. This episode made history as the first interracial kiss shown on TV.

Saldana's limited exposure to the "Star Trek" TV series and subsequent movies was intentional. After she got the part, she listened to advice from director J.J. Abrams. "I followed J.J.'s advice. He said, 'If I have to advise you guys at all, I would advise you not to watch [the original TV series]. Just inform yourself of the whole concept of 'Star Trek,' if you're not already a Trekkie or fan. I don't want you to cloud whatever contribution you guys can make yourselves to the role that you are jumping into.' I thought that was very encouraging." However, Saldana did meet with Nichelle Nichols to discuss the role and character of Uhura.

Star Trek received mixed reviews. Some critics and fans viewed the movie as a re-invention of the well-known *Star Trek* world and welcomed the new cast of young actors as a fresh approach to the series. But some were angry that so many changes were made to the basic *Star Trek* premise and complained that the movie swept away 30-plus years of *Star Trek* history in order to make a new beginning. Saldana's performance was widely praised, however. The *National Review* said that "Saldana smolders as a young Uhura," while *Entertainment Weekly* said "Saldana gives Uhura a sultry spark." According to *Daily Variety*, "Saldana is vibrant as the female crew member who bestows her favors on one officer to the exasperation of another."

Avatar

Saldana's next big screen role was in the 2009 blockbuster hit movie *Avatar*. In this 3D science fiction / fantasy movie, she played Neytiri, an entirely computer-generated character. The story of *Avatar* takes place in the year 2154, on the alien world of Pandora, a jungle-covered planet located in the Alpha Centauri system many light years from Earth. As the story begins, the audience learns that human negotiations with Na'vi natives of Pandora have turned violent. A corporate group is mining a rare mineral on Pandora that is needed to solve Earth's energy crisis. A former U.S. Marine named Jake is recruited to travel to the human outpost on Pandora and infiltrate the Na'vi, with the goal of removing obstacles to the mining operation. Humans cannot breathe in Pandora's atmosphere, but the Avatar Program allows human "drivers" to have their consciousness linked to a remotely controlled biological body that can survive in the toxic air. These avatar bodies are genetically engineered hybrids that combine human and Na'vi DNA.

> "I'm very proud to say I am a geek," Saldana boasted. "But I'm kind of a cool geek. I grew up in a very sci-fi home so I've seen a lot of sci-fi movies, from **Dune** to **Alien, 2001, ET, Batteries Not Included**…. All these films I go crazy for. But never **Star Trek**."

As Jake, in avatar form, is finding his way on Pandora, he gets into trouble, and Neytiri, a beautiful Na'vi female, saves his life. He is then taken in by her clan through a process involving many trials and tests. As Jake's relationship with Neytiri deepens, he learns to respect the Na'vi culture. He then faces the ultimate test as he leads the Na'vi in an epic battle that will decide the fate of an entire world.

Saldana has said that she pursued a role in *Avatar* because of the director, James Cameron. "He was why I got into movies," she revealed. "His female heroes—Ripley [from the *Alien* movies] and Sarah Connor [from the *Terminator* franchise]—showed me an actress can be an action hero." To prepare for the role of Neytiri, Saldana trained for six months, studying martial arts, archery, and horseback riding. She also had to learn the language of the Na'vi that was created for the movie. Because Neytiri is a computer-generated character, Saldana doesn't actually appear on screen in the movie. The film's innovative "motion capture technology for animation" means that all her movements, from ballet-like leaps to facial expressions, are translated into a cartoon version of herself. To accomplish this, Saldana and many of the other *Avatar* actors had to wear special bodysuits fitted with sensors as well as helmets laced with cameras. "It wasn't as easy as everybody thinks where you just show up and lend your voice and have these visual illustrators try to create a character out of it. Everything we did—95% of it—was translated onto the screen." To portray Neytiri, Saldana studied the movements of certain animals. "My character is very agile, a hunter and a warrior. We looked a lot at the feline kingdom for inspiration. And she's very playful, so we looked at dolphins."

> "
>
> To portray Neytiri in **Avatar**, Saldana studied the movements of certain animals. "My character is very agile, a hunter and a warrior. We looked a lot at the feline kingdom for inspiration. And she's very playful, so we looked at dolphins."
>
> "

Avatar was a runaway success with moviegoers and won 31 film industry awards, including three Oscars, while also being nominated for 53 additional awards. Critics, however, gave the film mixed reviews. "It's dazzling, engulfing, a techno-dream for the senses, but one that's likely to leave audiences at once amazed and unmoved," Ty Burr wrote in *Entertainment Weekly.* "[The use of 3D renders the whole world] heightened, popping, bolder than life.... It's the story and the characters that could have used another dimension or two." Writing in the *New York Times,* movie critic Manohla Dargis praised the film: "If the story of a paradise found and potentially lost feels resonant, it's because *Avatar* is as much about our Earth as the universe that Mr. Cameron has invented. But the movie's truer meaning is in the audacity of its film-making. Few films return us to the lost world of our first cinematic experiences, to that magical moment when movies really were bigger than life.... Movies rarely carry us away, few even try. What's often missing is awe,

Saldana as Neytiri, a fearless and beautiful warrior who is a member of Pandora's royal clan of Na'vi.

something Mr. Cameron has, after an absence from Hollywood, returned to the screen with a vengeance. He hasn't changed cinema, but with blue people and pink blooms he has confirmed its wonder."

Future Plans

Saldana has several projects lined up to follow her successes in *Star Trek* and *Avatar*. "I find myself looking for roles that are strong,'" she acknowledged. "I'm easily turned off from roles that are soccer moms or love interests. If you really want me to say no, tell me that I will be 'the chick in the flick.' I have an issue with that.... I don't feel that there are enough roles that resemble the American women nowadays in Hollywood. It's almost an insult when you read scripts and you see that the guy's the hero."

Saldana enjoys acting in science fiction movies because of the potential for strong female characters. However, she said, "I wish there were more genres in which women could have more opportunities to be presented as what we are. We're complex creatures, we're very intricate, we also have journeys. We can be the heroes and we can save everyone. We can also be vulnerable, and we can be saved as well, all in one person."

Saldana can be seen in the 2010 movie *Death at a Funeral*, a comedy about family mishaps, miscommunication, and mixups surrounding the funeral of the family's father. The story mixes the crazy behavior and unexpected problems of characters played by a large all-star cast led by Chris Rock and Martin Lawrence and also featuring Loretta Devine, Danny Glover, Regina

Saldana appeared with an all-star cast in the 2010 comedy Death at a Funeral.

Hall, Tracy Morgan and Luke Wilson. Saldana plays Elaine, a cousin who is badgered at the funeral by a persistent ex-boyfriend who demands that she break up with her current boyfriend and return to him. She also has a role in the 2010 movie *The Losers*, an adaptation of the DC-Vertigo comic book about members of a top-secret CIA team who plan revenge after they were left for dead on a dangerous mission. She plays Aisha, a blood-thirsty mercenary killer who thrives on close combat.

When planning her long-term career as an actor, Saldana hasn't been shy about acknowledging her dream of winning an Oscar some day. "I'm not going to be like, 'I just want to be known for my work,'" she declared. "No, I want that golden statue on my shelf. Whether it happens or not, it will not determine the kind of substance that I feel I contributed. But I want it.… Shoot for the stars and I'll settle for a cloud."

HOME AND FAMILY

Saldana lives with her boyfriend Keith Britton and divides her time between homes in New York City and Los Angeles. She has a dog named Calvin, a pit bull-pointer mix that she adopted from a shelter.

SELECTED CREDITS

Center Stage, 2000
Get Over It, 2001
Crossroads, 2002
Drumline, 2002
Pirates of the Caribbean: The Curse of the Black Pearl, 2003
The Terminal, 2004
Guess Who?, 2005
Star Trek, 2009
Avatar, 2009
The Losers, 2010
Death at a Funeral, 2010

HONORS AND AWARDS

Young Hollywood One to Watch Award (*Movieline* magazine): 2004, for her performance in *The Terminal*

FURTHER READING

Periodicals

Cosmopolitan, May 2009, p.104

Ebony, Mar. 2005
Entertainment Weekly, Aug. 21, 2009, p.88; Nov. 13, 2009, p.58; Jan. 29, 2010, p.24
Hispanic, June 2004
Interview, July 2004, p.32
Latina, May 2009; July 2009
US Weekly, Dec. 28, 2009, p.68
USA Today, Jan. 5, 2010, p.D2
Women's Health, May 2009

Online Articles

http://www.hollywoodtoday.net
   (Hollywood Today, "*Avatar* Heroines, Zoë Saldana and Sigourney Weaver," Dec. 19, 2009)
http://www.people.com
   (People, "*Avatar*'s Zoë Saldana Is Proud to Be a Geek," Dec. 21, 2009)
http://www.tvguide.com
   (TV Guide, "Zoe Saldana, no date)
http://movies.yahoo.com
   (Yahoo, "Zoe Saldana," no date)

ADDRESS

Zoë Saldana
International Creative Management
10250 Constellation Blvd.
Los Angeles, CA 90067

WORLD WIDE WEB SITES

http://www.zoesaldana.com
http://www.avatarmovie.com
http://www.startrekmovie.com
http://www.startrek.com

Sonia Sotomayor 1954-
American Supreme Court Justice
First Hispanic Justice on the U.S. Supreme Court

BIRTH

Sonia Sotomayor (pronounced *so-toe-my-OR*) was born on June 23, 1954, in the Bronx, the northernmost of the five boroughs that make up New York City. She was the daughter of Puerto Rican immigrants who came to the United States during World War II. Her father, Juan, had only a third-grade education and never learned to speak English. He worked as a welder after arriving in the United States. Her mother, Celina,

Sotomayor at the age of six or seven.

first worked as a telephone operator at a small hospital in the Bronx. She later earned her practical nurse's license and worked as a methadone clinic nurse and emergency room supervisor. Sonia has one younger brother, Juan, who grew up to become a doctor.

YOUTH

Sotomayor was born and raised in a housing project in the Bronx, a rough, working-class part of New York that experienced rising rates of crime and poverty during her childhood and adolescence. Fortunately, the Sotomayor family was able to obtain an apartment in the Bronxdale Houses, a complex that was much cleaner and safer than some of the other housing options in the Bronx. Unlike the graffiti- and trash-strewn housing that marred other parts of the Bronx, these residential apartments were, as Sonia recalled, "spacious and pristine."

The challenges of growing up in the Bronx became even greater for Sotomayor in 1962, when she was diagnosed with diabetes at age eight. Diabetes is a disease in which the pancreas is no longer able to produce insulin, a hormone that enables the body to process sugars in food. If left untreated, it can cause blindness, heart disease, and kidney problems. Sotomayor's family, however, was able to bring her diabetes under control through careful monitoring and daily injections of insulin. Today, Sotomayor continues to give herself daily insulin injections to manage her diabetes.

One year after Sotomayor was diagnosed with diabetes, her father suffered a fatal heart attack at the young age of 42. This sudden loss devastated the family and forced Celina Sotomayor to support and raise her children all by herself. She worked extra hours to put her children through private Catholic schools, and she even scrimped and saved to buy Sonia and her brother a full *Encyclopaedia Britannica* set. According to her children, their encyclopedia set was the only one in the entire housing project.

Celina Sotomayor also set firm guidelines of behavior for her children. "They had their rules," recalled one of Sonia's childhood friends. "She worked, and basically no one was allowed out of the house until she came home from work." In addition, she was a steady role model who taught her children the importance of education and the value of hard work. When Sonia was a teenager, for example, her mother returned to school to become a registered nurse. "My mom was like no student I knew," Sonia recalled. "She got home from school or work and literally immersed herself in her studies, working until midnight or beyond, only to get up again before all of us.... She had almost a fanatical emphasis on education.... She kept saying, 'I don't care what you do, but be the best at it.'"

An Early Passion for Justice

Young Sotomayor took her mother's lessons to heart. She became known in her neighborhood as both a spunky and principled kid. Her younger brother recalls that she frequently stepped in to defend him from local bullies. She also developed an early fascination with the adventures of popular crime-fighting heroes of the 1950s and 1960s. Her two favorites were Nancy Drew, a high-spirited girl detective featured in a series of children's books, and Perry Mason, a brilliant and idealistic lawyer who solved mysteries on a television series that broadcast from 1957 to 1966. "When I was nine or ten, I became enamored of Nancy Drew stories and I wanted to be an investigative detective like her," So-

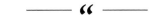

> *Celina Sotomayor was a strong role model who valued education and hard work. She set firm guidelines of behavior for her children. "They had their rules," recalled one of Sonia's childhood friends. "She worked, and basically no one was allowed out of the house until she came home from work."*

tomayor noted. When doctors told Sonia that her diabetes would prevent her from pursuing detective work, she was crestfallen. But her disappointment was short-lived. "I noticed that Perry Mason was involved in a lot of the same kinds of investigative work that I had been fascinated with reading Nancy Drew, so I decided to become a lawyer," she explained. "Once I focused on becoming a lawyer, I never deviated from that goal."

EDUCATION

Sotomayor attended Catholic private schools in the Bronx throughout her elementary and high school years. An excellent and hardworking student,

Sotomayor as a Princeton senior when she won the Pyne Prize, the highest academic honor granted to an undergraduate student.

she was class valedictorian when she graduated from Cardinal Spellman High School in 1972.

Sotomayor's fine academic record enabled her to gain admission into New Jersey's Princeton University, one of eight famous "Ivy League" colleges in the northeastern United States. Upon arriving on Princeton's campus in the fall of 1972, however, Sotomayor recalled that the school constituted "a very foreign experience for someone from the South Bronx." For one thing, Princeton had only begun admitting women a few years before, so most of the student body was male. In addition, she had grown up surrounded by Latino friends, classmates, and neighbors, but there were few other Latinos in Princeton's student body—and none on its faculty.

The sense of isolation and uncertainty that Sotomayor initially felt at Princeton grew worse when she realized that she did not possess the same level of background knowledge as her classmates, most of whom came from wealthy families and fancy prep schools. Determined to close this gap, Sotomayor devoted much of her freshman year to reading the works of Mark Twain, Jane Austen, and other famous writers taught in prep school literature courses. "She was very studious and intent on doing well in school," one of her friends recalled. "I remember her emerging sometimes in the early morning from her room, somewhat rumpled. I knew she spent all night working on a paper or studying.… If she had a project to do, she worked on it 100 percent."

Sotomayor soon overcame these initial struggles with her grit and determination. By her junior year she was not only posting top grades, but was also emerging as a leader of campus Latino groups. She earned top academic marks as a senior as well, enabling her to graduate summa cum laude ("with highest praise") with a bachelor's degree in history in 1976. In fact, Sotomayor was honored as a senior with the Pyne Prize, the school's highest academic honor for undergraduate students. This recognition marked the first time that Princeton had awarded the Pyne Prize to a Latino student.

Years later, Sotomayor described her four years at Princeton as "the single most transforming experience" of her life. Speaking at Princeton in 1996 to a group of Latino students, she explained that "it was here that I became truly aware of my Latina identity—something I had taken for granted during my childhood when I was surrounded by my family and their friends."

Armed with her degree from Princeton, Sotomayor decided to pursue a law degree at Yale, another famous Ivy League school bursting with wealthy and privileged students. Like she had done at Princeton, Sotomayor displayed both ambition and talent during her years at the Yale Law School. By the time she graduated in 1979, she had served a stint as editor of the prestigious *Yale Law Journal,* co-chaired the Latin American and Native American Students Association, and worked as managing editor of the Yale Studies in World Public Order program. "She had such a different path," recalled one of her law school friends. "There were so many people [at Yale] that had Roman numerals after their names and long histories of family members who had gone to Yale, and here was this woman who was from the projects, not hiding her views at all, just totally outspoken. She's one of those where, even at a school with great people, I knew that she was going to go on and do amazing things."

"She was very studious and intent on doing well in school," one of Sotomayor's college friends recalled. "I remember her emerging sometimes in the early morning from her room, somewhat rumpled. I knew she spent all night working on a paper or studying.... If she had a project to do, she worked on it 100 percent."

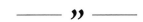

FIRST JOBS

After earning her law degree, Sotomayor left the leafy Yale campus for a position in New York City's office of the district attorney (DA). In a criminal case, the DA works as the prosecutor, the lawyer who represent the government in charging someone with a crime, while the defense attorney is the lawyer who represents the accused person. As an assistant DA, Sotomayor represented the city in numerous criminal cases involving robbery, assault, murder, rape, police brutality, prostitution, and other crimes.

"My work ran the gamut of criminal activity," she later said. "It was wonderful training for a lawyer."

Sotomayor admitted, however, that her work obtaining criminal convictions against alleged wrongdoers was sometimes difficult. "I had more problems during my first year in the office with the low-grade crimes—the shoplifting, the prostitution, the minor assault cases," she explained. "In large measure, in those cases you were dealing with … crimes that could be the product of the environment and of poverty. Once I started doing felonies, it became less hard. No matter how liberal I am, I'm still outraged by crimes of violence. Regardless of whether I can sympathize with the causes that lead these individuals to do these crimes, the effects are outrageous."

Sotomayor also acknowledged that some cases lingered longer than others. "It pains me," she said, "when I meet particularly bright defendants—and I've met quite a few of them—people who, if they had had the right guidance, the right education, the right breaks, could have been contributing members of our society. When they get convicted, there's a satisfaction, because they're doing things that are dangerous. But there are also nights when I sit back and say, 'My God, what a waste!'"

In 1984 Sotomayor left the DA's office for a job with the private New York law firm of Pavia and Harcourt. For the next several years she worked primarily on intellectual property issues and international commercial law. In 1988 she was promoted to partner in the firm.

CAREER HIGHLIGHTS

Launching a Career as a Judge

Sotomayor left private law practice and launched her career as a judge in 1991. That year, Republican President George H.W. Bush, acting on the recommendation of New York Democratic Senator Daniel Patrick Moynihan, nominated her to become a federal district judge in the Southern District of the State of New York. Sotomayor was honored by the nomination and happily accepted. When her nomination was confirmed in August 1992, she became the first American of Hispanic descent to be appointed to the federal bench in New York.

Sotomayor spent six years as a district judge. During this period she became known as a decisive, no-nonsense judge who had little patience for unprepared lawyers, political schemers, or legal games. Her most celebrated case during her tenure as a district judge came in April 1995, when she delivered a momentous ruling on a bitter eight-month-long legal battle between Major League Baseball owners and players over salary issues. This conflict

THE U.S. JUDICIAL SYSTEM

The court system, or judicial system, is one of the three branches of the federal government set out in the U.S. Constitution: the executive branch, the legislative branch, and the judicial branch. Each branch has specific responsibilities. The executive branch includes the president and the vice president. It also includes the Cabinet, a group of presidential advisers who are the heads of federal departments and agencies, including the departments of state, treasury, defense, justice, education, and others. The legislative branch is the Congress, including both the House of Representatives and the Senate. The Congress creates laws, collects taxes, declares war, ratifies treaties, and approves the president's nominations for certain positions, including federal judges. The judicial branch includes the nation's courts.

The federal judicial system, where Sotomayor served, is comprised of three different levels. The lower courts, the level at which most cases are originally tried (and where Sotomayor started her career as a judge), are the district courts. After a case is tried, if one side disagrees with the decision of the district court and wants to appeal it, the case would go to the next level, the court of appeals. There are 94 judicial districts in the U.S., and those districts are organized into 12 regional circuits, each of which maintains a U.S. Court of Appeals (also called circuit courts). The appeals (or appellate) court judges review the lower court's decision and either sustain it (agree) or overturn it (disagree). After that step, the case could be taken to the Supreme Court, the highest court in the land. The decision of the Supreme Court is final. At all three levels in the U.S. judicial system, federal judges are nominated by the president, confirmed by the Senate, and serve for life.

had arisen when team owners tried to sweep away longstanding free agent and salary arbitration systems. The players, who strongly supported these systems, had responded to this move by going out on strike. The conflict was so entrenched that the 1994 World Series had to be cancelled.

Sotomayor settled this clash by issuing an injunction (essentially a court order) against the team owners. She ruled that the owners had no legal right to unilaterally end Major League Baseball's free agent and salary arbitration systems. That ruling forced the owners to return to the bargaining table. A short time later, players and owners reached a new agreement that ended the longest work stoppage in professional sports history.

Moving to the Court of Appeals

In 1997 President Bill Clinton nominated Sotomayor to become a judge on the U.S. Court of Appeals for the Second Circuit. Judges on these appeals courts review legal decisions handed down by district courts, as well as those handed down by federal agencies. Cases heard in appeals courts are reviewed by three-judge panels, which have the power to reverse these decisions if a majority of the three judges feel that the lower court or agency has issued an unconstitutional or otherwise flawed decision.

> "The practice of law is perhaps the most diverse, eclectic exposure to life that you can receive," Sotomayor explained. "People come to you with their problems, and their cases cover a wide range of issues. For you to be able to practice law with the vision it requires, you have to be a very well-rounded person because whatever happens out in the real world, whether it involves business or family or technology, usually finds its way into the courtroom."

Sotomayor's nomination to the Court of Appeals was confirmed by the U.S. Senate on October 2, 1998. She loved working as an appeals court judge, in large measure because she enjoyed the intellectual challenge of hearing all sorts of different cases involving numerous complex legal issues. "The practice of law is perhaps the most diverse, eclectic exposure to life that you can receive," she explained. "People come to you with their problems, and their cases cover a wide range of issues. For you to be able to practice law with the vision it requires, you have to be a very well-rounded person because whatever happens out in the real world, whether it involves business or family or technology, usually finds its way into the courtroom."

Sotomayor's position on the Second Circuit also enabled her to keep living in her beloved New York City. Working from her home base—a stylish two-bedroom condominium in the city's vibrant Greenwich Village neighborhood—she loved to explore the city's many restaurant, theatre, sports, and nightlife options. She sometimes embarked on these adventures with current and former law clerks from her staff, many of whom she regarded as members of her extended family.

Sotomayor poses by her office window in 1998, after being confirmed by the U.S. Senate for a seat on the U.S. Court of Appeals for the Second Circuit.

On the bench, meanwhile, Sotomayor's reputation continued to grow. Lawyers who appeared before her court regarded her as smart and fair-minded, but they also knew that she could be tough on lawyers who were not ready for court. As one former Sotomayor clerk-turned-U.S. attorney stated, "[she] doesn't tolerate unpreparedness, nor should she."

During the course of her career on the appeals court, Sotomayor heard appeals of more than 3,000 cases and wrote about 380 majority opinions. The U.S. Supreme Court reviewed a total of five of these cases. It reversed the majority decision supported by Sotomayor on three occasions. The most highly publicized of these reversals came in June 2009, when the Supreme Court ruled by a narrow 5-4 margin that Sotomayor erred in supporting a decision by the city of New Haven, Connecticut, to toss out a promotion test used by the fire department. The Supreme Court majority ruled that white firefighters who had scored well on the test were unfairly denied promotions when the results were thrown out.

Nominated for the Highest Court in the Land

Sotomayor's life took a momentous turn in November 2008, when Democrat Barack Obama defeated Republican candidate John McCain in the presidential election to become the nation's 44th president. Sotomayor knew that Obama's victory might have enormous consequences for her. Political and legal analysts alike agreed that if Obama had an opportunity to fill an opening on the U.S. Supreme Court during his presidency, Sotomayor ranked as one of the top candidates. They believed that he would be attracted by her strong legal qualifications, her inspiring life story, and the prospect of nominating the first Latino American to the nation's highest court.

Sotomayor listened to this speculation with mixed feelings. She knew that a seat on the U.S. Supreme Court was the pinnacle of her profession. The nine justices who sit on the Supreme Court may hold office for life. The Supreme Court's job is to make sure laws passed by the legislative branch and regulations issued by the executive branch do not violate the U.S. Constitution, which is the cornerstone of all American law. The Court accomplishes this by interpreting the provisions of the Constitution and applying its rules to specific legal cases. Because the Constitution lays out general rules, the Court tries to determine their meaning and figure out how to apply them to modern situations. After the justices select a case for review—and they accept fewer than about 100 of the 6,000 cases presented to them each year—they first will hear arguments by the two opposing sides. They begin discussing the case, take a preliminary vote, and then

President Barack Obama and Vice President Joe Biden escort Sotomayor to the East Room of the White House, where the president introduced her as his nominee for the U.S. Supreme Court, May 2009.

one justice from the majority is assigned to write up the Court's opinion. Drafting an opinion is complex and time-consuming, and the whole process can take over a year. The Court's final opinion has tremendous importance, setting out a precedent that all lower courts and all levels of government throughout the United States are required to follow. The reasoning given in the opinion is also important, because it helps people understand the basis for the decision and how the ruling might apply to other cases in the future.

Despite the power and prestige associated with becoming a Supreme Court judge, Sotomayor was not sure that she wanted to rebuild a new life for herself in Washington DC, where the Supreme Court hears cases. "Sonia was happy being a Federal Appeals judge, loved her life in New York, and felt fulfilled," a friend noted. "She worried about having less time to spend with her mother, family, and friends, particularly given her mom's age and potential health complications."

In the end, though, Sotomayor decided that she would accept a nomination if it was offered. She knew that as the country's first Latino Supreme Court justice—and only the third woman justice in the long history of the

Court—she could be a role model and inspiration to millions of minority children across the country.

On May 1, 2009, Supreme Court Justice David H. Souter announced that he intended to retire. White House officials quickly contacted Sotomayor and a few other leading candidates to interview them for the Supreme Court opening. During the next few weeks, officials combed through the personal histories and legal decisions of the candidates, who also sat for long rounds of interviews with members of Obama's staff. Then, on the evening of May 25, Sotomayor received a telephone call from the White House saying that the president would like to speak to her. "I had my cell phone in my right hand and I had my left hand over my chest trying to calm my beating heart, literally," she remembered. "And the president got on the phone and said to me, 'Judge, I would like to announce you as my selection to be the next Associate Justice of the United States Supreme Court.' I caught my breath and started to cry and said, 'Thank you, Mr. President.'"

> **"I had my cell phone in my right hand and I had my left hand over my chest trying to calm my beating heart, literally," Sotomayor remembered. "And the president got on the phone and said to me, 'Judge, I would like to announce you as my selection to be the next Associate Justice of the United States Supreme Court.' I caught my breath and started to cry and said, 'Thank you, Mr. President.'"**

Before concluding their phone conversation, Obama asked her for two promises. "The first was to remain the person I was, and the second was to stay connected to my community," she said. "And I said to him that those were two easy promises to make, because those two things I could not change."

Enduring a Challenging Confirmation Process

When Obama announced that he intended to send Sotomayor's nomination to the U.S. Senate for confirmation, as required by law, he emphasized both her amazing personal story and her distinguished judicial career. The president also discussed "empathy"—the ability to understand and identify with another person's feelings and views. He said that Sotomayor possessed the empathy he was looking for in a Supreme Court justice.

Many observers warmly praised Obama's pick. Leaders from America's Latino communities expressed delight with the selection, as did progressive political activists, Democratic lawmakers, and many legal scholars. Republican congressional leaders and conservative pundits strongly criticized the choice, however. They charged, for instance, that "empathy" was simply a code word to describe a judge who favored changing laws to fit his or her liberal political beliefs. They pressed these claims even after Sotomayor supporters noted that Supreme Court Justice Samuel Alito—a conservative whose nomination a few years earlier had been embraced by Republicans—had trumpeted the value of empathy in his own Supreme Court confirmation hearings.

Conservative opponents of Sotomayor's nomination also highlighted the U.S. Supreme Court's June 2009 decision to overturn her ruling in the New Haven fire department case. As the days passed by, however, the main focus of Republican opposition coalesced around a statement that Sotomayor made back in 2001. During a speech that year to Latino law students, she had made reference to a favorite saying of Sandra Day O'-Connor and Ruth Bader Ginsberg, the first two female Supreme Court justices in U.S. history. After noting that O'Connor and Ginsberg were fond of stating that a "wise old woman" and a "wise old man" would come to the same conclusions, Sotomayor added that "I would hope that a wise Latina woman with the richness of her experiences would more often than not reach a better conclusion than a white male who hasn't lived that life."

Sotomayor's confirmation hearings before the Senate Judiciary Committee began on July 13, 2009. Over the next few days, Democratic Senators offered friendly questioning while Republican senators subjected her to intense cross-examination. The single greatest focus of Republican inquiry was her "wise Latina" comments of eight years before. Sotomayor tried to defuse the controversy by dismissing the statement as "a rhetorical flourish that fell flat." She explained that her statement was simply an effort "to inspire young Hispanics, Latino students, and lawyers to believe that their life experiences added value to the process." Finally, the judge tried to reassure skeptical Republicans by stating "unequivocally and without doubt: I do not believe that any ethnic, racial, or gender group has an advantage in sound judging."

As the questioning continued, Sotomayor remained calm and unruffled, reassuring the committee members that she would never let personal feelings influence her rulings. When the hearing was over, the committee voted 13-6 to endorse the nomination. On August 6, the full Senate voted in favor of

President Barack Obama and Vice President Joe Biden pose with Supreme Court justices prior to the investiture ceremony for Sotomayor, September 2009. From left: Associate Justices Samuel Alito, Ruth Bader Ginsburg, Anthony M. Kennedy, John Paul Stevens, Chief Justice John Roberts, President Obama, Associate Justice Sonia Sotomayor, Vice President Biden, Associate Justices Antonin Scalia, Clarence Thomas, Stephen Beyer, and retired Associate Justice David Souter.

Sotomayor's Supreme Court nomination by a 68-31 vote. When Obama heard the news, he declared that "this is a wonderful day for Judge Sotomayor and her family, but I also think it's a wonderful day for America."

Enjoying a Landmark Moment

Sotomayor was sworn into membership on the Supreme Court on August 8, 2009, at a ceremony led by Chief Justice John G. Roberts Jr. A few days later, at a White House reception organized to celebrate the event, she described her membership on the Court as "the most humbling honor of my life." But Sotomayor emphasized that her confirmation "would never have been possible without the opportunities presented to me by this nation.... I am struck again today by the wonder of my own life, and the life we in America are so privileged to lead."

Sotomayor also singled out her mother for special words of thanks. "I have often said that I am all I am because of her, and I am only half the woman she is." For her part, Celina expressed immense pride in her daughter. "I am proud of her, not because she is a Supreme Court justice, but because she is a good person," Celina said. "She has a big, beautiful, and kind heart."

During her first year on the Supreme Court, Sotomayor sided with the liberal justices, as many had predicted, on cases related to campaign speech, juvenile crime, religion, federal power, and criminal law. She showed little of the restraint that's common to many first-year Supreme Court justices. Starting out on the Court can be very difficult; in fact, Justice David Souter once said his first year was like "walking into a tidal wave." Yet as Sotomayor started the 2009-10 term, she seemed confi-

After being selected for the Court, Sotomayor called it "the most humbling honor of my life" and emphasized that it "would never have been possible without the opportunities presented to me by this nation.... I am struck again today by the wonder of my own life, and the life we in America are so privileged to lead."

dent and at ease. She was quick to question attorneys, rather than hanging back, as some justices have done at first. She has been described as well prepared for each case, with detailed questions and a businesslike manner. It's required a lot of time and hard work, but observers have said she relishes her new responsibilities. "This past year, I have often felt like I was living in a dream, wondering when someone was going to pinch me to wake me up," Sotomayor said in a speech to college graduates. "The hours can be long, but I have found that the long hours are painless when you are doing what you love."

HOME AND FAMILY

Sotomayor married high school sweetheart Kevin Noonan in 1976, just before entering Yale Law School. They divorced in 1983 without having any children. She remains close to her mother, brother, and many of her nieces, nephews, and cousins.

HOBBIES AND OTHER INTERESTS

Sotomayor likes to cook, work out, and attend ballet and theatrical productions. She is also a big fan of the New York Yankees.

SELECTED HONORS AND AWARDS

Pyne Prize (Princeton University): 1976
Outstanding Latino Professional Award (Latino/a Law Students Association): 2006

FURTHER READING

Periodicals

Current Events, Sep. 7, 2009, p.4
Latina, Dec. 2009-Jan. 2010, p.108
Los Angeles Times, June 8, 2010
National Review, June 22, 2009, p.28
New York, June 8, 2009, p.14
New York Times, Sep. 25, 1992; May 15, 2009, p.A21; May 27, 2009, p.A1; May 28, 2009, p.A16; June 5, 2009, p.A1; July 10, 2009, p.A1; July 15, 2009, p.A17; July 16, 2009, p. A18; Aug. 7, 2009, p.A1; Aug. 9, 2009, p.A12; Sep. 9, 2009, p.A12
New York Times Magazine, Nov. 27, 1983, p.118
New Yorker, Jan. 11, 2010, p.42
Newsweek, July 20, 2009, p.43; Aug. 31, 2009, p.29
People, Aug. 17, 2009, p.75
Time, June 8, 2009, p.24; June 15, 2009, p.23; June 22, 2009, p.35
Time for Kids, Sep. 18, 2009, p.4
USA Today, July 15, 2009, p.A10; July 16, 2009, p. A4; July 17, 2009, p.A7; Aug. 10, 2009, p.A4
Washington Post, July 25, 2010

Online Articles

http://www.abanet.org/publiced/hispanic_s.htm
(American Bar Association, "National Hispanic Heritage Month 2000, Profile—Week 4: Sonia Sotomayor," 2000)
http://www.dailyprincetonian.com/2009/05/13/23695
(Daily Princetonian, "At Princeton, Sotomayor'76 Excelled at Academics, Extracurriculars," May 13, 2009)
http://www.law.com/jsp/nylj/PubArticleNY.jsp?id=1202430720254&slretur n=1&hbxlogin=1
(New York Law Journal, "Sotomayor Is Pragmatic, Empathetic Lawyers Say," May 15, 2009)
http://topics.nytimes.com/top/reference/timestopics/people/s/sonia_soto mayor/index.html
(New York Times, New York Times Topics: Sonia Sotomayor, n.d.)

http://thecaucus.blogs.nytimes.com/2009/09/25/sotomayor-offers-details
  -on-her-nomination
  (New York Times, "Sotomayor Offers Details on Her Nomination," Sep.
  25, 2009)
http://www.washingtonpost.com/wp-dyn/content/article/2009/05/26/AR
  2009052600914.html
  (Washington Post, "Heritage Shapes Judge's Perspective," May 27, 2009)

ADDRESS

Sonia Sotomayor
U.S. Supreme Court
Supreme Court Bldg.
1 First Street NE
Washington, DC 20543

WORLD WIDE WEB SITES

http://www.oyez.org
http://www.supremecourtus.gov

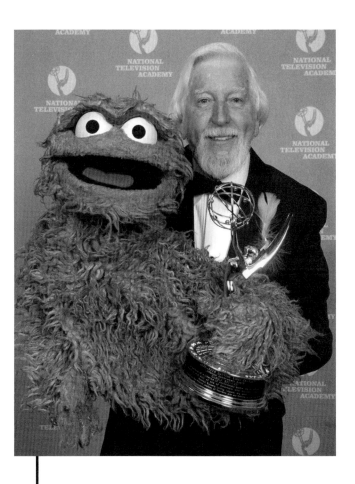

Caroll Spinney 1933-

American Puppeteer and Artist
Creator of Big Bird and Oscar the Grouch on
"Sesame Street"

BIRTH

Caroll Edwin Spinney was born on December 26, 1933, in
Waltham, Massachusetts, a western suburb of Boston. He
was the third and youngest son of Chester Spinney, who
worked in a watch factory, and Margaret Spinney, who had
left her home in England as a young girl to work in North
America. She was an aspiring fashion illustrator and designer
who put aside her career to focus on raising her sons, David,

Donald, and Caroll, who was so named because he barely missed being born on Christmas.

YOUTH

Spinney grew up in Acton, Massachusetts, a rural area west of Boston. He was so small as a child that he was nicknamed "Pee Wee" in first and second grade and felt self-conscious about his size. He would later bring these emotions from childhood to his most famous character, "Big Bird gets frustrated and a little insecure, because I certainly was. I was the small kid in the neighborhood and I was pushed around a lot," he remembered. "I always wanted people to like me, because I wasn't cool." In fact, he has said he was shy. "If the word 'nerd' existed back then, that's what I would've been considered—even though I don't like that word." He especially loved comics and drawing: "I drew all the time. If it was cold weather, when [I] came in from playing or sliding in the winter, I would then start drawing on my comic books."

> "Big Bird gets frustrated and a little insecure, because I certainly was," Spinney remembered. "I was the small kid in the neighborhood and I was pushed around a lot. I always wanted people to like me, because I wasn't cool."

Spinney was five years old when he first saw a puppet show, put on by some college students at a neighbor's day care. He enjoyed it so much he bought a monkey puppet at a rummage sale for a nickel and used a stuffed flannel snake his mother had made him as another prop. By age eight, he had built a puppet theater out of old crates and performed a show in his family's barn. He charged his neighbors and friends two cents a ticket, and after 20 minutes "everybody went away smiling," he recalled. "I already wanted to be a cartoonist when I grew up. After this show, I decided that I would also become a puppeteer." For a shy person who liked performing, puppetry made sense. When he stayed behind the curtain, he didn't feel awkward at all. "As a puppeteer you can hide whatever you are at the moment and be only what they see," he said. "And you could get the adults to laugh." For Spinney's next Christmas, his mother and his brother Donald created a Punch-and-Judy puppet theater with a complete set of puppets to go along with it. Spinney's mother also wrote scripts for her son's puppet shows.

Spinney was also interested in television, a new invention that was spreading across the country after World War II. He first saw a TV at the 1940

World's Fair. "I remember looking at it and thinking—the idea just came to me—a television looks a lot like a puppet theater. I wanted to do puppets on television. I hadn't even seen it done, but I knew that it could be." When TV first came to the Boston area in 1947 and the neighborhood doctor purchased a set, Spinney visited the house to see what was on. One of the children's programs he saw had a puppet skit that he knew he could have performed much better. It gave him confidence that he could turn his love of puppetry into a successful career. "I decided some day I'm going to be on the best TV kids' show," he recalled.

EDUCATION

In the early 1950s, Spinney graduated from Acton High School, where a teacher supported his career goal of becoming a puppeteer. Although his father wanted him to start working right away, Spinney entered the Art Institute of Boston's College of Art and Design. There he studied illustration and commercial art, thinking it would be a practical major. He supported himself by performing puppet

When Spinney learned how to keep his live audience entertained for 45 minutes, he was hooked. "Once I started performing live for the camera," he noted, "I knew that was what I wanted to do."

shows at birthday parties and holiday gatherings. He interrupted his studies to serve in the U.S. Air Force for four years, but after his service he returned to school and completed his degree in the late 1950s.

CAREER HIGHLIGHTS

Starting His First Television Show

When Spinney enlisted in the Air Force, he managed to pass a draftsman's exam and was stationed at a base in Las Vegas, Nevada. There he drew technical instructional charts and training aids such as a poster instructing "How to Bomb and Strafe." Because the weather in Las Vegas was so hot, Spinney performed his Air Force duties during the earliest part of the day, leaving his afternoons free. He used his spare time to put on puppet shows for local groups, and one such performance led to a contact with local television station KLAS. They hired him to draw advertising cards, then gave him time for his own children's program. "The Rascal Rabbit Show," using a white rabbit puppet his mother had made for him, debuted on KLAS-TV in 1955. When Spinney learned how to keep his live audience entertained for 45 minutes, he was hooked. "Once I started performing live for the

Spinney's characters from "Sesame Street": Big Bird and Oscar the Grouch.

camera," he noted, "I knew that was what I wanted to do." The show only lasted a couple of months, because the Air Force soon ordered him to transfer to Bitburg, Germany. He found a way to express himself there as well, contributing a comic strip to the local armed service newspaper.

When Spinney left the Air Force in 1957, he got an interview with the Walt Disney Company, which produced many of his favorite cartoons. Their offer to hire him as an animator would have fulfilled a long-time ambition, but the pay was so dismal he decided to return to Boston to finish his degree. While there he created animations for commercials and collaborated on the "Crazy Crayon" cartoon series. He discovered that creating animation wasn't as satisfying as performing for a live audience. "The only trouble with art is that it's very lonely. I don't get any applause until later," he remarked. In 1958, he auditioned for a Boston television station that was looking to create a new children's program. Although he didn't get the job, they called him later and asked if he would contribute to a television series for children that would air during the summer season. He soon was starring with singer Judy Valentine in "The Judy and Goggle Show," which was set inside a spaceship and included Goggle, his yellow bird puppet with "goggle" eyes. Although the show earned excellent ratings for its time slot, the station didn't have room in its schedule to broadcast it after the summer.

Instead, the same Boston station offered Spinney a job performing on "Bozo's Big Top," a successful children's show that franchised the character of Bozo the Clown to local stations around the United States. Starting in 1959, Spinney performed with hand puppets and acted in costume as several characters. These included Grandma Nellie, Bozo's clown grandmother; Kookie, a boxing kangaroo; and Mr. Lion, the "fastest draw alive." For the Mr. Lion segment, the costumed Spinney would write down a child's name and turn it into an animal drawing in less than 30 seconds. Although his first drawing challenge was on the spur of the moment, it became a regular feature of the show. Much of the show was unscripted. "We kind of made it up as we went along," he later remembered. "We had no writers. Sometimes it was quite funny. I wish I had tapes of it, because I think some of it must have been really bad." For most of his run on "Bozo's Big Top" Spinney performed in front of a live audience three days a week, but there was still something unsatisfactory about the job. "While what I was doing paid pretty well," he said, "it did not make me feel I had ever done anything really important."

That changed after a performance at the 1969 Puppeteers of America convention. Spinney had been experimenting with combining animation and puppetry, performing his characters against a screen that used film as moving scenery. For the convention, he built an elaborate stage and chore-

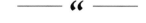

Spinney was excited about the prospect of working with Jim Henson, the creator of the Muppets. "I was somewhat in awe of him. The live shows I'd seen him put on—the ideas, the puppets, and the performances—were incredible.... When I saw Jim's commercials and TV appearances, I realized just how well puppets and television could be done."

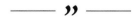

ographed a show that synchronized music, animation, and live performance of his cat puppet, Picklepuss, which he brought from "Bozo." On the day of the show, however, a misplaced spotlight hid the animated scenery and ruined the program. While waiting for someone to fix the light, Spinney improvised with Picklepuss and some shadow puppets. "My character, Picklepuss, in his struggles to save the day, ended up being funnier than my material," Spinney remembered. In the audience that day was Jim Henson, the legendary creator of the Muppets who was already nationally famous for his performances on "The Ed Sullivan Show." Henson invited Spinney to New York to talk about a job on a new children's program. Spinney was excited about the prospect of working with Henson. "I was somewhat in awe of him. The live shows I'd seen him put on—the ideas, the puppets, and the performances—were incredible.... When I saw Jim's commercials and TV appearances, I realized just how well puppets and television could be done."

Moving to "Sesame Street"

When Spinney met with Henson, he learned the Muppets would be working on a children's show for the Public Broadcasting System (PBS) called "Sesame Street." Its goal was to use the latest research about how children learn to create a television show that would teach them such simple concepts as counting and the alphabet. Henson was looking for a puppeteer to take two roles: a large, goofy bird and a grouchy character named Oscar. "I wondered what the Bird and Oscar would actually do, as there were no scripts available at this point," Spinney recalled. "I had no idea how they would fit in the show, or what voices I would use. Still, I was confident I could learn. I *had* to do this! I was being asked to work for someone who, in my mind, was the greatest puppeteer in history. This show *had* to work." Although it meant a large pay cut and a commute from Boston to New York City, Spinney agreed to join the show.

"Sesame Street" first aired in fall 1969, with Spinney's character of Big Bird only appearing for one or two minutes each episode. Henson originally pictured the character as a goofy country bumpkin who kept running into things. "He didn't have a clue about anything, and it seemed that he had no real purpose on the show except as a comic diversion," Spinney noted. "Certainly, he had no educational value." That changed when Spinney read a script that called for Big Bird to be upset because he couldn't join kids at day care. The puppeteer thought it sounded creepy for a goofy adult to want to go to day care, so "I said, 'Let's make sure the audience knows that he's a kid.' That way he could go to day care and play with the other kids." It also meant that Big Bird could learn things along with the audience. After playing the scene where Big Bird throws a tantrum because he can't join other kids at day care, the puppeteer remarked, "it felt very natural, and I knew that suddenly I had a real, human, complex character to work with. He was the too-big kid, much as I had been the too-little kid when I was his age."

The look of the Big Bird puppet also evolved with Spinney's feedback. When the puppeteer first began performing Big Bird, he couldn't see out of the costume. The first time he saw his performance on a monitor, he remembered, "I was shocked when I saw ... how much his head was flailing

"Sesame Street" hosts Gordon (Matt Robinson), Mr. Hooper (Will Lee), Susan (Loretta Lee), and Bob (Bob McGrath) stand with Big Bird on the set of the TV series in about 1969.

around and his feathers were all put on inverted so that the bottoms, the underside of the feathers were showing." The Muppet designers adapted the puppet by putting feathers with the shiny sides up, and reshaping his head. Eventually the puppet reached eight feet two inches tall, close to the limit that the five-foot ten-inch Spinney could reach. During that second year, Henson also rigged a monitor for him inside the suit, so Spinney could see what the camera was seeing and make sure Big Bird was looking in the right direction.

Because Spinney worked the controls of Big Bird's head with his hand, the suit was considered a "walkabout" puppet, not a costume. Spinney wore costume pants for Big Bird's legs, then raised his right hand above his head to work Big Bird's mouth. His left hand went in Big Bird's left wing, and a wire let him move the right wing in the opposite direction of the left. Because Big Bird's head weighed more than four pounds, Spinney couldn't stay in the suit much more than 10 minutes. Despite being limited to brief segments, Big Bird quickly became the most popular character on the show. Spinney received many fan letters addressed to Big Bird inviting him to come over and play.

> *Spinney was gratified when he saw his "Sesame Street" characters on a children's book cover along with several Disney characters. "What satisfaction I felt! Some of the most magical moments of my childhood were watching Disney cartoons," he recalled. "Seeing my characters dancing with Bugs and Mickey told me that I shared in those magic moments for other children. It hadn't hit me before. Now I knew that I had gotten to where I wanted to be."*

Spinney's other character for "Sesame Street," Oscar the Grouch, required a completely different approach. The puppeteer knew Oscar was supposed to live in a trash can, but he wasn't sure exactly how to flesh out the character. A chance encounter provided inspiration. "I was going to meet Jim to do a run-through on Oscar for the first time," Spinney recalled. "I was supposed to have a voice ready, and still couldn't decide when I got into a cab and the driver said, 'Where to, Mac?'" While the driver colorfully complained about the local mayor, the puppeteer added, "I just kept saying to myself, 'Where to, Mac? Where to, Mac?' and I realized that sounded just right." He used that voice on his first run-through with the puppet, having Oscar tell Jim Henson, "Get away from my trash can!" "That'll do nicely," Henson told Spinney, and the gruff but lovable Oscar became a regular on the show.

When in character Spinney often works with children, as in this encounter between Big Bird and students from the Overbrook School for the Blind.

Becoming a Television Pioneer

During its first season, "Sesame Street" was immediately hailed as one of the best children's programs ever, winning a Peabody Award and three Emmys—the first of more than 100 Emmys the show has won during its first 40 years. "I can't imagine we were acclaimed, it was so crude and amateurish," Spinney remembered. "But compared to what was on TV at the time as far as content, we were way ahead of them right from the start. Because this was the only show that really studied how to teach children." Still, the puppeteer almost left after the first year finished filming. He spent his summer performing on "Bozo's Big Top" in Boston and the station offered him his own "Picklepuss" show. Spinney decided to think it over for a month, but soon realized he was working in a dream job, reaching a larger audience than he could have imagined as a child. In November 1970 Big Bird was on the cover of *Time* magazine, and later Spinney saw his "Sesame Street" characters on a children's book cover along with several Disney characters and Bugs Bunny. "There were *my* characters, perfectly cartooned, dancing with my favorite cartoon characters from childhood," he recalled. "What satisfaction I felt! Some of the most magical moments of my childhood were watching Disney cartoons. Seeing my characters dancing with Bugs and Mickey told me that I shared in those magic moments for other children. It hadn't hit me before. Now I knew that I had gotten to where I wanted to be."

During the 1970s and 1980s, Spinney earned four Emmy Awards for individual performance and two Grammy Awards for contributing to the best children's recording of the year. He also received invitations for Big Bird and Oscar to guest star on other TV shows. He appeared on several variety shows and became a frequent guest of the game show "Hollywood Squares," eventually appearing on more than 140 episodes. Spinney's characters were also invited to appear at many public events. He made an appearance in 1971 with the Boston Pops, with Big Bird conducting the orchestra. This led to a series of tours in which Spinney's Big Bird would conduct a musical program; Spinney would perform in 10-minute segments, then go backstage to rest and take oxygen. He conducted groups across the U.S., Canada, and Australia, until the travel and effort became too exhausting. He also became a frequent visitor at the White House, making his first trip in 1971 at the invitation of First Lady Patricia Nixon and meeting every First Lady since then. Performing as Oscar, he shared a stage with Prince Charles of Britain.

Spinney's frequent television appearances led to many travel opportunities as well. In 1979 comedian Bob Hope invited him to join a special taped in China. The communist nation had long been closed to outsiders and had only recently opened itself to political and cultural exchanges with the United States. While taping "Bob Hope on the Road of China," Spinney's Big Bird did a song and dance number with Hope and also got a chance to entertain the local children. They were fascinated with Big Bird despite the language difference, and Spinney returned home, determined to explore the country further. He came up with the idea of having Big Bird discover he is related to the Phoenix of China, a legendary bird, and travel there to find her. The result was the 1983 program "Big Bird in China," which was a hit both in the United States and China.

Spinney also appeared in several movies as both Big Bird and Oscar, most notably taking a starring role in the 1985 feature *Follow That Bird.* The film begins with a social worker noticing that Big Bird doesn't live with other birds and sending him to Illinois to live with a family of dodos. His new family has no imagination and Big Bird misses his friends, so he decides to walk to New York City to get back to Sesame Street. At the same time, his Sesame Street friends go in search of the missing Bird, and Big Bird and his friends have many adventures along the way. While celebrity cameos livened up the film, "the person who seems to hold the movie together is Caroll Spinney, the Muppeteer who, under all those yellow feathers, plays the bird we would follow anywhere," remarked Jay Boyar, a critic for the *Orlando Sentinel.*

"'Sesame Street,' I've come to realize, is a big place," Spinney said. *"Sure, some characters become more popular than others for periods of time, but the show has always been a group effort in the service of our mission. Sharing and cooperation, getting along with others, and recognizing one another's strengths are some of our most important social messages, after all."*

Creating a Lasting Legacy

Although Spinney has worked on "Sesame Street" for more than 40 years, one episode in particular stands out in his mind. Actor Will Lee, who had played shopkeeper Mr. Hooper since the first season, died in late 1982 from a heart attack. The show's producers debated how to address the actor's departure and considered having the character retire. Finally they decided to deal with the issue of death head on. When Big Bird wants to give Mr. Hooper a portrait he drew, the adults on Sesame Street have to explain that death means Mr. Hooper will never be coming back. "When the scene ended, all the actors in the cast had genuine tears in their eyes," Spinney recalled. "We used the first take, because it was so real. I think this scene was the best one we did in all the … years of 'Sesame Street.' It was our tribute to Will Lee." Big

Big Bird reads to children on "Sesame Street."

Bird's drawing of Mr. Hooper—which the puppeteer drew himself—still remains a part of the set in Big Bird's nest.

Over 40 years, there have been many changes at "Sesame Street." Producers changed the format to include longer stories when research showed young viewers could follow them, and they made other adjustments as the average audience member became younger. Financial issues meant the number of episodes per season shrank from over 100 the first season to 26 in season 40. New characters came to the show; one in particular, a little red Muppet named Elmo, became even more popular than Big Bird. Spinney welcomed the changes as a chance to keep teaching kids. "'Sesame Street,' I've come to realize, is a big place," he said. "Sure, some characters become more popular than others for periods of time, but the show has always been a group effort in the service of our mission. Sharing and cooperation, getting along with others, and recognizing one another's strengths are some of our most important social messages, after all."

Even grouchy Oscar has a lot to teach children, according to his puppeteer: "I think [he] teaches kids that it takes all kinds in the world." Spinney said he finds Oscar a refreshing change after being sweet-natured Big Bird all day, and he insisted that Oscar is "not a villain, not horrible, … and although he can be rude and mean, he fundamentally has got a heart of gold." He explained that Oscar is a "perfectionist" who's passionate about trash. "He's into his thing, he's often alone, and when somebody intrudes on him, naturally he gets grouchy." If Spinney reads a script where Oscar crosses the line of being too rude, he will ask for changes. "Honestly, I'm often surprised at what he's going to say, but my mother and father were very funny and that's why it comes easy for me, or for the puppet."

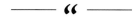

After performing as Big Bird and Oscar for over 40 years, Spinney revealed that "working the puppet has become something like touch typing. I don't have to think about it too much, and I can concentrate on expressing what Big Bird is thinking and feeling. I didn't create the puppet, and I don't write the scripts, but I guess what I do is bring Big Bird his soul.... He's the child that I wanted to be, the kind of person I think we all should be."

Spending more than half his life playing Big Bird and Oscar has earned Spinney many accolades. In 2000, the Library of Congress gave him the Living Legend Award for his work as Big Bird, while his television peers voted him a Lifetime Achievement Emmy Award in 2006. (He earned his fifth Emmy for individual performance the following year.) While he finds these kinds of awards satisfying, the puppeteer is most gratified by

The cast of "Sesame Street" on its 40th anniversary.

the response he gets from the public. When Spinney went on a book tour for his 2003 memoir *The Wisdom of Big Bird,* he had a chance to meet many fans who might otherwise not recognize him. "I've talked to dozens of people on this tour who say, 'You have no idea how important you were to our family,'" he recalled. "I don't know how I could have been so fortunate."

After performing as Big Bird and Oscar for over 40 years, Spinney revealed that "working the puppet has become something like touch typing. I don't have to think about it too much, and I can concentrate on expressing what Big Bird is thinking and feeling. I didn't create the puppet, and I don't write the scripts, but I guess what I do is bring Big Bird his soul.... He's the child that I wanted to be, the kind of person I think we all should be." Although he has been limited to two characters for a lengthy time, he said he never gets bored with the work. "There's a huge dramatic range," he remarked. "I've gone from blubbering tears to wild happiness. It's very satisfying." Besides, he added, "even though the Bird appears very birdlike and does birdy things like live in a nest, he really is as human as anyone on the show." Spinney's goal is to keep exploring his characters' humanity as long as he is physically able to do so. "When I no longer can hold that bird's head up where it belongs, then I guess I'll have to say, 'Hasta la vista,'" he commented. "It's just so much of a joy to do it. It's physically demanding, which keeps me in good shape. I'm not one who adores doing exercise, but the last thing I want to do at this point is retire."

MARRIAGE AND FAMILY

Spinney married his first wife, Janice, sometime in the 1960s. They had three children, Jessica, Melissa, and Benjamin, and divorced in 1971. Spinney met his second wife, Debra Jean Gilroy, at the Children's Television Workshop, where she worked as a secretary. They married in 1979 and moved to a country home in Woodstock, Connecticut. The couple also has a studio apartment in New York City, where they spend time during the shooting season of "Sesame Street."

HOBBIES AND OTHER INTERESTS

Throughout his years working as puppeteer, Spinney has continued working as an artist. He regularly draws cartoons, and when he can find the time he creates acrylic paintings, often featuring the character of Big Bird. Some of his works are for sale as prints or originals, and some he has donated to benefit charities.

SELECTED CREDITS

Television Series and Specials

"Bozo's Big Top," 1959-69
"Sesame Street," 1969-
"Hollywood Squares," 1976-80, 2001
"Christmas Eve on Sesame Street," 1978
"Bob Hope on the Road of China," 1979
"Big Bird in China," 1983
"Big Bird Brings Spring to Sesame Street," 1987
"A Muppet Family Christmas," 1987
"Big Bird in Japan," 1988
"Big Bird's Birthday or Let Me Eat Cake," 1991
"Elmo Saves Christmas," 1996

Films

The Muppet Movie, 1979
The Great Muppet Caper, 1981
Follow That Bird, 1985
The Adventures of Elmo in Grouchland, 1999

Books

How to Be a Grouch, 1976 (as Oscar the Grouch; author and illustrator)
The Wisdom of Big Bird (and the Dark Genius of Oscar the Grouch): Lessons from a Life in Feathers, 2003 (with J. Mulligan)

Recordings

Big Bird Sings!, 1973
Big Bird Leads the Band, 1977
Bounce along with Big Bird, 1985
Bird Is the Word!: Big Bird's Favorite Songs, 1995
Sesame Street: Oscar's Trashy Songs, 1997
A Sesame Street Christmas, 2002

HONORS AND AWARDS

Grammy Award for Best Recording for Children (The Recording Academy): two awards for "Sesame Street" recordings
Emmy Award (National Academy of Television Arts and Sciences): 1974, 1976, and 1979, Outstanding Individual Achievement in Children's Programming (with others), 1984, Special Classification of Outstanding Individual Achievement—Performers, and 2007, Outstanding Performer in a Children's Series (with Kevin Clash), all for "Sesame Street"
Hollywood Walk of Fame: 1994 (as Big Bird)
Living Legend Award (Library of Congress): 2000
Legacy for Children Award (Children's Discovery Museum): 2003
James Keller Award (The Christopher Awards, Inc): 2004
Emmy Award (National Academy of Television Arts and Sciences): 2006, Lifetime Achievement Award

FURTHER READING

Books

Davis, Michael. *Street Gang: The Complete History of Sesame Street*, 2008
Spinney, Caroll, with J. Mulligan. *The Wisdom of Big Bird (and the Dark Genius of Oscar the Grouch): Lessons from a Life in Feathers*, 2003

Periodicals

Atlanta Journal-Constitution, May 9, 2003, p.E6
Chicago Tribune, Nov. 14, 1989
Current Biography, 1999
Daily Variety, Mar. 17, 2006, p.A1
Los Angeles Times, Sep. 15, 1991, p.36; May 21, 2003
New York Times, Nov. 11, 1998
New Yorker, Nov. 9. 2009
Orlando Sentinel, Aug. 4, 1985, p.F1
People Weekly, Dec. 4, 2000, p.115
Television Quarterly, Fall 2006, p.61

Washington Post, June 22, 2008, p.A7
Winston-Salem Journal, Nov. 16, 1998, p.D1

Online Articles

http://www.emmytvlegends.org
  (Archive of American Television, "Caroll Spinney—Archive Interview,"
  May 12, 2001)
http://today.msnbc.msn.com/id/25193936
  (MSNBC, "As Big Bird, Caroll Spinney Loves Every Feather," June 16,
  2008)
http://www.npr.org
  (National Public Radio, "A Life Inside Big Bird," May 5, 2003)
http://www.npr.org
  (National Public Radio, "Voice of Big Bird, Oscar Wins Lifetime Award,"
  Apr. 27, 2006)
http://artsbeat.blogs.nytimes.com/2009/11/09/big-bird-responds
  (New York Times, "Big Bird Responds," Nov. 11, 2009)
http://www.nytimes.com
  (New York Times, "Public Lives: 30 Happy Years as an 8-Foot Tall Yellow
  Bird," Nov. 11, 1998)
http://www.topics.nytimes.com
  (New York Times, "Sesame Street," multiple articles, various dates)
http://content.usatoday.com/topics/topic/Caroll+Spinney
  (USA Today, "Caroll Spinney," multiple articles, various dates)

ADDRESS

Caroll Spinney
Sesame Workshop
One Lincoln Plaza
New York, NY 10023

WORLD WIDE WEB SITES

http://www.carollspinney.com
http://www.sesamestreet.org/onair/cast

Kristen Stewart 1990-

American Actress
Plays Bella Swan in "The Twilight Saga" Movies

BIRTH

Kristen Jaymes Stewart was born on April 9, 1990, in Los Angeles, California. Her mother, Jules, is Australian; she worked as a scriptwriter and script supervisor for movies and television shows. Her father, John, worked as a stage manager, producer, and director of television shows on the Fox network. Stewart has three older brothers.

YOUTH

Stewart grew up in Los Angeles. On vacations, her family often traveled to Australia to visit her mother's relatives and friends. That's where she discovered her love of surfing, a hobby she took up at an early age. She first learned to surf in Noosa Heads, a resort town in Queensland on the eastern coast of Australia. Noosa Heads is famous for its surfing beaches, which are common stops on the world competitive surfing circuit.

As a child, Stewart was not particularly interested in acting. Both of her parents and all of her brothers worked in the movie and television entertainment industry, but they all held jobs behind the camera. Stewart thought she might become a writer or director and never considered becoming an actor. "I never wanted to be the center of attention—I wasn't that 'I want to be famous, I want to be an actor' kid. I never sought out acting, but I always practiced my autograph because I loved pens. I'd write my name on everything."

BECOMING AN ACTRESS

Stewart started to change her mind about acting after taking part in her elementary school's holiday play one year. A talent agent happened to be in the audience, and her performance caught his attention. The next day, the agent called Stewart's parents to ask if she was interested in auditioning for acting roles. At first, her parents didn't like the idea. They were familiar with the movie and television industry and knew the challenges that child actors could face. Stewart was not sure about acting either, even though being in the school play had helped her realize that she liked performing on stage. After a lot of thought and discussion, she and her parents decided that she should try some auditions and see what happened. Stewart began auditioning for roles in movies and television shows when she was eight years old.

> "I never wanted to be the center of attention—I wasn't that 'I want to be famous, I want to be an actor' kid. I never sought out acting, but I always practiced my autograph because I loved pens. I'd write my name on everything."

When she was 10 years old, Stewart got her first acting role after more than a year of going to auditions. She was given a small non-speaking part in the Disney Channel movie *The*

Thirteenth Year, about a boy who discovers that his birth mother is a mermaid. This early experience helped convince her to continue her pursuit of an acting career.

CAREER HIGHLIGHTS

Almost from the beginning of her career, Stewart chose to follow a different path than most child actors. Rather than pursuing parts in television comedies and children's movies, Stewart wanted to play unusual young characters in serious dramatic movies. Her first speaking part was a small role in *The Safety of Objects*, an independent film released in 2001. The movie told the story of the overlapping lives of four families living in the same neighborhood, each struggling to cope with their own emotional problems. Stewart

Stewart appeared with Jody Foster in the 2002 thriller Panic Room.

played Sam Jennings, the tomboy daughter of a troubled single mother. Although the movie was not received well by critics or moviegoers, the experience helped Stewart in future auditions.

The First Big Break

Stewart landed her first big role with a leading part in the 2002 psychological thriller *Panic Room*. This film told the suspenseful story of a single mother and her daughter who become trapped when a group of thieves break into their home. Stewart auditioned for the role of Sarah Altman, the young daughter of the character played by Jodie Foster. The audition process was long and difficult, including six different tryouts. Stewart was disappointed when the part was given to a different actress. However, a conflict in scheduling forced the original actress to back out of the project, and Stewart was offered the role after all.

Critics were unenthusiastic about *Panic Room* as a whole, but Stewart was praised for her believable performance. Many commented that she and Foster resembled each other so much and related so well to each other in the movie that they appeared to actually be mother and daughter. One writer for *Variety* said that Stewart "delivered an assured performance that led some critics to compare her skills to Foster's early style." A critic for *Interview* liked the "toughness and maturity" of her acting. Stewart was nominated for a Young Artist Award for her role in *Panic Room*.

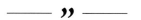

> "I started homeschooling because my teachers were failing me. I think it was just resentment—I made more work for them. But homeschooling is great; you can study what you want, which allows you to get more excited about what you're doing."

Stewart's successful performance in *Panic Room* led to her being cast in the 2003 film *Cold Creek Manor*. She played Kristen Tilson, the daughter of a couple who move their family into a house that they soon find seems to be haunted. This suspense drama did poorly with moviegoers and critics, although her performance earned her another Young Artist Award nomination.

Around this time, Stewart began homeschooling. Between going to auditions and acting in movies, it had become too difficult for her to conform to a traditional school schedule. Stewart missed a lot of school days when she was working on movies, and her grades began to suffer. "I started homeschooling because my teachers were failing me. I think it was just resentment—I made more work for them. But homeschooling is great; you can study what you want, which allows you to get more excited about what you're doing."

Soon after *Cold Creek Manor,* Stewart landed her first starring role in the 2004 movie *Catch That Kid*. She played the part of Maddy Phillips, a scheming 12-year-old super-spy. Maddy concocts an elaborate bank-robbing plan to get enough money to pay for the life-saving surgery needed by her dying father. This role allowed Stewart to show a different, lighter side of her acting ability. The movie also provided an opportunity for her to reach a younger audience, and it became a major hit with pre-teens. *Variety* called it a "breezy, teen-friendly caper," while a critic for the *Washington Post* said that her acting "perfectly captures the anxieties and frustrations of even the bravest pre-teen girl."

The Fast Track to Stardom

Stewart was beginning to make a name for herself as a talented and versatile young actress who could hold her own playing dramatic roles opposite

Stewart in a scene from Zathura, *based on the book by Chris Van Allsburg.*

adult actors with much more experience. She was offered many more roles, and she appeared in 10 films made from 2005 to 2008. Stewart soon found herself on her way to becoming a movie star.

Stewart's next big project was the 2005 Showtime television movie *Speak,* based on the popular novel by Laurie Halse Anderson. Stewart played the starring role of Melinda Sordino, a high school freshman who stops almost all verbal communication after being raped by an upperclassman. This role provided her with the opportunity to portray different aspects of the same character, as Melinda struggles to put her life back together. Her performance was praised by critics, who called Stewart "breathtaking" and "a wonderfully expressive actress." A critic for the *New York Times* said that her performance "creates a convincing character full of pain and turmoil."

Also in 2005, Stewart appeared in *Zathura,* based on the book of the same name by Chris Van Allsburg. She played the older sister of two boys who find that playing a mysterious board game has accidentally transported the family home to the far reaches of outer space. This role allowed her to showcase her comic acting skills. Then in 2006, she had a leading role in *Fierce People*, the strange and dramatic story of a group of people brought together for a summer at the country estate of an aging billionaire. Neither of these movies enjoyed much commercial success, but Stewart continued to be noticed for her growing talent as an actress. By this time, she was moving from one project to the next almost continuously.

―――― " ――――

"[Acting] just feels good. I find I want to do a movie because I love the script or I love the story. You have these themes in your mind, and you think about them incessantly, and then it's time to shoot the scene and you're like, 'Okay, you're going to be done with this in 15 minutes, so you'd better do it right.'"

―――― " ――――

Stewart appeared in three movies released in 2007. She had a starring role as Jess Solomon in *The Messengers,* a moderately successful supernatural thriller about a family that moves from the city to an old farm. The farm quickly becomes the focus of many strange and unexplained events. Stewart followed this with a starring role as Lucy Hardwicke in the comedy/drama *In the Land of Women.* This movie tells the story of a young man who is transformed by his encounters with the family of women who live across the street from his grandmother. *Variety* called her performance the high point of the movie. *Variety* also praised her bold performance in *Into the Wild*, the story of a young man who leaves everything behind to travel through the Alaskan wilderness. Stewart was nominated for a Young Artist Award for her portrayal of Tracy Tatro, a teenager who falls in love with the idealistic young drifter.

Stewart continued her full work schedule, appearing in four movies released in 2008. In the Hollywood satire *What Just Happened?*, she played the rebellious daughter of an overwhelmed studio executive. Critics praised her performance as one of the most memorable parts of the film. In *The Yellow Handkerchief*, she starred as Martine, a young woman on a road trip through Louisiana who helps a hitchhiker who has just been released from prison to reunite with his wife. Stewart also had a very small part in *Jumper*, the story of a young man who is able to teleport to any location in the world. She appeared in the movie's final scene. But it was her fourth movie of 2008, *Twilight*, that would catapult her to superstardom.

Twilight

Twilight is the film adaptation of the popular young adult book of the same name by author Stephenie Meyer, the first book in a series of novels filled with romance, danger, and suspense. Stewart stars as Bella Swan, a teenager who moves to a rural small town in Washington state and soon becomes fascinated with the mysterious and handsome Edward Cullen (played by Robert Pattinson). Edward seems equally fascinated by Bella, and trouble brews for the two teens. Bella discovers that Edward is not really a teenager at all, but is in fact a very old vampire. And Edward struggles with his nearly overwhelming feelings for Bella, knowing how dangerous it is for him to even be near her. As Bella and Edward realize they are falling in love, danger gathers around them, until Bella must make a choice that deeply affects them both.

Before she auditioned for the role of Bella, Stewart had not read the *Twilight* books. When she read the film script, she was attacted to the idea of portraying a teenage girl who is experiencing such intense feelings of attraction for the first time. "What I love about the story is that it's about a very logical, pragmatic girl who you think would never get swept into something that has this bizarre power," Stewart said. "It's not an easy love. That's what I like about it. It's the most strained, impossible love, and they are both willing to fight for it and die for it. That's what I was drawn to." Before filming began, Stewart read the *Twilight* books to get a deeper sense of the character she was to play.

Filming *Twilight* proved somewhat challenging because for the first half of the production, Stewart was only 17 years old. As a minor, she was restricted by laws governing underage actors, so she could only work a maximum of five hours per day. Because her character Bella is in almost every scene of the movie, this made the shooting schedule difficult to manage. When Stewart had her 18th birthday in the middle of the production, *Twilight*'s director presented her with a cake decorated with a clock and the words "Now you're on nights," meaning that from that point on, Stewart had to work full days.

One of the most highly anticipated movies of 2008, *Twilight* earned mixed reviews from movie critics. *USA Today* offered some harsh comments. "Despite questionable casting, wooden acting, laughable dialogue, and truly awful makeup, nothing is likely to stop young girls from swarming to this kitschy adaptation of Stephenie Meyer's popular novel.... Stewart and Pattinson lack chemistry. Her subtle acting does not serve her well in this overheated setting. As Bella, she seems to have two expressions: blank and slightly less blank." A reviewer for *Variety* called the movie "a disappointingly anemic tale of forbidden love that should satiate the pre-converted

Stewart (Bella) with Robert Pattinson (Edward) and Taylor Lautner (Jacob) in scenes from Twilight *and* New Moon.

but will bewilder and underwhelm viewers who haven't devoured Stephenie Meyer's bestselling juvie chick-lit franchise…. A supernatural romance in which the supernatural and romantic elements feel rushed, unformed, and insufficiently motivated, leaving audiences with little to do but shrug and focus on the eye-candy." But the review went on to praise Stewart's performance, saying "Stewart makes Bella earthy, appealing, and slightly withdrawn." The *Washington Post* also pointed to her performance. "*Twilight* works as both love story and vampire story, thanks mainly to the performances of its principals. Pattinson and Stewart want to convince you that their characters are an undead freak and the girl who, against all logic, loves him. Yet they do it not by selling you on what makes Edward and Bella so different, but by finding their flesh-and-blood humanity."

"I'm really proud of *Twilight*," Stewart declared. "I think it's a good movie. It was hard to do, and I think it turned out pretty good." Fans agreed, as the movie became an immediate blockbuster hit. Fans were particularly drawn to the relationship between Bella and Edward, and that interest was fueled by rumors that Stewart and Pattinson were romantically involved. There have been many reports in celebrity magazines that claim it's true, but neither Stewart nor Pattinson have been willing to confirm it. Before the movie was even released, appearances by the pair drew wild crowds, as when 6,500 fans crowded a room at the 2008 Comic Con in San Diego just to get a glimpse of the *Twilight* cast in person. "It feels so good to have something you love be received so hotly," Stewart said of *Twilight*'s runaway success. "But the physical manifestation of the success, from the screaming fans to the box office, is just crazy." Indeed, the film's take at the box office was more than impressive. It earned almost $193 million in the U.S. and $392 million worldwide, with an opening weekend take of almost $70 million.

Twilight also earned multiple awards, sweeping the 2009 Teen Choice Awards by winning 11 of the 12 categories in which it was nominated. These included Stewart's award for Choice Movie Actress: Drama and the Choice Movie Liplock award, which she shared with her costar, Robert Pattinson. *Twilight* also won five MTV Movie Awards, including Best Female Performance for Stewart's portrayal of Bella, and the Best Kiss award shared by Stewart and Pattinson. She is proud of all of the awards, but shy about being honored for kissing. "I need to get over it," she revealed, "but I'm so concerned with what I look like during kissing scenes."

The Twilight Saga: New Moon

In *The Twilight Saga: New Moon,* Bella delves deeper into the mysteries of the supernatural world. The movie continues the love story between Bella

The closeness and chemistry that Stewart and Pattinson have shown onscreen, as in this scene from New Moon, *have led many to conclude that they are dating in real life.*

and Edward, with all the passion, drama, suspense, and action of the original film. It starts with Bella's 18th birthday party going terribly wrong— she gets a minor paper cut that leads to a violent attack by one of the vampires. Edward knows he has to leave her to protect her, so he and his family leave town—and leave Bella heartbroken, numb, and alone. For solace she turns to her old friend Jacob, a member of the mysterious Quileute Indian tribe, who has a supernatural secret of his own. Things begin to develop between Bella and Jacob, but she still pines for Edward. He appears to her only when she's in danger, so she begins throwing herself into ever-more dangerous situations in hopes of summoning him. But finally, Bella goes too far.

When *The Twilight Saga: New Moon* was released in late 2009, it drew a mixed response from critics. The *New York Times* called it "the juiceless, near bloodless sequel." *Salon* criticized its pacing, complaining that "The movie is essentially a string of brooding speeches, often delivered in the woods, with very little interesting connective tissue in between.'" The *Boston Globe* called it "an anemic comedown after the full-blooded swoon of last year's *Twilight.…* [In most] respects, the movie's a drag— paced like a dirge and cursed with dialogue and a goopy musical score …

that bring out the book's worst day-time soap tendencies. But what can you expect from an installment that keeps the central duo of human Bella and vampire Edward apart for an extended 500-page sulk?" Others, though, enjoyed the movie's melodramatic aspects. *Slate* magazine called it a "juicebomb," a term to describe guilty pleasures, movies the reviewer couldn't intellectually defend but still loved. "*The Twilight Saga: New Moon,* like its 2008 predecessor *Twilight,* is a classic juicebomb. Mopey, draggy, and absurdly self-important, the movie nonetheless twangs at some resonant affective chord. This viewer, at least, was catapulted back to that moment of adolescence when being mopey, draggy, and absurdly self-important felt like a passionate act of liberation. The *Twilight* movies are schlock, but they're elegantly appointed, luxuriously enjoyable schlock, and the world they take place in—the densely forested, perpetually overcast, vampire-and-werewolf-ridden town of Forks, Wash.—feels like a real, if fantastical, place."

> "What I love about the [Twilight] story is that it's about a very logical, pragmatic girl who you think would never get swept into something that has this bizarre power," Stewart said. "It's not an easy love. That's what I like about it. It's the most strained, impossible love, and they are both willing to fight for it and die for it. That's what I was drawn to."

But whatever critics had to say about the film as a whole, they routinely praised Stewart. "The performances are uniformly strong, especially by Stewart, who is turning into a fine young actress," wrote the *Washington Post.* "Despite melodrama that, at times, is enough to induce diabetes, there's enough wolf whistle in this sexy, scary romp to please anyone." And *Salon* wrote that "Stewart is much better than she needs to be for this material: Even in the most emotionally heightened scenes, she intuitively eases up on the clutch—miraculously, nothing she does feels overdone or overthought."

Despite reviewers' ambivalence about the film, fans were smitten, turning out in droves as soon as it opened. *New Moon* earned almost $143 million on its first weekend, making it the biggest opening of 2009 and the third biggest opening behind only *The Dark Knight* and *Spider-Man 3.* Since its opening, *New Moon* has earned more than $296 million in the U.S. and almost $710 million worldwide. Fan interest was fueled by the ongoing rumors that Stewart and Pattinson were dating in real life.

The Twilight Saga: Eclipse

In 2010, Stewart appeared in *The Twilight Saga: Eclipse*, the third installment in the series. In this film, Bella awaits high school graduation while grappling with the choice to become a vampire or remain mortal and commit to either Edward or Jacob. This choice is even more difficult because she knows that her decision will impact the course of the war between vampires and werewolves. The Cullens band together with their sworn enemies, the wolf pack, to protect Bella. And in the process, Edward and Jacob become allies as they fight against other vampires.

Reviews of the movie were mixed. Some criticized the dialogue, the acting, and the directing, while others praised it as the best film yet in the series, particularly the romantic scenes and the exciting action sequences. Critic Betsy Sharkey offered this praise in the *Los Angeles Times*. "*The Twilight Saga: Eclipse* is back with all the lethal and loving bite it was meant to have: The kiss of the vampire is cooler, the werewolf is hotter, the battles are bigger, and the choices are, as everyone with a pulse knows by now, life-changing." Ann Hornaday wrote in the *Washington Post* about the difficult choices faced by Bella. "With all the talk about the Big Change to come after graduation, with Bella longing for physical intimacy with Edward and Edward valiantly resisting, the cardinal *Twilight* themes of longing, chastity, and protection are stronger than ever," Hornaday argued. "More deeply psychological than the first two, *Eclipse* goes further not just in advancing the story but also in illuminating the tension that Bella embodies—between autonomy and surrender." Reviewer David Germain from AP highlighted the film's appeal. "Meyer's millions of fans know what they want in a good Twilight movie," Germain wrote, "and they are going to love *Eclipse*." Indeed, fans turned out en masse to see the film, which broke all box-office records on its release, earning almost $65 million in its opening weekend. To date, *Eclipse* has earned more then $300 million in the United States and more than $689 million worldwide.

Stewart will return to the role of Bella in two additional movies based on the final novel in the series, *Breaking Dawn*. Fans were thrilled to learn that this long novel would be made into two movies, rather than condensed into one. In this episode from the saga, Bella is married and pregnant with a unique, supernatural child. The two films adapted from *Breaking Dawn* are scheduled for release in 2011 and 2012.

Stewart with Jesse Eisenberg in a scene from Adventureland.

Taking Roles in Other Films

Between the *Twilight* movies, Stewart has worked on several other films. In fact, the success of the first film transformed her career. For example, *The Cake Eaters*, a movie that Stewart had completed before *Twilight*, had never been released. After the phenomenal success of *Twilight*, that movie suddenly had a 2009 release date and a poster that featured Stewart prominently. "If it was not for *Twilight*, I'm not sure *The Cake Eaters*, a film I dearly love, would have seen the light of day," Stewart remarked. In *The Cake Eaters*, she played Georgia, a young woman suffering from a debilitating disease. A reviewer for the *New York Times* praised her "tough, strong performance," and *Variety* called her acting excellent. A movie critic for the *Buffalo News* said, "Stewart is a superb young actress, and this is probably the most impressive thing she has yet done on film."

Stewart had a leading role in the 2009 comedy *Adventureland*, a story that takes place in 1987 and focuses on the experiences of a group of young people working at an amusement park in Pittsburgh, Pennsylvania. Stewart plays Em Lewin, who she described as "fairly damaged. She has an odd number of hang-ups. It's too much for her. Any time you don't like yourself people won't treat you well." The movie was not very successful in theaters, and it drew mixed reviews from critics. A reviewer for *USA Today* described the movie as a "bittersweet, if uneven, coming-of-age comedy" and said that Stewart's acting was "sullen and low-key." But *Entertainment Weekly* said that Stewart had "a cutting sharpness that draws you right to her pale, severe beauty."

In 2009 Stewart had a starring role in *Welcome to the Rileys*, a complex drama in which she played a teenaged stripper and prostitute. The story focuses on the makeshift family that gradually forms when her character joins up with a married couple who are grieving the death of their own daughter. In 2010 she appeared in *The Runaways*, the biographical story of the 1970s rock band of the same name. The band was led by lead singer and guitarist Joan Jett, played by Stewart, and Cherie Currie, played by Dakota Fanning. *The Runaways* was an all-girl rock group at a time when rock and roll was a bastion of blatant male sexism, and the band was one of several that challenged that attitude. Stewart won praise from movie reviewers for her portrayal of Jett, as in this comment from A.O. Scott in the *New York Times*. "Stewart, watchful and unassuming, gives the movie its spine and soul," he declared. "Cherie may dazzle and appall you, but Joan is the one you root for, and the one rock 'n' roll fans of every gender and generation will identify with."

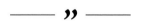

"If there is anything you really want to do, you have to give it a shot," Stewart stressed. *"Otherwise you're going to hold onto it forever and just regret it. You should have no regret."*

Though she may have been reluctant initially to become an actress, Stewart now enjoys the challenge of making movies. "With acting, every story is different, and you're constantly playing different people, so you're never sure if you'll be able to pull it off. At the end it can be like the greatest thing in the world, but you have to second-guess yourself a little." Stewart has also said "[Acting] just feels good. I find I want to do a movie because I love the script or I love the story. You have these themes in your mind, and you think about them incessantly, and then it's time to shoot the scene and you're like, 'Okay, you're going to be done with this in 15 minutes, so you'd better do it right.'"

Overall, Stewart has earned consistently high praise from movie critics. One *Variety* writer said that Stewart is "an exceptionally poised young film actress with a knack for challenging roles as troubled adolescents" and that she impresses "audiences and critics alike with her realistic performances and her choice of projects." A writer in *Interview* said that her acting always "comes off 100 percent natural."

Even with all of her success, Stewart still isn't sure that she wants to stick with acting forever. "I want to go to college for literature," she stated. "I want to be a writer. I mean, I love what I do, but it's not all I want to do—be a professional liar for the rest of my life." But Stewart is happy that she made that long-ago decision to go on her first audition. "If there is anything you really want to do, you have to give it a shot," she stressed. "Otherwise you're going to hold onto it forever and just regret it. You should have no regret."

HOME AND FAMILY

Stewart lives in Los Angeles with her parents, a cat, and a border collie named Oz. She says she has "no plans to move any time soon. I'm really tight with my family and besides, I think it would be a little weird to have a big, sprawling place all on my own."

HOBBIES AND OTHER INTERESTS

When she is not busy filming or preparing for a movie, Stewart enjoys playing guitar and reading. She says her books are among her most prized possessions. "If my house were burning down, I'd be running out with all of my books." She also likes Big Band music and has recently taken up swing dancing. Stewart has also been an avid surfer since childhood. She visits Australia as often as she can, both for surfing and to visit friends and family there. "I love Australia and we have a lot of great family and friends down there. I can't wait to get back."

SELECTED CREDITS

The Safety of Objects, 2001
Panic Room, 2002
Cold Creek Manor, 2003
Catch That Kid, 2004
Speak, 2005
Zathura, 2005
Fierce People, 2006
In the Land of Women, 2007
The Messengers, 2007
Into the Wild, 2007
The Yellow Handkerchief, 2008
What Just Happened?, 2008
Twilight, 2008
The Cake Eaters, 2009
Adventureland, 2009

The Twilight Saga: New Moon, 2009
The Twilight Saga: Eclipse, 2010
The Runaways, 2010

HONORS AND AWARDS

MTV Movie Awards: 2009 (two awards), Best Female Performance and Best Kiss (with Robert Pattinson), for *Twilight;* 2010 (two awards), Best Female Performance and Best Kiss (with Robert Pattinson), for *The Twilight Saga: New Moon*

Teen Choice Awards: 2009 (two awards), Choice Movie Actress: Drama and Choice Movie Liplock (with Robert Pattinson), for *Twilight;* 2010 (four awards), Choice Movie Actress—Fantasy, for *The Twiligth Saga: New Moon,* Choice Summer Movie Star—Female, for *The Twilight Saga: Eclipse,* Choice Movie Liplock and Choice Movie Chemistry (with Robert Pattinson), both for *The Twilight Saga: New Moon*

FURTHER READING

Books

Hurley, Jo. *Kristen Stewart: Bella of the Ball,* 2009

Periodicals

Entertainment Weekly, Nov. 14, 2008, p.30; Apr. 10, 2009, p.36; May 29, 2009, p.26; Nov. 20, 2009, p.30
Girls' Life, Apr./May 2007, p.37
Interview, Mar. 2006, p.167; Jan. 2007, p.136; Nov. 2007, p.110
New York Times, Nov. 13, 2009; Nov. 20, 2009; June 29, 2010
Newsweek, Mar. 30, 2009, p.60
People, June 15, 2009, p.68; Nov. 2009 (special *New Moon* edition)
USA Today, Apr. 1, 2008, p.D1; Apr. 3, 2009, p.D13
Vanity Fair, Apr. 2007, p.201

Online Articles

http://www.mtv.com
   (MTV, "*Twilight* Star Kristen Stewart Talks *New Moon,* Future Sequels," Mar. 17, 2009)
http://www.nytimes.com
   (New York Times, "Media Vampires Beware," Nov. 13, 2009)
http://topics.newsweek.com/entertainment/movies/2009/twilight.htm
   (Newsweek, "Kristen Stewart," "*Twilight,*" collected articles, multiple dates)

http://www.people.com/people/kristen_stewart
  (People, "Kristen Stewart," collected articles, multiple dates)
http://www.teenink.com/nonfiction/celebrity_interviews
  (TeenInk, "Actor—Kristen Stewart," no date)
http://www.usatoday.com/life/movies/news/2009-03-31-kristen-stewart
  _N.htm
  (USA Today, "Kristen Stewart: Some People Think They Know Her, But
  …" Apr. 2, 2009)
http://www.variety.com
  (Variety, "Kristen Stewart: Biography," 2009)

ADDRESS

Kristen Stewart
Summit Entertainment
1630 Stewart Street, Suite 120
Santa Monica, CA 90404

WORLD WIDE WEB SITES

http://www.twilightthemovie.com
http://www.newmoonthemovie.com
http://www.eclipsethemovie.com
http://www.stepheniemeyer.com/twilightseries.html

Photo and Illustration Credits

Front Cover Photos: Beyoncé: NBC Photo/Virginia Sherwood; Hillary Rodham Clinton: U.S. State Department Photo; LeBron James: UPI/Michael Bush/Landov; Caroll Spinney as Big Bird: AP Photo/Mark Lennihan.

Beyoncé/Photos: Photo by Music World Entertainment/Nickelodeon via Image.net (p. 11); CD cover: THE WRITING'S ON THE WALL © 1999 Columbia Records/Sony BMG Music Entertainment. All Rights Reserved. (p. 14); Rick Diamond/WireImage (p. 16, top); Movie still: GOLDMEMBER. Photo by Melinda Sue Gordon/SMPSP © 2002 New Line Productions, Inc. All Rights Reserved. (p. 16, middle); CD Cover: DANGEROUSLY IN LOVE © 2003 Legacy/Columbia/Sony BMG Music Entertainment. All Rights Reserved. (p. 16, bottom); Courtesy MTV Networks (p. 19); Movie still: DREAMGIRLS. David James © 2006 Dreamworks LLC & Paramount Pictures. All Rights Reserved. (p. 21); CD Cover: I AM … SASHA FIERCE © 2008 Sony BMG Music Entertainment. All Rights Reserved. (p. 24); NBC Photo/Virginia Sherwood (p. 26).

Justin Bieber/Photos: Pamela Littky/ © 2010 Universal Music Group (p. 31); Pamela Littky/ © 2009 Universal Music Group (p. 34); Giulio Marcocchi/Sipa Press/KIDS_gm.177/0903291339 via Newscom (p. 36); Kevin Winter/Courtesy of Nickelodeon 2010 Kids' Choice Awards (p. 38); CD: MY WORLD. Island Records/ © 2010 Universal Music Group (p. 40).

Charles Bolden/Photos: NASA/Bill Ingalls (p. 43); NASA (pp. 46, 48); NASA/Johnson Space Center (p. 50); NASA/Bill Ingalls (pp. 53, 54).

Drew Brees/Photos: AP Photo/Eric Gay (p. 59); Courtesy Purdue University Sports Information (p. 62); AP Photo/Paul Spinelli (p. 64); AP Photo/Eric Gay (p. 67); John Gress/Reuters/Landov (p. 69); Scott Clarke/ESPN (p. 71); AP Photo/Kevin Terrell (p. 72).

Ursula Burns/Photos: Lonnie Major/Courtesy of Xerox Corporation (p. 77); Newscom (p. 80); Courtesy of Xerox Corporation (p. 83); Stephanie Kuykendal/Bloomberg via Getty Images (p. 85); Courtesy of Xerox Corporation (p. 86).

Robin Chase/Photos: © 2007 Tanit Sakakini (p. 91); Family photo, courtesy Robin Chase (p. 92); Courtesy Zipcar, Inc. (pp. 94, 96); © Stephen Oakley (p. 99).

Hillary Rodham Clinton/Photos: Official Portrait of Secretary of State Hillary Clinton. Courtesy, State Department (p. 103); Courtesy of William J. Clinton Presidential Library (p. 106); Photo from *Persistence of Spirit* Collection donated by Arkansas Democrat. Courtesy, Arkansas History Commission. (p. 109); U.S. Department of Defense (p. 111); AP Photo/Doug Mills (p. 112); AP Photo/Gerald Herbert (p. 114); Chris Fitzgerald/CandidatePhotos via Newscom (p. 117); Official White House photo by Pete Souza (p. 118, top); U.S. State Department photo (p. 118, middle and bottom).

Gustavo Dudamel/Photos: Mathais Bothor/Deutsche Grammophon/Courtesy Thirteen/WNET New York/PBS (p. 125); Chris Christodoulou/Courtesy Thirteen/WNET New York/PBS (p. 127); Deutsche Grammophon/UMD/Universal Music Group (p. 130); John Bohn/Boston Globe/Landov (p. 133); Mathew Imaging/Courtesy Thirteen/WNET New York/PBS (p. 134); AP Photo/Mark J. Terrill (p. 136).

Eran Egozy and Alex Rigopulos/Photos: Courtesy, Reverb Communications (p. 141); Courtesy, Reverb Communications (p. 143); DVD Cover: AMPLITUDE © 2003 Sony Computer Entertainment America Inc. Developed by Harmonix Music Systems. (p. 147); DVD Cover: GUITAR HERO Game engine code © 2005 Harmonix Music Systems Inc. Developed by Harmonix Music Systems. © 2005 RedOctane, Inc. All Rights Reserved. (p. 150); THE BEATLES: ROCK BAND screenshot © 2009 Harmonix Music Systems, Inc. All Rights Reserved. (p. 153, top); ROCK BAND 2 screenshot © 2008 Harmonix Music Systems, Inc. All Rights Reserved. (p. 153, middle); ROCK BAND screenshot © 2008 Harmonix Music Systems, Inc. All Rights Reserved. (p. 153, bottom).

Neil Gaiman/Photos: Mark Sullivan/WireImage (p. 157); Xinhua/Landov (p. 159); Book cover: THE SANDMAN (Volume One); PRELUDES & NOCTURNES by Neil Gaiman. Published by DC Comics. Cover and compilation © 1991, 1995 DC Comics. All Rights Reserved. Cover and publication design by Dave McKean. (p. 162); Book cover: THE DAY I SWAPPED MY DAD FOR TWO GOLDFISH (HarperCollins Children's Books). © 1997, 2004 by Neil Gaiman and Dave McKean. (p. 164); Movie still: CORALINE © LAIKA, Inc. All Rights Reserved. (p. 167, top); Book cover: CORALINE (HarperCollins Publishers). Text © 2002 Neil Gaiman. Illustrations © 2002 Dave McKean. Jacket art © Dave McKean. Jacket design by Hilary Zarycky. (p. 167, middle); Movie still: CORALINE © LAIKA, Inc. All Rights Reserved. (p. 167, bottom); Book cover: MIRRORMASK © 2005 The Jim Henson Company (HarperCollins Children's Books). Text © 2005 by Neil Gaiman and Dave McKean. All Rights Reserved. (p. 169, top); Movie still: MIRRORMASK © 2005 The Jim Henson Company, Inc. All Rights Reserved. (p. 169, middle); Book cover: MIRRORMASK: THE ILLUSTRATED FILM SCRIPT OF THE MOTION PICTURE FROM THE JIM HENSON COMPANY. Script, storyboards, and artwork © 2005 The Jim Henson Company (William Morrow/imprint, HarperCollins Publishers).Text © 2005 by Neil Gaiman and Dave McKean. All Rights Reserved. (p. 169, bottom); Book cover: THE GRAVEYARD BOOK (HarperCollins Children's Books) Text © 2008 by Neil Gaiman. Illustrations © 2008 by Dave McKean. (p. 172).

Tavi Gevinson/Photos: Astrid Stawiarz/Getty Images (p. 177); Heather Charles/MCT/Landov (p. 180); Patrick Kovarik/AFP/Getty Images (p. 183); AP Photo/Jennifer Graylock (p. 185).

Hugh Jackman/Photos: Antonio Nava/Landov (p. 189); Movie: X-MEN ORIGINS: WOLVERINE. Photo by James Fisher. (p. 192); Zuma Photos/Newscom (p. 194); Movie still: X2: X-MEN UNITED. Kerry Hayes/SMPSP ™ © 2003 Twentieth Century Fox. X-Men character likenesses: ™ © 2003 Marvel Characters, Inc. All Rights

Reserved. (p. 196); Movie still: X-MEN 3: THE LAST STAND. Kerry Hayes/SMPSP
™ © 2006 Twentieth Century Fox. X-Men character likenesses: ™ © 2006 Marvel
Characters, Inc. All Rights Reserved. (p. 198); Movie still: X-MEN ORIGINS:
WOLVERINE. Photo by James Fisher. (p. 200); Movie still: HAPPY FEET © 2006
Warner Bros. All Rights Reserved. (p. 202, top); Publicity still: FLUSHED AWAY ©
2006 Dreamworks Animated (p. 202, middle); Movie still: FLUSHED AWAY © 2006
Dreamworks Animated (p. 202, bottom).

Jesse James/Photos: TV still: JESSE JAMES IS A DEAD MAN/Spike TV (p. 207);
PRNewsFoto via Newscom (p. 210); Courtesy of Discovery Channel/PRNewsFoto
via Newscom (p. 212); AP Photo/Jean-Marc Bouju (p. 215); TV still: JESSE JAMES IS
A DEAD MAN/Spike TV (p. 217).

LeBron James/Photos: Marc Serota/Getty Images (p. 221); Book: SHOOTING STARS
(2009 The Penguin Press) by LeBron James and Buzz Bissinger. Copyright © LeBron
James. All rights reserved. Photo by Patty Burdon. Jacket Design by Darren Haggar.
(p. 223); Bob Leverone/TSN/Icon SMI/via Newscom (p. 226); AP Photo/Mark Duncan (p. 229); AP Photo/Duane Burleson (p. 231); Adam Hunger/Reuters/Landov (p.
234); AP Photo/Phil Long (p. 237).

Taylor Lautner/Photos: Kevin Winter/Getty Images for KCA (p. 241); DVD: THE AD-
VENTURES OF SHARKBOY AND LAVAGIRL © Buena Vista Home Entertainment, Inc. (p. 244); Movie: THE TWILIGHT SAGA: NEW MOON. Kimberley
French/ © 2009 Summit Entertainment, LLC. All rights reserved. (p. 246, top and
bottom); Movie: TWILIGHT. Deana Newcomb/ © Summit Entertainment, LLC. All
rights reserved. (p. 246, middle); Chris Polk/Getty Images for KCA (p. 249); Movie:
THE TWILIGHT SAGA: ECLIPSE. Kimberley French/ © 2009 Summit Entertainment, LLC. All rights reserved. (p. 251); DVD: VALENTINE'S DAY © 2010 New
Line Cinema/Warner Bros Entertainment Inc/Warner Home Video. All rights reserved. (p. 253).

Chuck Liddell/Photos: TV still: GUYS CHOICE AWARDS 2008/Spike TV (p. 257);
Courtesy, Cal Poly Athletics Media Relations (p. 259); UPI Photo/Roger Williams via
Newscom (p. 262); Francis Specker/Landov (p. 265); ABC/Adam Larkey (p. 267).

Mary Mary/Photos: UPI Photo/Arianne Teeple via Newscom (p. 271); Album cover:
THANKFUL © 2000 Legacy/Columbia/Sony Music Entertainment (p. 274); Album
cover: THE SOUND © 2008 Columbia/Sony Music Entertainment (p. 277); Jason
Merritt/Getty Images (p. 279).

Christianne Meneses Jacobs/Photos: Photo by Marc Jacobs/Courtesy Christianne
Meneses Jacobs (pp. 283 and 286); Photo by James Dyrek/Courtesy Christianne
Meneses Jacobs (p. 289); Photo by Rodney Choice/Courtesy Christianne Meneses
Jacobs (p. 292).

Melinda Merck/Photos: Courtesy of the ASPCA ® (pp. 295, 297, 300, and 302).

Stephenie Meyer/Photos: Ingo Wagner/dpa/Landov (p. 307); Book cover: TWILIGHT
(Little, Brown and Company). Text copyright © 2005 by Stephenie Meyer. All rights
reserved. Jacket design by Gail Doobinin. Jacket photo by Roger Hagadone. (p. 310);
Movie still: TWILIGHT © Summit Entertainment, LLC. All rights reserved. (p. 313);
Movie poster: NEW MOON © 2009 Summit Entertainment, LLC. All rights re-

served. (p. 315); Movie still: ECLIPSE © 2010 Summit Entertainment, LLC. All rights reserved. Photo by Kimberley French. (p. 316); John Shearer/WireImage (p. 319).

Orianthi/Photos: Meeno/ © 2009 Geffen/Universal Music Group (p. 323); Chapman Baehler/ © 2009 Geffen/Universal Music Group (p. 325); Movie: MICHAEL JACKSON'S THIS IS IT © 2009 Columbia Tristar/Sony Pictures Entertainment, Inc. All rights reserved. (p. 328); Michael Becker/PictureGroup/FOX via AP Photo Images (p. 330).

Alexander Ovechkin/Photos: Jim McIsaac/Getty Images (p. 335); AP Photo/Jacques Boissinot (p. 336); Mitchell Layton/Getty Images (p. 339); AP Photo/Tom Mihalek (p. 341); AP Photo/Pablo Martinez Monsivais (p. 344).

Brad Paisley/Photos: ABC/Katherine Bomboy (p. 349); CD Cover: WHO NEEDS PICTURES © 1999 Arista Records/BMG Entertainment. All Rights Reserved. (p. 352); AP Photo/The Tennessean/Randy Piland (p. 354); ABC/Katherine Bomboy (p. 356); CD Cover: AMERICAN SATURDAY NIGHT © 2009 Arista Nashville/ Sony BMG Music Entertainment. All Rights Reserved. (p. 359); Official White House photo by Pete Souza (p. 361).

Keke Palmer/Photos: PRNewsFoto/Nickelodeon via Newscom (p. 365); Movie still: TYLER PERRY'S MADEA'S FAMILY REUNION © 2006 Lions Gate Entertainment. All rights reserved. Photo by Alfeo Dixon. (p. 367); Movie still: AKEELAH AND THE BEE © 2006 Lions Gate Entertainment. All rights reserved. Photo by Saeed Adyani. (p. 369); Movie still: THE LONGSHOTS. © 2008 The Weinstein Company. All rights reserved. Photo by Tony Rivetti Jr./Dimensions Films. (p. 371); AP Photo/Lisa Rose (p. 372).

Paramore/Photos: © 2009 FBY/Wea/Fueled By Ramen/Warner Elektra Atlantic Corporation. (p. 377); Album cover: ALL WE KNOW IS FALLING © 2005 FBY/Wea/Fueled By Ramen/Warner Elektra Atlantic Corporation. (p. 380); © 2007 FBY/Wea/Fueled By Ramen/Warner Elektra Atlantic Corporation. (p. 383); © Debbie VanStory/RockinExposures/iPhoto via Newscom (p. 385); Album cover: BRAND NEW EYES © 2009 FBY/Wea/Fueled By Ramen/Warner Elektra Atlantic Corporation. (p. 387).

Candace Parker/Photos: Greg Ashman/CSM/Landov (p. 393); Dwain Scott/WireImage (p. 395); Courtesy of Tennessee Athletics Media Relations (p. 397); AP Photo/Paul Connors (p. 401).

David Protess/Photos: AP Photo/M. Spencer Green (p. 405); AP Photo/Michael S. Green (p. 408); Steve Kagan/Time Life Pictures/Getty Images (pp. 410, 413); AP Photo/Beth A. Keiser (p. 415); Brian Cassella/Chicago Tribune/MCT (p. 417); Nancy Stone/Chicago Tribune/MCT (p. 419).

Albert Pujols/Photo: AP Photo/Rob Carr, File (p. 423); Diamond Images/Getty Images (p. 425); Scott Rovak/AFP/Getty Images (p. 427); Peter Newcomb/Reuters/Landov (p. 428); AP Photo/Tom Gannam (p. 432); George Burns/ESPN (p. 434).

Zoë Saldana/Photos: Movie: DEATH AT A FUNERAL © 2010 Screen Gems, Inc./Sony Pictures Entertainment, Inc./Columbia Tristar marketing Group. All rights reserved. Photo by Phil Bray. (p. 439); DVD: CENTER STAGE © 2001 Sony Pictures Home

Cumulative General Index

This cumulative index includes names, occupations, nationalities, and ethnic and minority origins that pertain to all individuals profiled in *Biography Today* since the debut of the series in 1992.

For cumulative general, places of birth, and birthday indexes, please see biographytoday.com.

511

CUMULATIVE GENERAL INDEX

Places of Birth Index

The following index lists the places of birth for the individuals profiled in *Biography Today*. Places of birth are entered under state, province, anb/or country.

Canada

573

Michigan

Applegate, K.A. . . . . .Jan 00
Askins, Renee . . . . .WorLdr V.1
Bell, Kristen – *Huntington Woods* . . .Sep 05
Canady, Alexa – *Lansing* . . . . . .Science V.6
Carson, Ben – *Detroit* . . . . .Science V.4
Carter, Regina – *Detroit* . . . . .Sep 07
Curtis, Christopher Paul
 – *Flint* . . . . .Author V.4
Galeczka, Chris – *Sterling Heights* . .Apr 96
Horvath, Polly – *Kalamazoo* . . .Author V.16
Jenkins, Jerry B. – *Kalamazoo* . .Author V.16
Johnson, Magic – *Lansing* . . . . .Apr 92
Joy, Bill – *Detroit* . . . . .Science V.10
Kiraly, Karch – *Jackson* . . . . .Sport V.4
Krone, Julie – *Benton Harbor* . . . . . .Jan 95
LaHaye, Tim – *Detroit* . . . . . . Author V.16
Lalas, Alexi – *Royal Oak* . . . . .Sep 94
Lautner, Taylor – *Grand Rapids* . . . .Sep 10
Mallett, Jef – *Howell* . . . . .Apr 09
Mohajer, Dineh – *Bloomfield Hills* . . .Jan 02
Mohammed, Warith Deen
 – *Hamtramck* . . . . .Apr 09
Page, Larry – *East Lansing* . . . . .Sep 05
Riley, Dawn – *Detroit* . . . . .Sport V.4
Scieszka, Jon – *Flint* . . . . .Author V.9
Shabazz, Betty – *Detroit* . . . . .Apr 98
Small, David – *Detroit* . . . . . . Author V.10
Van Allsburg, Chris – *Grand Rapids* .Apr 92
Ward, Lloyd D. – *Romulus* . . . . .Jan 01
Watson, Barry – *Traverse City* . . . . .Sep 02
Webb, Alan – *Ann Arbor* . . . . .Sep 01
Williams, Serena – *Saginaw* . . . . .Sport V.4
Winans, CeCe – *Detroit* . . . . .Apr 00

Minnesota

Burger, Warren – *St. Paul* . . . . .Sep 95
Douglas, Marjory Stoneman
 – *Minneapolis* . . . . .WorLdr V.1
Hartnett, Josh – *St. Paul* . . . . .Sep 03
Madden, John – *Austin* . . . . .Sep 97
Mars, Forrest Sr.
 – *Minneapolis* . . . . .Science V.4
McNutt, Marcia
 – *Minneapolis* . . . . .Science V.11
Murie, Olaus J. . . . . .WorLdr V.1
Paulsen, Gary – *Minneapolis* . . .Author V.1
Ryder, Winona – *Winona* . . . . .Jan 93
Schulz, Charles
 – *Minneapolis* . . . . .Author V.2
Scurry, Briana – *Minneapolis* . . . . . .Jan 00
Ventura, Jesse – *Minneapolis* . . . . .Apr 99

Weinke, Chris – *St. Paul* . . . . .Apr 01
Winfield, Dave – *St. Paul* . . . . .Jan 93

Mississippi

Bass, Lance – *Clinton* . . . . .Jan 01
Brandy – *McComb* . . . . .Apr 96
Clemons, Kortney – *Meridien* . . . . . .Sep 07
Favre, Brett – *Gulfport* . . . . .Sport V.2
Forman, Michele – *Biloxi* . . . . .Jan 03
Hill, Faith – *Jackson* . . . . .Sep 01
Jones, James Earl
 – *Arkabutla Township* . . . . .Jan 95
McCarty, Oseola
 – *Wayne County* . . . . .Jan 99
McNair, Steve – *Mount Olive* . . .Sport V.11
Payton, Walter – *Columbia* . . . . . . .Jan 00
Rice, Jerry – *Crawford* . . . . .Apr 93
Rimes, LeAnn – *Jackson* . . . . .Jan 98
Roberts, Robin – *Pass Christian* . . . .Jan 09
Spears, Jamie Lynn – *McComb* . . . .Sep 06
Taylor, Mildred D. – *Jackson* . . .Author V.1
Williams, Hayley – *Meridian* . . . . . .Apr 10
Winfrey, Oprah – *Kosciusko* . . . . . .Apr 92;
 Business V.1
Wright, Richard – *Natchez* . . . . .Author V.5

Missouri

Angelou, Maya – *St. Louis* . . . . .Apr 93
Champagne, Larry III – *St. Louis* . . .Apr 96
Eminem – *Kansas City* . . . . .Apr 03
Goodman, John – *Affton* . . . . .Sep 95
Heinlein, Robert – *Butler* . . . . . .Author V.4
Hughes, Langston – *Joplin* . . . .Author V.7
Lester, Julius – *St. Louis* . . . . . .Author V.7
Limbaugh, Rush – *Cape Girardeau* .Sep 95
Miller, Shannon – *Rolla* . . . . .Sep 94
Nye, Naomi Shihab – *St. Louis* . .Author V.8
Parker, Candace – *St. Louis* . . . . . . .Jan 10
Spade, Kate – *Kansas City* . . . . .Apr 07

Montana

Carvey, Dana – *Missoula* . . . . .Jan 93
Horner, Jack – *Shelby* . . . . .Science V.1
Jackson, Phil – *Deer Lodge* . . . . .Sport V.10
Lowe, Alex – *Missoula* . . . . .Sport V.4
Paolini, Christopher . . . . .Author V.16

Morocco

Hassan II – *Rabat* . . . . .WorLdr V.2
Newsom, Lee Ann . . . . .Science V.11

Myanmar

see Burma

Nebraska

Buffett, Warren – *Omaha* . . . .Business V.1
Cheney, Dick – *Lincoln* . . . . .Jan 02

Birthday Index

BIRTHDAY INDEX

Biography Today

General Series

Biography Today **General Series** includes a unique combination of current biographical profiles that teachers and librarians — and the readers themselves — tell us are most appealing. The **General Series** is available as a 3-issue subscription; hardcover annual cumulation; or subscription plus cumulation.

Within the **General Series**, your readers will find a variety of sketches about:

- Authors
- Musicians
- Political leaders
- Sports figures
- Movie actresses & actors
- Cartoonists
- Scientists
- Astronauts
- TV personalities
- and the movers & shakers in many other fields!

ONE-YEAR SUBSCRIPTION

- 3 softcover issues, 6" x 9"
- Published in January, April, and September
- 1-year subscription, list price $66. **School and library price $64**
- 150 pages per issue
- 10 profiles per issue
- Contact sources for additional information
- Cumulative Names Index

HARDBOUND ANNUAL CUMULATION

- Sturdy 6" x 9" hardbound volume
- Published in December
- List price $73. **School and library price $66 per volume**
- 450 pages per volume
- 30 profiles — includes all profiles found in softcover issues for that calendar year
- Cumulative General Index, Places of Birth Index, and Birthday Index

SUBSCRIPTION AND CUMULATION COMBINATION

- $110 for 3 softcover issues plus the hardbound volume

For Cumulative General, Places of Birth, and Birthday Indexes, please see www.biographytoday.com.

Biography Today **will be useful in elementary and middle school libraries and in public library children's collections where there is a need for biographies of current personalities. High schools serving reluctant readers may also want to consider a subscription."**
— *Booklist,* American Library Association

"Highly recommended for the young adult audience. Readers will delight in the accessible, energetic, tell-all style; teachers, librarians, and parents will welcome the clever format [and] intelligent and informative text. It should prove especially useful in motivating 'reluctant' readers or literate nonreaders."
— *MultiCultural Review*

"Written in a friendly, almost chatty tone, the profiles offer quick, objective information. While coverage of current figures makes *Biography Today* a useful reference tool, an appealing format and wide scope make it a fun resource to browse." — *School Library Journal*

"The best source for current information at a level kids can understand."
— Kelly Bryant, School Librarian, Carlton, OR

"Easy for kids to read. We love it! Don't want to be without it."
— Lynn McWhirter, School Librarian, Rockford, IL

1992

Paula Abdul
Andre Agassi
Kirstie Alley
Terry Anderson
Roseanne Arnold
Isaac Asimov
James Baker
Charles Barkley
Larry Bird
Judy Blume
Berke Breathed
Garth Brooks
Barbara Bush
George Bush
Fidel Castro
Bill Clinton
Bill Cosby
Diana, Princess of
  Wales
Shannen Doherty
Elizabeth Dole
David Duke
Gloria Estefan
Mikhail Gorbachev
Steffi Graf
Wayne Gretzky
Matt Groening
Alex Haley
Hammer
Martin Handford
Stephen Hawking
Hulk Hogan
Saddam Hussein
Lee Iacocca
Bo Jackson
Mae Jemison
Peter Jennings
Steven Jobs
John Paul II
Magic Johnson
Michael Jordon
Jackie Joyner-Kersee
Spike Lee
Mario Lemieux
Madeleine L'Engle
Jay Leno
Yo-Yo Ma
Nelson Mandela
Wynton Marsalis
Thurgood Marshall
Ann Martin
Barbara McClintock
Emily Arnold McCully
Antonia Novello

Sandra Day O'Connor
Rosa Parks
Jane Pauley
H. Ross Perot
Luke Perry
Scottie Pippen
Colin Powell
Jason Priestley
Queen Latifah
Yitzhak Rabin
Sally Ride
Pete Rose
Nolan Ryan
H. Norman
  Schwarzkopf
Jerry Seinfeld
Dr. Seuss
Gloria Steinem
Clarence Thomas
Chris Van Allsburg
Cynthia Voigt
Bill Watterson
Robin Williams
Oprah Winfrey
Kristi Yamaguchi
Boris Yeltsin

1993

Maya Angelou
Arthur Ashe
Avi
Kathleen Battle
Candice Bergen
Boutros Boutros-Ghali
Chris Burke
Dana Carvey
Cesar Chavez
Henry Cisneros
Hillary Rodham Clinton
Jacques Cousteau
Cindy Crawford
Macaulay Culkin
Lois Duncan
Marian Wright
  Edelman
Cecil Fielder
Bill Gates
Sara Gilbert
Dizzy Gillespie
Al Gore
Cathy Guisewite
Jasmine Guy
Anita Hill
Ice-T
Darci Kistler

k.d. lang
Dan Marino
Rigoberta Menchu
Walter Dean Myers
Martina Navratilova
Phyllis Reynolds
  Naylor
Rudolf Nureyev
Shaquille O'Neal
Janet Reno
Jerry Rice
Mary Robinson
Winona Ryder
Jerry Spinelli
Denzel Washington
Keenen Ivory Wayans
Dave Winfield

1994

Tim Allen
Marian Anderson
Mario Andretti
Ned Andrews
Yasir Arafat
Bruce Babbitt
Mayim Bialik
Bonnie Blair
Ed Bradley
John Candy
Mary Chapin
  Carpenter
Benjamin Chavis
Connie Chung
Beverly Cleary
Kurt Cobain
F.W. de Klerk
Rita Dove
Linda Ellerbee
Sergei Fedorov
Zlata Filipovic
Daisy Fuentes
Ruth Bader Ginsburg
Whoopi Goldberg
Tonya Harding
Melissa Joan Hart
Geoff Hooper
Whitney Houston
Dan Jansen
Nancy Kerrigan
Alexi Lalas
Charlotte Lopez
Wilma Mankiller
Shannon Miller
Toni Morrison
Richard Nixon

Greg Norman
Severo Ochoa
River Phoenix
Elizabeth Pine
Jonas Salk
Richard Scarry
Emmitt Smith
Will Smith
Steven Spielberg
Patrick Stewart
R.L. Stine
Lewis Thomas
Barbara Walters
Charlie Ward
Steve Young
Kim Zmeskal

1995

Troy Aikman
Jean-Bertrand Aristide
Oksana Baiul
Halle Berry
Benazir Bhutto
Jonathan Brandis
Warren E. Burger
Ken Burns
Candace Cameron
Jimmy Carter
Agnes de Mille
Placido Domingo
Janet Evans
Patrick Ewing
Newt Gingrich
John Goodman
Amy Grant
Jesse Jackson
James Earl Jones
Julie Krone
David Letterman
Rush Limbaugh
Heather Locklear
Reba McEntire
Joe Montana
Cosmas Ndeti
Hakeem Olajuwon
Ashley Olsen
Mary Kate Olsen
Jennifer Parkinson
Linus Pauling
Itzhak Perlman
Cokie Roberts
Wilma Rudolph
Salt 'N' Pepa
Barry Sanders
William Shatner

600

Elizabeth George
 Speare
Dr. Benjamin Spock
Jonathan Taylor
 Thomas
Vicki Van Meter
Heather Whitestone
Pedro Zamora

1996

Aung San Suu Kyi
Boyz II Men
Brandy
Ron Brown
Mariah Carey
Jim Carrey
Larry Champagne III
Christo
Chelsea Clinton
Coolio
Bob Dole
David Duchovny
Debbi Fields
Chris Galeczka
Jerry Garcia
Jennie Garth
Wendy Guey
Tom Hanks
Alison Hargreaves
Sir Edmund Hillary
Judith Jamison
Barbara Jordan
Annie Leibovitz
Carl Lewis
Jim Lovell
Mickey Mantle
Lynn Margulis
Iqbal Masih
Mark Messier
Larisa Oleynik
Christopher Pike
David Robinson
Dennis Rodman
Selena
Monica Seles
Don Shula
Kerri Strug
Tiffani-Amber Thiessen
Dave Thomas
Jaleel White

1997

Madeleine Albright
Marcus Allen

Gillian Anderson
Rachel Blanchard
Zachery Ty Bryan
Adam Ezra Cohen
Claire Danes
Celine Dion
Jean Driscoll
Louis Farrakhan
Ella Fitzgerald
Harrison Ford
Bryant Gumbel
John Johnson
Michael Johnson
Maya Lin
George Lucas
John Madden
Bill Monroe
Alanis Morissette
Sam Morrison
Rosie O'Donnell
Muammar el-Qaddafi
Christopher Reeve
Pete Sampras
Pat Schroeder
Rebecca Sealfon
Tupac Shakur
Tabitha Soren
Herbert Tarvin
Merlin Tuttle
Mara Wilson

1998

Bella Abzug
Kofi Annan
Neve Campbell
Sean Combs (Puff
 Daddy)
Dalai Lama (Tenzin
 Gyatso)
Diana, Princess of
 Wales
Leonardo DiCaprio
Walter E. Diemer
Ruth Handler
Hanson
Livan Hernandez
Jewel
Jimmy Johnson
Tara Lipinski
Jody-Anne Maxwell
Dominique Moceanu
Alexandra Nechita
Brad Pitt
LeAnn Rimes
Emily Rosa

David Satcher
Betty Shabazz
Kordell Stewart
Shinichi Suzuki
Mother Teresa
Mike Vernon
Reggie White
Kate Winslet

1999

Ben Affleck
Jennifer Aniston
Maurice Ashley
Kobe Bryant
Bessie Delany
Sadie Delany
Sharon Draper
Sarah Michelle Gellar
John Glenn
Savion Glover
Jeff Gordon
David Hampton
Lauryn Hill
King Hussein
Lynn Johnston
Shari Lewis
Oseola McCarty
Mark McGwire
Slobodan Milosevic
Natalie Portman
J.K. Rowling
Frank Sinatra
Gene Siskel
Sammy Sosa
John Stanford
Natalia Toro
Shania Twain
Mitsuko Uchida
Jesse Ventura
Venus Williams

2000

Christina Aguilera
K.A. Applegate
Lance Armstrong
Backstreet Boys
Daisy Bates
Harry Blackmun
George W. Bush
Carson Daly
Ron Dayne
Henry Louis Gates, Jr.
Doris Haddock
 (Granny D)

Jennifer Love Hewitt
Chamique Holdsclaw
Katie Holmes
Charlayne Hunter-
 Gault
Johanna Johnson
Craig Kielburger
John Lasseter
Peyton Manning
Ricky Martin
John McCain
Walter Payton
Freddie Prinze Jr.
Viviana Risca
Briana Scurry
George Thampy
CeCe Winans

2001

Jessica Alba
Christiane Amanpour
Drew Barrymore
Jeff Bezos
Destiny's Child
Dale Earnhardt
Carly Fiorina
Aretha Franklin
Cathy Freeman
Tony Hawk
Faith Hill
Kim Dae-jung
Madeleine L'Engle
Mariangela Lisanti
Frankie Muniz
*N Sync
Ellen Ochoa
Jeff Probst
Julia Roberts
Carl T. Rowan
Britney Spears
Chris Tucker
Lloyd D. Ward
Alan Webb
Chris Weinke

2002

Aaliyah
Osama bin Laden
Mary J. Blige
Aubyn Burnside
Aaron Carter
Julz Chavez
Dick Cheney
Hilary Duff

Billy Gilman
Rudolph Giuliani
Brian Griese
Jennifer Lopez
Dave Mirra
Dineh Mohajer
Leanne Nakamura
Daniel Radcliffe
Condoleezza Rice
Marla Runyan
Ruth Simmons
Mattie Stepanek
J.R.R. Tolkien
Barry Watson
Tyrone Willingham
Elijah Wood

2003

Yolanda Adams
Olivia Bennett
Mildred Benson
Alexis Bledel
Barry Bonds
Vincent Brooks
Laura Bush
Amanda Bynes
Kelly Clarkson
Vin Diesel
Eminem
Michele Forman
Vicente Fox
Millard Fuller
Josh Hartnett
Dolores Huerta
Sarah Hughes
Enrique Iglesias
Jeanette Lee
John Lewis
Nicklas Lidstrom
Clint Mathis
Donovan McNabb
Nelly
Andy Roddick
Gwen Stefani
Emma Watson
Meg Whitman
Reese Witherspoon
Yao Ming

2004

Natalie Babbitt
David Beckham
Francie Berger
Tony Blair

Orlando Bloom
Kim Clijsters
Celia Cruz
Matel Dawson Jr.
The Donnas
Tim Duncan
Shirin Ebadi
Carla Hayden
Ashton Kutcher
Lisa Leslie
Linkin Park
Lindsay Lohan
Irene D. Long
John Mayer
Mandy Moore
Thich Nhat Hanh
OutKast
Raven
Ronald Reagan
Keanu Reeves
Ricardo Sanchez
Brian Urlacher
Alexa Vega
Michelle Wie
Will Wright

2005

Kristen Bell
Jack Black
Sergey Brin & Larry
    Page
Adam Brody
Chris Carrabba
Johnny Depp
Eve
Jennie Finch
James Forman
Wally Funk
Cornelia Funke
Bethany Hamilton
Anne Hathaway
Priest Holmes
T.D. Jakes
John Paul II
Toby Keith
Alison Krauss
Wangari Maathai
Karen Mitchell-
    Raptakis
Queen Noor
Violet Palmer
Gloria Rodriguez
Carlos Santana
Antonin Scalia
Curtis Schilling

Maria Sharapova
Ashlee Simpson
Donald Trump
Ben Wallace

2006

Carol Bellamy
Miri Ben-Ari
Black Eyed Peas
Bono
Kelsie Buckley
Dale Chihuly
Neda DeMayo
Dakota Fanning
Green Day
Freddie Highmore
Russel Honoré
Tim Howard
Cynthia Kadohata
Coretta Scott King
Rachel McAdams
Cesar Millan
Steve Nash
Nick Park
Rosa Parks
Danica Patrick
Jorge Ramos
Ben Roethlisberger
Lil' Romeo
Adam Sandler
Russell Simmons
Jamie Lynn Spears
Jon Stewart
Joss Stone
Hannah Teter
Brenda Villa
Tyler James Williams
Gretchen Wilson

2007

Shaun Alexander
Carmelo Anthony
Drake Bell
Chris Brown
Regina Carter
Kortney Clemons
Taylor Crabtree
Miley Cyrus
Aaron Dworkin
Fall Out Boy
Roger Federer
Will Ferrell
America Ferrera
June Foray

Sarah Blaffer Hrdy
Alicia Keys
Cheyenne Kimball
Keira Knightley
Wendy Kopp
Sofia Mulanovich
Barack Obama
Soledad O'Brien
Jamie Oliver
Skip Palenik
Nancy Pelosi
Jack Prelutsky
Ivan "Pudge"
    Rodriguez
Michael Sessions
Kate Spade
Sabriye Tenberken
Rob Thomas
Ashley Tisdale
Carrie Underwood
Muhammad Yunus

2008

Aly & AJ
Bill Bass
Greta Binford
Cory Booker
Sophia Bush
Majora Carter
Anderson Cooper
Zac Efron
Selena Gomez
Al Gore
Vanessa Hudgens
Jennifer Hudson
Zach Hunter
Bindi Irwin
Jonas Brothers
Lisa Ling
Eli Manning
Kimmie Meissner
Scott Niedermayer
Christina Norman
Masi Oka
Tyler Perry
Morgan Pressel
Rihanna
John Roberts Jr.
J. K. Rowling
James Stewart Jr.
Ichiro Suzuki
Karen P. Tandy
Marta Tienda
Justin Timberlake
Lee Wardlaw

2009

Elizabeth Alexander
Will Allen
Judy Baca
Joe Biden
Cynthia Breazeal
Michael Cera
Miranda Cosgrove
Lupe Fiasco
James Harrison
Jimmie Johnson
Heidi Klum
Lang Lang
Leona Lewis
Nastia Liukin
Demi Lovato
Jef Mallett

Warith Deen
  Mohammed
Walter Dean Myers
Michelle Obama
Omarion
Suze Orman
Kenny Ortega
Robert Pattinson
Chris Paul
Michael Phelps
Rachael Ray
Emma Roberts
Robin Roberts
Grayson Rosenberger
Dinara Safina
Gloria Gilbert Stoga
Taylor Swift
Shailene Woodley

2010

Beyoncé
Justin Bieber
Charles Bolden
Drew Brees
Ursula M. Burns
Robin Chase
Hillary Rodham Clinton
Gustavo Dudamel
Eran Egozy & Alex
  Rigopulos
Neil Gaiman
Tavi Gevinson
Hugh Jackman
Jesse James
LeBron James
Taylor Lautner

Chuck Liddell
Mary Mary
Christianne Meneses
  Jacobs
Melinda Merck
Stephenie Meyer
Orianthi
Alexander Ovechkin
Brad Paisley
Keke Palmer
Paramore
Candace Parker
David Protess
Albert Pujols
Zoë Saldana
Sonia Sotomayor
Caroll Spinney
Kristen Stewart